A Theory of Narrative

A
Theory
of
Narrative

RICK ALTMAN

 Columbia University Press

NEW YORK

Columbia University Press
Publishers Since 1893
New York   Chichester, West Sussex
Copyright © 2008 Columbia University Press
All rights reserved
Library of Congress Cataloging-in-Publication Data
Altman, Rick, 1945–
   A theory of narrative / Rick Altman.
       p. cm.
   Includes bibliographical references and index.
   ISBN 978-0-231-14428-5 (cloth : alk. paper)—ISBN 978-0-231-14429-2 (pbk. : alk.
paper)—ISBN 978-0-231-51312-8 (ebook)
   1. Narration (Rhetoric)   2. Narrative art.   I. Title.
PN212.A47 2008
700.4—dc22   2007053035

Columbia University Press books are printed on permanent and durable acid-free paper.
This book is printed on paper with recycled content.
Printed in the United States of America
c 10 9 8 7 6 5 4 3 2 1
p 10 9 8 7 6 5 4 3 2
References to Internet Web sites (URLs) were accurate at the time of writing. Neither the author nor Columbia University Press is responsible for URLs that may have expired or changed since the manuscript was prepared.

In memory of

Frederick Jerome Altman

1915–2006

Contents

Acknowledgments

A Theory of Narrative owes its existence to the support of many institutions and individuals. Several chapters were drafted while I was a Fellow of the Cornell Society for the Humanities. Others were developed during my tenure as a University of Iowa Faculty Scholar. Portions of the theory have been worked out in lectures at Bryn Mawr College, the University of Delaware, Hobart and William Smith Colleges, the University of Illinois, the University of Michigan, Cornell College, the University of Montreal, and the University of Iowa; presented at the annual meetings of the Modern Language Association, the Society for Cinema and Media Studies, and the Midwest Modern Language Association; or published in *Diacritics, Medievalia et Humanistica, Olifant, Wide Angle,* and *South Atlantic Quarterly.* I am especially grateful for the interdisciplinary intellectual support I have found in the University of Iowa Department of Cinema and Comparative Literature, and for released time and research assistance provided by the College of Liberal Arts and Sciences and the Graduate College at the University of Iowa. Several graduate research assistants have helped me in this project—thanks especially to Erica Stein and her keen editorial eye. At every step of the way, I have enjoyed active assistance from the Columbia University Press team responsible for producing this book: Jennifer Crewe, Afua Adusei, Roy Thomas, Cynthia Garver, and Milenda Lee. I have also benefited substantially from the comments of two particularly astute outside readers.

A Theory of Narrative would never have seen the light of day had it not been for the many years of discussion, support, and judicious editing that my wife, Janet Elizabeth Gurkin Altman, has contributed to this project.

This book is dedicated to my father, who taught me to think broadly, to avoid gallicisms, and to write with a general reader in mind. This was the last book to benefit from his careful editing. I will miss our weekend telephone editing sessions.

Note

Translations from French and Old French are by the author. Translations from other languages are from the edition listed in the bibliography.

A Theory of Narrative

ONE What Is Narrative?

Among human endeavors, few are more widely spread or more generally endowed with cultural importance than narrative—the practice of storytelling. Not only are stories universally told, stored, and analyzed, but also they regularly occupy a place of honor in society. Stories constitute the bulk of sacred texts; they are the major vehicle of personal memory; and they are a mainstay of law, entertainment, and history. As Italian theorist and philosopher Benedetto Croce put it, "Where there is no narrative, there is no history" (1951:26). Omnipresent and culturally privileged, narrative gains much of its power from its ability to change form easily and repeatedly. However different the media that serve as a given story's vehicles—however distinct the oral, written, illustrated, or film versions of a particular narrative—we readily recognize a story's ability to be translated into different forms and yet somehow to remain the "same" story. Clearly, narrative exists independently of the media that give it concrete form. Eminently transformable, narrative has been carried wherever human beings have gone. Applied to each new mode of communication, narrative has remained ever present, ever up to date. An essential strategy of human expression and thus a basic aspect of human life, narrative commands our attention. If we would understand the ways in which humans interact, we must take up the challenge of narrative. What is it? How does it make meaning?

The importance of narrative has long been recognized. From Aristotle to the present, virtually every major critic and theorist has had something to say about the art of narrative. Indeed, contemporary accounts of narrative have been so heavily marked by past treatments that scholars have often unknowingly accepted an unreasonably limited definition of narrative, thus arbitrarily restricting narrative's full historical range. In the pages that follow, I outline several notions about narrative that have been repeated often enough to pass for received wisdom. By highlighting the tacit limits associated with these traditional definitions of narrative, I also point up the extent to which recent narrative theorists have adopted and systematized these limits. This rapid overview leads to a proposal for a new definition of narrative, open to a more inclusive range of texts and experiences.

It is time to break free from the traditional understanding of narrative and the limited forms of analysis that it has produced. Once narrative itself is redefined, the way lies open to revise our notions of narrative analysis, narrative kinds, and narrative history. While this may seem an unreasonably vast program, we cannot renew our understanding of narrative piecemeal. Only by taking on the full spectrum of problems associated with narrative can we achieve the goal of seeing narrative anew.

The Traditional Understanding of Narrative

Historically, definitions of narrative have been tightly tied to a particular type of plot. Of all the aspects that characterize narrative, only a few have been singled out for special attention, thus privileging a particular type of narrative and making it all but impossible to give adequate treatment to the full historical range of narrative. This tendency began with Aristotle's *Poetics*. Primarily formulated as commentary on the art of tragedy, the insights of the *Poetics* have nevertheless been regularly applied to a broad spectrum of narrative texts. Book VI of the *Poetics* informs us that a tragedy is impossible without action, but a tragedy may exist without characters (1909:13). Aristotle's treatment of plot in Book VII helps us understand just what he means by action. A work should be long enough, he suggests, "to allow of the hero's passing by a series of probable or necessary stages from misfortune to happiness, or from happiness to misfortune" (16). Having adopted Homer's *Odyssey* as model and reference, Aristotle regularly figures texts as a series of connected actions, with textual structure configured in terms of matched situations (such as misfortune and happiness). Definition and structure thus reinforce each other all too neatly.

Already implicit in the *Poetics*, the convenient coincidence of plot-based definitions of narrative and plot-based notions of structure has dominated Western narrative theory since the Aristotelian revival of the late Renaissance. Though sixteenth-century neo-Aristotelian treatises by Lodovico Castelvetro, Julius Caesar Scaliger, and Torquato Tasso are most often cited in this regard, the key moments are actually two very public quarrels that took place in seventeenth-century France. During the mid-1630s, the French intelligentsia was heavily invested in what came to be called the "Quarrel over *Le Cid*," a wide-ranging literary debate nominally targeting Pierre Corneille's tragicomedy *Le Cid* but also dealing more broadly with questions of appropriate playwriting standards. Most important for the history of narrative theory is the eventual agreement on the necessity to respect what is called a "unity of action." Adapted from Aristotle, the notion of unity of action involves the need to build a play around a single unbroken plot thread, eschewing competing story lines, unnecessary characters, and unrelated episodes. Within a decade, French tragedies and tragicomedies would systematically abandon their epic and pastoral precedents in favor of plots adhering to the unity of action ideal.

Nearly half a century after the infamous Quarrel of *Le Cid*, a similar high-level confrontation developed around Madame de Lafayette's novella, *La Princesse de Clèves*. Only after a series of anonymous book-length critiques would this cause célèbre be laid to rest. Though the debate touched on several questions involving narrative content and construction, one conclusion is especially important for our purposes. Previously applied only to serious theater, the notion of unity of action would—thanks to the "Quarrel of *La Princesse de Clèves*"—for the first time be directly applied to the art of narrative prose. Henceforth, the multiple plots of romance and epic would no longer be acceptable in French prose narrative. Closely followed by William Congreve and others in England, this prescriptive approach soon became a tacitly accepted European standard of narrative composition and thus eventually of novel writing. Stories must be coherent; they must have a distinct beginning, middle, and end; they must connect their parts through clearly motivated causes; and they must expunge any material unrelated to this unity of action. It is easy to see how biographical form became the standard for the early novel in both France and England: use of a single omnipresent protagonist is no doubt the easiest and most efficient way to assure unity of action.

What influence did the twin quarrels of *Le Cid* and *La Princesse de Clèves* have on the definition of narrative? Since they treat the question of "What kind of narratives should be composed?," it is entirely reasonable to assume that they would have no effect on the quite different question of "What counts as a narrative?" But this assumption fails to acknowledge the effect of prescriptive theorizing on the very language used to define literary categories. Before the late Renaissance revival of Aristotle, stories employed extremely diverse strategies. With the rise of neoclassical standards, not only was this variety attenuated but also the very notion of what constitutes a narrative was retooled to match neoclassical prescriptions of proper narrative construction. The new definition of narrative adopted during this period was carefully matched to novelistic production. Fallen from grace, many prior narrative traditions were no longer considered worthy of attention and thus were no longer taken into account in defining narrative itself. Romance, epic, pastoral, sacred history, the *fabliau* and other comic tales—all of these were effectively written out of the definition of narrative by developments associated with the rise of the novel.

Reinforced by two centuries of novel writing, twentieth-century narrative theory settled comfortably into this neo-Aristotelian tradition. Just as Aristotle's narrative theory depended heavily on Homer's *Odyssey* and Sophocles' *Oedipus Rex*, so Percy Lubbock treated the novels of Henry James as his master text (1921) and Roland Barthes took the work of Balzac as the archetype of narrative (1953, 1970). Other critics have similarly referred to a long tradition of novelists from Daniel Defoe and Samuel Richardson to Gustave Flaubert and Marcel Proust. Whether the hero in question is Lazarillo de Tormes, Tom Jones, Emma Bovary, or Isabel Archer, the twin biographical and psychological traditions of the novel clearly reinforce a definition of narrative that is dependent on action and built around "the hero's passing by a series of probable or necessary stages from misfortune to happiness, or from happiness to misfortune." This approach understandably guided the work of the neo-Aristotelian Chicago critics. It also clearly surfaced in the quest-oriented model that dominated Anglo-American criticism during the third quarter of the twentieth century. Following a Jungian lead, Joseph Campbell popularized the notion of the "monomyth," according to which all myth is understood to follow a single quest-related pattern (1956). The influential writings of Canadian theorist Northrop Frye systematized Campbell's basic insight and applied it to an extraordinarily broad literary corpus (1957). This plot-oriented tradition has been continued in Peter Brooks's emblematically titled *Reading for the Plot* (1984) and J. Hillis Miller's *Reading Narrative* (1998).

It is thus hardly surprising to find that a contemporary manual of basic literary terms systematically defines everything related to narrative in terms of plot. Those who look up the term "narrative" in Sylvan Barnet, Morton Berman, and William Burto's *The Study of Literature: A Handbook of Critical Essays and Terms*—a literary manual first published in 1960 and still in use today—are bluntly told to "see plot" (1960:317). Those who seek the term "character" receive the same instructions (272). Together, Aristotle, the novel, and the quest myth have produced an ineluctable effect on Anglo-American notions of narrative: if you want to know anything at all about narrative, *see plot*.

Key texts by French structuralist theoreticians Roland Barthes (1966), A. J. Greimas (1966), and Gérard Genette (1972, 1983) codified and intensified the tendency to define all narrative in terms of a specific plot type. At the height of structuralist activity, a *Poétique* article by Karlheinz Stierle, quoting A. C. Danto's description of the "basic structure of all narrative texts," defined narrative as follows (1972:178):

x is f at t_1

g happens to x at t_2

x is h at t_3

For Danto and Stierle, as for Aristotle, all narratives have a beginning, middle, and end. In other words, narrative is not just a set of materials but is a quite specific method of organizing those materials. Narrative definition is ineluctably bound to plot, and the plot in question is always of a particular kind.

At first, it might seem that this definition of narrative involves not just plot but character as well. After all, without "x," there can be no narrative. In practice, however, the structuralist approach to narrative is just as efficacious as its Anglo-American counterpart in nudging character out of the picture in favor of plot. For example, in Roland Barthes's often-quoted 1966 essay, "Introduction to the Structural Analysis of Narratives," characters are treated only through the actions they perform, at a level identified as that of "actions." In defense of this marginalization of characters, Barthes says: "From its very beginnings, structural analysis has refused to treat characters as essence." Influential Russian formalist Boris Tomachevski, he points out, "went so far as to deny any narrative importance to characters" (1966:16). He might also have quoted the opinion of Vladimir Propp, like Tomachevski an important formalist influence on structuralist narratology. "In the study of the folktale," affirms Propp, "the only important thing to know is *what* the characters do; *who* does something and *how* he does it are questions of secondary importance" (1970:29).

The opening chapter of Edward Branigan's *Narrative Comprehension and Film* offers an especially clear example of the stakes involved in current definitions of narrative. "In a narrative," affirms Branigan, echoing Aristotle, "some person, object, or situation undergoes a particular type of change and this change is measured by a sequence of attributions which apply to the thing at different times. Narrative is a way of experiencing a group of sentences or pictures (or gestures or dance movements, etc.) which together attribute a beginning, middle, and end to something" (1992:4). This definition leads Branigan to quote Tzvetan Todorov (1971:39) regarding the five basic stages of a narrative:

1. A state of equilibrium at the outset
2. A disruption of the equilibrium by some action
3. A recognition that there has been a disruption
4. An attempt to repair the disruption
5. A reinstatement of the initial equilibrium

These five stages depend on a series of relationships, thus producing what Branigan represents as a standard pattern of narrative, conveniently symbolized as: A/B/–A/–B/A.

Note that this description is offered not as an analysis but as a definition. Just as neoclassical prescriptions regarding appropriate narrative composition eventually determined neoclassical definitions of narrative, so structuralist theorists have regularly elevated analytical insights to definitional claims. The stakes of this approach become clear when Branigan applies Todorov's prescriptions to a sample narrative, a simple limerick:

There was a young lady of Niger
Who smiled as she rode on a tiger.
    They returned from the ride
     With the lady inside
And the smile on the face of the tiger.

Working from a definition of narrative that requires not only a beginning, middle, and end but also an A/B/–A/–B/A structure, Branigan affirms that "the reader discovers that the narrative did not begin with 'lady,' or 'youth,' or the place of 'Niger,' as its initial term ('A') because none of those beginnings will yield a macro-description of the required kind" (1992:5). In order to read this limerick as a narrative, Branigan insists, we may construe it in only one way. We must take "smile" as an initial term, thereby producing the following sequence of transformations (5):

A   smile
B   ride
–A   [swallowed: a horrible pleasure?]
–B   return
A   smile

Convinced that narrative involves a time-bound sequence of actions performed by a single protagonist, Branigan takes a limerick that apparently tells the story of two characters—a lady and a tiger—and reconfigures it as the story of a smile.

Let us for a moment imagine a slightly different limerick relating similar events involving similar characters:

A dashing young smile from Niger
Graced a damsel astride a fierce tiger
    But during their ride
     The smile changed sides
And came home safe on the teeth of the tiger.

This second limerick corresponds much more satisfactorily to Branigan's account: a smile goes for a ride, changes sides, and returns transformed. The anthropomorphization of the smile in this limerick justifies treating the smile as protagonist and thus as organizing principle of this narrative. But if *this* limerick corresponds neatly to Branigan's analysis, then how do we explain application of the same analysis to Branigan's initial limerick, in sum a quite different poem? Might there exist a definition of narrative that is capable of capturing the difference between the two limericks rather than forcing us to roll them into one?

A thumbnail examination will bring some clarity to these questions. Analyzing Branigan's limerick as a poem, without privileging its narrative component, I note the mismatch of the rhyming terms "tiger" and "Niger"—the one south Asian and the other African. This evocation of colonial locations necessarily colors appreciation of the two characters in Branigan's limerick: one dominant and self-confident, the other dominated and subservient. Instead of transforming an initial situation regarding a single protagonist, the ending involves a reversal of situations involving two characters: the dominant, self-confident character eventually proving to be weak and overconfident, while the apparently dominated and subservient character deploys unexpected strength. Far from playing the role of protagonist, the smile is parametric to the lady and the tiger—the common test whereby their differences are made to surface.

In this parable of colonial overconfidence and insufficiency, the one structural claim that an analysis cannot possibly maintain is that the lady's smile and the tiger's smile are the same. On the contrary, the analysis—and a fortiori our definition of narrative—must recognize the irreducible difference between the lady and the tiger. But this cannot be done with summary terms constituted by substantified verbs ("smile," "ride," "return"), since these suppress the original subjects, thereby dissimulating the characters with which they were originally associated. Instead, we need a method capable of bringing to the fore the oppositions constitutive of this particular narrative: lady/tiger, culture/nature, human/animal, dominant/recessive, apparent knowledge/effective knowledge, and so forth. Branigan's analysis, based on Todorov's neo-Aristotelian definition of narrative, squeezes the original limerick into a straitjacket. In order to make the limerick speak the type of narrative that his definition requires, Branigan must produce a reading that is quite distant from the limerick he started with. To be sure, he does read the poem as a narrative, but a broader definition of narrative might have permitted him to see yet another narrative, one more consistent with the text's characteristics. The poem that I read in Branigan's limerick—the parallel and eventually inverted stories of colonizer and colonized—fails to match the definition of narrative through which Branigan's narrative analysis must pass. Like Noël Carroll, who quietly slips from an analytical statement about the history of narrative texts ("narratives typically represent *changes* in states of affairs"; 2001:26) to a definitional statement ("narratives represent change"; 28), Branigan constructs a definition so centered on *change* that it proves unable to attend adequately to questions of *difference*.

This cursory glance at the neo-Aristotelian approach to narrative espoused by Todorov and Branigan suggests that we must revisit the question of narrative definition, especially since this approach is so widely shared, as several recent overviews of narrative theory clearly reveal (O'Neill 1994, Onega and Garcia Landa 1996, Abbott 2002, Rimmon-Kenan 2002, Herman and Vervaeck 2005, Phelan 2006). Because definitions often serve prescriptive purposes, they sometimes quietly diminish the very phenomena they are meant to illuminate. In order not to impoverish narrative, our definition must go beyond the Aristotelian tradition. The section that follows proposes a more open definition of narrative, designed to facilitate a broader spectrum of analyses.

The Nature of Narrative Revisited

Existing definitions of narrative share several shortcomings. Most are based on a limited corpus, stress a single characteristic, and take one type of narrative as representative of the entire class. To avoid these problems, I have respected the following precepts:

1. Useful definitions must be based on a willfully diverse corpus. Examples produced during a single historical period (e.g., the recent past) or by a limited group (e.g., culturally acceptable writers) do not constitute an

adequate sample. It is up to the theorist to guard against a corpus that is artificially limited by a combination of personal taste, ease of access, historical trends, or hidden cultural preferences. This has long been a serious problem in defining narrative, from Aristotle's dependence on the *Odyssey* and *Oedipus* to Lubbock's exclusive attention to the work of Henry James, Barthes's regular reference to Honoré de Balzac, and other theorists' tendency to base their notions of narrative on the novel alone. Virtually the sole narrative theorists to actively diversify their corpus have been Milhail Bakhtin (1968, 1981) and the team of Robert Scholes and Robert Kellogg (1966) and Scholes, Kellogg, and James Phelan (2006).

2. Good definitions maintain a balance between restriction and inclusion. Definitions must be restrictive, clearly excluding inappropriate examples, in order to target accurately the specific phenomena under investigation. At the same time, self-consciously inclusive definitions avoid unreasonable exclusion of potentially useful examples. The history of narrative definition has so often been marked by a desire for exclusion that we are currently in particular need of inclusiveness (though the inclusive efforts of Smith 1981, O'Neill 1994, Abbott 2002, and Prince 2003 deserve recognition).

3. Multiple-operator definitions are preferable to definitions based on a single criterion, because the latter rarely do justice to the phenomenon under study. While single-criterion systems allow for easy classification, they match up poorly with the complexity of a category like narrative and are of little use in the analytical process.

4. Subcategories must not be confused with the category itself (e.g., men for humans). In particular, a common approach to narrative organization (e.g., a beginning-middle-end structure) must not be taken as part of narrative's very definition. Because they disenfranchise no potential subcategories, "equal-opportunity" definitions are to be preferred.

Respecting these four precepts, the definition developed below is organized into three basic areas. *Narrative material* encompasses the minimal textual characteristics necessary to produce narrative. *Narrational activity* involves the presence of a narrating instance capable of presenting and organizing the narrative material. *Narrative drive* designates a reading practice required for narrative material and narrational activity to surface in the interpretive process.

Narrative Material

Most definitions of narrative assume that action alone is sufficient to define narrative. Two major innovations characterize the present definition: recognition that narrative material is insufficient by itself to define narrative, and insistence on character as a defining characteristic on a par with action.

ACTION

Narratives require action. Without action, we may have portraiture, catalogue, or *nature morte*, but not narrative. A telephone, a car, and a detective do not produce a narrative until they are set in motion by a series of actions: the telephone rings, the detective answers then jumps in the car. Seen in this way, actions are like verbs creating contact among the separate substantives populating a narrative.

Nearly every definition of narrative mentions action, though several recent theorists have preferred the term "event" (Toolen 1988:7, Miller 1998:46, Abbott 2002:12, Prince 2003:58). Rarely, however, do theorists recognize the very real complexity of this apparently simple requirement. Just what counts as "action" for the purpose of defining narrative? In scientific terms, there is no doubt that sunshine requires the action of heat-producing explosions. Why is it, then, that the sun's shining provides no more than atmosphere in one text (thus failing to constitute an action and contribute to that text's narrativity), but in another (e.g., a story of the sun's decision to continue shining in spite of humanity's wrongdoing) it counts as the action necessary to narrative? Questions like this imply that narrative cannot be defined by action alone, for even the recognition of action as such (i.e., acknowledgment that a particular action is sufficiently salient to count as action for purposes of narrative definition) cannot be achieved independently of other factors.

Actions appear so central to narrative that theorists often summarize narratives in terms of their actions alone. Narratives are typically referred to as representing a rise and fall, loss and recovery, or desire and acquisition. Gérard Genette (1980) first describes narrative as the expansion of full subject/verb sentences but then proceeds to organize his study according to the verbal aspects of his examples alone. Branigan summarizes the lady/tiger limerick as smile/ride/swallow/return/smile. This use of verb-based cover terms, as

William Hendricks (1973) notes, effectively disguises the aspects of narrative that depend on something other than action.

CHARACTER

In definitions of narrative, virtually no attention has been paid to the notion of character. Aristotle goes so far as to proclaim that character is simply unnecessary. Barthes and the structuralists relegate character to a dependent position. Anglo-American theorists have been similarly effective in excluding character from definitions of narrative. Though several volumes have been devoted to the study of characters in novels and films (Harvey 1965, Price 1983, *The Filmic Character* 1997), only exceptionally has character been given substantial play in constructing definitions of narrative (Scholes and Kellogg 1966, Chatman 1980, Rimmon-Kenan 2002, and Scholes, Kellogg, and Phelan 2006). No doubt the main reason for this oversight is the assumption that actions necessarily imply actors; designation of the actor as a defining characteristic would thus be redundant. If by definition an actor becomes an actor only by performing an action, then the action itself is primary and mention of the actor superfluous.

This logic is doubly flawed. First, as we know from our experience with the theater and cinema, actors are in fact neither engendered solely by their actions nor fully defined by them. Actors are also repositories of potential actions, existing independently of any specific completed action. The names of a film's starring actors in the opening credits create in us expectations regarding actions not yet realized, thereby convincing us that their characters exist independently of their actions. Second, this logic confuses the notion of "actor"—the one who performs an action—with the very different notion of "character." What is a character? And how is a character different from the actor who performs the actions necessary to a narrative? The answer to these questions is best approached as a function of the medium serving as a particular narrative's vehicle. In theater, human bodies serve as the vehicle for telling stories. As long as Sarah Bernhardt remains at the level of theater's bodily vehicle, she remains Sarah Bernhardt. She may laugh and cry or rant and rave, but she remains an actress and not a character. When she speaks, it is the body of Sarah Bernhardt that speaks; the words and actions remain on the level of the narrative's vehicle. Once she becomes Camille (in Alexandre

Dumas's play *La Dame aux Camélias*), however, Sarah Bernhardt is no longer the agent of her actions. Now the agent is another entity, separate from the actress and thus divorced from the bodily vehicle on which theater depends. Just as Camille is one level removed from Sarah Bernhardt, and thus from the "language" that serves as the vehicle for theater, so all characters exist at a level different from that of their narrative's vehicle. When we view a comic strip, we are looking at a series of lines until the process of representation turns those lines into represented forms. Without going through this process, we can never perceive a character but only a drawing. Reading a novel we first encounter words, not characters (just as theater offers actors before characters). The letters "D-a-v-i-d-C-o-p-p-e-r-f-i-e-l-d" do not at first designate a character—an entity existing at a level different from that of language itself. Certain events must take place before we will recognize "David Copperfield" as a character rather than as a simple name.

The key to this process may be found in the flights of fancy attributed by Jorge Luis Borges to his character Funes the Memorius. Constantly challenged by the classifications on which abstract thought depends, Funes is particularly troubled by the fact that the same name is used to designate phenomena that to him seem quite distinct: "It bothered him that the dog at three fourteen (seen from the side) should have the same name as the dog at three fifteen (seen from the front)" (1964:65). What Funes describes with such naïve accuracy is precisely the process that leads to readers' and viewers' recognition of a character. We look at the comic strip and see one image, then an instant later see a second image. The two images are demonstrably different, just like the views of the dog from the side and the front. Yet for us to construe this comic strip as narrative, we must give the same character name to both images. In a very real sense this is (as Borges cleverly implies) the way in which all knowledge is created: in order for phenomena to be memorized and turned into knowledge, we must renounce nominalism in favor of the abstract categories of realism. Narrative knowledge depends on this level of abstraction—we must abandon the media used to express and communicate the narrative in favor of a constructed, abstract level where the figure in frame one (seen from the side) and the figure in frame two (seen from the front) and the name used in frame three ("Goofy") are all recognized as referring to the same character. None of these taken alone actually is the character, but all three refer to the character, in the process erasing the primary graphic and linguistic levels. The development of characters thus participates in the creation of a "diegesis," a posited level independent of the textual vehicle.

The example provided by Funes the Memorius suggests in the simplest possible manner the extent to which the notion of character depends on multiple reiterations of the character. As long as there is only one picture of the dog, then Funes has no problem, precisely because he still identifies the graphic language and the dog. Only when the second image appears does Funes's frustration arise, for now he must contend with a contradiction between the physical level (the level of the vehicle), where he sees two different pictures, and the abstract level (the diegetic level), where there is only one character. Only with the introduction of the second example does this contradiction—and thus the character—appear. Far from being a synonym of "actor" (the one who does the acting) or "subject" (the one who sets the verb in motion), the term "character" is a technical term properly applied only to a limited range of actor-subjects. Among narrative theorists, only Seymour Chatman (1980:107ff), Gerald Prince (1982:71ff), and Mieke Bal (1985:25) have recognized the complexity and specificity of the notion of character.

Just as two distinct views are necessary to establish the existence of a character—an entity existing at a level different from the text's vehicle—so are two views necessary to determine what counts as an action for purposes of narrative definition. The term "action," when used as a criterion for narrative, is not simply an everyday term designating activity of all types but operates instead as a technical term dependent on a network of textual relationships. Thus sunshine usually does not count as a narrative-defining "action," but the sun's continuing to shine in spite of human shortcomings might very well qualify. Why should these two actions have different effects on a text's narrativity? What are the real differences hidden in this seat-of-the-pants distinction? In the first case, both the sun and the act of shining exist in a vacuum, whereas in the second case, the sun has been established as a character and the action of shining is set in relation to the possibility of the sun's not shining. Just as establishment of an actor as a character requires a minimum of two connected views of the actor, so qualification of an action as narrative-defining requires that an activity be valorized by a related activity—a transformed version of the activity that

(a) increases the saliency of both activities, (b) identifies the activity as a narrative variable, and thus (c) turns the simple activity into a narrative-defining action.

If the sun shines when it does by the simple continued revolution of heavenly bodies, then narrative is absent, but if the shining of the sun is set in relation to the non-shining of the sun, or the shining of the moon, or any other related activity capable of drawing attention to the process of the sun shining, then we recognize the kind of action that is necessary to narrative.

The existence of narrative depends on the simultaneous and coordinated presence of action and character. Narratives are not made of characters here and actions there but of characters acting. Indeed, it is the very fact that a character acts that permits us to recognize successive images as representing the same character. Conversely, it is through association with a character that simple activities become narrative-defining actions. For analytical purposes, action and character may reasonably be separated, but it is only as two angles on the same process that we encounter and experience action and character. This leads us to a second set of defining characteristics, precisely dependent on the way in which we encounter action and character.

Narrational Activity

It is often said that the world is full of stories all happening simultaneously. Yet the world is not itself a story. Neither the city of Brussels nor the battle of Waterloo is a story in and of itself. Yet both contain the material necessary for narrative. How is it that a city or a battle can be transformed into a narrative? Two processes, both narrational in character, are necessary to that transformation.

FOLLOWING

One of the most characteristic aspects of narrative involves the reader's sense of following a character from action to action and scene to scene. A bird's-eye view of a city, or a detailed description of a battle, no matter how many individual actors and activities are visible, will provide at most the material for narrative. Not until the narrator begins to follow a particular character will the text be recognizable as narrative. Or, to put it more accurately, not until a particular character is followed will we sense the activity of a narrator, thereby defining the text as narrative. Stendhal's *The Charterhouse of Parma* follows Fabrice del Dongo across the battlefields of Waterloo; in *Les Misérables* Victor Hugo animates the same battle by alternately following the Olympian decision-maker Napoleon and the pusillanimous scavenger Thénardier. It is this process of following that turns these accounts into narrative.

Imagine a long shot of the Grand Central Station waiting room. The camera doesn't move as it captures hundreds of hurried commuters scurrying about. Suddenly the camera tracks in to focus on a single, nervous individual looking at the clock. As she moves across the floor, the camera pans to follow her. At first the space is neutral, unvectored, narratively flat. When the camera focuses on a single individual and follows her, however, we recognize that we are being cued to read this scene as narrative. Followed, the character serves as a vector defining the space before us. As she becomes a character, thanks to the process of following, so her activities—previously indistinguishable from all the other activities visible in the image—turn into narrative-defining actions. Constitutive of narrative, the process of following thus simultaneously activates both character and narrator.

The process of following brings two different levels into clearer focus. Until the camera begins to follow a particular person, turning her into a character and foregrounding her actions, the process of narration remains entirely transparent, with no apparent separation between narrational and diegetic levels. With the introduction of following, concentrating attention on a particular character, we paradoxically also sense the existence of a narrational instance—some one, some thing, some system deciding who should be followed. The process of following thus simultaneously highlights character and narrator, diegesis and narration. It is precisely this simultaneous emphasis on two different levels that constitutes narrative. Without following, we have only an unvectored chaos, capable of producing narrative but not yet doing so; with following, we not only concentrate attention on a character and the character's actions, thus satisfying the first set of conditions for the existence of narrative, but we also implicitly reveal the existence of a second, narrational level. The author authors the words (sounds, images, etc.) of the text, but these are not where the narrative lies. The narrator narrates the diegetic level, which is where the narrative is located. All texts have a primary vehicle (or vehicles); narrative in addition constructs a diegesis beyond the primary vehicle and offers a narrator as a necessary filter between reader and diegesis. The process of following is the initial and primary evidence of that narrator's activity. (For a review of "no-narrator" approaches to narrative definition, see Herman, Jahn, and Ryan 2005:396–97.)

FRAMING

A substantial contradiction exists between two familiar but quite different ways of using the term "narrative." On the one hand, the term is regularly used to designate a type of material that is easily recognizable, even in small chunks. Used in this way, the term aptly describes our categorization activity as we browse through a stack of books, sort a bunch of films, or surf a series of television channels. Sampling only a portion of each text, we readily determine whether or not it is a narrative text. Once we establish—and it happens very rapidly indeed—that the text features characters, action, and following, we quickly identify it as narrative. Yet this "snapshot" approach contrasts strongly with narrative theoreticians' most common use of the term. From Aristotle to Branigan, theorists insist that narratives always have a beginning, middle, and end; that narrative endings must echo narrative beginnings in a significant manner; and that this arrangement is fundamental to the very notion of narrative. Texts lacking this structure are thus commonly not accepted as narratives. The contradiction here is quite clear. If it is necessary to observe the entirety of a text in order to acknowledge it as narrative, then what is it that channel surfers are recognizing? How can narrative be at the same time something that is identifiable piecemeal and something requiring the experience of complete texts?

The only way out of this quandary is to recognize two standard uses of the term "narrative," appropriately coexisting but easily distinguished. The first case, where narrative is discernible from small textual samples, involves recognition of what we might call "*some*" narrative, whereas the second case is concerned with the definition of "*a*" narrative. Daytime television soap operas offer a good example of "some" narrative. No matter when we tune in, we are rapidly convinced that we are dealing with a narrative text; yet no matter how long we watch, we never reach closure. Unlike most novels and films, soaps are all middle; we nearly always confront them in medias res and leave them before a satisfactory conclusion is reached. Yet we never doubt their narrativity. At every point we acknowledge that they are narrative in nature; that is, we recognize in them "some" narrative.

How do the texts touted as narrative by theoreticians differ from soaps? That is, how does "a" narrative differ from "some" narrative? The main difference at work here is the process of framing. In deciding whether a text is narrative, we are usually concerned only to know whether it contains characters, action, and following. But when theorists concentrate on a common narrative pattern, they are analyzing questions of framing, not content. Just as a shot of the crowds in Grand Central Station becomes narrative (in the sense of "some" narrative) only when a character is followed, thus revealing narrational activity, so a series of events becomes narrative (in the sense of "a" narrative) only when those events are framed, thus revealing yet another type of narrational activity. By itself, daily life cannot be said to constitute narratives, however much narrative material it may provide. But when a naturalist novelist cuts daily life into slices, thus delimiting and framing it, the narratives implicit in daily life may be revealed.

To recognize "some" narrative, all we need are narrative material and following, but "a" narrative is recognizable only when it has been fully framed. In one sense, then, it is the very process of framing that gives a text its beginning and end. Without framing, texts are all middle; by the very act of framing, texts gain a beginning and end. Note that this definition of framing says nothing about necessary correspondences between beginnings and endings. Framing delimits the text but does not guarantee any particular internal textual organization—thus avoiding the Aristotelian pitfall of making one among many possible types of textual organization part of narrative's very definition.

Narrative Drive

The preceding descriptions of minimal narrative criteria assume that narrative material and narrational activity are always located within the text. Upon careful inspection, however, this assumption proves poorly justified. Let us return for a moment to our Grand Central Station crowd scene, the one that becomes narrative only when it is invested with narrational activity. When the narrational activity is provided by a camera tracking a particular character, then we can confidently affirm that the narrational activity is intratextual. But suppose a spectator recognizes on the screen a star actor among all the other unrecognized faces. Or imagine that a spectator sees a good friend in the crowd. Or perhaps a graduate student writing a dissertation on facial types notices someone with the type of face she is currently treating. In all these cases there is every likelihood that the spectator will follow one individual throughout the scene, just as if the camera had chosen to focus on that character. In other words, it is entirely imaginable that the narrator responsible for narrational activity can be the spectator or reader (supported by powerful social institutions like the film industry, the family, or the educational system). As Michael J. Toolen puts it, narrative is not just a sequence of non-randomly connected events but a *"perceived* sequence of non-randomly connected events" (1988:7; my italics), a position shared by Luc Herman and Bart Vervaeck (2005:52–54).

A similar situation obtains regarding every aspect of narrative material and narrational activity. Virtually any situation can be invested with character/action characteristics, as well as with following and framing. Indeed, this is what anthropologists, archaeologists, historians, doctors, car mechanics, and myriad others are doing as they strive to make sense of social customs, ancient stones, and physical symptoms. Identifying the characters and actions meaningful to their specific context, these "spectators" perform the narrational function of following individual characters and framing separate narratives. For one, this might mean charting the destruction of a civilization by farmers' inability to adjust to new climatic conditions; for another, it might mean following the ramifications of foreign matter introduced into the gas tank. For these professionals, the very process of exercising their profession involves creating a narrative out of details that are not necessarily in and of themselves narrative.

We may appropriately term this tendency to read texts as narratives "narrative drive." Narrative drive can derive from many sources: personal interests, professional mandates, or social expectations. While it may be conditioned by textual characteristics, it can never be wholly dependent on elements that are internal to the text. In other words, without narrative drive on the part of the reader, texts are not read as narrative. Conversely, though narrative drive usually arises in response to specific textual factors, a strong narrative drive can generate the very factors necessary for recognition of narrative. Imagine a line, a simple line drawn across the page. One would be hard put to claim that this line satisfies any of the requirements for narrativity outlined above. Yet the reader who is strongly driven to treat this text as narrative can do so with little difficulty. Somewhere, the line will seem a little bit thinner or a tone fainter. Recognizing the continuity of the line through thick and thin, we turn the line into a character named "the line" (like Borges's dog, recognizably the same at different points in spite of demonstrable differences), and the thinning into an event worthy of recognition as an action. Thus our simple straight line turns into a narrative in which "the line" first "thins," then "thickens"—character/action units that characterize narrative material. By following the line and delimiting the text to the surroundings of the line's thinning and rethickening we have implicitly provided the narrative activity necessary for narrative. A strong case of narrative drive has produced a narrative where none was apparent. On virtually any set of givens, this process may be repeated.

Paradoxically, there exists similar evidence for the converse of this principle. However narrative a text may appear to some, a lack of narrative drive can always threaten the text's narrativity. For some, the action and dialogue of a love scene may disappear entirely in favor of contemplating the portrait of a beautiful woman or an attactive man. A battle scene may lose its narrative focus entirely when the members of a Civil War re-creation society watch the scene, attentive not to its narrative stakes but to making a catalogue of the weapon types used by Union and Confederate soldiers. My favorite example of the lack of narrative drive appears in the Blackhawk Films version of D. W. Griffith's classic thriller short, *The Lonedale Operator*. Instead of stressing the growing love affair between the train engineer and the telegraph operator, Blackhawk's version provides an insert describing the locomotive visible on the screen. Rather than attend to the burglars' attack, another insert explains that the locomotive is pointing in the wrong direction. Initially distributed to railroad fans, Blackhawk's infamous version of *The Lonedale Operator* substitutes what we might whimsically term "locomotive drive" for "narrative drive." Far from constituting an unusual situation, this case actually exemplifies the extremely common circumstance where a text read by some as narrative is harvested by others for entirely different purposes. Depending on the "reading formation" espoused by the reader at the moment of a particular reading, a text can move in and out of the narrative category, whether or not it displays narrative material and narrational activity.

The one thing we can claim with great assurance is that whenever narrative drive causes a text to be read as narrative, the reading will foreground narrative material and narrational activity. Though these interconnected levels may reasonably be analyzed separately, they have immediate impact on each other. The very process of following convinces us of the existence of a character; similarly, the process of framing lends such importance to certain events that they readily appear as the actions required by narrative. Whether through recognition of conspicuous textual elements or by dredging up entirely submerged textual factors, narrative drive always produces salient narrative material and narrational activity. While narratives may be read in many ways, the reading of a narrative as narrative always involves the presence of narrative material, the implementation of narrational activity, and the deployment of narrative drive.

A New Approach to Narrative Analysis

Whether they are constructed of words, images, sounds, or bodies, all narratives depend on the process that I have termed "following." Revealing narrational activity while organizing the narrative material, the process of following contributes heavily to narrative rhetoric and meaning. In the ensuing pages, narratives are thus analyzed through the filter provided by following. Surprisingly, this mode of approaching narratives has never been previously attempted. Several new terms are thus necessary.

Following-Unit

Analysis of a random group of narratives quickly reveals enormous variation in the following process. Some narratives resolutely follow the same character from beginning to end (Henry in Stephen Crane's *The Red Badge of Courage* or Julien Sorel in Stendhal's *The Red and the Black*), while others regularly alternate between two characters or groups (Virtues and Vices in

Prudentius's *Psychomachia* or Pyncheons and Maules in Nathaniel Hawthorne's *House of Seven Gables*); still others follow many different characters during the course of the narrative (Victor Hugo's *Notre-Dame de Paris* or Leo Tolstoy's *War and Peace*). Furthermore, the length of time any particular character is followed varies enormously. In Flaubert's *Madame Bovary*, Charles is followed only until he encounters Emma; from that point on we follow Emma almost exclusively for the rest of the novel. In Longus's *Daphnis and Chloe*, we follow Daphnis for a short stretch, then switch to Chloe, then back to Daphnis, and so forth, always alternating in brief segments. In the average action film, culminating combats are typically handled through formulaic alternation between the principals—a shot or two for the hero, a shot of the bad guy, and so on, with no more than a few seconds spent on either character at any one time. To analyze these texts as narratives, we need to be able to conceive them as a succession of "following-units": that is, as a series of segments each made up of that portion of the text where a character (or group of characters) is followed continuously.

The operative concern here is "following," not "point of view." Virtually every recent general study of narrative deals with the concept of point of view (Chatman 1980:74–160,184–203, Genette 1980:161–262, Bal 1985:100–115, Martin 1986:130–51, Genette 1988:41–144, Chatman 1990:147–262, O'Neill 1994:58–131, Van Peer and Chatman 2001, Abbott 2002:62–75, Rimmon-Kenan 2002:72–86), but none treat the process of following. It is essential to distinguish between the concept of point of view and the notion of following. Point of view always involves, however transitorily, the use of a character as a secondary filter of information (as opposed to the Olympian narrator common to most pre-modern narrative). For this reason, the notion of point of view is applicable only to selected texts; indeed, an identifiable point of view may exist in only a small portion of even those texts. Following, in contrast, is essential to the very category of narrative: wherever there is narrative there is following. Segmentation of narratives by point of view would thus leave enormous holes; several centuries would be skipped over, as would major portions of most pre-modern novels. Segmentation by following-unit, however, covers the entire narrative portion of every text treated as narrative.

In some texts, division into following-units is a simple task indeed. Medieval Grail romances such as the anonymous thirteenth-century *Queste del*

Saint Graal regularly interrupt the story of one knight to say "And now the story follows Galahad (or Lancelot, or Gawain) instead." In this case, each following-unit is neatly delimited by the narration process itself. In many dialogue-oriented nineteenth-century novels, however, following-units are anything but discrete. For example, a character may be followed to a protracted scene involving several dialogues among multiple characters, with another character followed away from the scene. When do we stop following the first character and begin following the second? No exact answer is possible. Nor is the process of separating a narrative text into following-units ever a mechanical, scientific affair. Just as different levels of narrative drive must necessarily affect the narrative status of a text, so differing investments may lead two perfectly competent readers to segment the same text into following-units quite differently.

Modulations

Once narrative texts are conceived as a series of following-units, the question of transitions between following-units forces itself on us. In some stories, the narrator simply stops talking about one character and shifts to another. In others, great care is taken to justify movement from one character to another within the logic of the tale. Borrowing a notion from Jean Rousset's *Forme et signification* (1964:117–22), I term all transitions from one following-unit to another "modulations."

Modulations are of three main types. One following-unit may modulate to another by bringing characters into contact within the diegetic space. True to the classical French theatrical doctrine termed "liaison des scènes," this method operates scenically, reducing the narrator's need to intervene in the course of the narrative. Far more common in earlier narrative, and still operative today primarily in popular narrative, is a modulation method that depends not on physical contact in the diegetic world but on some characteristic that two characters share and that can be played up by the narrator. The western's stereotypical "Meanwhile, back at the ranch" operates in just this fashion. We follow the Lone Ranger (or Hopalong Cassidy or Randolph Scott) for the space of one following-unit, while he is out hunting the outlaws. Then the narrator's "Meanwhile, back at the ranch" justifies a modulation back to the imperiled women struggling to defend the ranch house against marauding rustlers. This modulation depends on the fact that both the Lone Ranger and the women at the ranch are placed in the same time frame. A third type of modulation abandons any such logic, simply jumping to a new character without any obvious justification for the introduction of a new following-unit.

Employing terminology introduced by Roman Jakobson (1956) and augmented by Gérard Genette (1966), I call the first type of modulation "metonymic," the second "metaphoric," and the third "hyperbolic." While Jakobson initially proposed the terms metonymic and metaphoric to distinguish between different types of figurative language (characterized, respectively, by syntagmatic and paradigmatic connections), the terminology may also be productively applied to narrative modulations.

Metonymic modulations depend on direct spatial contact within the diegesis. Frequently justified by the act of seeing, metonymic modulations can easily be established simply by manipulating the location of characters. For example, in *Notre-Dame de Paris* Victor Hugo elegantly modulates from an indoor scene between the soldier Phoebus and his fiancée Fleur-de-Lys to a following-unit featuring the gypsy girl Esmeralda simply by having Phoebus and Fleur-de-Lys step out onto the balcony where they can be seen by Esmeralda. A similar device is used in scores of films featuring characters with binoculars: from a following-unit featuring the plotting criminals we cut to a long shot with a binocular mask, followed by a medium shot of an investigator looking through binoculars. The metonymic simplicity of this movement is often appropriated or even parodied by enterprising narrators. A transitional intertitle from Rupert Julian's *The Phantom of the Opera* explains that "melody floats through hall and corridor, even to the executive offices, where a strange deal is being closed," thus employing sound's ability to bend around corners to establish a metonymic modulation where no visual contact is possible. Similarly, but with increased whimsy, François Truffaut follows up the first murder in *The Bride Wore Black* with a shot of a scarf floating in the sky over the city where the murder took place. As the scarf eventually lights on a tropical plant, we can just make out a jet plane in the background. We then continue to follow a woman inside the plane, thus concluding a lengthy and clever modulation which, against all odds, has been based on spatial contiguity.

Metaphoric modulations depend on a quality shared by the characters followed in successive following-units. From Alexandrian romances and classical epics to dime novels and adventure films, the sole shared quality is often time. With the hero on one side of the Mediterranean and the heroine dragged off by pirates to the other side, parallel presentation of simultaneous actions is a convenient device indeed, with regular metaphoric modulations joining the star-crossed lovers (through such connectors as *interea, cependant*, or *meanwhile*). Even in contemporary romances, the tradition of justifying a modulation from one lover to the other through simultaneous sleepless nights remains strong. Most metaphoric modulations involving simultaneity reinforce the sharing of time with some other shared activity: parallel preparations for battle, similar thoughts, matching songs. Even before Vincente Minnelli's film version of *Gigi* brings the title character into contact with her eventual love-match Gaston, a modulation from the one to the other has been justified by the similarity of their attitudes and songs; to her naïve "I Don't Understand the Parisians" corresponds his world-weary "It's a Bore."

With a little imagination, metaphoric modulations can be devised for virtually any situation. Novels can establish metaphoric connections with no more than a "No less disheartened was x," "Similarly challenged was y," or "Pondering the same problem was z." Comic strip artists regularly take advantage of color, size, or position to justify modulation from one character to another. Visually sensitive filmmakers like René Clair and Rouben Mamoulian often modulate from one character to another simply by superimposing an object from one shot onto a similarly shaped object from the previous shot. The creation of clever metaphoric modulations is itself a stylistic flourish indulged in by authors from every era.

Hyperbolic modulations abandon the careful spatial or conceptual ties characteristic of their metonymic and metaphoric counterparts. Recognizing that most traditional poetry uses figurative language based on metonymic or metaphoric connections, but that the baroque figures of the French Renaissance poet Jean de Sponde regularly eschew such relationships, Gérard Genette (1966) suggests that we recognize the latter as "hyperbolic" in nature (as compared with the more traditional "parabolic" figures characterized by metonymic or metaphoric links). Hyperbolic figures go out of their way to bring together objects or experiences that seem to have little in common. Just as surrealists touted strange connections like the junction of an umbrella and a surgery table, so hyperbolic figures thrive on the unexpected, the apparently unconnected. In the same manner, while metonymic and metaphoric modulations always foreground the relationships that justify them, hyperbolic modulations systematically evacuate any sense of relationship between successive following-units.

The basic hyperbolic modulation is thus the one popularized by the Grail romances: "The story now leaves x and begins with y." No explanation, no connection, no sense of spatial or conceptual leading. Indeed, in the Grail romances we soon sense that the fundamental questions that readers must ask—the Grail questions—involve an inquiry into this very lack of information. Why x? Why y? Who are they and how do they differ? Do they have something in common in spite of the hyperbolic modulation's silence on that question? There is something inviting about the technique shared by so many nineteenth-century and early-twentieth-century novels, whereby the character followed in one chapter or section is replaced—after a short white space on the page—by a different character in the next chapter or section. Every hyperbolic modulation tempts us to ask: "How did we get here from there?" What justifies the progression of *Notre-Dame de Paris*, *War and Peace*, André Gide's *Lafcadio's Adventures*, André Malraux's *Man's Fate*, Thornton Wilder's *The Bridge of San Luis Rey*, or any of the many other novels that regularly modulate without apparent justification from character to character? Mysterious, underjustified, lacking any apparent connections, hyperbolic modulations always seem to introduce questions about narrative structure that metonymic and metaphoric modulations effectively avoid.

Following-Pattern

Every narrative text may usefully be understood as a series of individual following-units, joined by modulations and arranged in a particular manner. Each narrative text thus displays a specific "following-pattern." Our perception of any given narrative is heavily marked by the interdependence of individual following-units and the overall following-pattern perceived in the text. By the same token, the pattern perceived in any given text depends in part on the range of patterns we have previously experienced. One of the major missing links in our understanding of narrative is a general account of the various following-patterns that characterize narrative organization. As the pages to come will reveal, the history and practice of narrative have long been dominated by three major following-patterns. Implicitly recognized and emulated by practitioners, these three following-patterns have regularly been invested with specific functional and symbolic purposes. Without a detailed account of this aspect of narrative expression, our understanding of narrative must remain incomplete.

The task that lies ahead is thus a daunting one. Narrative analysis, typology, and history must be rethought from a new standpoint. This is a tall order, apparently calling for simultaneous advances on several fronts. To avoid tackling too many problems at once, I begin by analyzing a single representative text that challenges received notions of narrative definition and structure. The lessons derived from that analysis are then applied to a series of similar texts, permitting the recognition of a first basic following-pattern. This process is then repeated with exemplary texts representing a second and then a third fundamental following-pattern. After this broad survey, a first conclusion assesses the overall theoretical ramifications of the approach taken in this book. Remaining questions regarding the applicability of this new method are treated in a second conclusion.

TWO   The Song . . . of Roland?

As it is usually told, *The Song of Roland* is the tragic story of a youthful warrior who makes the successive mistakes of incurring his stepfather Ganelon's ire and assuming that his rearguard can, by itself, repel the Saracen attack perfidiously engineered by Ganelon. As a result of Roland's hubris, the entire rearguard is killed, including his best friend Oliver. Blowing his horn with his last breath, Roland finally summons the main force, which, under Charlemagne's command, eventually avenges his death not once but twice—first against Marsile's local army and then against Baligant's combined legions.

Behind this apparently simple summary lurk several problems. This Roland-centered approach reminds us that the title of the poem is a nineteenth-century creation, added shortly after this early twelfth-century manuscript (Bodleian ms. Digby 23) of a late-eleventh-century text was discovered in 1832. Indeed, Roland's death just over halfway into the poem has led some critics to claim that the text as a whole is not unified (and thus may be an amalgam of separate sources), while other readers have gone to great lengths to show that the final half of the poem can be justified as a continuation of Roland's story. Both camps share two fundamental assumptions: that the first half of *Roland* is organized around the title character and that a work is unified only if all its principal aspects can be explained in terms of a single hero. Analysis of the text's following-pattern offers an entirely different hypothesis.

The Following-Pattern

Just what is the shape of *Roland*'s following-pattern? The question is more easily asked than answered: scores of different individuals and groups are followed during the course of the manuscript's 293 stanzas and 4,002 verses. As soon as we have been introduced to Charlemagne, the narrator's attention jumps to the Saracen camp for the first of six council scenes. There we meet the pagan king Marsile, who fears the wrath of the Christian armies. Soon we are in the midst of the Christian camp, where the pagan messengers tender offers of peace. There follows the famous scene where Roland nominates his stepfather Ganelon for the dangerous assignment of carrying a response to Marsile. We then follow Ganelon and Blancandrin, the pagan messenger, to Saragossa, where Ganelon persuades the Moors to attack Roland and the rearguard at Roncevaux. Once Ganelon has given a false report to Charlemagne, the French are shown riding toward their homeland, while the Saracens are represented maneuvering their yet-to-be-formed army to ambush the yet-to-be-formed rearguard. After Charlemagne's two prophetic dreams, we eventually witness both Ganelon's nomination of Roland for the dangerous rearguard assignment and Marsile's formation of his squadrons.

When the battle begins, we follow an increasing number and variety of characters. Some following-units treat an entire army in summary fashion; others offer close-ups of individual combats in which pagan and Christian knights are followed alternately and independently. As the Christian force dwindles in both strength and numbers, attention is concentrated on the successive deaths of the French heroes—first Roland's friend Oliver, then bishop Turpin, and finally Roland himself. The second battle is handled in much the same way. We spend more time following the pagan commanders as they prepare for the second battle than we do with Charlemagne's grief or his plotting of revenge. We witness the organization of the infidel army, as well as the formation of the Christian ranks. Before the battle begins, we flash back and forth many times from one side to the other, finishing with an overview of both armies, treated in a single description. Finally, Baligant and Charlemagne meet in single combat. Like their armies, the two commanders are described with plural phrases applying to both warriors.

Even Charlemagne's victory and the general pagan surrender are not enough to remove all opposition to the cause of Christian justice, however. Nor does the victory in Spain eliminate all pagans from the following-pattern. Once the French have been followed home, we must still watch Pinabel and Thierry fight a judicial duel to decide Ganelon's fate. This fight, like the earlier ones, is built of alternating glimpses of the two combatants. When Thierry wins the fight, we turn to Ganelon and his thirty sympathizers, who are duly executed. Not until we have followed the pagan queen Bramimonde to the baptismal font, however, can we return to Charlemagne, whom we leave as we found him at the beginning—with the prospect of still another city to wrest from the hands of the pagans.

Most critics have read *The Song of Roland* quite selectively, following the causal chain that begins when Roland nominates Ganelon as messenger and ends with Roland's death or Charlemagne's revenge. To make sense of the text in this manner, scholars typically concentrate on only a few passages, primarily those relating to Roland's motivation and eventual death. But we have only to look at the extraordinary variety of characters followed to realize that, even when alive, Roland is hardly at the center of the text. The following-pattern's characteristic alternation between two warring forces precludes concentration on any one individual. Instead, the following-pattern offers another stable element. Throughout the text, the following-pattern's constant alternation keeps us ever aware of the perpetual conflict. Roland may die, Charlemagne may cross temporarily to the other side of the mountain, and scores of warriors attract the narrator's attention only to disappear from view forever—but the alternation of the following-pattern never ceases. Even when the French troops have returned to France, the poet finds an opponent to sing about: the battle between Pinabel and Thierry is a microcosm of the whole work in terms of both theme and form. But so is every confrontation, for we are never limited to only one side of things. Now a Frenchman closes on an unsuspecting pagan and with a flash of hard steel lays open his brain; now a valiant pagan, incensed, responds by decapitating a Christian with one swift blow. Not only battles but also parallel council and travel sequences mirror the overall structure, which is constantly emphasized by the alternating following-pattern.

I	Background of the French situation (1a)
II	The Saracens decide to sue for peace (1b–7a)
III	Roland nominates Ganelon to serve as messenger (7b–26)
IV	Ganelon convinces the pagans to ambush the rearguard (27–52)
V	Ganelon lies to Charles (53–54)
VI	The French ride toward France (55a)
VII	The Saracens ride toward Roncevaux (55b)
VIII	Charlemagne's prophetic dreams (56–57)
IX	Ganelon designates Roland as rearguard leader (58–68a)
X	The Saracen squadrons are formed (68b–79a)
XI	The rearguard hears the Saracen forces approaching (79b)

FIGURE 2.1 The beginning of *The Song of Roland,* linear representation (stanza numbers in parentheses)

Schematically, the familiar Roland-centered reading of the first part of the text may be represented as in fig. 2.1. This linear configuration aptly reflects the method that novel-oriented critics have applied to this text ever since they succeeded in dubbing it *The Song of Roland.* Relating each action to the preceding and succeeding ones, they have seen this first quarter of *Roland* as a cause-and-effect progression stemming from Ganelon's rage at having been chosen by his stepson for a dangerous mission. Interest has thus been concentrated on the results of Ganelon's treachery, on the background of the Roland-Ganelon relationship, and on Charlemagne's tragic foreknowledge of his nephew's danger. The individual has been placed at the center, with the rest of the Christian army, the entire pagan force, and both sets of divinities treated as secondary.

What is at stake here is not the importance of Roland's and Ganelon's respective roles. The real question lies further on: To what extent is *Roland*'s structure patterned on the linear cause-effect chain constituted by Ganelon's machinations and Roland's resultant death? A careful assessment clearly reveals the importance of the following-pattern's rhetorical effect. In *The Song of Roland*, the following-pattern succeeds in transforming the linearity of the plot into a balanced, spatial structure. If the biographical form of a typical novel tends to equate structure and plot, deriving the one from the other, *Roland* opposes structure

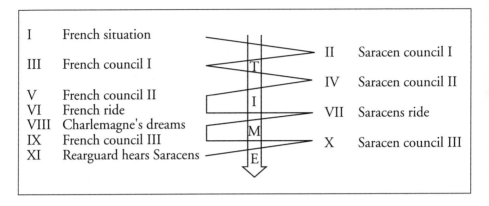

FIGURE 2.2 The beginning of *The Song of Roland*, zigzag representation

to plot, seeking stasis through the balanced pattern suggested by the alternating arrangement of following-units. This alternation invites us to reorganize our perception of the first section of *Roland* according to the pattern represented in fig. 2.2. As the slope of the zigzag line representing the following-pattern indicates, the alternation at first shows temporal continuity, with textual progression replicating the flow of diegetic time. As the climax of this first section approaches, however, there is an increasing tendency to obliterate the time continuum, with the same time represented twice, once on each side of the Pyrenees.

We can perhaps best recognize the difference between the two diagrams—and the differing approaches to narrative structure that they represent—by analyzing our own eye movements as we look at the diagrams. The first diagram, representing *Roland* as a single line, naturally draws our eyes progressively down the page in a more or less continuous fashion. The second diagram by no means does away entirely with motion down the page, but it adds an extremely important horizontal component. Our eye movements from left to right and back again disguise our vertical movement—almost to the point of making us forget our vertical progress altogether. The whole point of *Roland*'s zigzag following-pattern is to make us construe the text not in terms of temporal development but as a spatial balance of opposing forces. The spatialization of time in *Roland* serves at every moment to underline the conflict pitting Christian forces against pagan legions.

Throughout *The Song of Roland* an alternating following-pattern is augmented by parallel scenes and the doubling of time in order to underline the *theomachia* that generates the poem's basic structure. Charlemagne's battle with Baligant takes up where the rearguard's skirmish with Marsile left off. Repeatedly, alternation between the two sides culminates in the forging of both armies or warriors into a single description, as represented in fig. 2.3. The first three following-units take up over one-third of the sequence and strictly respect the continuity of time. As the battle begins, however, the following-units are systematically shortened, averaging only one stanza apiece throughout the general combat that constitutes the first phase of the battle. Increasingly, parallel actions are treated as occurring concurrently. During the final duel between Baligant and Charlemagne the following-units are further reduced to less than one-third of a stanza apiece. Thoroughly fragmented, time now serves the spatial opposition of the two leaders, their armies, and their divinities. Even in those passages where time cannot be doubled, such as dialogue interchanges, the poet has cast the opposing speeches from the same mold, thereby emphasizing the parallelism of the two sides rather than a temporal or cause-and-effect relationship.

Dividing *Roland* into following-units reveals many of the poem's distinctive characteristics. It shows how time is deemphasized by repetition of the same time segment. It demonstrates the extent to which psychological motivation and linear development are sacrificed to formal juxtaposition. It reveals that meaning depends not on narrative progress but on the nearly static contrast of two diametrically opposed groups. It also draws our attention to the problem of modulation between following-units. Taking advantage of the many similarities between the warring forces, *Roland* demonstrates a marked preference for metaphoric modulations. Instead of just jumping to the other side, or depending on the flow of time to justify a change of focus, the narrator arrests time by concentrating on the similarities between the two sides.

This technique is substantially aided by the poet's mastery of verse structure. *Roland*'s verses are all built in the same manner, with a four-syllable hemistich followed by a six-syllable hemistich. Repeatedly, identical or similar hemistichs are used to justify passage from one side to the other, with the reiterated hemistichs often placed at the start of successive stanzas. In the heat of the Roncevaux battle we move from Roland to his foes in the following manner:

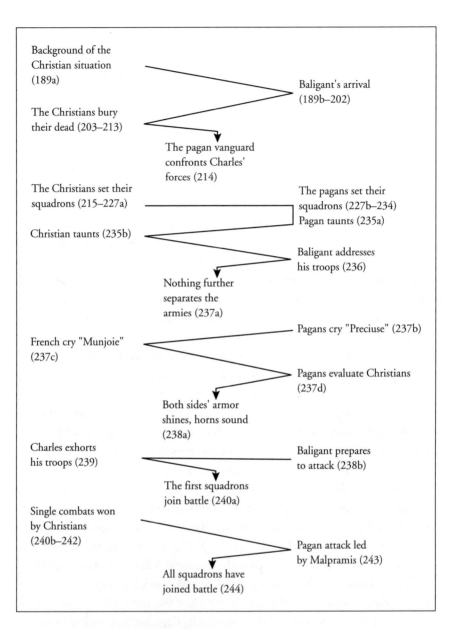

Background of the
Christian situation
(189a)

Baligant's arrival
(189b–202)

The Christians bury
their dead (203–213)

The pagan vanguard
confronts Charles'
forces (214)

The Christians set their
squadrons (215–227a)

The pagans set their
squadrons (227b–234)
Pagan taunts (235a)

Christian taunts (235b)

Baligant addresses
his troops (236)

Nothing further
separates the
armies (237a)

French cry "Munjoie"
(237c)

Pagans cry "Preciuse" (237b)

Pagans evaluate Christians
(237d)

Both sides' armor
shines, horns sound
(238a)

Charles exhorts
his troops (239)

Baligant prepares
to attack (238b)

The first squadrons
join battle (240a)

Single combats won
by Christians
(240b–242)

Pagan attack led
by Malpramis (243)

All squadrons have
joined battle (244)

FIGURE 2.3a *(Above and opposite page)* The battle between Charlemagne and Baligant (stanza numbers in parentheses)

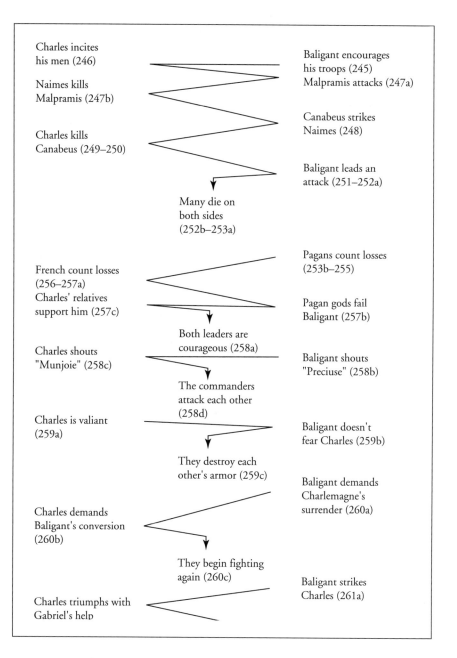

Charles incites
his men (246)

Baligant encourages
his troops (245)
Malpramis attacks (247a)

Naimes kills
Malpramis (247b)

Canabeus strikes
Naimes (248)

Charles kills
Canabeus (249–250)

Baligant leads an
attack (251–252a)

Many die on
both sides
(252b–253a)

Pagans count losses
(253b–255)

French count losses
(256–257a)
Charles' relatives
support him (257c)

Pagan gods fail
Baligant (257b)

Both leaders are
courageous (258a)

Charles shouts
"Munjoie" (258c)

Baligant shouts
"Preciuse" (258b)

The commanders
attack each other
(258d)

Charles is valiant
(259a)

Baligant doesn't
fear Charles (259b)

They destroy each
other's armor (259c)

Baligant demands
Charlemagne's
surrender (260a)

Charles demands
Baligant's conversion
(260b)

They begin fighting
again (260c)

Baligant strikes
Charles (261a)

Charles triumphs with
Gabriel's help

FIGURE 2.3b

When Roland sees the accursed host . . . (stanza 144)

When the pagans saw that there were few Frenchmen . . . (145)

So strong is the rhythm of *Roland*'s verse structure that even single nouns—when carefully paired—are sufficient to provide the parallelism necessary for metaphoric modulation, as in this simple move from Baligant to his Christian foe:

The Emir calls to his army. (245)

The Emperor entreats his Frenchmen. (246)

Throughout *Roland*, formulaic repetition is used as a basis for modulation between the two sides. Early in the battle, the Saracen knight Margariz

Spurs his horse, gets set to strike Oliver.

His shield he breaks beneath its pure gold buckle. (103)

In the next stanza, Margariz's Christian counterpart, Roland,

Spurs his horse, gets set to strike Chernuble.

His helmet he breaks where the carbuncles shine. (104)

As often occurs, the formal parallelism justifying modulation is here used to introduce a substantive distinction between Saracen and French warriors: whereas Oliver's body is protected by God from Margariz's blow, Roland's sword slices Chernuble in half.

Based on similarities between Christians and pagans—but highlighting their differences—metaphoric modulations provide smooth transitions from one following-unit to the next, at the same time emphasizing the fundamental differences that underlie the poem's general structure. Paired speeches often use repeated formulaic language to concentrate attention on a basic difference between the two sides. Just when all looks hopeless for the French rearguard, the end of one stanza initiates an echo:

The Archbishop says: "Accursed are those who do not fight hard!

Charles is returning, he will avenge us well." (159)

To which the beginning of the next stanza responds:

> The pagans say: "In an evil hour we were born!
> On a terrible day for us the sun has today risen;
> We have lost our lords and our peers;
> Charles is returning, the valiant one, with his great army." (160)

Though they have lost all their friends and will soon die themselves, the French retain the Christian virtue of hope, while the pagans, despite their victory, give in to despair.

Because it depends on parallelism rather than sequential or cause-and-effect relationships, metaphoric modulation heightens *Roland*'s characteristic tendency toward spatialization. When Turpin attacks Malquiant, he hits him so hard

> That he strikes him dead on the green grass. (121)

After that, Grandonie attacks Gerin. But what do we mean by "after that"? If we mean, "in the next stanza," then we are right, but if we mean, "in the following moment," we do violence to *Roland*'s painstakingly constructed metaphoric modulations. The poet has carefully located Grandonie's action not on a time continuum ("after that") but in a world of space, for the next stanza begins

> On the other side is a pagan, Grandonie. (122)

From reading novels we have become accustomed to equating a text's temporal flow to that of the diegesis. *Roland*'s combination of an alternating following-pattern and repeated use of metaphoric modulation requires a change in our reading habits. When Grandonie hits Gerin so hard

> That he strikes him dead on a high rock (122)

thereby echoing the language of the previous stanza, we begin to understand why the poet is so anxious to keep us from structuring our reading according to a simple one-after-the-other perception of verses or stanzas. The language just used for Turpin's victory over Malquiant is repeated in order to induce us to read the succeeding stanzas as *counterposed* rather than subsequent actions. Together, the alternating following-pattern and metaphoric modulations transfigure the text, forcing it into a spatial mold uniquely suited to the balance that informs *Roland*'s structure.

Symmetry

Differing reading strategies shed light differentially. The way we configure a text has important ramifications for the extent to which various aspects of the text achieve saliency. When *The Song of Roland* is considered in traditional terms, as a series of events laid out in cause-and-effect fashion along a time line, salient aspects of the text include such novelistic concerns as character psychology and motivation. When the alternating following-pattern is emphasized, however, attention is drawn to entirely different aspects of the text. Instead of stressing the effect that one character has on another, readers who attend to the following-pattern are bound to notice that the text's characters are created in pairs. Charlemagne and Marsile both have nephews, Roland and Aelroth, who by virtue of their parallelism must meet in single combat. Tradition told the poet that Archbishop Turpin had accompanied Charlemagne to Spain, thus calling for a Saracen counterpart, Siglorel the magician, whom Turpin kills on the battlefield. The pagan divinity must be tripartite—Apollo, Mohammed, and Tervagant—to mirror the Christian Trinity. *Counter*part characters, *counter*feit gods, *counter*attacks designed to *counter*act. We look in vain for historical antecedents for most of the pagan aspects of the poem, for the Christians' adversaries are generated formally, not historically.

Surprisingly, this principle extends even to *Roland*'s geography. Witness the example of Saragossa, where the first Saracen council takes place, and the makeshift camp where the French are installed at the beginning of the action. Now Saragossa is a city, not a country town; even the poet must have known that, because he considered Saragossa important enough for Charlemagne to bother to capture it. Another age—or another type of text—would have shown us the narrow streets and spacious courtyards, the moats and drawbridges, the merchants with their strange wares, the ladies with their bizarre costumes. Even the poet's contemporaries painted cities with towers and turrets, temples and trellises. What do we find in *Roland?* An orchard, a pine tree, another tree, a silk cloth, a throne. Why should the poet bother to describe the city at all, if this is all he can muster? What is there about this description that particularizes Saragossa? This doesn't even sound like a city. It sounds more like a glorified campsite. It sounds, in fact, exactly like the encampment of Charlemagne: just an orchard, a pine, another tree, a silk cloth, a throne. There is no *city* of Saragossa, there are only Marsile's locus and Charlemagne's locus: a Saracen camp and a French camp. Just enough detail is furnished that each locus unfailingly evokes the other. Everyday realism and the historical characteristics of the Saracens play no more than a bit part in the overall drama where the fates of Christian and pagan are weighed in the balance. Only a *counter*weight can provide a *counter*balance.

Reading *Roland* as a linear progression is not unlike reading a poem while ignoring everything but the poem's linguistic structures. Until the reader recognizes that the poem is divided into verses and stanzas, none of the poem's characteristic rhymes or patterns is likely to reach the surface. Once the poem's distinctive units are acknowledged, however, all kinds of relationships seem to jump off the page. From the very start, readers of *Roland* are compensated for attending to the following-pattern by the way in which division of the text into following-units stresses salient material. The second half of the opening stanza, for example, takes us to Saragossa, where we meet the Saracen king Marsile. According to the last line of the stanza,

It cannot be helped, misfortune will reach him there. (1)

For several stanzas we witness the first Saracen council scene, returning to the French only when the Saracen messengers arrive in Charlemagne's camp. In one sense, the flow of these stanzas is both temporally and spatially continuous, for all we are doing is following the messengers from one camp to another. The poet's choice of language breaks us out of this continuum, however, by marking the beginning of the French council scene with a familiar hemistich:

It cannot be helped, they [the messengers] will deceive him somewhat. (7)

The French council scene is thus yanked out of an apparent temporal continuum and repositioned as a counterpart to the Saracen council. By placing the parallel verses both at the end of a stanza and at the start of parallel council scenes, the poet successfully reinforces the alternating following-pattern. Just as the presence of rhyming words at the end of each verse confirms that a poem is constructed by verses, this careful deployment of formulaic hemistichs offers a sure sign of the importance of following-units in *Roland*.

When writing verse, poets must obey more than the simple rules of grammar. They must regularly attend to questions of rhythm and rhyme over and above linguistic concerns. A similar program governs the construction of *The Song of Roland*. Just as the poet's choice of a particular word at the end of one verse creates constraints regarding the choice of the final word of the next verse, so *Roland*'s alternating following-pattern calls for a similar type of rhyming. The presentation of every Christian action or character creates not a cause demanding an effect but a type demanding a pagan countertype. Every Christian motif creates a "slot," to use Karl Uitti's term (1973:91), for its pagan counterpart. Baligant does not appear because history records his presence but because the return of Charlemagne creates a slot for a foe comparable in power and in stature to the French emperor. In "balance of power" politics, alliances are made not because of friendship but because the balance must be maintained. The form dictates the action and not vice versa. A similar structural principle holds true at all levels of *Roland*.

When Charlemagne returns to find the rearguard slaughtered, it is late in the day. To allow immediate revenge, Charlemagne asks God to prolong the day (179). Even this miracle of prolonged daylight creates a slot that must be filled on the pagan side as well. As soon as Baligant appears, he makes his way to Saragossa by the light of lanterns reflected in the facets of his innumerable jewels (190). The pagan Emir knows how to extend daylight quite as well as his Christian counterpart. Once the parameter of the slot is set—here "prolonged daylight"—transferral to the other side seems almost automatic.

Simple but effective, *Roland*'s slot composition gains much of its power from the context for comparison that it so clearly provides. Each time a slot is filled, a parallel is created between the two sides. While this relationship is initially based on similarity, it offers the opportunity to recognize difference as well. Take the case of Charlemagne's and Baligant's similar ability to prolong daylight. When we first meet Baligant, we know little about him, having been told only that he is old, powerful, and an enemy to the Christian cause. Our first view of the emir shows him illuminating the night with his lanterns and jewels. But what does it mean to say that he has lanterns and jewels? That we can know only by comparing the treatment of Baligant to the corresponding Christian slot. When we do so, we immediately understand the import of Baligant's trappings: lanterns and jewels are to Baligant as God is to Charlemagne. The emir has stolen the fire of the gods. If Charlemagne is a model Christian, in every way subservient to his Lord, Baligant is Lucifer, "the bearer of light," intent on expanding his own kingdom. Here humility, there pride. Only by spatializing the narrative, by perceiving subsequent following-units as balanced and parallel, can we proceed to the important task of discovering divergences between those sections of the text which at first seemed similar and symmetrical.

The concluding combat between Baligant and Charlemagne drives the point home. When Baligant dons his armor, the process is described at length (228), a description directly modeled on Charlemagne's arming a few stanzas earlier (215). So close is the resemblance between the two passages that no fewer than five hemistichs are repeated in the two descriptions. When the two commanders finally cross swords, their similarities are stressed by application of the same terms to both adversaries. In one stretch, the two warriors are the common subject of twelve successive plural verbs. Some critics have not hesitated to castigate *Roland*'s poet for this technique. Eugene Vance says that "instead of taking the trouble to differentiate between his characters . . . he invites us to see double, as if a single knight fought against himself in a mirror" (1970:76). Why indeed would such a gifted poet tarnish a highly ornamental set piece by repeating the same lines used elsewhere?

It is precisely the similarities between the two knights that reveal their crucial differences. The more traits they share, the more the specificity of their differences stands out. We were led to juxtapose these two passages because of their formal and verbal similarities; now we must inquire as to the differences exposed by those similarities. Charlemagne's sword is named "Joyous," for the relics it contains, whereas Baligant's sword is dubbed "Precious," because it is encrusted with valuable jewels (228). Where the French emperor has the Christian virtue of joy and relics of the saints, the pagan emir has naught but pride and earthly goods. Baligant thus insists that the French king surrender to him and become his vassal. In response, Charles invites the pagan emir to surrender not to him but to God and to become

Christian (260). It is hardly surprising that the ultimate distinction between the two warriors—the separation of the quick from the dead—should be engineered by the angel Gabriel, who intervenes in favor of Charlemagne (261–62). The entire account serves to demonstrate the equality of the two warriors in all domains save one: their religion. The final line of the Baligant description perfectly encapsulates the difference:

> God! what a baron he could be, if only he were Christian! (228)

Vance is right to note the poet's tendency to recycle language, but only by recognizing the function of that repetition can we fully appreciate *Roland*'s minimalist technique.

Throughout *The Song of Roland* this same procedure is used, employing symmetrical presentation as a basis for differentiation:

1. Set up parallels through use of an alternating following-pattern.
2. Reinforce those parallels through repetition of formulaic language.
3. Establish significant differences within that context of parametric similarity.

In this manner, the poet successfully creates a context for highlighting the most important distinctions.

Integration

Analysis of *Roland*'s following-pattern reveals a structure based on alternating and symmetrical presentation of Christians and pagans. Far from being organized around a single individual, as the modern title implies, the text depends on parallelism between two homogeneous groups. With few exceptions, individuals are subordinated to the group, acting as placeholders or representatives rather than as characters with personal motivation. Individuals do exist, however, if only because of each group's need for a leader. Though *Roland*'s following-pattern is structured primarily by alternation between two groups, it also depends on a regular change of scale, zooming in and out between individuals and groups. In addition to the Christian-pagan axis of symmetry, we must therefore recognize a secondary axis that is dependent on the relationship between the individual and the group. Characters are constantly defined by their relationship to these complementary axes. If the presence of a *French* commander brings into being a slot for his Saracen mirror image, the presence of a French *commander* implies an army that includes several levels of officers and soldiers. On the one hand, a relationship of symmetry, generated by the irreducible conflict of opposing worldviews; on the other hand, a relationship of integration, involving a hierarchy of vassals and lords.

The most important function of the text's integrative axis is its ability to energize the text. The very nature of symmetry produces situations that are static, absolute, and general in nature. *Roland*'s dynamic aspect is generated by exceptions that activate the text's integrative axis. Taken together, these two principles make possible the rather jerky and uncertain forward movement of the text. Two different types of stasis characterize *Roland*. The first, which provides the text's initial situation, involves a balance between two forces with the same concerns, similar characters, and a shared desire to occupy Spain; the second occurs when all the pagans have been either killed or converted, concluding the story. The text exists only as long as a balance is maintained, only until the first type of stasis is replaced by the second.

Roland tends toward the universal, toward the elimination of every exception. Far from presenting this movement as a linear progression, however, the poet cleverly disguises this passage from a differentiated to a unified world behind a mask of static opposition. Throughout the text, generalizations are carefully juxtaposed with assertions of exception. Each general statement provides a projection into the future, a foreshadowing of that moment at the end of the text when absolute domination will be realized, whereas each exception represents the present, when the disputed land is still shared and balance is still possible. Universal statements kill the text, for the text depends on balance and is undone by unity. Positing an exception reverses the tendency toward the death of the text by renewing the possibility of balance. To remove the exception is thus to progress in time, toward unity; but by opposing rules to exceptions, the poet spatializes that temporal dimension, defining change through opposition rather than as linear progression.

From the very first stanza of *Roland*, the universal/exception opposition draws attention through the technique of enjambment:

Right down to the sea he [Charlemagne] conquered the proud land.
Not a castle is left before him;
Neither wall nor city remains to be stormed,
Except Saragossa, high up on a mountain. (1)

The Saracen-French conflict is here redefined in terms of the totality-individuality spectrum. Charles's motivating force is the desire to conquer all of Spain; Marsile's sole wish is to remain the lone exception, the one Spanish chief to save his city from the ferocious idol-smashing plunderers of the French army. Without the enjambment "Except Saragossa" and the exception it implies, the poem's first stanza would be its last. The general statement represents not a fact but a goal; the exception is a temporary device for maintaining the text's life.

Lest we miss the initial importance of exception in energizing *Roland*'s plot, the next stanza repeats the technique, even to the enjambment and initial placement of the word "Except":

Not a single pagan will respond a word,
Except Blancandrin from Deep Valley Castle. (2)

As long as Marsile's men all maintain the same attitude, the plot languishes; if Blancandrin were to remain silent, the first Saracen council scene would be the last. Modulating from the group to the individual, the poet introduces an exception that gives the story new impetus. A similar situation obtains in the first French council scene:

The French are quiet, except for Ganelon. (15)

Seen from a distance, the following-pattern always seems to stress alternation between two groups. But seen from up close, modulation between the group and the individual takes on an equally important role.

Throughout the battle scenes, the plot gathers new impetus by repeated use of the same technique. The poet measures an army's success not solely by the number killed but by the number left as well:

Of the twelve [Saracen] peers ten are dead;
Except for two none remain alive. (102)

The text thus remains defined by a balance between the two sides, all the while measuring the current situation against eventual universalization. When the tide turns against the French in the Roncevaux battle, the universal/exception relationship is reversed. The previous example, tending toward ultimate eradication of the twelve pagan peers, is now matched by an exception (again highlighted through enjambment) foreshadowing elimination of the French force:

All are dead, these French knights,
Except sixty, that God has spared:
Before they die, they will exact a heavy price. (127)

The poet thus succeeds in energizing the plot (=change) without disturbing the fundamental opposition (=stasis). At every important juncture the poet repeats this pattern, each time rescuing the text from the eclipse that would accompany the attainment of a unified world.

Alternating between Christians and pagans, but also between individuals and groups, the *Roland* poet at times seems to shift from one project to another. While stressing the symmetrical axis, the poet makes no bones about his preference for one group over the other. When he is working along the integrative axis, however, the poet sometimes calls into question the values of those very Christians whose merit he has just lauded in contrast to pagan shortcomings. Moving from one Christian knight to another, and from individual warriors to the group and back—often aided by formulaic repetition of whole hemistichs—the poet establishes a context for comparison among Christians that complements the more obvious contrast between foes. Roland in particular often suffers from the comparisons engendered by this movement along the integrative axis. When Oliver pleads with Roland to sound his horn, in order to summon Charlemagne to defend the rearguard, Roland offers a surprisingly self-serving reason for refusing. He responds:

To die is better than for me to be dishonored. (86)

Only by reading this verse in the context of other verses with the exact same initial hemistich can we fully understand Roland's attitude. Shortly, with the rearguard's destiny no longer in doubt, Roland finally recognizes the need to call for Charlemagne's help. Oliver varies Roland's response only slightly, but by now we have learned the importance of such apparently minute differences when they occur within a context of similarity. Replacing Roland's self-consciousness with a contrasting group-consciousness, Oliver says:

To die is better than for us to be dishonored. (128)

Earlier, Ganelon had characterized Charlemagne as someone who believes that

To die is better than to abandon his barons. (40)

Roland's preoccupation with his own reputation directly contradicts his commander's desire always to serve his vassals. It is hardly surprising, then, that Roland's words should be echoed in the final judicial duel not by Thierry, who emphasizes the vassal's duty to his lord, but by Pinabel, whose most persuasive argument is his immense physical strength. Like Roland, Ganelon's champion claims that he can win the fight single-handed. Like Roland, he puts his relatives and his own reputation above his country's survival. Like Roland, he claims that

To die is better than for me to be dishonored. (284)

In *Roland*, as elsewhere, men are measured by the company they keep; reacting like Pinabel hardly reflects well on Roland.

Nor does Roland impress us when he imitates the pagans' desire for booty rather than the higher concerns of Turpin and Oliver. Once again, the device of repeated hemistichs draws attention to the comparison. Where Turpin invokes his king and his religion:

My lord barons, Charles has left us here;
For our king we must surely die.
Help to uphold Christianity! (89)

where Oliver refers to God and country:

> My lord barons, remain on the field!
> In God's name, look to it
> That you strike hard, both receiving and giving!
> We must not forget Charlemagne's insignia. (92)

Roland turns instead to fame and fortune:

> My lord barons, hold your horses!
> These pagans are looking to be martyred.
> Today we shall win a handsome and heavy booty;
> No king of France ever had such a valuable one. (91)

Not only is Roland more concerned with personal wealth than with duty, but also he seems more interested in competing with the king than in serving him. Roland's speeches consistently reveal an undertone of ambition, a hint that Roland would be more comfortable as a lord than as a vassal: unlike other French knights, who are defined primarily by their fealty to Charles, Roland is characterized by his quick anger and interest in personal gain. He is even reputed to have captured a city without his commander in chief's order (184).

Longing for the individuality associated with the heroes of legend, Roland fears above all that a "bad song" might be sung about him. Yet, for all his pride and rejection of the group ideal, Roland returns at the end of his life to his Christian duty, humbling himself before God, confessing his sins, and now, finally asking for Charlemagne's protection. Though he clearly shares responsibility with Ganelon for the French defeat, his final confession underlines the fact that it is never too late to return to one's Christian duties. Ganelon's death offers a clear contrast. Whereas Roland joins his hands, the feudal symbol of unity and communal service, Ganelon is torn limb from limb, the traditional punishment for treason against one's sovereign. Through his treachery, Ganelon cost Charlemagne his "right arm"; now Ganelon must lose his.

Roland's final diptych, juxtaposing Ganelon's death by drawing and quartering with the pagan queen Bramimonde's conversion to Christianity, provides a doubly fitting conclusion for the text's integrative axis. The effect of treason is to pull a nation apart, individual ambition destroying the efforts and goals of the community. Conversion is the exact inverse of treason, because it reduces disunity, integrating a world that once was divided. Conversion and treason, integration and separation: these are the actions that energize *The Song of Roland*, for community is the highest value that the text has to offer. To betray one's king is to destroy that community, to become a convert is to restore it. To understand fully why treason and conversion are conceived as diametrical opposites we have only to consider how pervasive was the medieval application of feudal principles. By his treason against God, Satan was considered the commander in chief of all traitors, the lord of all non-Christians and traitors to the feudal system. There are, it would seem, two ways to join Satan's legions:

1. Wrong placement on the Christian/pagan axis of symmetry.
2. Wrong placement with respect to the individual/group integrative axis.

Roland's two endings—Ganelon's death and Bramimonde's conversion—thus correspond to two different rhetorical tasks. The text must stress right belief, but it must also preach community-oriented action.

Polarity Adjustment

If the overall structure of *The Song of Roland* can be configured as symmetry around a primary axis, and the action of any given episode can be explained by reference to a secondary axis, that of the individual's integration into the group, the relationship of one episode to another is best understood by reference to two related operations: replacement and polarity adjustment.

As we move through the text, alternating between sides, we observe an endless variety of faces. From character to character, from group to group, we move according to a logic of "slots," each character calling forth his mirror image among the enemy, according to the role that each plays within his group. This primacy of function over personality carries with it an assumption of interchangeability. Once characters are killed or depart, their slots are filled like the ranks of an army in battle. As each new pair of following-units gives way to the next, new characters take the stage, but their relationship remains stable and thus representative of the duality governing *Roland*'s overall structure. Initially leaders of the vanguard, Roland and Oliver must be replaced when they are assigned to the rearguard; there are jobs to be done, and the commander must fill the empty slots. When the rearguard is slaughtered, the main French force replaces it. A similar operation substitutes Baligant and his army for Marsile and his decimated forces. Even Charlemagne cedes his place in the final episode to his vassal Thierry, for a judicial duel against Ganelon's replacement Pinabel.

Unlike tales built around the life of an individual, *The Song of Roland* has no convenient stopping point. Its replacement principle permits it to go on and on by simple variation in the size and identity of the group implied. In his conflict with Ganelon we may focus on Roland, but soon he is seen as part of the rearguard, which is rapidly replaced by the main force representing all Christendom. Individual units take part in a wider opposition and thus cannot be perceived as ends in themselves. By the same token, a group can be represented by any one of its individuals—from the emperor battling his opposite number to the scrawniest of youths defending his king's rights. The same is true of the enemy, which is never without a replacement for a fallen champion. Just as Baligant takes over from Marsile, the final stanza alerts us to a new pagan uprising in the land of Imphe. *Roland* is a saga not of change but of survival. It dramatizes not a one-time affair but the continuing need to protect the empire against outsiders. In theory (and in practice, as numerous sequels attest), the text is never ending; the operation of replacement can expand its basic structure indefinitely.

Is *Roland* then fundamentally the same from beginning to end? In one sense we must say that it is, for here there is little of the education that characterizes the Bildungsroman, little of the quest and discovery common in romance, little of the mystery and solutions of the detective novel. In another sense, however, *Roland* is constantly evolving, constantly redefining its terms as adjustments are made in the identity of its polarities. Each section of the text presents a conflict between polar opposites, but from one section to another the specifics of the polarity may shift, isolating a new variable. By offering a slightly different comparison, each subsequent opposition provides further insight into the qualities and beliefs requisite for victory. *Roland* is thus a text not of *becoming*, like Goethe's *Wilhelm Meister* or Flaubert's *L'Éducation sentimentale*, but of constant *definition*.

When Roland forms the rearguard, Charlemagne offers him half the army, but he refuses, instead instructing Walter to choose only knights from "our land." As the text specifically informs us, the Christian forces are thus represented in the ensuing combat only by the Francs de France, the knights hailing from the French royal domain of which Paris is the center. Throughout the struggle, Roland's men fight as much for the honor of their province as they do out of duty to their emperor and God. When the sun grows dim to mark Roland's death, only this limited France grows dark. The battle at Roncevaux is thus neither the clash of the Holy Roman Empire with the Arab world nor an encounter between Christianity and pagandom but a confrontation of two smaller sections. This limitation is clearly reflected in a careful choice of vocabulary. Roland's foes are termed "Saracens," a term used thirty times before the Baligant episode but only twice thereafter, and then only to designate the natives of Iberia. Baligant's forces are instead referred to as "Arabs," a designation not used at all during the first battle. In like manner, the French expression for their homeland (*Tere major*), used several times during the Roncevaux episode, does not occur at all during the encounter between Charlemagne's and Baligant's full forces.

Whereas the Roncevaux ambush was limited to regional foes, the second combat is clearly defined as the affair of the entire empire. Roland was able to gather his rearguard in the short space of two stanzas, but nine are necessary for Charlemagne to appoint squadrons from the far corners of his domain. With the new polarity comes a new approach: neither personal pride nor national honor will encumber Charles the way it did Roland, for his responsibilities, like his army, cover the entire nation. Charlemagne's victory thus corresponds to a shift from Roland's local and personal concerns to a resolutely community-oriented stance. The contrast between Roland's defeat and Charlemagne's victories provides a clear lesson for a country about to embark on the most international effort of the Middle Ages. In 1095, Pope Urban II preached the first of a series of crusades requiring the solidarity of the entire Christian world. This was a time when many must have been recalcitrant, unwilling to fight alongside their enemies of recent years. It is not hard to imagine the reaction of a typical Franc de France: "Who will go? Will you?" "Not me—fight side by side with a German, not on your life!" *Roland*'s polarity adjustment offers a fable of the dangers of self-sufficiency, an invitation to pool energy and make a unified stand against the infidel foe.

To understand the idea of a common enemy, and to take arms together, men as different as Bretons and Bavarians had to conceive of themselves as similar, deemphasizing their differences in favor of their common Christianity. Accordingly, the emphasis given to nationality and heroic virtues in the Roncevaux episode is transferred in the next battle to God and religion. If Roland's efforts seem almost secular in nature, with constant reference to individual valor, opportunities for plunder, and talk of the kind of song that heroes inspire, the combat against Baligant is from the very beginning a religious crusade, for the pagan commander as well as for his Christian counterpart. The last few stanzas of the Charlemagne-Baligant duel offer an apt emblem of the episode's concern for polarity adjustment. The parallel description of the two commanders nullifies the importance of individual force and courage by making the two men equal in those terms, thereby highlighting the variable of religion. The physical situation exactly mirrors the structure: just as the commanders are divested of all their secondary attributes, so are they deprived of every element of their armor. Stripped to their tunics, they fight "skin to skin," ready to grapple over the basics. Using the word "my" six times in six verses, Baligant asks his foe to render homage to him. In response, Charles offers a different approach, exhorting Baligant to serve God, "the omnipotent king" (260). Never demanding homage to himself, Charlemagne reveals that even the French emperor serves a higher King. Unlike Roland and Baligant, Charlemagne is consistent in his feudal vision of the world. Expecting service from his vassals, he expects, in turn, to give service to his Lord.

In keeping with the principle of replacement operations, Charlemagne's victory over Baligant does not bring the text to a close but simply prepares the way for a new opposition. The combat betwen Pinabel and Thierry continues the process of polarity adjustment, correcting misconceptions that the first two battles might have engendered. At Roncevaux, the French were attacked by surprise. When Baligant appears with his army, Charlemagne's forces do not shrink from battle, but neither do they provoke it themselves. The judgment of Ganelon continues this shift, requiring a faithful Frank actually to provoke Pinabel in order to assure justice. Roland's warmongering in the first part proved so counterproductive that a correction is now needed. Lest we assume that Roland's bravado is his main problem, a new duality is offered, suggesting through Thierry's zeal that concern for God's justice is the only parameter that counts.

The poet's careful manipulation of the word "wise" brings this point home. At the outset of the Roncevaux episode, a famous verse assures us that "Roland is courageous and Oliver is wise" (87). We soon discover that Roland's valor succeeds only in causing the slaughter of his squadrons, while Oliver's wisdom, had Roland listened to it, might have saved the twelve peers and their friends. From the first battle on, valor is clearly suspect and wisdom highly prized. When Charles appoints a court to try Ganelon, he therefore chooses "the wisest men of all" (267). To our surprise, these wise men prove unwilling to take action. If they are so wise, then why are they afraid to uphold the right and seek justice? Clearly, they are too wise, and not courageous enough. They have only the kind of wisdom that led Ganelon to claim

> I was the messenger to Marsile;
> By my wisdom I saved myself. (273)

Thierry's action proves that wisdom alone cannot suffice. The judges are wise but Thierry is courageous. By standing up for the right, Thierry provides a partial rehabilitation of Roland's values. Roland's fault, we now see, was not his bellicose nature but his desire for personal glory. If Roland's death taught us to abhor pride and self-sufficiency, Thierry's timely courage teaches us that with the right intentions anyone may stand alone. To keep us from assuming that strength is inherent in the individual—as we once may have assumed that evil is inherent in the person of the foe—the poet deliberately paints Thierry as "a kind of Everyman," as Karl Uitti has called him (1973:105):

> Meager was his body, and skinny and twisted,
> Black his hair and his face sort of brownish;
> He is certainly not big, but neither is he too small. (277)

No broad shoulders and white hat for Thierry. Lest we misunderstand the source of Charlemagne's strength, the battle is repeated with someone simple playing the role of hero—clearly his strength must come from God. Kings we are not, but if a skinny brown-faced runt with black hair can protect his kingdom and God's justice, then most certainly we can as well.

One final diptych serves to dissolve any lingering doubts. "I am a Frenchman," some might say, "I have nothing to fear." Others might consider that past sins make them unworthy. The destruction of Ganelon, followed by Bramimonde's baptism, puts an end to such thoughts. Ganelon's example serves as a reminder that "wise" men, even when they are French, can be subjected to a horrible death and eternal damnation. Bramimonde's experience reveals that no measure of wrongdoing can prevent a repentant sinner from achieving salvation.

Seen from a distance, *Roland*'s incessant combats appear all too similar. Handsome Christian knights clash repeatedly with ugly pagan warriors, their differing physiognomy and religious practices constantly highlighted. Yet the poem's alternating following-pattern succeeds in stressing other values as well. By establishing similarities between the two sides, *Roland* creates a context within which more specific differences may be detailed. Each battle thus emphasizes its own particular concerns, slightly adjusting the polarity as the text progresses. At first, these three encounters seem virtually identical, with the same glittering armor, the same flashing swords, the same final deathblows. When we look more closely, however, we discover that the process of polarity adjustment has shifted the emphasis with each new combat:

I. Roland and the rearguard vs. Marsile's army

Christian	vs.	pagan
French	vs.	Saracen
weakness	vs.	strength
vanity/individualism	vs.	group orientation

II. Charlemagne vs. Baligant

Christian	vs.	pagan
Holy Roman Empire	vs.	Arab world
strength	vs.	strength
humility/group orientation	vs.	vanity/individualism

III. Thierry vs. Pinabel

Christian	vs.	Christian
French	vs.	French
weakness	vs.	strength
humility/group orientation	vs.	vanity/individualism

Though *Roland* initially appeared to be about religious difference, its second and third battles together offer a new interpretation. By matching adversaries marked by equivalent strength or similar nationality and religion, the final encounters shift the text's emphasis from religion to group orientation. The first battle repeatedly invokes the differences between the combatants' religions, but it also stresses the surprise nature of the Saracen attack and the overwhelming superiority of Marsile's forces. We might easily come away from this episode understanding that the outcome was caused entirely by Ganelon's treachery and the pagans' strength. However, the hand-to-hand combat between Charlemagne and Baligant effectively eliminates physical superiority as an operative variable. Similarly, the judicial duel between two Christians shunts attention away from religion as the all-powerful difference that it once appeared.

Though it began as a religious epic, *The Song of Roland* ends as a feudal fable stressing fealty, a cautionary tale warning against elevation of personal concerns above respect for the welfare of the group. While it stresses Christianity throughout, *Roland*'s shift from narrow nationalism to a more inclusive concern for the entire empire displaces the emphasis from religion as such to a broad concept of Christendom, along with allegiance to Christian leaders. Making a similar point in another way, we may say that the effect of *Roland*'s polarity adjustment is to transfer emphasis from the primary axis of symmetry, dependent on religious difference, to the integrative axis, with its accent on the relationship between the individual and the group.

THREE Dual-Focus Narrative

T *he Song of Roland* displays the characteristics of a narrative type that I call "dual-focus." The narrator follows no single character throughout but instead alternates regularly between two groups whose conflict provides the plot. Because the group rather than an individual plays the lead role, individuals serve primarily as placeholders, defined by the group, rather than as characters whose development constitutes an independent subject of interest. Succeeding following-units typically portray the two sides engaged in similar activities. This parallelism induces comparison of the two sides and is the source of the text's main rhetorical thrust. Each new pair of following-units is related to the previous pair by the principle of replacement. The text's structure resembles that of an equal-arm balance. When a member of one group changes sides or refuses to fight, the balance of power is destroyed and the plot is set in motion. The text ends when the two sides are reduced to one, by death or expulsion, or through marriage or conversion.

Within this basic pattern two separate but complementary models may be discerned. The first operates as if the two opposed groups carried the same magnetic charge. As the text progresses and the two sides come closer together, the group that is more firmly fixed repels the other from its field. Fixation is effected by the text's rhetorical dimension, eliciting the reader's sympathy for one side over the other. This pattern, which I call "dual-focus epic," normally concludes with the elimination or containment of the side condemned by the text's rhetoric. Many of the texts that display this pattern are popular in nature, ranging from the medieval popular epic to comic strips and science fiction, and from the Gothic novel and *roman feuilleton* to the Hollywood western. Other dual-focus epics are religious in nature, including major portions of the Old Testament, the New Testament book of Revelation (Apocalypse), Hesiod's *Theogony*, and the Babylonian Genesis known as *Enuma Elish*. Wherever there is religion, there is of course parody, as evidenced by works as diverse as the early *Batrachomyomachia* ("Battle of the Frogs and Mice"), the *Roman de Renart*, the Renaissance mock epic, and Jonathan Swift's *Battle of the Books*. Many texts that have normally been read, like *Roland*, as the stories of individual heroes, make more sense when they are returned to their rightful place in the dual-focus tradition. Later we shall have occasion to see why Homer's *Iliad* and Vergil's *Aeneid* should be placed among this number.

Dual-focus narrative is not restricted to literary texts. It extends to historical narratives like Thucydides' *History of the Peloponnesian War*, Tacitus's account of the aftermath of Nero's death in the first book of his *History*, and Augustine's *City of God*, as well as historical fictions from Flaubert's *Salammbô* to the films of Sergei Eisenstein. The cinema is a favorite medium for the development of dual-focus potential, in such films as D. W. Griffith's *Birth of a Nation*, Jean Renoir's *Grand Illusion*, Luis Buñuel's *Viridiana*, and scores of popular favorites like Merian C. Cooper and Ernest B. Schoedsack's *King Kong*, Cecil B. De Mille's *Unconquered*, and Gordon Douglas's *Them!* The plastic arts have also long borrowed the form and thematic concerns of dual-focus epic, from the high culture of Romanesque Last Judgment scenes to the commercial simplicity of magazine advertisements showing two washing machines and two equal-sized boxes of detergent, the lowly Brand X and the New! Improved! Will-get-your-clothes-one-hundred-percent-brighter Brand Y. In all these texts, irreducible differences place the two sides in opposition, creating pressure that ultimately leads to domination by one of the two groups.

Another group of texts, which I call "dual-focus pastoral," shares almost all the characteristics of dual-focus epic. Dual-focus pastoral texts retain the alternating following-pattern and parallelism, group-conscious and apsychological characters, progression by replacement, and a plot that operates according to a balance mechanism, accompanied by the basic dual-focus tendency to suppress the temporal flow in favor of static spatial structures.

The difference between the two forms stems from a simple shift in the relationship between the two mirror-image groups. If dual-focus epic sets one side against the other, like similarly charged magnets laying equivalent claims to the same space, dual-focus pastoral features magnets with opposite charges, two sides that seek union. Whether or not the primary identity of the two sides in dual-focus pastoral is sexual (as it usually is in Western literature), one side is almost always associated with a strong male factor, while the other is given a strong female identity. The union that brings the text to a close is thus assimilated to marriage, whether between individuals, families, countries, or philosophies. As in dual-focus epic, the two sides are ultimately reduced to one, that reduction marking the end of the text.

Like its epic counterpart, dual-focus pastoral proliferates in popular literature. From the Alexandrian romance as represented by Heliodorus's *Aethiopica* or Longus's *Daphnis and Chloe*, to a Renaissance pastoral novel like Honoré d'Urfé's *Astrée*, all the way to the Hollywood musical, dual-focus pastoral has survived nearly unchanged. Western society has always found a place for this dual-focus complement to the more highly regarded epic form, as we see in the Old Testament books of Ruth and Song of Songs, medieval romances like Boccaccio's *Filostrato*, Chrétien de Troyes's *Cligés*, the Provençal *Roman de Flamenca*, or *Aucassin et Nicolette*'s clever parody, and modern love stories as diverse as Nathaniel Hawthorne's *House of Seven Gables* and James Cameron's *Titanic*. In fact, dual-focus pastoral has often been combined with dual-focus epic, as in the amorous diplomacy of Esther in the Bible, the *Nibelungenlied*, and Honoré de Balzac's *Les Chouans*, or the thrills and then chills of Geoffrey Chaucer's *Troilus and Cressida*, Robert Wise's *West Side Story*, and Vittorio De Sica's *The Garden of the Finzi-Contini*. The genre of melodrama in particular has shown a continuing capacity to merge the two forms, for the combination of a villain, a damsel in distress, and a dashing young savior offers a compact method of satisfying the needs of dual-focus epic and pastoral alike.

Beginnings

Let us begin with a metaphor, a touchstone to which we can return from time to time to validate our results: dual-focus narrative is a chess game, a balanced confrontation where the two sides move alternately according to a simple set of rules, each piece having a limited function meaningful only in terms of the larger fate of its side. The battle takes place in time, yet strategy must be conceived in space, the opponent's position remaining fully as important as the attacker's plans. How then does this game begin? What action must be performed in order for the match to start? White moves first, but much has taken place before White can advance the first pawn. Two actions precede White's first move, and precede it they must, for without the chessboard and the pieces the competition cannot begin.

Two simple procedures characterize the creation of the dual-focus world. First, a contested space must be created, limited on all sides and clearly displaying its major axis of symmetry. What kind of a match would it be if the threatened pieces could simply maneuver off the board in order to escape the attack? Second, the players must be divided into two equivalent groups, clearly identifiable by a difference in color, uniform, language, sex, or other differentiation device. A football game begins in just this way. The day before, there were men all over the field, running this way and that, chaotic, helter-skelter, chasing passes onto the cinder track and errant kicks into the stands. The next morning, the groundskeepers appear, outlining the playing surface in bright white chalk. When game time arrives, the teams pour out of the chute onto the field, the home team clearly identified by its gold helmets and black uniforms, the visitors resplendent in their green and white. The game can now begin, because the formless mass of the day before has achieved differentiation through the magic effect of white lines and color-coded uniforms. The undefined, unbounded battleground has now been marked off and delimited, and the players' allegiances identified.

Whatever their scope, dual-focus texts must effect this definition by differentiation. Exposition and creation thus become quite literally synonymous. Borrowing from an earlier tradition, the beginning of Ovid's *Metamorphoses* neatly summarizes the doctrine of creation by separation with its implied parallels between God, the universe, and its elements on one side and the narrator, the text, and language on the other:

Before land was and sea—before air and sky
Arched over all, all Nature was all Chaos,
The rounded body of all things in one,

The living elements at war with lifelessness. . . .
No living creatures knew that land, that sea
Where heat fell against cold, cold against heat—
Roughness at war with smooth and wet with drought.
Things that gave way entered unyielding masses,
Heaviness fell into things that had no weight.
  Then God or Nature calmed the elements:
Land fell away from sky and sea from land,
And aether drew away from cloud and rain. (1958:3)

The cosmogonic act creates a world and a language, but not just any world, not just any language. Both are built on the principle of binary opposition, so that the war of the words can adequately describe the battle of the elements, those of the text as well as those of the world.

If Ovid's style depends on a series of oppositions, it is clearly because only a nominal, dichotomized style can properly evoke the world seen from a dual-focus perspective. When Augustine writes his *Confessions*, he evokes his past sins and shows by what actions, by what thoughts, he changed his life. He has no room for balanced opposition of noun to noun, of clause to clause, because the whole point of his account is to reveal not the static binary nature of the world but man's opportunity for change. When Augustine turns to history, however, his style turns along with him. *The City of God* rewrites the history of mankind as the unceasing opposition between two cities. Consequently, its style appears to be generated by the simplest of computers, the use of any noun immediately calling forth its mirror-image counterpart. *The City of God* (but not *The Confessions*) clearly operates according to dual-focus principles.

The lexicon of dual-focus texts resembles that of our chess metaphor. The game cannot be played until and unless every "white bishop" is given a corresponding "black bishop." Dual-focus vocabulary is thus double, containing both a parameter of comparison ("bishop") and a uniform identifying allegiance ("white" or "black"). In fact, dual-focus vocabulary is doubly double. If the contrast between a white bishop and a black bishop activates the text's axis of symmetry, the juxtaposition of a white bishop and a white king feeds the text's integrative axis. This bipartite status of dual-focus words requires a two-part analytical process like that used above for *The Song of Roland*:

1. Organization of the text into pairs of actions, characters, or following-units defined according to the same parameter.
2. Comparison of the two elements in each pair in order to isolate the characteristics particular to each side.

As used by Ovid, "heat" and "cold" are not two different, independent words but the same word with opposite signs. To read these terms successfully, we need to recognize heat and cold not as separate terms but as the two parts of a dual concept, containing both a parameter of comparison (heat) and a marker of allegiance (the opposite plus and minus signs). Only in this way can we make sense of dual-focus narrative's characteristic method of organizing texts and worlds.

In keeping with dual-focus modes of understanding, the Old Testament God is said to have created the elements not individually but in pairs. Darkness is not *created*, it is *separated* from light, thereby simultaneously constituting both paired elements. Woman is not created separately from man, she is separated *wo-man*, from man. Even the Jewish people are by no means created, in the modern sense of that word; instead, they are differentiated. Just as the Tower of Babel story explains the dispersion of a single language into many, the Genesis account of Adam's descendants shows how a single family gave rise to many nations, with Israel in the center and its enemies in outlying lands. Out of sibling rivalry situations, Genesis generates the foes that plague Israel throughout the Old Testament. From the line of Cain come the herdsmen who live in tents, those who have no fixed home. Ham, who gazed on his father's nakedness, gives rise to a long list of Israel's traditional enemies, including the Babylonians, Egyptians, Assyrians, and Philistines. Lot, Abraham's nephew who slept with his daughters, is the father of the Moabites and Ammonites. The Edomites descend from Esau, whose intermarriage with foreigners suggests that he "despised his birthright" long before he was formally robbed of it by a conspiracy of his mother and younger brother, Jacob. Only with the reunion of Joseph and his would-be fratricidal brothers at the end of Genesis does the pattern of sibling rivalry cease, now that the Israelites and their enemies are well defined. This separation stage reaches its culmination at the beginning of Exodus with the Passover, reaffirming separation of the world into Jew and non-Jew.

The subsequent giving of the law to Moses on Mount Sinai thus entails little new material. It is simply a recognition of already established principles, a codification of the reasoning behind the previous differentiation of the world into two radically different groups and value systems. Cain set himself before God ("You shall have no other gods before me"), and so killed his righteous brother ("You shall not kill"). Ham committed an act of perversion with his sleeping father ("Honor your father and your mother"). Joseph's brothers were envious of his privileged position in the family circle, and so they sold him into slavery ("You shall not covet"). And so on. Once the Chosen People have reached the Promised Land, the chess game can begin, for Genesis has provided not an undifferentiated world equally available to all but a carefully laid out playing field with a set of mirror-image players, and Exodus has codified the rules by which the game is to be played. The rest of the Old Testament reads like a list of permutations generated by this junction of a series of enemies and a list of laws.

As the Old Testament establishment of the Law clearly reveals, one of the most important aspects of dual-focus narrative is the development of a language suited to description of the text. The binary opposition of Cain to Abel, of Lot to Abraham, of Esau to Jacob, and so forth not only splits the world into separate groups but also provides new vocabulary with every division, new terms particularly appropriate to the text's dual-focus world. Just as the arrangement of chessmen on the chessboard identifies white versus black as a meaningful opposition, so the division of Noah's sons into Ham versus Shem and Japheth defines "Honor your father" versus "Shame your father" as a meaningful opposition and thus as an important critical tool. Dual-focus texts require readers to remember the differences established in the exposition and to use them as critical vocabulary.

Less formulaic in style and structure than sacred texts, dual-focus novels often delay presentation of their constitutive dualities until the reader has already become familiar with the characters and their contexts. Émile Zola's *Le Ventre de Paris* thus remains, for half of its length, a very confusing novel indeed. Florent, whom we expect to become the main character of a typical biographically shaped novel, has just returned from political prison in Cayenne. He moves in with his sausage-making half-brother, finds a job supervising the sale of fish in the central Paris market, and in general serves as our eyes, nose, mouth, and ears as Zola introduces us to the belly of Paris, its delights and excesses. We learn about the operation of Les Halles and the life of its denizens, but we remain in doubt about the novel's direction. Florent has a few quarrels, makes a friend or two, perhaps even falls in love, but we are never sure because we enjoy no interior views of his personal desires or his revolutionary plotting.

In the absence of a clear sense of the novel's structure we have no idea what to look for. For us the text remains chaotic, just as the market does for Florent, until he leaves the city with his friend Claude. During their excursion to Nanterre (then a garden spot well outside of town), Claude explains the world to Florent. The market runs not according to a set of laws handed down by the government, says Claude, but according to one of the oldest laws in the universe, the war between the Fat and the Thin (whence the novel's usual English title). Suddenly, the people and smells, places and sounds, tastes and animosities of Les Halles come into sharp focus. For fully half the novel we had floundered in the watery confusion of the fish market and lingered without obvious purpose among the fattening delights of the pork butcher's shop, café-hopping like a Parisian student unsure how to organize his day. Before, we had been vaguely following Florent, though by no means continuously. Now that the text has received definition, now that we have a vocabulary for ordering the many sensations that the text provides, the following-pattern as well becomes more clearly defined. From now on the text's dual-focus status becomes apparent, with regular alternation and opposition between two camps, the Fat and the Thin.

What Zola holds off until the middle of *Le Ventre de Paris*, the cinema often provides in a film's opening footage. Around the time of World War I, movie houses didn't wait even that long. A melodrama might be introduced in such a fashion as to leave little doubt about the necessary critical vocabulary:

You may
Applaud the Hero
and
Hiss the Villain

Defining the owner's expectations regarding the conduct and class of the audience, lantern slides often preceded the show, displaying a message like this:

Gentlemen will *please* remove their hats, *others* must

In much the same way, dual-focus films sometimes organize the credits preceding the action not in order of the actors' appearance but according to their distribution within the film. Charlie Chaplin's *Great Dictator*, for example, arranges the credits in two separate but parallel lists: "People of the Palace" and "People of the Ghetto."

Whereas literature exists only in time, placing each word after the preceding one, cinema has the ability to work in space as well, thereby gaining an additional method of dividing the world. Alfred Hitchcock's *Notorious* is one of many films that opens on a trial scene viewed from a doorway at the back of the courtroom, with the camera carefully stationed right on the room's axis of symmetry. The center line of the frame thus corresponds exactly to the center line of the courtroom, both real and filmic space thus being exactly split between the accused German traitor and the U.S. prosecutor. The opening frames of Vittorio De Sica's *Garden of the Finzi-Contini* introduce a bevy of white-shirted bicyclists intent on traversing a high, solid, stone wall in order to reach the object of their summer joy, a tennis court, on the other side. We have so little idea who these young people are that we concentrate instead on the battle with the wall. There, as they stand dejectedly in the street, our eyes and our sensitivities are trained to see the world as space, divided by the walls of social distinction. Within lies the private domain of the Finzi-Contini, Ferrara's most powerful family, while on the outside waits youth, powerless until it has been recognized by the Cerberus who eventually opens the gate. Before characters even have names, De Sica's clever exposition implies, they are defined by the space they inhabit and the walls that bound them.

Even when cinema works sequentially, it often provides spatial definition for dual-focus films. Once Jean Renoir has shown us the French officers' quarters in the opening scene of *Grand Illusion*, he rapidly provides a parallel scene identifying the stakes of the initial scene. After Maréchal (Jean Gabin) and de Boeldieu (Pierre Fresnay) have been shot down, they are brought to the German headquarters commanded by von Rauffenstein (Erich von Stroheim). In many ways the two places are similar: on both sides there is music, drinking, and talk of women. Temporary army camps, we easily imagine, cannot differ much from one side of the line to the other. And yet there are differences. The French soldiers listen to a popular song and babble on in familiar language about the squadron's shared girlfriend, while in the German camp we hear a Strauss waltz and multilingual conversation about the capitals of the world. Renoir goes beyond national difference—the expected parameter of opposition in a war film—to redefine the French camp as common and the German camp as aristocratic. In this masterful movie where the popular/aristocratic dichotomy slowly replaces the French/German clash, Renoir has from the very beginning provided the two vocabularies necessary for analysis of the film.

Dual-focus pastoral operates in much the same way, deploying the same techniques of thematic, linguistic, and character differentiation used in its epic counterpart. At once the most naïve and the most sophisticated of the Alexandrian romances, Longus's *Daphnis and Chloe* goes Henry Fielding's *Tom Jones* one better. "Two Foundlings," it might be called, for the text begins with parallel discoveries. Daphnis is found in the woods, being nursed by a goat. Chloe is discovered in the grotto of the nymphs, where a ewe gives her suck. The most obvious opposition emphasized by these paragraphs is the male/female difference, for *Daphnis and Chloe* is the story of the two foundlings' accession to the sexual knowledge of their parents' generation, but readers who see no more than a biological opposition in these opposed paragraphs are missing a chance to learn how to read the text. Dual-focus expositions offer a lesson in critical approaches in addition to introduction of the dramatis personae. Just as the Old Testament's meaning is implicit in the divisions highlighted by sibling rivalry (Chosen People/others, Promised Land/periphery, virtue/vice), so the opening paragraphs of *Daphnis and Chloe* provide the tale's basic differences and parameters, as represented in fig. 3.1. Every opposition, however simple, eventually plays a part in Longus's story. With no further information than that provided by the distance separating the opening paragraphs, we can proceed to a clear understanding of Daphnis's and Chloe's sexual strivings.

Hawthorne handles the problem of dual-focus pastoral exposition quite differently in his *House of Seven Gables*. Instead of introducing the pair of young people who will provide the novel's love interest, he begins with Colonel Pyncheon's illegitimate bid to snatch a plot of land from Matthew Maule, its rightful owner. On the one hand, a colonel, a man of the sword;

Daphnis	*name*	Chloe
male	*sex*	female
oak grove	*location*	grotto
straight	*shape*	curved
convex	*surface*	concave
dry land	*element*	spring water
(Pan)	*god*	Nymphs
older	*age*	younger
ivory sword	*token*	golden anklet
Lamon	*father*	Dryas

FIGURE 3.1 Initial oppositions in *Daphnis and Chloe*

on the other hand, a carpenter named after an apostle. Soon the two families laying claim to the same land achieve increasing diffentiation. The new house on "Maule's Lane, or Pyncheon Street, as it were now more decorous to call it" (1851:18) may belong to the Pyncheon clan, but it is built by a Maule, thus perpetuating their claim to an interest in the property. Even after the Maules seem to have abandoned hope, the two families' parallel claims continue to retain the narrator's attention. The Pyncheon approach to the problem of real estate is typically feudal and aristocratic, based "on the strength of mouldy parchments," while the Maules know no other claim than "their own sturdy toil" (26), the method of a new class whose development in this country was an item of keen interest to Hawthorne. The well of nobility has run dry, he implies, just as the Maule well, its water once so sweet and plentiful, went sour the day that the Pyncheons took over. All this took place many generations before Hawthorne's narrative begins, yet the effects of the original distinction between Pyncheon and Maule linger on, informing the plot until such time as the two families can become reunited once again, through the romance of Phoebe Pyncheon and Holgrave the daguerrotypist. Just as Longus uses a dual exposition to associate his two foundlings with differences that will be essential to the remainder of the story, Hawthorne succeeds in making his young lovers carry important thematic baggage by beginning with the quarrel between their ancestors.

The Hollywood musical often goes to great lengths to establish parallelism between male and female principals. MGM's 1940 version of *New Moon* (directed by Robert Leonard) begins with two simultaneous shipboard songs. On deck, Jeanette MacDonald sings in the elegant garb of the aristocracy. Cut to Nelson Eddy, singing behind bars in the hold. Just as *The Song of Roland* reinforces parallels by the use of repeated formulaic language, so *New Moon* draws the two songs together by using the same editing sequence for both stars, with similar shot changes punctuating the lyrics at exactly the same spots for both renditions. But paired songs need not be simultaneous or similarly edited if they display parallel concerns. After Maurice Chevalier's opening praise of "Little Girls" in *Gigi*, director Vincente Minnelli offers us a diptych of songs that create a connection between Gigi (Leslie Caron) and Gaston (Louis Jourdan) even before we see them together. Once Gigi has expressed her frustration with Paris life in "I Don't Understand the Parisians," Gaston's "It's a Bore" gives voice to a similar displeasure with life in the French capital. Virtually any aspect of a film can be used to establish parallelism between the male and female leads. In Thornton Freeland's *Flying Down to Rio*, back-to-back writing desks and paired cables establish the parallelism between Gene Raymond and Dolores del Rio. In W. S. Van Dyke's *Sweethearts* and Minnelli's *The Band Wagon*, mirror-image sets are used to reinforce the Eddy-MacDonald and Astaire-Charisse contrast.

Whether epic or pastoral, dual-focus texts systematically present their action as generated by preexisting categories. Exposition of those categories thus takes on enormous importance, for it is only through connection of individual characters to long-established groups and values that dual-focus narrative can operate. This is why so many dual-focus texts begin in medias res, stressing a constitutive conflict or difference even before we meet the characters involved. In many cases, the background of the main characters is withheld until the dual-focus parameters are set. Not until Superman has had the opportunity to bring many criminals to justice do we learn the story of his birth, and then only as an explanation of his sensitivity to kryptonite. In *The Song of Roland* we learn of Roland's prowess in fighting the Saracens, but only in later epics do we learn about his childhood and early exploits. As the alternating following-pattern clearly reveals, dual-focus texts are not about personal growth and decisions but about the differences between categories and the characters or groups that embody them.

Principles of Opposition

Dual-focus exposition characteristically involves creation of an entire universe—not just two opposed camps and the world around them but also the language necessary to describe that world. Unable to exercise personal control over their surroundings, dual-focus heroes at best understand the laws that govern their world and act accordingly, thereby attracting to themselves the adjectives that identify the elect in the linguistic system imposed by the narrator. Dual-focus characters are part of the created world; they cannot escape their position. Nor can they, like a picaresque protagonist oppressed by this week's master, simply walk out and create a new universe. The dual-focus world is finite, with laws and language delineated from the outset.

Chess players derive a certain thrill from knowing that their resources are limited and that neither the rules nor the board can be stretched. The winning strategy is not to expand capabilities, as one of my childhood opponents used to do by slipping an extra piece on the board when I was looking elsewhere, but to maximize efficiency with the available resources. A black bishop is a black bishop; it cannot become a white one. The words *black* and *white* are not available for transfer in the chess text as *scared* and *courageous* are in Stephen Crane's *Red Badge of Courage*. Whatever Jean-Paul Sartre may say, in the dual-focus world essence precedes existence. To understand the role that language plays in this system, we can do no better than to meditate on Isabel MacCaffrey's pertinent remarks about *Paradise Lost*: "Milton makes his words take sides; the objects of the poem, both animate and inanimate, along with other names, are aligned in opposing ranks and forced to participate in the War in Heaven that is being continued on earth" (1959:101). In this section I examine the diverse methods employed by dual-focus narrators to make "words take sides," thereby revealing the dynamics—or rather statics—of dual-focus opposition.

Of all our critical terms, perhaps the most problematic is the term "hero." Because it combines affective and formal implications, the designation "hero" often implies more than is meant. While neologisms like "protagonist" and "antihero" facilitate reference to central characters who are not necessarily heroic, they provide little help with the inverse situation, the heroic character who is not necessarily central but who by virtue of heroic action is often assumed to occupy a central position. As with "character," problems associated with the term and concept of "hero" have been largely neglected by critics and theorists alike (though see Mieke Bal's lucid pages in *Narratology* on "The Problem of the Hero," 1985:91–93).

Perhaps the most common result of this terminological quandary is the sort to which *The Aeneid* has regularly been subjected. Traditional criticism has treated Vergil's epic as the story of Aeneas, the hero of Rome's founding, the symbol of Roman power, and the classic example of Roman virtue. The first six books, in this traditional view, correspond to the wanderings of Odysseus, while the last six derive from *The Iliad*. Yet critics acknowledge that Aeneas is neither the instigator of the plot nor an individual independent of his exemplary status, nor even a character altogether capable of self-definition. In short, Aeneas corresponds to the affective content of our term "hero" but not to any of its structural implications. He is emphatically not followed throughout most of *The Aeneid*. Not only does he share the following-pattern with Dido and Carthage, as well as with Turnus and the Italians, but equal time is also given to the gods and their quarrels.

Aeneas is a hero, no doubt, but not because he is an individual. Instead of becoming a hero, Aeneas is born one. His very existence is predicated on his ability to represent exemplary Roman traits. In one sense, Aeneas is not a character in the traditional sense at all but a synecdoche, a figure representing in miniature, on a human scale, the secrets of Roman power and domination over the rest of the world. Because it is the literary property of the Roman cause, Aeneas's character is not available to Aeneas to be defined through his own actions. Aeneas cannot create himself, because he has already been defined by his function. Aeneas is a hero all right, but in the dual-focus sense of that term. He is the group personified.

From the very exposition of *The Aeneid*, the dualistic nature of Vergil's epic is apparent. As in *The Song of Roland*, the very first line introduces to us the man with whom the book closes, but once again that man is left behind before we have read ten lines, ceding his place to the one enemy who stands between him and his home. For it is the goddess Juno who first merits the narrator's full attention. Not until all her quarrels are exposed, along with her support of the Greeks against the Trojans and of Carthage against Latium, does the narrator bring us back to Aeneas. By this time the design is clear: Aeneas will be constantly buffeted by all the storms that Juno can send to force him off his course or delay him. Dido and Turnus, Aeolus and Allecto may be only temporarily opposed to Aeneas, but Juno always is. Traditional criticism considers that *The Aeneid* belongs entirely to one character, yet the following-pattern constantly pairs Aeneas with a matching lover or a comparable combatant.

Only within the last half-century has *The Aeneid*'s dualism been recognized. Emphasizing the "great conflict throughout the whole poem between light and darkness" (1962:171), Viktor Pöschl has masterfully analyzed the manner in which Vergil subjects the structure of his epic to tension between two fundamental forces:

> Vergil's Jupiter is the symbol of what Rome as an idea embodied. While Juno as the divine symbol of the demonic forces of violence and destruction does not hesitate to call up the spirits of the nether world . . . Jupiter is the organizing power that restrains those forces. Thus, on a deeper level, the contrast between the two highest divinities is symbolic of the ambivalence in history and human nature. It is a symbol, too, of the struggle between light and darkness, mind and emotion, order and chaos, which incessantly pervades the cosmos, the soul, and politics. . . . The struggle and final victory of order—this subduing of the demonic which is the basic theme of the poem, appears and reappears in many variations. The demonic appears in history as civil or foreign war, in the soul as passion, and in nature as death and destruction. Jupiter, Aeneas, and Augustus are its conquerors, while Juno, Dido, Turnus, and Antony are its conquered representatives. The contrast between Jupiter's powerful composure and Juno's confused passion reappears in the contrast between Aeneas and Dido and between Aeneas and Turnus. The Roman god, the Roman hero, and the Roman emperor are incarnations of the same idea. (17–18)

One of the leitmotifs of Pöschl's study is Goethe's insistence, expressed in a letter to Friedrich Schiller (8 April 1797), that each scene must symbolically represent the whole. It is precisely *The Aeneid*'s dual-focus structure that permits Vergil to follow this precept so scrupulously. Just as the exposition must be double, so every part of the work depends on the alternating following-pattern's constant invitation to compare and contrast the juxtaposed parties. If Aeneas's wanderings are relegated to an included story, it is not solely to permit the book to begin in medias res but also to avoid giving the impression that Aeneas himself is the poem's subject, he must not be made to appear so. Even Aeneas's final victory shows him as part of a diptych, his patience and humanity opposed to Turnus's irrational anger and barbarism. Like other early epics that show Moses and the Israelites fleeing from Pharaoh or the Greeks laying siege to Troy, *The Aeneid* portrays a battle between continents, a fight reminiscent of the wars that pitted Hannibal's elephants against the ordered legions of the Imperial Army. Vergil's universe is clearly that of the concentrically organized Old Testament, for the true antonym of "Citizen of Rome" is not "Citizen of Carthage" but "barbarian." Those who enjoy Roman citizenship have all the rights of the world's most powerful, most civilized nation; outsiders have none. Ingroup, outgroup— always the spatial distinction of a line drawn around the group in order to distinguish inclusion from exclusion. Those Italians who are willing to accept peaceful cohabitation may perhaps gain the advantages of citizenship, but the shameless fornication of a Dido or the barbaric fighting style of a Turnus must forever exclude them.

To emphasize citizenship is to play up the importance of foundation, whether of Rome in *The Aeneid*, the Promised Land in the Old Testament, or socialist Russia in Eisenstein's *Battleship Potemkin*. Foundation of a still existent state—along with worship of the founders—offers a theme that effectively reinforces audience homogeneity. Dual-focus narrative creates continuity between the distant past and the living present by means of a series of replacement operations. Just as Latium will be the new Troy, Augustus will be a scion of Aeneas's line. Even when the relationship is more or less facetious, as in René Goscinny and Albert Uderzo's comic strip *Astérix le Gaulois*, the continuity from text to audience is immediately apparent. Vergil affords readers every opportunity to identify with individual characters, to participate in their dilemmas, and to learn from their reactions, yet the overall structure of *The Aeneid* calls for group reaction rather than individual identification. Because the text is about Rome rather than any particular individual, it might manage without Aeneas, but it cannot dispense with some sequence of circumstances leading to the founding of Rome.

Interestingly, when the classical epic sought a method of increasing psychological interest, the approach adopted remained decidedly dual-focus. Instead of following a single character exclusively, concentrating all attention on his motivations and decisions, the Christian writer Prudentius introduced a measure of psychological complexity into his *Psychomachia*, some four centuries after Vergil, by transferring *The Aeneid*'s successive diptychs into the theater of the mind. Whereas character traits are always externalized in Vergil's epic, with one set of attitudes attributed to Aeneas and another to his successive foes, Prudentius begins the long process of internalizing character psychology, using Virtues and Vices as his warriors and psychological allegory as his mode. In many ways—obvious to anyone who has read both texts—Prudentius is an inferior writer to Vergil, yet to Prudentius goes the credit for discovering an influential method of bending dual-focus strategies to psychological purpose. Nearly forgotten, *Psychomachia* deserves revival, for together with Augustine's *City of God* it provided the foundation for a thousand years of medieval dual-focus narrative, in the visual arts as well as in literary, religious, and historical texts.

Prudentius's text is built around seven hand-to-hand combats between Virtues and Vices, resulting in peace and the building of a new temple. Just as the Decalogue in Exodus renders explicit the dualities of Genesis, detailing the markers that distinguish Jew from non-Jew, so Prudentius codifies much of the Vergilian material. At the same time, he draws heavily on Old Testament parallels, thus effecting one of the first important syntheses of classical and Judeo-Christian dual-focus narrative. The second combat, in which Chastity meets Lust (Libido), clearly parallels the Aeneas-Dido relationship, for Juno's strategy involved throwing Dido soul and body at Aeneas. The next fight presents the outcome of the Dido-Aeneas relationship, with Long-suffering (Patientia) battling Wrath (Ira). Like Dido, frustrated at her inability to debauch her counterpart, Ira eventually runs herself through with a sword. The rest of Prudentius's epic operates in much the same way. Virtues named Lowliness (Humilitas), Soberness (Sobrietas), and Reason (Ratio) match Aeneas's *pietas*, while Vices identified as Pride (Superbia), Indulgence (Luxuria), and Greed (Avaritia) neatly sum up the barbarism of Turnus and his allies Camilla, Mezentius, and Juno. The end of *Psychomachia* offers additional parallels to the founding of Rome. Just as Concordia sets foot inside the new temple, she is attacked from within by Discordia—an obvious reference to Roman mythology and the well-known sibling rivalry between Romulus and Remus.

On the surface, *Psychomachia* seems no more than a militant Christian text, with no explicit reference to *The Aeneid*. The examples cited are not classical but traditional Old Testament types: Job and Solomon, Judith and Holofernes, David and Goliath. Yet the choice and order of Virtues and Vices reveal the extent to which *Psychomachia* offers a psychological codification of Vergil's epic. By combining classical and Christian psychology, Prudentius solved one of the Renaissance's thorniest problems well over a millennium too soon. By using psychological labels and by making the human mind the battleground of his epic, Prudentius began a progression whose implications lead directly out of the dual-focus mode.

Dual-focus epic, as exemplified by the Old Testament, *The Aeneid*, and *Psychomachia*, operates according to what we might call "concentric dualism." Value is allocated to opposed groups differentially, as if one group were nearer to the source of value than the other. Geography is thus always hierarchical in nature. Those closest to the center are valued most highly, for in the center is Jerusalem, the Temple, the Ark of the Covenant. In the words of Mircea Eliade (1959), the Promised Land is *cosmos*, the outlying regions *chaos*, and Jerusalem the *axis mundi*. Surprisingly, dual-focus pastoral often follows the same model. Though some dual-focus pastorals (such as *Daphnis and Chloe*) approximate equal treatment of male and female, thereby approaching a more egalitarian diametrical dualism, the more common method involves a sense of underlying inequality—of concentric dualism—as if dual-focus pastoral were simply a disguised version of dual-focus epic.

Because courtship is regularly treated as conquest in Western literature, women are repeatedly identified with territory to be occupied and won. Having conquered Italy, Aeneas simultaneously lays claim to the land and to the local king's daughter, Lavinia. By concentrating attention on the clash between the villain and the young lover, popular melodramas effectively conceal the lover's interest in occupying the young lady's property. Though Hollywood musicals typically end with a marriage of apparent equals, closer scrutiny often reveals a substantial imbalance in the couple, almost always to the benefit of the man and the detriment of the woman. From Maurice Chevalier and Fred Astaire to Gene Kelly and Elvis Presley, the guy typically gets top billing and the better half of the deal. In Fred Zinneman's *Oklahoma!*,

Laurie may realize her dreams by marrying Curly, but when the cowhand weds the farmgirl he acquires her farm as well.

Daphnis and Chloe offers not only one of the most charming of all dual-focus pastorals but a myth of artistic interpretation as well. Longus reveals characters in the very act of learning that the world can be understood only in terms of a binary principle. At first, lacking knowledge, Daphnis and Chloe gather none of the fruits of their love. Only after the facts of life are passed on to them by nature and their elders will the two star-crossed lovers enjoy physical lovemaking. The overall pattern of replacement operations is typical of dual-focus pastoral: by marrying, children of different families gain the right to engender and raise their own family, thereby constituting a new generation. This saga of birth and repopulation reverses the epic tale of death and destruction, the two forms fitting neatly together as part of the larger dual-focus vision. At first nourished by goat and sheep, Longus's pastoral pair are soon discovered by parallel peasant families, then eventually passed on to their rediscovered aristocratic parents. This series of parental replacement operations is not complete until the children born to the newlyweds are, in turn, confided to the care of a goat and a ewe. In this cyclical arrangement, the only change that takes place over the course of the text is replacement of one generation by its successor.

For that change to come about, however, Daphnis and Chloe must learn what the previous generation already knows. Taking his thematic material from the text's fundamental male/female distinction, Longus portrays a *boy* and a *girl* learning what those sexual designations mean. For children to become parents, they must first learn to understand and to represent their sex. Since the cyclical nature of human existence depends on sexual categories, Daphnis and Chloe must learn to be defined by those categories in much the same way that Esther must accept and reveal her Jewishness or Aeneas his Roman virtue. Daphnis's and Chloe's new knowledge represents the actualization of a natural reality rather than the kind of learning associated with traditional definitions of narrative. Instead of becoming something that they previously were not, they move closer and closer to perfect representation of their divine archetypes: Pan, whose altar is by a tree (the masculine principle), and the Nymphs, who are worshiped in a grotto (the female principle).

Daphnis and Chloe exist in a world apart, a domain where the gods, people, and nature live in perfect concord, for the gods are the shepherds' foster parents, and the animals their charges and constant companions. As long as the young lovers remain within this context the following-pattern strictly obeys the principle of alternation between male and female, goat and sheep. Protected by its peaceful isolation, this pastoral society is nevertheless not totally shut off from the outside world. At regular intervals, the calm and naïveté of pastoral seclusion are interrupted by incursions from the world of experience and violence beyond. Dual-focus pastoral alternation between Daphnis and Chloe thus shares the text with dual-focus epic alternation and conflict between the pastoral society and its less peaceful neighbors. Outside intervention is necessary because Longus's shepherds are doomed to perpetual ignorance as long as they remain isolated. They try to imitate the lovemaking of sheep and goats, but they soon find it unsuitable for humans.

In lovemaking there is also an element of violence, Daphnis discovers to his horror. From the start, the violent outside world is defined as the erotic realm of the wolf. When Daphnis and Chloe take their herds out to pasture, "Eros contrived trouble for them. A she-wolf from the adjoining countryside harried the flocks" (1953:7). Only when Daphnis has himself fallen into the trap set for the wolf will he bathe himself before Chloe, thus lighting in her the low fire of young love. The flames are fanned as Dorcon, an experienced cowherd "who knew not only the name but the facts of love" (10), challenges Daphnis to a contest, resulting in a first kiss between the two foundlings. Daphnis then for the first time finds Chloe beautiful. When autumn comes, Daphnis is carried off by pirates, then is carried away by a view of Chloe's naked body as she bathes to celebrate his return: "That bath seemed to him to be a more fearful thing than the sea" (18). But the young lovers cannot satisfy their longings without the good offices of Lykainion (whose name means "the little wolf"), a city wench who has long had her eyes on Daphnis. Knowledge gained outside the pastoral world turns out to be required for procreation of life within pastoral bounds. Daphnis and Chloe must learn the lesson of Eros: they must capture the wolf instinct and turn it to their own purpose. In the words of Paul Turner, "they cannot become mature human beings until they have come to terms with the 'wolf' element in human nature" (1968:21).

Before they can come to terms with Eros, however, they must learn to interpret their world. Like the reader faced with the hidden pattern of a book, Daphnis and Chloe can make no progress in their understanding of the world until they discover its organizing principles. Nature is the text, Daphnis and Chloe are its readers. Progressively, the lovers perform for us the task of elucidating the text's polarity adjustment process. Not until Daphnis first bathes himself before Chloe does she discover beauty. Delightfully naïve, she sets out to answer a simple question: What produces beauty? Daphnis bathed and he was beautiful, she thinks; perhaps if I bathe myself I too will be beautiful. But her bath changes nothing. When Daphnis pipes, that too makes him beautiful in her eyes; but when she pipes, it is to no avail. Action, Chloe discovers, is not essential but incidental, a hypothesis that she proves by her ineffectual metaphorizing:

> I am sick for sure, but what the malady is I do not know. I am in pain, but can find no bruise. I am distressed, yet none of my sheep is missing. I feel a burning, yet am sitting in thick shade. How many times have I been pricked by brambles, yet I never cried; how many times have bees stung me, but I never lost my appetite. The thing that pricks my heart now is sharper than those. Daphnis is beautiful, but so are the flowers; his pipe makes fine music, but so does the nightingale—but flowers and nightingales do not disturb me. Would I could become a pipe, so that he might breathe upon me, a goat, that I might graze in his care! Only Daphnis did you make beautiful; my bathing was useless. (1953:9)

Daphnis fares no better when Chloe's first nude bath leads him to discover beauty. At first, these would-be lovers mistakenly assume that all texts are the same, that each one can be compared to all the others without any loss of meaning. "They wanted something, but knew not what" (13).

What they lack is a clear understanding of the differences between their two bodies. In the dual-focus pastoral world it is difference, not change, that carries meaning. Like Montessori pupils, Daphnis and Chloe must learn to grasp the relationship between the peg and the pegboard, matching similar shapes and noting the difference between convex and concave configurations. If the young inhabitants of the pastoral world are slow to learn how their bodies differ, it is in part because those who have already discovered Eros take this knowledge for granted. Philetas thinks he is teaching them how to requite their love by suggesting "kisses and embraces and lying together with naked bodies" (1953:22), but he has left out the essential fact. He treats the young lovers as if they were both the same, as if they were exact mirror images one of the other. When Daphnis lies with Lykainion, however, he discovers the small but all-important flaw in the mirror. Chloe resembles him in all ways but one, he learns. Finally, in this binary principle, he gains the knowledge needed to read the world.

But Lykainion's warning about the violence of lovemaking keeps Daphnis from running to Chloe and putting his newfound knowledge into practice. Just as the pastoral world cannot be self-perpetuating without letting a bit of Eros through a break in its walls, so Daphnis cannot make love to Chloe without causing her to bleed: "Chloe would soon have become a woman if the matter of the blood had not terrified Daphnis" (1953:46). Never, in the course of Longus's tale, does Daphnis resign himself in a psychologically motivated manner to the "matter of the blood." Instead, Longus handles the problem ritually, exploiting the divine affinities apparent since the story's opening paragraph. At first goat and sheep, Daphnis and Chloe adjust to their roles as man and woman in two different ways. After learning a lesson in human anatomy, they perform the myths in which Pan enacts his sexual role with the Nymphs. When Daphnis's foster father Lamon passes down the knowledge of his generation in the form of the Pan-Syrinx story, the two youths act out the tale, thus rendering explicit their relationship to Pan and Syrinx. Pan tried to persuade Syrinx to give in to his desires, but Syrinx refused a partially human lover. Hiding among the reeds, Syrinx was soon accidentally cut down by Pan. When he realized what he had done, Pan bound the reeds together, thereby inventing the flute. This etiological account reveals that lovemaking does indeed have a bestial element, while recognizing that beauty and music owe their very existence to the deflowering of a woman. The lesson is clear: for love to be requited, man's bestial side must tear woman apart.

Once Daphnis learns this lesson he does his best to convey it to Chloe through another story about Pan. This time the goat god is courting the nymph Echo, who "avoided all males, whether human or divine, for she loved maidenhood" (1953:45). It would have been better for her, though, had she surrendered to Pan, for out of jealousy he tore her limb from limb and scattered her all over the land. And so it is, explains Daphnis, that today she returns our music like some antiphonal chant. Remembering the time when he and Chloe had competed verbally, alternately launching sallies "antiphonally . . . like an echo" (40), Daphnis expects Chloe to understand the parallel between their own situation and the story of Echo. Indeed, the Echo myth elegantly demonstrates the functioning of the flaw in the dual-focus mirror. Pan with his pipe makes sounds, but their beauty is complete only when Echo has responded with her chorus. The two are complementary, but different—Pan is the phallus, with his pipe, while Echo is the concave circle of hills that returns Pan's compliment.

As recounted in *Daphnis and Chloe*, the Echo myth aptly describes more than just a single pastoral pair. For the antiphonal method is the basic mode not only of pastoral but also of dual-focus narrative as a whole. From Theocritus to Vergil and on to the Italian Renaissance, "amoebic" verse is the fundamental medium of the pastoral experience. Whether between two shepherds in a singing match or two lovers competing in fun against each other, the basic principle of this type of verse is contained in its name: *amoibé* or change. The formal similarities of succeeding verses create a mirror effect, but the amoebic aspect of the verse introduces the mirror's flaw. It is instructive to compare the type of change inherent in amoebic verse to the type we associate with the novel of education. The novel portrays a character moving through time, changing as she goes, generating the text's structure, which becomes increasingly based on change-over-time as the text progresses. In amoebic verse the situation is radically different, dependent instead on difference-over-space. The *amoibé* occurs not between one time and the next but between one character and another. Daphnis and Chloe may make significant progress in terms of their own personal education, but the text as a whole deemphasizes that progress in two distinct ways: the one cyclical (the end repeats the beginning), the other amoebic (constantly measuring the difference between Daphnis and Chloe rather than between one situation and the next). Interest is thus transferred from diachronic movement to the text's synchronic dimension. We measure change not along the text's temporal axis, as in the Bildungsroman (from ignorance to experience, for example), but at right angles to that temporal development.

From the formulaic repetitions of *The Song of Roland* to the antiphonal duets of the Hollywood musical, dual-focus narrative rejects change-over-time in favor of the amoebic principle of difference-over-space. What makes it so easy to construct comparisons is the formulaic nature of the fundamental distinctions around which dual-focus texts are built. In one sense, dual-focus characters don't even have names—they are defined instead by their position. The name "Satan" means opponent, as does the Old French equivalent, *averser*, used throughout *The Song of Roland*. Even the word "enemy" is none other than *in* plus *amicus*, "not-friend." Dual-focus epics are thus populated with characters who, structurally speaking, may be identified as *friend* and *not-friend*. The system's duality is regularly carried in character names, from Hesiod (Law/lessness), Old Testament judges (Gideon's other name is Jerubbaal, meaning "contend with Baal"), and medieval religious texts (Anti/christ) to comic strip heroes (the Avenger), science-fiction films (*Them!*), and westerns (out/laws). Indian myth takes the system one step farther. Not only is Ahi the water dragon known as Vṛtra, meaning the evil one or simply the adversary, but Vṛtra is overcome by Indra the fertility god who is also known as Vṛtrahan, the slayer of Vṛtra the opponent. Dual-focus epic always depends on the opposition of a Vṛtra to a Vṛtrahan, an adversary to an adversary killer, a foe to a friend, an other to a self. Dual-focus pastoral follows a similar route, opposing male to fe/male and man to wo/man. The rhyme is built in, because the underlying structure always already depends on the presence of rhyming characters and values.

Replacement Operations and Polarity Adjustment

Concentrating on principles of opposition, I have thus far paid little attention to the development of dual-focus texts over time. In one sense, this is appropriate, because dual-focus narratives work very hard to highlight static oppositions and questions of space. Dual-focus texts are not without plots, but those plots always seem to serve the text's fundamental duality. Much has been written about the structure of novelistic plots, but most novel-based conclusions simply don't apply to dual-focus strategies. A new analysis is needed, stressing the specificity of the dual-focus approach.

Our guiding metaphor thus far has been the chess game, with its clear opposition between equivalent but opposite players. We have now reached the limits of this metaphor's usefulness. The chess analogy exemplifies quite well the text's synchronic aspect, but it has less to say about the diachronic progression of the text. Another metaphor now suggests itself, one that is central to both classical and Christian dual-focus traditions. Throughout *The Iliad* and then again at the end of *The Aeneid* we are told that the king of the gods holds the fate of mortals in his hand as he would hold an equal-arm balance, with the Greeks or Aeneas on one side and the Trojans or Turnus on the other. Christian mythology borrows this motif, transferring it from the battlefield to the soul and calling it *psychostasis* or the weighing of the soul. With St. Michael holding the scale, good deeds fill one pan and bad acts the other. As in the classical motif, the pan that outweighs the other is the winner. Once weighing has taken place, the soul's fate is decided and the text is finished.

Dual-focus texts are conceived as a process of weighing. Beforehand, the scale is stable. Afterward, the scale once again achieves stability. Only in between, during the process of weighing, does the scale oscillate. In order to continue, the text must avoid permanent resolution of its seesawing motion. The opening section of this chapter argued that dual-focus texts typically begin by a process of splitting, which organizes an initial chaotic situation into two antithetical principles, groups, or characters. This split presides over the text's synchronic component, but something else is needed to initiate the dual-focus diachronic dimension. The Old Testament book of Judges offers useful insight into this process. The Pentateuch serves to establish a claim to power and value, with the Israelites separated from those around them, valorized by a special covenant with God, and organized according to laws prescribing the conduct required for extension of that privileged relationship. Joshua, the book directly following the Pentateuch, completes the establishment of the Israelites—with God's help they reach the Promised Land, where they enjoy a position of power and stability. But in stability there is no text. The book of Judges exists not because everything continues to run along smoothly but because the people of Israel continually "did what was evil in the sight of the Lord" (a formula that is repeated no fewer than eight times: Judges 2:11, 3:7, 3:12, 4:1, 6:1, 8:34, 10:6, 13:1). Whenever the Israelites stray from the source of their strength—the Law and its Giver—they empower their foes and mobilize a new section of the text. To the periods when the people of Israel are obedient and dominate the land from the Jordan to the sea, the text accords not one word, for the continued existence of the text depends on maintaining the suspense—literally and figuratively—during which no one knows which way the scales will tilt. Judges becomes a model for the remainder of the Old Testament, which oscillates between straying from the Law, with a consequent loss of power, and periodic returns to the power engendered by proper belief and action.

Dual-focus rhetoric firmly allies readers with one side, but the diachronic aspect of dual-focus texts requires a rupture between sympathy and power. The plot isn't set in motion until the fate of the rhetorically privileged side appears to be in doubt. A real-world example may be of some use here. For decades during the twentieth century, world politics depended heavily on the notion of a "balance of power." As long as a power balance subsists, this dual-focus theory asserted, the gates of war remain closed. But when the Soviets sent Sputnik into orbit, the newspapers were suddenly cluttered with comparative graphs, terms of imbalance like "gap" or "lag," and new versions of the perennial Ivan-Johnny contrast, all triggered by fear that the imbalance might turn into war—the larger text that balance of power politics attempts to keep from being written. "What made war inevitable," Thucydides says at the beginning of *The Peloponnesian War*, "was the growth of Athenian power and the fear which this caused in Sparta" (1954:25). It is here that Thucydides begins his text, and not with a detailed account of the years of peace preceding the war, for the breakdown of the balance of power and the text are simultaneous and in a sense synonymous. In *The Song of Roland* only a few lines are needed to relate Charlemagne's successful Spanish campaign. For seven years, the Holy Roman Emperor had achieved a continuous string of victories, yet the poet shows no interest in that portion of history. What attracts the poet—what constitutes a dual-focus plot—is the breakdown of Christian unity, the consequent reduction of Christian strength, and thus the challenge to Christian superiority. Just as each episode in Judges begins when the people of Israel stray from God and his Law, so *Roland* is set in motion by Ganelon's straying from his feudal responsibilities.

Ganelon belongs to a class of characters that we may conveniently label as "middlemen." Refusing to be fully defined by the duality that organizes the text's synchronic existence, middlemen cross the line that separates the text's two constitutive groups, thereby disturbing the delicate balance between the two sides. Homer's *Iliad* offers a particularly clear example of the functioning of dual-focus middlemen. Ever since Aristotle's attempts to squeeze *The Iliad* into the biographical mold that he applied to *The Odyssey*, Homer's martial epic has been consistently misread, the Trojan war being treated as a function of Achilles' anger rather than vice versa. In short (with the exception of a few passages in Whitman 1958 and Sheppard 1969), *Iliad* criticism has suffered from the same problem that has so long plagued *The Aeneid* and *The Song of Roland*: a fundamentally dual-focus text has been read as if it had only a single focus. *The Iliad* makes much more sense when it is treated as a dual-focus epic triggered by Achilles' alienation from his group, thus producing an imbalance between Trojans and Greeks. The mechanism by which Achilles becomes a middleman deserves attention, because it demonstrates especially clearly the dual-focus tendency to handle every situation in binary fashion. The middleman is not an independent category lying between Greeks and Trojans but is instead generated out of an internal conflict formally identical to the larger Greek-Trojan battle.

At the outset Chryses brings the wrath of Apollo down on the Greeks for their unwillingness to return his daughter Chryseis, but when she is sent home, their safety seems assured. Agamemnon, however, is far from satisfied; he resents losing Chryseis and thus resolves to replace his lost prize with Achilles' captive Briseis. This series of replacement operations, substituting one anger for another, forces Achilles into the role of opponent. It is Achilles' plea to Zeus (through his mother Thetis) and not Chryses' invocation to Apollo that spells the beginning of the Greeks' misfortune. Not until Book XVI, where Achilles reverses his original plea to Zeus, will the Greeks' fortune change, and not until Achilles himself decides to reenter the combat in Book XIX will the Trojans' fate be sealed. *The Iliad* is not Achilles' book but a clever combination of international and intranational strife. It is Achilles' role at the intersection of the book's two conflicts (the Greek-Trojan battle and the quarrel with Agamemnon) that forces him into the role of middleman. This composite formula will become the model for many a later dual-focus text, including the Hollywood western and several generations of superhero comic books.

Once the dual-focus text has been set in motion by the creation of an initial imbalance (through defection of a middleman, breakdown of group unity, or divergence from the Law), the text proceeds according to a series of replacement operations. Instead of operating through a clear cause-and-effect pattern, each new confrontation seems to be generated automatically, in response to a clear textual need. When one foe is vanquished, another arises, as if out of thin air, to take his place. No bad guy, no text. In Eugène Sue's immensely popular 1830s serial novel, *Les Mystères de Paris*, we run through three more or less independent series of adversaries. As soon as the heroic Rodolphe is freed from the threats posed by Bras-rouge and the Maître d'école, the Martial family jumps in to join La Chouette and her evil designs; no sooner are they out of the way than Polidori and Jacques Ferrand present their ugly faces and even uglier schemes. Where did they come from? Who knows? Who cares? Readers are given no more reason to care about the origin of these foes than about the reasons for the timely appearance of new antagonists for Batman, Superman, James Bond, or Wonder Woman. Throughout the dual-focus tradition, adversaries are generated not through a traditional cause-and-effect process but as a necessary function of the text's structure.

Just as the technique of replacement operations operates quasi-automatically, so are dual-focus actions generated mechanically out of a small number of well-known principles. Because dual-focus characters are usually defined by relationship to a principle or group, they typically act more as placeholders than as independent beings with lives of their own. The opening scene of John Ford's *Wagonmaster* presents the Cleggs brothers robbing a store. As they leave, the clerk grabs a gun and wings the head of the gang. "Uncle Shiloh" instantly turns and says: "You shouldn't of done that." As if by rote he then shoots down the clerk. The way Shiloh sees it, he has no choice; an affront requires response. "Well I guess I'm gonna haf t'kill ya now" is the basic motif of this necessary reaction common to all but the most sophisticated dual-focus fiction. Where other modes have psychology and motivation, dual-focus narrative depends on automatic mechanisms like honor codes, talion laws, and allegiance to one's group (be it national, religious, or sexual). As Northrop Frye puts it apropos of comedy, dual-focus characters remain in "ritual bondage" (1957:168) to a particular idea or category, thus depriving them of the independence enjoyed by characters in other modes.

The same principle applies to the progression of the dual-focus text itself. Systematic deployment of metaphoric modulations moves us from side to side in a manner that depends more on formal parallelism than on character choice. The alternating following-pattern thus seems to arise from the underlying dual-focus structure rather than from plot considerations. Consider Xenophon's short Alexandrian romance known as *An Ephesian Tale*, which recounts the love story between Anthia and Habrocomes. When we read lines like "Anthia for her part was no less smitten" (1953:73), we probably don't think twice about how we have modulated from Habrocomes to Anthia. Upon reflection, however, we recognize two separate acts of communication. On the one hand, the narrator provides information about Anthia ("Anthia . . . was . . . smitten"); on the other hand, he draws on an underlying parallelism to justify the movement from Habrocomes to Anthia (". . . for her part . . . no less . . ."). Each action calls for a matching action, and thus, automatically, for modulation to the counterpart character. The familiar convention of sleepless nights works in the same fashion. "Habrocomes pulled his hair and ripped his clothes," we are told. As if by rote, the text then tells us that "Anthia too was in deep distress" (73–74).

Thanks to replacement operations and metaphoric modulation, the dual-focus alternating following-pattern moves us through the text in a way that seems automatic and unchanging. A simple story like *An Ephesian Tale* progresses through a series of oppositions, first alternating between the young lovers Anthia and Habrocomes, then, once they are separated, between their successive captors. At first, this simplicity appears representative of dual-focus narrative as a whole—we always seem to be alternating between Romans and barbarians, Christians and pagans, friends and foes, men and women. Because each new following-unit apparently involves a 180-degree reversal, we have the sensation of always returning to the exact same location, thus repeating the same opposition. A closer look suggests that more is going on in dual-focus texts. As we move through a series of replacement operations, instead of exactly repeating the same opposition again and again we encounter small but meaningful differences in the parameter of opposition. This "polarity adjustment" offers a minimalist but powerful method of making meaning, characteristic of dual-focus narrative.

In *The Song of Roland*, the importance of the Christian-pagan opposition is eventually compromised by the introduction of additional dualities: group orientation versus individualism, humility versus pride, strength versus weakness, and so forth. This process is facilitated by the dual-focus tendency to oppose clusters of characteristics rather than single features. With each alternation, with each metaphoric modulation, an opportunity exists to vary the properties contained in any given cluster, thereby nearly imperceptibly adding an important new consideration. From a distance, the text may appear monotonous, endlessly repeating the same opposition, with the same clear rhetorical effect, but upon closer inspection we discover a less obvious program.

D. W. Griffith's controversial masterpiece, *The Birth of a Nation*, offers a fascinating example of the opportunities available through polarity adjustment. The first half of Griffith's film alternates between two parallel families, the Stonemans in the North and the Camerons in the South. Before the outbreak of the Civil War, we witness the friendship of the younger sons—eventually destined to meet in battle—as well as the nascent romance of Elsie Stoneman and Ben Cameron. When war comes, we continue our alternation between Union and Confederate sides. As the film progresses, however, the contrast between North and South progressively diminishes in favor of the qualities shared by these noble foes. Little by little, we shift from opposition between the Stonemans and Camerons to a celebration of their hidden commonality—of their shared patrician whiteness—now opposed to the supposedly barbaric qualities of the "Negro race." Having grabbed our attention by stressing the pathetic side of internecine strife, Griffith now slides to his real topic, the superiority of one race over the other. What appeared to be the historical tale of North versus South has turned into a biased account of white versus black. Just as photographers must deal with the problem of parallax, and cartographers must adjust for the slight difference between true North and magnetic North, readers of dual-focus narrative must remain ever attentive to a slippage in the polarities around which the text is built.

Endings

Through replacement operations, metaphoric modulation, and polarity adjustment, the alternating following-pattern of dual-focus narrative is eventually suspended by reduction of the text's two constitutive foci to one. In dual-focus epic, this process involves destruction or exile of one group. In dual-focus pastoral, reduction is effected through a merger of the two sides. Many texts combine the two approaches. Most descriptions of narrative endings assume that they relate to the body of the text in a manner that is entirely uncharacteristic of dual-focus narratives. Typically used to describe narrative conclusions are paired terms like cause-effect, question-answer, and problem-solution (e.g., Richardson 1997:92, Miller 1998:46, Carroll 2001:32, Abbott 2002:12). None of these is adequate to describe the way in which dual-focus texts end. Instead, the necessary concepts are reversal and apocalypse. Two early Christian examples will prove especially useful for understanding the role of endings in dual-focus narrative.

One of the most influential early Christian texts was *The Martyrdom of Saint Perpetua and Saint Felicitas,* which became the literary model for the important genre known as the *passio* or martyr's life. In only a few pages, this moving text portrays two separate battles. The dominant battle is the one implied by the title: Perpetua, Felicitas, and their friends are questioned, beaten, and slaughtered by the Romans. The day before she is to die in the arena, however, Perpetua has a dream depicting a second battle. Thrust into the arena alone, she is soon attacked by the Devil disguised as an Egyptian, whom she defeats in single combat. In real life under the Romans, Perpetua dies a horrible death, but in her dream she leaves the arena victorious. In its simplicity, this account of martyrdom eloquently demonstrates the double binarity of dual-focus apocalyptic endings. An apparently primary distinction opposes the Christians to the Romans, but that antagonism is eventually trumped by a more important contrast between dingy reality and glorious dream life. Perpetua's vision cannot possibly be understood as an effect of a preceding cause. Instead, it must be seen as a reversal of the previously presented circumstances, a radical adjustment of polarities. In Perpetua's flesh-and-blood martyrdom, the operative distinctions involve physical power; in her dream, the outcome depends on spiritual power.

A similar pattern emerges from the familiar story of Dives and Lazarus (Luke 16:19–31), among Jesus' parables the most commonly depicted in medieval art. This exemplary tale about a rich man and a poor leper is typically recounted in a double diptych. The first image reveals Dives on the left, seated at his table, enjoying the fruits of this world, while Lazarus crawls into a corner on the right, his sores licked by dogs. This first panel is usually drawn or sculpted quite realistically, by medieval standards. The second image, however, is clearly the product of imagination rather than observation. On the left, the rich man burns in the fires of Hell; on the right, Lazarus reposes happily in the comforting bosom of Abraham. The variations on this theme are manifold—on the façade of the south porch at Moissac, in the capital of Vézelay's south aisle, in Herrad of Lansberg's *Hortus Deliciarum*—but the effect is always the same. This world is revealed as nothing but a degraded realm where people are not situated in their rightful place. The connections between the two diptychs include nothing that we can clearly identify as cause and effect, nor are there any strong temporal markers connecting the two panels. This is not a depiction of before and after but of here and hereafter, of the fallen world and eternal life.

Throughout the history of dual-focus narrative, a similar textual organization has held sway. The first part of the text depicts a world of "reversed circumstances," as one Horatio Alger character put it. The conclusion rights that wrong by reversing the reversal. In many cases, this configuration clearly represents a reaction to a very real historical situation. Before emancipation, African Americans developed a large variety of narrative songs that offered an otherworldly response to the slavery they were made to endure in this world. These "Negro Sprituals" borrowed Old Testament metaphors and apocalyptic mythology as the basis for stories of heavenly triumph over human misery. When Southern whites were defeated in the Civil War, they too sought the kind of comfort easily provided by the magic of polarity adjustment. No text makes the otherworldly nature of the solution more obvious than Griffith's *Birth of a Nation*, where the white-robed riders of the Ku Klux Klan seem to float in out of a vision, expressing Southern aspirations of vengeance.

Defeated by the British, the Irish imagined a new life in the land across the sea, thereby shedding their identity as losers to the British in favor of a new identification with the American revolutionaries who defeated the British. Many times over, Irish songs thus repeat the double diptych of defeat at the hands of the British reversed by a triumphal new life in America. In Dion Boucicault's celebrated "Oh! Paddy Dear (The Wearing of the Green)," the first verse laments past losses and their effect on daily life in the defeated homeland, while the second imagines a new life for the Irish in a land "where rich and poor stand equal in the light of freedom's day." Though America may be a real place, it serves the same function in Irish song as dream does for Perpetua or heavenly vision for Lazarus. Because justice in this world seems faulty, dual-focus texts invent apocalyptic realms of perfect justice. Inverting previous events, apocalypse is formally equivalent to revenge, repeating the same stories with the roles reversed.

Transferred to dual-focus pastoral, this Last Judgment mentality produces fascinating results. Like its epic counterpart, dual-focus pastoral begins with "reversed circumstances," but of a different sort. Instead of starting with a defeat or an exile, dual-focus love stories typically begin with a mismatch: the eventual lovers are matched to the wrong partners. The Hollywood musical—often a particularly transparent bearer of dual-focus pastoral structures—regularly begins by introducing same-sex friends or a mismatched heterosexual couple. For the film to progress, the "wrong" couples must be done away with, so that the "right" matches can be concluded. In Minnelli's *An American in Paris*, Gene Kelly is paired first with Oscar Levant (wrong sex) and then with Nina Foch (too old) before eventually finding Leslie Caron, who had previously been coupled with Georges Guétary (too old). In order to drive the point home, Kelly also finds the time to dance with a group of children (too young) and a grey-haired woman (too old). The minute Kelly sights Caron, we have no doubt which characters should be matched and how the film will end. Just as comedy audiences know from the start that the *senex* is an inappropriate match for the attractive young woman, who must instead be matched to someone her age, so musical audiences have a keen notion of what passes for justice in the dual-focus pastoral world. If dual-focus epic implicitly closes on the motionless end of a battle (aptly figured in *Psychomachia* illustrations by the image of a Virtue standing triumphantly over the corresponding recumbent Vice), dual-focus pastoral ends with a freeze-frame of the couple's final clinch, thereby extending the "right" match into eternity.

Dual-focus narrative typically stretches between two eternities, two absolutes. Before the text there was nothing but chaos; with the end of the text comes the end of time. Time is the enemy; it is a fallen notion. Only in the clarity of Apocalypse and Last Judgment (even when that notion is reduced to no more than a freeze-frame) can the fall into time be reversed. Given to absolutes, dual-focus narratives often assign values in a manner that is abundantly clear. "Pagans are wrong and Christians are right" (79), we are boldly assured in *The Song of Roland*. In dual-focus pastoral, a similar sense of rightness is produced by paired close-ups, a significant exchange of glances, or the convention of parallel sleepless nights. This clarity engenders a context of reader confidence that effectively undermines traditional notions of cause and effect. Why do Kelly and Caron get together at the end? Is it because of this or that action? No, it is above all because they are "Fated to Be Mated," as Fred Astaire puts it apropos of his relationship with Cyd Charisse in Rouben Mamoulian's *Silk Stockings*.

Dual-focus endings thus involve a type of causality that is far removed from the logic of the detective novel. Does Aeneas defeat Turnus because he is courageous or because he is fated to do so? Is Turnus killed because he has wantonly slaughtered Pallas or simply because he is cast in the role of the villain? Does Thierry's victory over Pinabel at the end of *Roland* prove that he is in the right, or is it the fact that he is in the right that causes him to win? In Exodus 17 the Israelites fight the Amalekites while Moses stands atop the hill holding the rod of God; whenever he holds up his hand, Israel prevails, but the Amalekites dominate when he lowers his hand. Do the Israelites win because Moses keeps his hand raised, or vice versa? In medieval iconography, are individuals sent to heaven because of their good deeds or because the angels outweigh the devils on Michael's scale? Does Superman win because he has superpowers or because his opponents are evil?

The traditional hair-splitting responses to questions like these are quite unnecessary in the dual-focus context, for the questions themselves reveal a misunderstanding of the normal dual-focus approach to causality and judgment. We moderns have a hard time handling the notion that battle outcome and judgment of right and wrong might be both synonymous and simultaneous. In the judicial battles that constitute the locus classicus of dual-focus clashes, one side is not right because their man won, nor did their man win because that side was in the right. Rather, the two are synonymous, simultaneous, and incontrovertible. The concepts of *in*justice, of mistaken decisions, and of appeal are possible only in a fallen world. Once the apocalyptic moment has been reached, the outcome and the right are the same and inseparable. The judge is not a man, who might be considered fallible, but Jupiter, God, or the equally infallible (and equally prejudiced) Olympian narrator. There are thus no wrong judgments, because the moral code and the particular judgment are not separable. Instead of development, dual-focus narratives offer a stable rhetoric and a corresponding—and entirely predictable—last judgment.

Because they substitute predictable judgments for cause-and-effect plots, dual-focus texts also must, in large part, do without the suspense typically associated with other types of narrative. The same ability that permits dual-focus narrators to alternate between one side and the other typically provides not only present knowledge of all the characters but also knowledge of the future. Everything leads the reader to identify with this Olympian narrator. To a surprising extent, we share not only his prejudices but also his knowledge. The subject is either historically predictable (Rome was indeed founded) or generically predictable (we know how musicals end). At the same time, however, we have good cause to identify with the characters who receive the narrator's most sympathetic treatment. Placing ourselves in their skins, we share their limited perspective. We thus find ourselves in the contradictory position of simultaneously identifying with an all-powerful narrator and with limited characters. As Charlemagne we cannot understand his dreams, but as the narrator we understand them perfectly well. Dual-focus readers thus find themselves split—both Olympian narrator and limited character, both sure of the outcome and repeatedly in doubt. Dual-focus suspense is thus no suspense at all, in the normal sense of the term, but a tearing apart of the spectator, a rending to which we voluntarily submit in order finally to celebrate a renewed wholeness.

Uncle Remus enacts dual-focus ritual suspense in a particularly clear manner. Joel Chandler Harris's stories invariably begin with the little boy's question about the fate of Brer Rabbit. Based on doubt and curiosity, these queries about time, about specific events, about what happened next are designed to heighten suspense. But the narrator's answer is always couched in terms of universals, of essences, and of relationships that don't change over time. For example, in chapter six, the little boy inquires: " 'Uncle Remus, did the Rabbit have to go clean away when he got loose from the Tar-baby?' To which Uncle Remus retorts: " 'Bless gracious, honey, dat he didn't. Who? Him? You dunno nuthin' 'tall 'bout Brer Rabbit ef dat's de way you puttin' 'im down' " (1965:24). That is, if the boy has ritual curiosity, Uncle Remus has ritual knowledge, which he must impart to the boy. Just as each dual-focus text posits exception only to squelch it, so dual-focus narratives permit suspense only to demonstrate—to those who are within the circle—that suspense is never truly possible. If you know about Brer Rabbit, then there is no suspense, for his fate is fully predictable on the basis of his well-defined character. The dual-focus narrator turns us all into gods. We provisionally forget the outcome (which we have known all along from tradition, from generic knowledge, or from internal evidence) only in order to reenact the distance between narrator and audience, between the divine and the human. The end of the text represents the joining of the two, that moment when all knowledge is shared and theophany can take place.

The Dual-Focus System

This chapter has described several structures common to texts characterized by an alternating following-pattern, thereby making a case for the existence of a common but previously unrecognized type, which I have called dual-focus. The particular traits thus far educed include:

- A following-pattern that alternates between opponents or lovers
- Regular movement between the two sides by means of metaphoric modulation
- An exposition establishing two equivalent and opposed individuals, groups, or principles
- Progression of the text by replacement rather than cause-and-effect connections
- Characters who operate as representatives of a group or category rather than as independent beings who develop or change
- A plot that results from a temporary imbalance between the two sides and that proceeds by removal of exceptions and restoration of unity
- An imbalance that produces the plot, often engendered by the action of characters ("middlemen") who refuse to follow the dictates of their group, category, or sex
- Importance of the law, tradition, nature, or other established systems
- Negation of time through suspension, circularity, and spatialization
- Textual completion and return to a stable situation that depend on the reduction of two groups to one, through elimination or merging

This final section is devoted to constructing a coherent model that is capable of explaining the relationships connecting these apparently disparate characteristics.

The chess game metaphor evoked earlier provides useful insight. Descriptions of chess matches usually concentrate on the thirty-two pieces whose mobility is essential to the game, taking for granted the existence of the sixty-four-square chessboard across which those pieces are moved. Just as a chess match cannot be understood by studying the moves of a single side, so the underlying logic of the match cannot be grasped without recognizing the relationship between the players and the space constituted by the chessboard. As in chess, the fundamental logic of dual-focus epic involves two rivals *laying claim to the same space*, with the text representing the weighing of their respective claims. The contested space may take on diverse identities, from a plot of land disputed by ranchers and farmers or the hand of a woman desired in marriage by rival suitors, to the place on a housewife's grocery list fought over by competing detergents in commercials of the "Brand X" type. Whatever its nature, however, the contested space must be conceived as limited. As in chess or football, going out of bounds is not permitted, and resolution cannot be achieved by expansion of the available space. The claim of both sides is to a specific space, interchangeable with no other.

For a text to work in a dual-focus manner, it must establish a space (or series of spaces) and introduce two separate groups laying claim to that space. As Genesis 13:6 says of Lot and Abram, "The land could not support them both together" (New English Bible), or as the Revised Standard Version puts it, "The country was not large enough for both Abraham and Lot." The same motif appears repeatedly. The Italian peninsula is not big enough for both Aeneas and Turnus. Either Charlemagne or Marsile must be driven out of the Iberian peninsula. Or as so many western antagonists implicitly put it: "This territory ain't big enough for the both of us."

A simple example, featuring two versions of the "same" story, will help explain how this process operates. Imagine this sequence of events:

> A group of men sight an isolated house and decide to burglarize it. They develop a strategy and then put their plan into action. First, one of the group delivers a falsified note designed to lure the menfolk away, in the process emptying the bullets from the only gun in the house. Then the would-be burglars approach the house as a group, successively breaking down doors until they reach the inner sanctum where the objects of their desires are located.

The progress of the burglars is like a syntagmatic chain. They start in the bushes, cross the road, climb the stairs, force the front door, go through the entrance hall, break into the living room, force the inner sanctum door, and finally reach their quarry. This is a story that takes place in time, depends on cause-and-effect progression, and operates by metonymic modulation. In short, it is not a dual-focus text. When D. W. Griffith based *The Lonely Villa* on this scenario, however, he turned the story into something else. Instead of concentrating on the would-be burglars, he alternates between the burglars and the house-dwellers. Each room becomes a fortress that mother and daughters defend against the attackers. Instead of treating the burglars' assault in a progressive or developmental manner, Griffith emphasizes the repetitive nature of the successive stages of their attack. This he does by organizing each shot in a rigorously parallel manner. Each frame is filled in such a way as to identify the left and right edges with one group or the other, thus charging each edge with an affective value. In the first shot, the burglars hide under a bush on the lower left; a road cutting diagonally across the screen separates them from the front door of the house, their first objective. In subsequent shots, whether interior or exterior, whether of the burglars, the women, or the absent husband, the configuration is always the same: the left edge of the frame represents danger, the right edge safety. Inside the house this effect is achieved only by careful camera positioning. In each room, both edges of the frame coincide precisely with doors: the one on the left barricaded against the thieves' entrance, the one on the right soon used as an exit to the next room.

Each shot thus represents a new contested space, with that contestation figured by the left-right tension between the burglars and the embattled women. Whereas my version of the story stressed time, causality, and metonymic modulation, Griffith's version depends on spatial organization, replacement, and metaphoric modulation. This transformation comes about (as suggested in Altman 1981b) because Griffith has reorganized a series of rooms—present in my version as a syntagmatic chain—into a paradigmatic situation four times repeated. As we move from the besieged women to the attacking men and back, we continue to look at a frame that maintains the same structure. In my story, the house was the object of the burglars' desire, not a contested space. The alternating following-pattern, coupled with the rigorous adherence of each shot to a single paradigm, turns the film into a series of identical units, related by replacement, each generated by the basic dual-focus model. Because emphasis is laid not on the syntagmatic relationship between any two units but on the opposition between attackers and attacked within the unit, time is not sensed as a salient element of the story. I have previously used the image of the Archangel Michael's weighing of the souls to represent dual-focus narrative. It comes as no surprise that this action should be called *psychostasis* in Greek. *Stasis*, or weighing, is precisely what takes place in the static dual-focus world—and weighing involves spatial opposition, not temporal progression.

The timeless quality of spatial contestation is nowhere more beautifully exemplified than in Hawthorne's *House of the Seven Gables*. Maule has a plot of land that Pyncheon jealously covets; only this particular plot will do. So Pyncheon, after the custom of the times, simply has Maule hanged for witchcraft and usurps his property. But like the names of the novel's actors, "the wrong-doing of one generation lives into the successive ones" (1851:vi). The impossibility of escaping a legacy of evil is figured throughout the text by a compression of time and by transmission of the original opponents' characteristics to succeeding generations. The Maules, who built old Pyncheon's house, are consistently characterized by their sturdy toil, while the Pyncheon talents lie more in the domain of papers and words, deeds and laws. Even the day is divided between these two families: the Pyncheons' days belong to them, but their nights and their dreams belong to the Maules. Later generations of Pyncheons even look like their ancestors. The family's history "seemed little else but a series of calamity, reproducing itself in successive generations, with one general hue, and varying in little, save the outline" (273).

Page after page is devoted to assuring the reader that no time has passed since the initial scenes, that today is like yesterday and tomorrow no different. The circular movement of local history is thus represented by an organ-grinder's dancing figures, their arms and legs flying all about, but always returning to their original place. In the end this is indeed what happens, for the daguerrotypist turns out to be a Maule and in love with a Pyncheon. Together they reverse their ancestors' quarrel. Their love makes the land whole again, unifies the day once more with the night, the working class with the aristocracy: "They were conscious of nothing sad nor old. They transfigured the earth, and made it Eden again, and themselves the two first dwellers in it. The dead man, so close beside them, was forgotten. At such a crisis, there is no death; for immortality is revealed anew, and embraces everything in its hallowed atmosphere" (1851:347). In *The House of Seven Gables* the fundamental dual-focus tendency to subordinate time to space becomes a guiding theme.

Dual-focus narrative's constitutive contest over space regularly appears in the Western dual-focus pastoral tradition as an identification of woman with land—the contested space itself. The sexual equality that *Daphnis and Chloe* is so careful to stress cannot be carried into the realm of land. When winter comes and the two lovers are separated, it is Daphnis who wanders far from home while Chloe stays put, just as Pan is represented in the book's included stories as a philanderer, while his partners are identified with the land (Syrinx as a swamp, Echo as the hills). This asymmetry permeates *The Aeneid*, where Aeneas is the landless wanderer and Dido and Lavinia the symbols of Carthage and Italy. To marry, for Aeneas, is to acquire land, a home, a country. In Hesiod's *Theogony* the father of the gods is called Uranus—Father Sky. This anthropomorphic vision of the universe, inspired by the position of the sky lying atop the earth, is completed by identification of the mother of the gods as Gaea—Mother Earth. This configuration is carried over into learned mythology through the garden topos, whereby woman is a limited and circumscribed space of highly desirable, extremely beautiful real estate. The same conception enters popular mythology in a variety of ways. Vocabulary used to describe land is regularly derived from woman's body and vice versa. The Grand Tetons and the *mons veneris* are perhaps the two best-known examples, but any erotic novel will supply more. Instead of choosing women at random, dirty jokes consistently return to the farmer's daughter—and land is not the only thing that gets plowed in farmer's daughter jokes. Fertility, seeding, sowing wild oats—the double application of these terms clearly identifies them as direct descendants of the Gaea-Uranus myth.

Though primarily associated with epic combats, the Old Testament recounts many pastoral tales as well, systematically built around identification of woman with the land. The book of Ruth begins as the story of a famine, yet it ends not with the expected reaping of plenty but with the birth of Jesse and the listing of his descendants. A saga about the bounty of the land is thus characteristically transferred to female fertility. The famine plot, stressing land, the harvest, and gleaning, runs parallel to the tale of Ruth and Boaz, each in need of a mate. The stories are tied together by equating Ruth with the unproductive earth. She is the empty vase, lack, famine, whereas

Boaz represents the seed, the provider, food, plenty. Ruth's connection with the land is explicitly recognized when Boaz offers Ruth in marriage to her next of kin, as the Law requires in the case of widowed women. "The day you buy the field from the hand of Naomi," he says, "you are also buying Ruth the Moabitess" (4:5). Woman is land; to acquire one is to acquire the other as well. Without a man, Ruth's land is infertile, but without a woman, Boaz cannot engender a son to further the line of Abraham. Only through the symbiotic relationship between man and woman can the parallel problems of famine and family be solved.

The Old Testament book known as Song of Songs or the Song of Solomon presents a similar sexual symbiosis, but with a radically different significance. This mysterious text, a favorite of medieval commentaries, is one of the prime sources for the Christian doctrine of mystic marriage. The woman in this tale of love is described by an elaborate and extended metaphor as Israel herself. She is a rose of Sharon, a lily of the valleys, beautiful as Tirzah and comely as Jerusalem; her hair is like Gilead, her neck like the tower of David, her eyes pools in Heshbon, her nose like a tower of Lebanon; her head crowns her as Mount Carmel dominates Israel. She is the blessed, the beloved, the Promised Land itself. He, however, is like an altar:

> His head is the finest gold; his locks are wavy, black as a raven. His eyes are like doves beside springs of water, bathed in milk, fitly set. His cheeks are like beds of spices, yielding fragrance. His lips are lilies, distilling liquid myrrh. His arms are rounded gold, set with jewels. His body is ivory work, encrusted with sapphires. His legs are alabaster columns, set upon bases of gold. His appearance is like Lebanon, choice as the cedars. (5:11–15)

Only one passage in the entire Old Testament matches the ornateness of this one: the section of I Kings 6–7 where Solomon builds the temple of the Lord. In Song of Songs the lover becomes a symbol of God himself, but not as some numinous, omnipresent being. The lover is the Ark of the Covenant, reposing in the Holy of Holies on the Temple Mount in Jerusalem, repeatedly identified throughout the Old Testament as the navel of the earth (e.g., Ezekiel 5:5 and 38:12). The term "navel" is of course a euphemism. In the mythology of the eastern Mediterranean it signifies the woman's sexual organ, the place where male and female sexual principles meet, which is precisely what they do in Song of Songs. The coupling of man and woman takes place in the spring, for each year God gives himself to his people, thus rendering all things fertile. Now that God has won the land for his people (in the preceding dual-focus epic books of the Old Testament), He makes love to the land so that new life might burst forth.

Built around contested space, both epic and pastoral varieties of dual-focus narrative thus display a fascinating complementarity. As Valentine de Saint-Point puts it, rather crudely, in the "Futurist Manifesto of Lust 1913,"

> After a battle in which men have died, IT IS NORMAL FOR THE VICTORS, PROVEN IN WAR, TO TURN TO RAPE IN THE CONQUERED LAND, SO THAT LIFE MAY BE RE-CREATED. (1973:71; emphasis in the original)

If dual-focus epic reduces two competitors for the same land to one, dual-focus pastoral offers the opportunity for repopulation through the fertile marriage of sky and land. Together, epic and pastoral perpetuate a closed dual-focus system featuring stable population and unchanging existence. Though some texts concentrate their attention on only one of these modes, many others combine the two, offering in a single package a coherent recipe for long-term stability.

In its dualism, its spatial orientation, its neglect of time, and its concern for long-term stability, dual-focus narrative consistently operates according to the model developed by Mircea Eliade to describe "traditional" societies. In *Cosmos and History: The Myth of the Eternal Return*, Eliade shows why many societies have no pronounced view of history, why they don't experience time as a continuum. In these societies the world is divided into two fundamentally different spaces. The village and all land that has been cleared for habitation or cultivation are "cosmos"; all cosmic actions have an archetype, symbolically repeating the acts of the gods ab initio. All other land—sea, forest, alien village—is "chaos," so termed because it has no celestial archetype, no function within the divine scheme. Within this concentric universe, all power and value derives from the hallowed center, the *axis mundi* or world navel, where heaven, hell, and earth meet. Reality and value depend on the opposition of cosmos to chaos and on repetition of certain paradigmatic gestures, thus producing "an implicit abolition of profane time, of duration, of 'history'" (1959:35). Just as Griffith deemphasizes the syntagmatic chain of events in *The Lonely Villa* by presenting a cyclical repetition of the archetype established in the opening shot, so Eliade's traditional societies draw attention away from the passage of time by stressing the relationship of each moment to a preestablished model. Through its alternating following-pattern, its replacement operations, and its paradigmatic "slotting," dual-focus narrative reproduces this configuration.

Though dual-focus narrative is hardly limited to traditional societies, it is not surprising to discover that many dual-focus texts have a distinctly popular origin or appeal, including oral epic, serial novels, westerns and musicals, dime novels and comic books. Many of the exceptions to this rule involve conscious attempts at re-creation of a previously popular form (*The Aeneid*, John Milton's *Paradise Lost*, Renaissance pastorals like Honoré d'Urfé's *L'Astrée*). The mind-set associated with primitive, peasant, or popular culture reproduces many of the most insistent dual-focus patterns and themes. This connection clearly derives from common assumptions about the organization of the world. Whatever is cosmos cannot be chaos. Whatever is Christian cannot be pagan. Whatever is female cannot be male. Social organization and narrative stucture alike depend on this "zero-sum" approach. When Zeus holds the fate of Greeks and Trojans in the balance, the rules of the game—and of fixed-arm scales—dictate that the fate of one group must reverse that of the other. For there to be a winner (plus value), there must also be a loser (minus value). The sum is always zero.

Past studies of narrative have usually assumed that all narrative texts can be assimilated to a single model. Vladimir Propp's *Morphology of the Folktale* provides a useful example. One of the formative texts of literary semiotics, Propp's study takes for granted that all Russian folktales are sufficiently similar to deserve to be studied together. Propp's followers regularly expanded this claim to the entirety of narrative, applying his results to texts as diverse as French novels and Hollywood westerns. I take an entirely different position here. Instead of assuming that all narratives have the same characteristics, I insist that variation according to different following-patterns and divergent underlying structures produces substantial differences among narrative texts. Instead of treating all narratives as fundamentally identical, we must recognize that different narrative types operate according to different rules.

Because Propp conceives narrative as a linear configuration, he describes only the syntagmatic aspects of his texts. For him, every Russian folktale takes the form of "The hero did this" and then "The hero did that." At pains to deal with the stretches of text that deal with an antagonist rather than the hero, he regularly folds this material into the hero's story—as others have done with *The Iliad*, *The Aeneid*, or *The Song of Roland*. Yet the texts analyzed by Propp have a paradigmatic component that escapes Propp's syntagmatic analysis. (Claude Lévi-Strauss 1976 and Mieke Bal 1985:30–33 are among the few theorists to have recognized this problem.) Or to put it in the terms of this chapter, Propp's texts regularly display the alternating following-pattern characteristic of dual-focus narrative. Instead of "The hero did this" and then "The hero did that," we consistently find "The hero did this" and then "The antagonist did that." In short, the majority of Propp's folktales are dual-focus texts. They must be seen not as representative of all narrative but as participating in the specific tradition of dual-focus narrative.

FOUR

Hester's Speculation

The dual-focus system is organized as if by divine fiat. Characters are subordinated to prearranged categories. Textual progression depends on an omniscient and omnipotent narrator. Decided from the outset, the locus of value remains invariable. Dual-focus texts thus adopt the ultrarealist position in the problem of universals. General categories are seen as real, concrete entities, whereas the particular objects, individuals, or statements that embody them are considered mere "accidents." Single-focus narrative, to which we now turn, offers a radically different approach, tending toward the nominalist solution to the problem of universals. According to this system, categories are nothing but abstractions derived from individual cases, names given to express the similarity of certain, quite concrete, particulars. Single-focus narrative typically transfers freedom and authority from the narrator and the divine to an individual liberated from the tyranny of prearranged categories and thus capable of personally creating value. Where characters once left questions of good and evil to their superiors, now individual decisions, desires, and defeats are the ones that count.

The movement from dual-focus to single-focus narrative is thus that of Prometheus, of Lucifer, of Adam, for it is the very fire of the gods that single-focus protagonists must steal in order to escape from the dual-focus universe, where they were imprisoned within the narrow walls of group orientation, preexistent universals, and narratorial whim. It is precisely this progression that Nathaniel Hawthorne portrays in his 1850 novel, *The Scarlet Letter*. From the start, it is clear that the prison, "a wooden edifice, the door of which was heavily timbered with oak, and studded with iron spikes," with "its beetle-browed and gloomy front" (1962:38), serves as a figure for Puritan narrowness of thought, morality, and conduct. The "iron-clamped oaken door" (39) is associated not only with the "force and solidity" (40) of the Puritan character, but also with "the grim rigidity that petrified the bearded physiognomies of these good people" (39):

> It was an age when what we call talent had far less consideration than now, but the massive materials which produce stability and dignity of character a great deal more. The people possessed, by hereditary right, the quality of reverence; which, in their descendants, if it survive at all, exists in smaller proportion, and with a vastly diminished force in the selection and estimate of public men. (168)

Hawthorne's novel begins as it does, with Hester Prynne's exit from prison, so that she may symbolize the modern world's liberation from the moral, philosophical, and legal chains of an earlier world and "a people amongst whom religion and law were almost identical" (40).

The Centrality of the Margins

Perhaps the most striking aspect of Hawthorne's tale of Puritan Boston is his refusal to bend his narrative technique to Puritan law. The Puritan fathers, like the ultrarealists of medieval theology, saw their laws as concrete, preexisting humanity, and oblivious to accidental variation among individuals. Those who failed to obey the law were treated as freaks of nature—morally reprehensible beings who must be so identified by imprisonment, public exposure, exile, or death. With value in the center, the eccentric individual could lay no claim to public sympathy and but little to the very status of personhood. Yet Hawthorne builds his entire novel around a single unconventional individual, whom he follows nearly exclusively from beginning to end. Though Hawthorne's narrator enjoys a level of knowledge shared by none of his characters, in one domain the narrator is clearly subordinated to Hester Prynne. Waiting expectantly at the prison door for "our narrative, which is now about to issue from that inauspicious portal" (39), Hawthorne reveals from the start that he is unable to tell his story until an outcast, an adulteress, a common criminal should free herself from the confinement imposed by oak and iron.

Far from considering Hester simply an accidental, and thus unimportant variation from the Puritan universal, Hawthorne builds his entire narrative around an individual case. For Hester *is* his narrative; without her, the novel cannot exist. Without Achilles, the fight and *The Iliad* proceed apace. Without Roland, the combat still continues. When Vashti fades from Ahasuerus's court, Esther is there to take up the slack. But should Hester remain in prison, should she be sentenced to death rather than to wear the symbol of her sin, then Hawthorne's novel would be stillborn. If the following-pattern of *The Scarlet Letter* concentrates almost exclusively on Hester Prynne, it is because her eccentricity makes her an appropriate subject for a novel. In a dual-focus text she would be reduced to conformity or expelled. Here, however, Hester's very individuality identifies her as a worthy subject.

The visual configuration of the opening scene highlights and explains the narrator's interest in Hester Prynne. When she steps into the open air, "as if by her own free-will" (42), Hester becomes like a magnet, drawing all attention to herself, reorienting a haphazard arrangement of similar people into a centered composition reminiscent of a Renaissance nativity:

> But the point which drew all eyes, and, as it were, transfigured the wearer,—so that both men and women, who had been familiarly acquainted with Hester Prynne, were now impressed as if they beheld her for the first time,—was that SCARLET LETTER, so fantastically embroidered and illuminated upon her bosom. It had the effect of a spell, taking her out of the ordinary relations with humanity, and inclosing her in a sphere by herself. (43)

Why do those who knew her see her as if for the first time? Something has occurred that goes deeper than a simple change of costume, yet that change clearly figures the quasi-philosophical gap separating Hester from the crowd. The townspeople dress as realists, conforming to a universal costume that disguises, subsumes, indeed denies all individuality. Hester's attire, however, "which, indeed, she had wrought for the occasion, in prison, and had modelled much after her own fancy, seemed to express the attitude of her spirit, the desperate recklessness of her mood, by its wild and picturesque peculiarity" (43). The Puritan process is here reversed. Instead of conforming to the prearranged model implicit in Puritan dress, Hester has externalized her innermost feelings in the fantasy of her dress. It is this tendency to begin with the particular rather than the general—to favor accidents over categories—that distinguishes both *The Scarlet Letter* and the class of texts to which it belongs.

The internalization motif associated with Hester's punishment underlines this new epistemology. To highlight the importance of personal experience, Hawthorne twice measures the distance between the prison and the pillory. Measured by the ruler, that preexisting unindividualized universal, "It was no great distance from the prison-door to the market-place." But a shared yardstick is not the only gauge applied. "Measured by the prisoner's experience, however, it might be reckoned a journey of some length" (43). It is a small point, but one that is not lost in Hawthorne's persistent concern to subordinate the world to Hester's experience rather than vice versa. Just as length can no longer be considered in absolute terms, neither can standards of punishment. When the older gossips call for still harsher penalties to be heaped on Hester, the youngest of the group cries out in recognition of the psychological impact of Hester's sentence. Punishment, she implies, is not an external quantity, measurable by any universally applicable standard. Conversely, no external judgment may any longer be taken as a necessary indication of sin. Once Hester spies her former husband in the crowd, her place on the pillory actually becomes a comfort to her. Public exposure, the very term of her sentence, is thus transmuted into shelter. In the new ethic represented by Hester's conduct, the only effective punishment takes place in the privacy of face-to-face human relations. Meanwhile, the corollary to this principle is demonstrated by Arthur Dimmesdale, Hester's partner in crime. His experience demonstrates that joy exists only in the privacy of the individual conscience and cannot be guaranteed by the admiration of the gathered throng.

The Scarlet Letter's opening scene progressively reveals an implicit limitation that has been self-imposed by the narrator. Just as the story cannot begin until Hester emerges from her prison, so the flow of words and scenes is subordinated to the central character: the spatial metaphor is indeed applicable, with those on the perimeter of the circle relating to each other only through the adulteress placed at the center. From a conversation about Hester we follow the gaze of the gossips to the prison door, from which Hester at last emerges. Once Hester has been described, we move back up that line of vision to observe the gossips' reaction. Returning to Hester, we follow her to the scaffold, only to be subjected once more to her logic: "Her mind, and especially her memory, was preternaturally active, and kept bringing up other scenes than this roughly hewn street of a little town, on the edge of the Western wilderness" (45). Where Hester's mind wanders, there we must follow, for the narrator has voluntarily become subservient to the character, masking his gaze behind hers rather than maintaining the typical dual-focus stance of domination and superiority.

Only when Hester returns from her mind's vision to that of her eyes do we see the activities taking place around her, and then only selectively, for in a sense Hester's vision not only surveys the scene, it creates the scene, according to the workings of her own mind. Her eyes, it seems, are the pen with which the text is written. Wherever she looks, the object of her vision is described by the narrator, as if he were her amanuensis rather than she his creation. When she looks at the crowd from her privileged position above, Hester selects one person to concentrate on, someone who by generally accepted social standards has a right to be considered part of Hester's story. In the social world, Hester's husband is vested with rights over his wife; in Hawthorne's narrative, however, Roger Chillingworth gains existence only when Hester's gaze calls him into being. The novel's technique thus directly contradicts the Puritan moral and legal code, according to which a woman, once married, must remain subservient to her husband no matter what the state of her inner desires. The narrative technique chosen by Hawthorne replicates Hester's physical and mental adultery, for it accords her the right to choose her own partners.

Breaking out of dual-focus constraints, Hester claims the right to compose her own story, to create her own life, the two now becoming synonymous in a fashion that is totally foreign to dual-focus disdain for the fate of the individual. Even Dimmesdale, Hester's lover, merits a place in the text only when she chooses. In the opening scene, she refuses to name her fellow sinner; the pastor thus passes out of the tale until such time as Hester once again brings him into it, at the governor's mansion. Even then, her insistence that he speak on her behalf is necessary to call his words into being. Only later will Hester's husband or partner be seen separately from her, and then only long enough to elucidate Hester's situation and the difficult decision she must make.

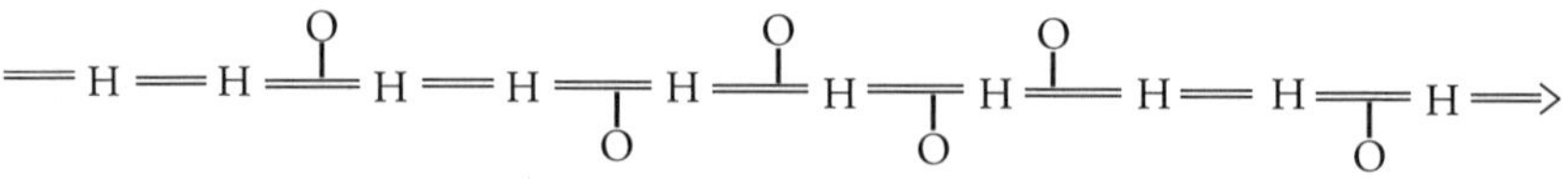

$$=\text{H}=\text{H}\overset{\text{O}}{=}\text{H}=\text{H}\overset{}{\underset{\text{O}}{\mathsf{T}}}\text{H}\overset{\text{O}}{=}\text{H}\overset{}{\underset{\text{O}}{\mathsf{T}}}\text{H}\overset{\text{O}}{=}\text{H}=\text{H}\overset{}{\underset{\text{O}}{\mathsf{T}}}\text{H}\Longrightarrow$$

FIGURE 4.1 *The Scarlet Letter* as experienced through Hester (H, Hester; O, forces of order)

The following-pattern of *The Scarlet Letter* thus differs radically from what we have seen in dual-focus narrative. Its skeleton is a simple straight line describing the progression of a single central character. Like most single-focus texts, Hawthorne's novel introduces secondary characters through the protagonist, clearly identifying them as structurally subservient. Movements away from the center are typically produced by some form of metonymic modulation tying the secondary character directly to the protagonist, thereby maintaining the illusion that the protagonist, and not the narrator, is in control of the story. When we leave Roger Chillingworth, after having heard his conversations and watched him observe Hester on the scaffold, we do not move directly to the assembly of magistrates who will speak the words of reproach and ask the questions that could just as well have been put on Chillingworth's lips, for a metaphoric movement of this type—from the offended one to those who speak for him—would set up a second focus of action, independent of Hester's power. We would thus return to the domain of dual-focus narrative, with its characteristic opposition between the orderly forces of civilized life and those who would challenge order and civilization.

Hawthorne steers us away from this dual-focus reading by making us pass through Hester each time we move from one aspect of her surroundings to another. From Chillingworth we return to Hester along the path of her gaze, sharing her vision and witnessing the effect on her mind, before moving to the magistrates who are now introduced through their spatial relationship to Hester, rather than through a parallel to the wronged husband whom, in a sense, they represent. Because the narrative material is filtered through Hester, the text is experienced as represented in fig. 4.1.

Were it not for the narrator's persistent following of Hester, the preponderance of metonymic modulation, and limitation of interior views to the

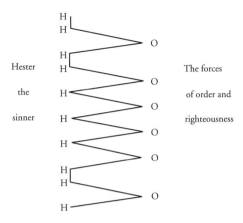

FIGURE 4.2 *The Scarlet Letter* represented as conflict

central character, the same material might well have been perceived by the reader as in fig. 4.2. The topic of *The Scarlet Letter*'s opening scene might reasonably lead us to expect this type of dual-focus presentation. The scene is built around the law and transgression; it apparently opposes the prison to the open space around it; everyone in the scene either defends or decries Hester's situation. Yet Hawthorne effectively keeps us from configuring this scene in a dual-focus manner. Seen from above, the scene would appear to be adversary in nature as well as presentation, but Hawthorne never lets us view the scene from above. Instead, we are drawn into the scene through Hester's own experience: we see what she sees. Instead of presenting the clash between the law and an outlaw, the scene is built as a chain of experiences either perceived or induced by the woman who climbs the scaffold. Hawthorne's technique robs everything in the created world of its independence, attaching all events and characters instead to Hester's destiny. In a very real sense, *The Scarlet Letter* has transferred the narrator from a dual-focus position in the divine regions above to a new existence in the human world, for Hester herself has stolen the narrator's fire. Claiming the right to create a law of her own, a religion suitable for the workings of her own conscience, Hester simultaneously usurps control of the narrative.

Speculation

The interaction between narrator and protagonist in *The Scarlet Letter* is no mere technical problem. As in dual-focus narrative, the relationship between the novel's narrator and its characters sums up an entire world-view. Operating like the law and those who enforce it in Hester's Puritan world, dual-focus narrators know where value is located and thus organize the narrative to highlight the source of value and the consequent duties of the individual. Hawthorne's narrator pretends neither to such knowledge nor to such control. Releasing characters into a novelistic space that remains to be created, the narrator places a pen at the service of Hester Prynne's eyes and concerns. Instead of preceding her actions and her thoughts, value must be created by them. *Speculation* is thus the novel's—and Hester's—mode of being: speculation in all its connotations, from the etymological visual sense to the familiar moral, philosophical, and economic meanings. Those around Hester have divided the world in two—the sinless and the sinners—and identified normal life with sinless-ness, life within the law. Hawthorne reverses that perspective, defining the human condition as that of the sinner. What makes Hester an appropriate subject for a single-focus novel is precisely her unwillingness to live within the law, coupled with her ability to build a new life around her lawlessness:

> Her sin, her ignominy, were the roots which she had struck into the soil. It was as if a new birth, with stronger assimilations than the first, had converted the forest-land, still so uncongenial to every other pilgrim and wanderer, into Hester Prynne's wild and dreary, but life-long home. (60)

Hester's life in the new world, like Adam's, begins with sin, and with the knowledge that it brings of every creature's fallen condition, for Hester now has "a sympathetic knowledge of the hidden sin in other hearts" (65). She knows that every citizen of Boston shares her sinful condition, yet she alone is empowered to explore the implications of sin. Those around her live in a sham world, protected by the fact that the law holds them sinless. Hester alone accepts her condition and with it the possibility of re-creating the world through the freedom of speculation.

The effect of Hester's speculation is nowhere more clearly revealed than in the recurrent motif of the maze. In the well-defined topology of dual-focus narrative, labyrinthine structures represent chaos, the diametrical opposite of orderly, civilized space. The implications of this arrangement need hardly be spelled out: the maze must be avoided in favor of the familiar order of civilized life, just as the Puritans evade the labyrinthine ways of moral speculation by respecting their clearly delineated laws. For Hester, no such solution is possible. From the very beginning, her mind harbors two value systems: the one imposed on her from without, the other provided by her human experience. The very fact that, unlike her fellow citizens, she cannot consider the two as coinciding leaves her "in a dismal labyrinth of doubt" (73). Hester's labyrinth is not external trial but an entanglement of her own making. At any time she is free to return to life within the law, yet she repeatedly rejects this simple exit from her mental maze.

Far from fleeing the maze, Hester continues to choose it. Instead of seeking refuge in the stable values of Puritan life, she accepts the labyrinth as the fundamental condition of human life:

> Thus, Hester Prynne, whose heart had lost its regular and healthy throb, wandered without a clew in the dark labyrinth of mind; now turned aside by an insurmountable precipice; now starting back from a deep chasm. There was wild and ghastly scenery all around her, and a home and comfort nowhere. At times a fearful doubt strove to possess her soul. (120)

Like a person wandering about in a real maze, Hester is constantly confronted with two paths, of which she can choose but one. Her conduct can therefore not be produced by simple replication, as dual-focus behavior can be generated. Repeatedly facing a fork in the road, she must instead *choose* a line of behavior, deriving her action not from a universal but from the very accidents of her particular life. The knowledge that the two paths are not equally good produces doubt; the inability to know for sure which is better produces anxiety. As long as people are "wandering together in this gloomy maze of evil, and stumbling, at every step, over the guilt wherewith we have strewn our path" (126), the cost of sin must be paid in the coin of doubt and anxiety, guilty reminders of the fallen human condition, a heavy price to pay for the privilege of establishing one's own individuality.

There is, of course, another solution to the problem, which Hawthorne investigated in his next novel, *The House of the Seven Gables*, but this path Hester steadfastly refuses—that is, to renounce individuality and the claim to private experience in favor of a happy return to the communitarian and predetermined behavior of an earlier Eden, thereby refusing the implications of original sin and individual knowledge. Far from turning back toward an existence that she could not consider as Edenic in spite of the law's unambiguous assurance, Hester learns from her ordeal to find a home in the very exile that constitutes her punishment:

> She had wandered, without rule or guidance, in a moral wilderness; as vast, as intricate and shadowy, as the untamed forest, amid the gloom of which they were now holding a colloquy that was to decide their fate. Her intellect and heart had their home, as it were, in desert places, where she roamed as freely as the wild Indian in his woods. (143)

The decisive meeting between Hester and the minister takes place on the very border of the wilderness because this is where Hester has learned to live. With one foot in civilization and the other in new, uncharted lands, she has constantly felt torn between these two aspects of her personality. Now the time has come for decisions to be made, for Hester to admit that she prefers the wilderness, if only Dimmesdale will escape with her. When he agrees to her proposal, he is immediately identified with the freedom that the wilderness affords: "It was the exhilarating effect—upon a prisoner just escaped from the dungeon of his own heart—of breathing the wild, free atmosphere of an unredeemed, unchristianized, lawless region" (144). Recalling the physical liberation of the opening scene, the forest meeting reveals the human psyche freed from its lifelong submission to a religion of mechanical replication, an ethic devoid of concern for context, and a psychology requiring the sacrifice of individual desire.

The tragedy lies in Dimmesdale's inability to adapt to this new life. Whereas Hester has had long years to develop her capacity for confronting the unknown, the minister has sacrificed to his social and religious standing any possibility of learning the lessons of liberation. Even the tragedy of the ending, however, only underlines the importance of Hester's experience all the more. In a world where our sinful condition is taken seriously, where human experience is recognized as the maze that Hester knows it to be, only lonely grappling with doubt and anxiety can eventually teach us how to become comfortable in a new home amidst the labyrinthine ways of the moral wilderness. As R. W. B. Lewis has remarked, "the valid rite of initiation for the individual in the new world is not an initiation *into* society, but, given the character of society, an initiation *away from it*" (1978:346).

What Hawthorne so poignantly suggests through the maze motif, he portrays even more clearly through the speculative nature of Hester's thoughts and decisions, from her original crime of passion to its fully considered reaffirmation in the latter half of the novel. Only when Hester has been firmly established at the center of the narrative does the narrator move away from her long enough to depict the relationship between her husband and her lover. This sequence culminates in Dimmesdale's nocturnal vigil on the scaffold, where Hester finally discovers the minister's reduced condition and thus the effect of her decision to respect her husband's request to hide his real identity. This sequence constitutes the cause for which the following chapter, "Another View of Hester," presents the effect. This second half of the typical single-focus before-and-after diptych reveals the first signs of change induced by Hester's forced isolation. Her decision to support the minister in his weakness is presented not just as a change of mind but as a radically new type of decision:

> She decided, moreover, that he had a right to her utmost aid. Little accustomed, in her long seclusion from society, to measure her ideas of right and wrong by any standard external to herself, Hester saw—or seemed to see—that there lay a responsibility upon her, in reference to the clergyman, which she owed to no other, nor to the whole world besides. The links that united her to the rest of human kind—links of flower, or silk, or gold, or whatever the material—had all been broken. Here was the iron link of mutual crime, which neither he nor she could break. (1962:115–16)

Here indeed is a new standard of decision-making, and a radically new use for the iron that previously served only to imprison. Having "cast away the fragments of a broken chain" (119), Hester is now free to participate fully in the "electric chain" (111) that she, Dimmesdale, and little Pearl—"the connecting link between those two" (112)—formed as they stood together on the scaffold.

Human beings cannot cast off their bonds entirely. At best they can substitute one chain for another. But they can, if they will, choose their chains, and there lies the telling difference. "Like all other ties," Hawthorne admits, the new link of mutual crime "brought along with it its obligations" (116); but because the new chain is freely chosen, those obligations are all the more welcome.

Before her vigil with the minister, Hester had committed a crime, as evil a crime as the Puritan code recognizes. Yet in spite of her sin, she nonetheless respects her vows of marital obedience when ordered by her husband to keep the secret of his identity. By the time she finally witnesses the results of this obedience, however, "her life had turned, in a great measure, from passion and feeling, to thought" (119). The significance of her new "sin," her decision to stand beside her partner in crime rather than her legal husband, thus takes on immeasurably more significance than the original sin. For Dimmesdale, for the continued strength of the chain that binds them, Hester knowingly takes upon her conscience a rejection of all the legal ties that once bound her to Roger Chillngworth: "She marvelled how she could ever have been wrought upon to marry him! She deemed it her crime most to be repented of, that she had ever endured, and reciprocated, the lukewarm grasp of his hand, and had suffered the smile of her lips to mingle and melt into his own" (127). We are most assuredly in the realm of a new law when Hester the adulteress can declare legal marriage to be the greatest crime.

The Triumph of Individual Conscience

It is certainly no accident that Hester should be associated by Hawthorne with the antinomianist Ann Hutchinson or the reformer Martin Luther, for her tendency to predicate value on the decisions of the individual conscience rather than on the community's religious or legal system clearly reflects Reformation reaction against medieval doctrine and the Roman church:

The world's law was no law for her mind. It was an age in which the human intellect, newly emancipated, had taken a more active and a wider range than for many centuries before. Men of the sword had overthrown nobles and kings. Men bolder than these had overthrown and rearranged—not actually, but within the sphere of theory, which was their most real abode—the whole system of ancient prejudice, wherewith was linked much of ancient principle. Hester Prynne imbibed this spirit. She assumed a freedom of speculation, then common enough on the other side of the Atlantic, but which our forefathers, had they known of it, would have held to be a deadlier crime than that stigmatized by the scarlet letter. (1962:119)

More than just a reminder of the liberating effect of the Protestant Reformation, or a token of the New England Reformation, which had produced Henry David Thoreau's *Civil Disobedience* only a few months before *The Scarlet Letter*, Hester embodies a parable of reformation, a fable of the changes that take place within human minds, with the capacity to reform the status of every object and action.

Many years earlier (in 1837), in "Endicott and the Red Cross," Hawthorne had already formulated a primitive version of this tale. Usually cited in connection with *The Scarlet Letter* because it contains the physical prototype of Hester Prynne, a woman bearing a scarlet letter "thought to mean Admirable, or anything rather than Adulteress" (1962:224), "Endicott" bears still more important structural relationships to the later novel. Having received notice from the governor that the king of England is about to endanger Puritan freedom of worship, Endicott, the commander of a company of Puritan soldiers, the very symbol of order, obedience, and authority, reveals his belief in a principle beyond that of duty to one's sovereign. " 'The Governor is a wise man—a wise man, and a meek and moderate,' said Endicott, setting his teeth grimly. 'Nevertheless, I must do according to my own best judgment' " (225). Ordering his soldiers to form around him like the gossips who surround Hester at the outset of *The Scarlet Letter*, Endicott speaks a language that Hester will not discover until the second half of the novel: "Wherefore, I say again, have we sought this country of a rugged soil and wintry sky? Was it not for the enjoyment of our civil rights? Was it not for liberty to worship God according to our conscience?" (226). "Who shall enslave us here?" he asks. "What have we to do with this mitred prelate,—with this crowned king? What have we to do with England?" (227). Seconds later, Endicott unsheathes his sword and rends the Red Cross completely out of the banner.

In Hawthorne's narratorial comment we clearly witness the allegorizing approach that Hester's speculation suggests:

> With a cry of triumph, the people gave their sanction to one of the boldest exploits which our history records. And forever honored be the name of Endicott! We look back through the mist of ages, and recognize in the rending of the Red Cross from New England's banner the first omen of that deliverance which our fathers consummated after the bones of the stern Puritan had lain more than a century in the dust. (227)

Like Hester Prynne, Endicott is a symbol of the revolution that occurs when people transfer authority from powerful temporal superiors to the small voice of conscience within. "What we did had a consecration of its own" (140), Hester claims to the minister. Conscience, and not the church, is the ultimate measure of consecration. The "electric" chain that holds people together is ultimately stronger than the ironclad oaken door that keeps them apart.

Though Hawthorne does not fully investigate the ramifications of this new system, he does suggest some of its necessary consequences. The much-discussed scarlet letter itself becomes one of his methods for the systematic but oblique revelation of the new role and importance of individual judgment in Hester's world. Variously described by characters within the novel as representing Adulteress, Able, and Angel, the letter "A" has received still wider interpretation from critics. D. H. Lawrence constructed a veritable lexicon around Hester's symbol, from Alpha and Abel to Adam, Adama, Adorable, Adulteress, Admirable, America, Mater Adolerata, and beyond (2003:85–86). What does the scarlet letter mean? Different things to different people. The first gossip to comment on Hester's richly embroidered "A" gives vent to emotions that sound suspiciously like the product of jealousy:

> "She hath good skill at her needle, that's certain," remarked one of the female spectators; "but did ever a woman, before this brazen hussy, contrive such a way of showing it! Why, gossips, what is it but to laugh in the faces of our godly magistrates, and make a pride out of what they, worthy gentlemen, meant for a punishment?" (1962:43)

The next onlooker is less concerned by Hester's needlework skills than she is enraged by Hester's rich gown, when she has naught but rags of rheumatic flannel. Continuing to provide a mirror for the deepest emotions of those around her, Hester's "A" calls up the hidden sin of the youngest woman in the group, revealing her secret knowledge of the inner price exacted by sin. "Do not let her hear you!!" she whispers. "Not a stitch in that embroidered letter, but she has felt it in her heart" (43). When Hester later appears at the governor's door, the bond-servant who greets her reveals in like manner his concern for the shine and delicacy of upper-class finery, "perhaps judging from the decision of her air and the glittering symbol in her bosom, that she was a great lady in the land" (76).

The public's inability to consider the scarlet letter as an objective symbol soon frees Hester's badge from negative connotations altogether. Eminently practical and fundamentally more concerned with day-to-day necessities than with strict application of the Law, the common people of Boston soon reveal their work ethic by refusing "to interpret the scarlet 'A' by its original signification. They said that it meant Able; so strong was Hester Prynne, with a woman's strength" (117). Proof that Hester has effected some transformation in the mental patterns of her fellow Bostonians is clearly revealed in their new and infinitely more nuanced view of her "A" at the end of the novel: "The scarlet letter ceased to be a stigma which attracted the world's scorn and bitterness, and became a type of something to be sorrowed over, and looked upon with awe, yet with reverence too" (185). Even little Pearl infuses the embroidered letter with the only value system that she knows. When her mother discards the letter, Pearl is convinced that she herself has been rejected, that she has lost her mother's love. Only when the letter has been returned to its accustomed place will the child, once again sure of maternal affection, return to her mother's arms. Thus Hawthorne transfers the locus of meaning from objects to minds, from action to vision. Just as Hester creates a new value system through speculative thinking, so is meaning derived from considerations of point of view—"speculation" in its etymological sense.

In dual-focus narrative, where action is not divorced from meaning, the flow of the story depends largely on a relatively straightforward presentation of actions and words. In *The Scarlet Letter*, where meaning depends on purpose, thought, and intention, a narrative technique of a different sort is called for.

Without internal views of the characters, we have no way of evaluating or understanding them. The old system stressed punishment rather than guilt, result rather than intention. It is significant that Hester is punished not for adultery but for the visible result of adultery. Had she not become pregnant, the punishment would never have been exacted. Yet the reader's view is not that of the magistrates. The narrator's attention to the characters' inner lives provides a necessary component of the new internalized system. To Dimmesdale's parishioners, he appears the very type of sainthood, a sinless individual entirely devoted to God. The novel affords the reader a view that the public will never have. Not only are we privy to Dimmesdale's sinful past but also we witness his concern over "the contrast between what I seem and what I am!" (137–38) and thus judge him accordingly. Chillingworth, too, is evaluated according to this same method. The public sees him as a talented doctor who exhibits devotion to his patient beyond the call of medical duty. Yet we can have little sympathy for him. The old system condemned above all else those acts that threaten the community and its values, but we know that Chillingworth has committed the Unpardonable Sin because we have seen him violate the sanctity of the individual conscience.

In the same way, we learn to have a high opinion of Hester's virtue because we can see both that her illegal actions are motivated by concern for Dimmesdale's health and salvation and that her virtuous actions are no longer engendered by the habit of lawfulness but by a deeper, more freely chosen purpose: "With nothing now to lose, in the sight of mankind, and with no hope, and seemingly no wish, of gaining any thing, it could only be a genuine regard for virtue that had brought back the poor wanderer to its paths" (116). Even the very accusation of sinfulness and the right to erase its marks are now removed from the public arena. When Reverend Wilson offers to remove the scarlet letter from Hester's breast in exchange for the name of her fellow sinner, she shows that she has a far deeper understanding of punishment and repentance than he. "Never!" she cries. "It is too deeply branded. Ye cannot take it off. And would that I might endure his agony, as well as mine!" (53). Renewing this motif, Dimmesdale later rejects the Puritan tenet that the society and its representatives are solely responsible to decide who is guilty and who is not. Taking his accusation into his own hands, he too usurps the role formerly exercised only by God's own magistrates on earth.

If conscience would claim the right to judge the individual's own guilt, then it must take on as well the responsibility to reveal that guilt.

The Scarlet Letter's subjective approach to reality, its insistence on the mediatory effect of individual conscience and vision, leads directly to a new relationship between time and values. In dual-focus narrative, the value structure exists outside of time—before time, as it were. From day to day, from year to year, the same actions retain the same value. The victory that takes place at the end of the text, at the end of time, is no more than fulfillment of what has been apparent all along. When the true and princely identity of the lover has finally been discovered, he and his chosen bride are finally freed to exercise fully their functions as male and female; yet they have all along been performing according to the sexual parameters that define them. Nothing new, in terms of value structure, takes place at the end, save that the level of dream is transferred to that of reality. In dual-focus epic, where all the characters similarly incarnate specific values from the start, valuation depends not on their actions but vice versa. The value structure thus remains at all moments the same; its consistent, convenient codification by laws testifies to this fact. From the point of view of values, time doesn't exist in dual-focus texts. The system remains static. Just as we can choose any action in Puritan society and evaluate it adequately by reference to fixed laws, so we can perform a sampling operation anywhere in the dual-focus text and measure the value of the actions there performed by reference to the code of values glorified by the text.

In *The Scarlet Letter* no such operation is possible. People change, and since single-focus value depends on individual intention, value structures change as well. For individuals who live within the law, every action is sure, its value uncompromised by considerations of past or future. For Hester Prynne, however, every act becomes an economic speculation, an investment of present capital in a personal view of the future. When Hester agrees to keep the secret of Chillingworth's true identity, she does so in part out of marital duty but also out of utilitarian motives, based on an assumption that the future will be brighter if she conceals the truth. Soon, however, Hester discovers that her dutiful silence has been poorly invested, for it contributes to Dimmesdale's demise. Deciding that she must reverse her original decision, she tells the minister that her revelation is provoked by concern for truth (139), but our internal views of Hester have already revealed that she is no longer tied to the old morality and its universal laws of marital fidelity and honesty. This is no simplistic Cornelian opposition of mutually exclusive universals but the occasion for a radical reworking of the concept of honesty. Hester's decision is based not on invariable law but on the projected effect of individual action. She believes that Dimmesdale's pain will be relieved by her revelation and that his peace is more important than any other consideration: "Hester saw—or seemed to see—that there lay a responsibility upon her, in reference to the clergyman, which she owed to no other, nor to the whole world besides" (116).

Or seemed to see—there's the rub. No final evaluation is ever possible in this new world of doubt and anxiety. Hester must always predict the potential future value of every action in this value-market. She must always wager the present on the future. Her experience has taught her that wrong choice is possible, that value is not stable but can be lost—a danger not faced in the Puritan legal system. Yet value can be won as well. If her decision to permit Chillingworth to separate her from Dimmesdale leads to radical desexualization, and loss of the sun's life-giving power, her change of heart, reestablishing her links with the minister, contributes to a transfiguration of her whole being. Her cap is removed, releasing the femininity of her long hair. The crimson flush returns to her cheek:

> Her sex, her youth, and the whole richness of her beauty, came back from what men call the irrevocable past, and clustered themselves, with her maiden hope, and a happiness before unknown, within the magic circle of this hour. And, as if the gloom of the earth and sky had been but the effluence of these two mortal hearts, it vanished with their sorrow. All at once, as with a sudden smile of heaven, forth burst the sunshine, pouring a very flood into the obscure forest, gladdening each green leaf, transmuting the yellow fallen ones to gold, and gleaming adown the gray trunks of the solemn trees. (145)

Human rhythms are no longer subservient to those of nature; nature instead reflects the decisions of each individual. The world becomes a speculum, a mirror in which men and women see the values of their own consciences reflected. Hester's new decision has not simply restored her to the previous level, it has brought to her a "happiness before unknown," a surplus of value produced in the market of conscience by her speculation. Yet even this moment is transitory. The parable of the talents makes it abundantly clear that only a constant reinvestment of one's freedom can produce the desired result. At every moment we must reformulate our being, not in terms of an impersonal, static legal system but in terms of the potential effects of a particular decision on a specific future.

Hester's daughter Pearl objectifies this speculation. "Of great price,—purchased with all she had,—her mother's only treasure" (66), Pearl evokes Christ's teaching on the kingdom of heaven, a value both absent and future, attainable only by abandoning all traditional values. Those who follow the law need not undergo this radical emptying of the self with each transaction. Every decision that Hester makes, on the contrary, is "purchased with all she had." Because her actions reflect not an impersonal system but her very soul, each action engages the self, risks the self in a wholly new fashion. Sin—as well as righteousness—must now be reinterpreted from the standpoint of its effect on the future. The present thus becomes connected to both past and future in a new way, unknown within the dual-focus realm. Because decisions remain forever subject to change, the effect of one moment on another must be subjected to repeated analysis. Yet there are aspects of the past that we cannot change. Pearl exists, along with the "sin" that gave her life. We are thus condemned to evaluate the present as a function of past and future. Decisions of value no longer exist in a timeless present, oblivious to past sins and future potential.

The seeds of *The Scarlet Letter*, it would seem, are those of the typically dual-focus eternal triangle: a young and saintly hero contends with an old, jealous, devilish husband for the heart of a desirable maiden. The Man of God versus the Emissary of Satan. But this is neither the substance nor the form of Hawthorne's novel. *The Scarlet Letter* turns this typical dual-focus pattern inside-out, revealing just enough of the two men for us to understand the hesitations, the decisions, and the development of the woman. Concentrating on her instead of them, the novel internalizes strife and predicates its action on psychic progress rather than territorial struggle. If Hester is unable to remain mistress of her physical fate until the end—the minister's confession and death clearly demonstrating the cost of mistaken decisions—she nevertheless shows, in the conclusion, that her long apprenticeship to solitary life and speculation has provided her with the force and independence necessary to maintain her individualism and develop her progressive ideals. What is at stake in *The Scarlet Letter* is nothing less than the place of the sinner in the literary and social world. Dual-focus narrative simply expels eccentric individuals. Hester's story offers a new view of both world and text, where every individual is acknowledged as a sinner and thus becomes the protagonist of her own text.

FIVE   Single-Focus Narrative

D ual-focus narratives begin by division into two antithetical groups or principles, both striving to govern the same space. The text serves to resolve the conflict and reduce duality to unity, subordinating all aspects of the narrative universe to a single, well-established system protected by rules assuring its continued existence and coherence. On this note of continuing unity, established values, and eternal return, dual-focus texts conclude. It is at precisely this point that single-focus texts begin. The dual-focus world is a cloistered realm: self-contained, timeless, oblivious to all but its own perpetuation. Those who would escape its bounds or regulations are promptly reduced to nothingness by exclusion from the text. Contrary to the characteristic self-sufficiency of dual-focus narrative, single-focus texts typically begin by an escape from the timeless stability of dual-focus values.

Either subservient and properly integrated into society or excluded as out-laws, dual-focus characters derive their identity from without, like children born into their parents' religion. Dual-focus narrators endow characters with an identity, then accord attention to one character or another as they please. Single-focus narrators operate entirely differently. Not only do they accord liberty of conscience to individual characters, but also they consent to follow selected characters from incident to incident rather than measure each action by a preordained law, excluding exceptional individuals from the text. Whereas dual-focus characters are imprisoned from the start in a system that they cannot leave without also abandoning the text and thus their own lives, single-focus protagonists are represented as having *chosen* the single-focus mode over the dual-focus system into which they were born. It is this choice, inspired by the birth of personal desire, that captures the narrator's attention and subordinates the following-pattern to a single protagonist.

The Birth of Desire

We can best understand the specificity and importance of single-focus desire by contrasting the very different status of desire in the typical dual-focus pastoral plot, the "mythos of spring," as Northrop Frye would have it. Whether in an Alexandrian romance like *Daphnis and Chloe*, Renaissance pastoral, Molièresque comedy, or American musical, at the heart of the plot lies a pair of young lovers thwarted by mistaken identity, persistent rivals, or the ever-present *senex* (old man). In each case, the plot turns on a series of binary oppositions (male/female, young/old, inside/outside) defining categories and determining character behavior. Desire in this situation is either "natural"—called forth, reinforced, and justified by one's category—or entirely unnatural. Daphnis desires Chloe and vice versa, but only as a function of their sexual categories. Conversely, the *senex* violates his categorical imperative by becoming his son's rival; he must eventually learn to act his age or risk exclusion from the new society formed around the young lovers.

If we sense a connection between the archetypal comic plot and the rite of spring, it is precisely because the characters' roles are ritually determined. The lovers' desire is a function not of their individuality but of the awakening earth pushing through them. As trees bring forth blossoms, as animals go into heat, so comic lovers play out their designated roles, gathering around them all who represent the New Year, while excluding supporters of the Old. Procreation is the normal result of these biologically grounded desires.

In single-focus narrative, however, desire for the opposite sex represents veiled narcissism, a thinly masked desire for selfhood and transcendence. Tristan doesn't want Iseult; he wants obstacles, peril, and ultimately death (*Tristan and Iseult*). If Faust reels from desire to enjoyment with Gretchen, and yet in enjoyment longs for desire, it is because his true desire is to be like the gods (Goethe, *Faust*). Emma Bovary wants neither Rodolphe nor Léon but the ability to realize dreams (Flaubert, *Madame Bovary*). Julien Sorel yearns not for Mathilde but for control (Stendhal, *The Red and the Black*). Gatsby desires Daisy less than the power to destroy time and relive the past (Fitzgerald, *The Great Gatsby*). Guido doesn't want La Dolce Vita but something beyond life (Fellini, *La Dolce Vita*). The individual born of desire is always Adam, Lucifer, Prometheus. Caring less for the apple than its forbidden status, single-focus protagonists seek individuality by rejecting the codes established by the combined forces of God, father, and society.

No one has more eloquently described the relationship between noncategorical desire and a thirst for transcendence than Augustine, in the famous episode of the pear tree recounted in *Confessions* II:

> The pears certainly were beautiful, but it was not the pears that my miserable soul desired. I had plenty of better pears of my own; I only took these ones in order that I might be a thief. Once I had taken them I threw them away, and all I tasted in them was my own iniquity, which I enjoyed very much. For if I did put any of these pears into my mouth, what made it sweet to me was my sin. (1963:47)

To eat, to seek nourishment, is a natural human activity, necessitated by our physical makeup. Augustine's theft serves not to underline the biological needs he shares with others but to establish his individuality, to free him from categorical definition. Augustine's desire thereby deprives the pears of their own specific identity. Seen from his perspective, they are not pears but signs of his individuality. Instead of being defined by biological processes and the law, Augustine seeks to redefine the world in terms of his own subjective vision and desire, thus abandoning the status of creature in favor of the role of creator. Augustine's desire to become author of his own self, as he soon realizes, is none other than a yearning for the Author of All Being, a desire to be like God. Just as single-focus passion seeks self-definition rather than procreation, so Augustine's appetite for pears serves not to satisfy a hunger for food but to quench a thirst for authorship.

In first-person narration, single-focus longing for self-creation is mirrored by a desire to tell one's own story, listing accomplishments or confessing faults as markers of individuality. No such direct relationship exists in third-person narration, yet the narrator's decision to follow the protagonist to the near exclusion of others clearly reveals the force and function of the central character's desire. The narrators of Homer's *Iliad* and Vergil's *Aeneid* recount battles like mountaintop observers, concentrating first on one, then on another of the participants as they look down from their privileged belvedere. Dual-focus narration thus appears as separate from and superior to dual-focus action, for it is the aloof and omniscient narrator who seems to make the decisions about how the story will be told. The single-focus situation is quite different. .

Jane Austen's *Pride and Prejudice* is usually treated as the story of the Bennet household. Yet repeatedly during the novel, one of the five daughters leaves the family mansion to follow her own destiny elsewhere. Jane visits Caroline Bingley and stays with her aunt in London; Elizabeth walks in the rain to the Bingley mansion, visits Charlotte Lucas Collins at the Rosings parsonage, and travels northward with her aunt and uncle; Lydia vacations in Brighton, whence she runs off to London. The male characters are just as active in their wanderings. Mr. Bennet scours London in search of Lydia; Mr. Bingley shuttles between Netherfield and London; Wickham follows his regiment from Meryton to Brighton before fleeing to London; Darcy moves between Netherfield, London, Rosings, and Pemberley. Dual-focus treatment of these numerous comings and goings would no doubt involve careful pairing of male and female characters with highlighted scenes featuring their parallel thoughts: Jane's and Bingley's mutual doubts about each other's affections, Elizabeth's and Darcy's seriocomic misestimations of each other, Lydia's and Wickham's devil-may-care desire, perhaps even Mr. and Mrs. Bennet's radically different levels of involvement in their daughters' affairs of the heart. Yet no such pairing exists in the following-pattern of *Pride and Prejudice*. Indeed, of all the many trips made by the novel's large cast of characters, none can induce the narrator to leave the Bennet household save those made by Elizabeth. For, as E. M. Halliday has so aptly put it, "even a sleepy reader of this book must be well aware, before he has read very far, that it is Elizabeth Bennet's story" (1966:431).

Whereas dual-focus narrators enjoy Olympian freedom and powers, the narrator of *Pride and Prejudice* appears to have accepted voluntary submission to the whims of Miss Elizabeth Bennet, following her wherever she goes, letting all others disappear from the narration whenever they leave Elizabeth's side. It is not that this narrator does not *know* as much as that of *The Iliad* or *The Aeneid*; all are "omniscient" by traditional standards of narrative analysis. The difference lies in a voluntary limitation accepted by the narrator of *Pride and Prejudice*: following Elizabeth around like a reporter assigned to write her biography, independently of any interesting news occurring around her, this narrator gives an impression of subservience. As in *The Scarlet Letter*, the narrator of *Pride and Prejudice* seems less like the creator of a story, or even the objective recorder of history, than the amanuensis of the heroine. Throughout the single-focus tradition, the narrator appears to have abandoned all decisions to the character who is followed.

By usurping the dominant position in the following-pattern, the protagonist becomes the subject in relationship to whom all other characters and things remain objects. In dual-focus narration, the subject-object dichotomy is constantly broken down by the alternating following-pattern, which makes each focus subject and object in turn. Because both are subject as well as object, neither is either. This parallelism, this balancing, depends on a system where all members fulfill their categorical role. The enemies in dual-focus epic are pitted against each other not through personal desire but by a slot logic where they represent forces or groups that exceed individual interests. The very language of subject/object distinctions is inappropriate to texts like Prudentius's *Psychomachia*, where the characters' very names identify both their allegiance and their specific role. Is Ira (Wrath) subject and Patientia (Long-suffering) object, or vice versa? Generated by the tension between Virtue and Vice, they cannot be considered in terms of the subject/object dichotomy.

In the same manner, Dido's suicidal wrath and Aeneas's long-suffering *pietas* can never be reduced to the one-sidedness of a subject/object relationship because Dido and Aeneas are but specific embodiments of a more general quarrel between Jupiter and Juno in the heavens above. The same situation obtains in dual-focus pastoral, where the text's very plot is designed to neutralize subject/object distinctions. According to the Neoplatonic philosophy that presides over Honoré d'Urfé's *L'Astrée*, true love emanates not from individuals but from a higher order identifying two souls as destined for mating from their very birth. Dual-focus lovers desire not their opposite sex counterpart but fulfillment of their role within the system.

Suppose, however, that one partner refuses to return the other's love. Suddenly the lover's ego-investment increases, her desire is transferred from simple fulfillment of a categorical role to questioning of her very self. Rather than exemplifying sexuality, the character's desire becomes invested with individuality. The loved one loses his independence and becomes redefined as a marker of the lover's own state. This reorientation of the dual-focus love plot in subject/object terms provided one of the earliest and simplest methods of freeing the love theme for single-focus usage. An analogous method treats love or sensual desire as a forbidden fruit. Here desire is generated not as an exemplification of the character's sexual category (as it is in, say, *Daphnis and Chloe*), but *in spite of* a more complex, culturally defined category (for example, the category of married woman in Madame de Lafayette's *La Princesse de Clèves*). Instead of accommodating individuals to their biological or cultural category (the traditional function of dual-focus initiation), single-focus desire represents a purposeful attempt to evade either biological necessities like nourishment and procreation or the laws that provide individuals with their categorical starting points.

In fact, single-focus narrative often specifically identifies the protagonist as *not* fulfilling the expected biological role. One of the oldest of Western single-focus forms, the Christian saint's life, commonly begins by a turning away from the twin requirements of society and nature. Just as the infant Saint Nicholas is traditionally represented in medieval statuary as refusing his mother's breast (thereby expressing his preference for heavenly sustenance), so Saint Anthony, in the oldest and most influential of Christian vitae (Athanasius, *Life of Saint Anthony*), begins his saintly career—and his text—by abandoning his possessions and the world of men. In like manner, the Old French *Vie de Saint Alexis*, one of the most widely imitated of medieval vernacular saints' lives, chooses the young man's marriage night as his moment of separation both from human nature and tradition:

> When he saw the bed and looked at the girl
> Then he remembers his heavenly Lord
> Whom he prefers to any earthly prize. (2000:vv. 56–58)

Alexis's "wedding" to the church rather than to a charming virgin, Anthony's bouts with sexual temptation, Nicholas's refusal of his mother's breast (Otloh, *Life of Saint Nicholas*), Cuthbert's preference for prayer and spiritual sustenance over earthly food (Bede, *Life of Saint Cuthbert*), Hilarion's fasting (Jerome, *Life of Saint Hilaron*), Martin's decision to abandon his military career (Sulpicius Severus, *Life of Saint Martin*), Guthlac's voluntary isolation (Felix, *Life of Saint Guthlac*)—all devolve from what Gregory the Great ("Homilies on Ezechiel") calls "supernal desire," the desire for transcendence that leads men to seek values above biology or society.

Having once shunned categorical functions, individuals remain free to apply their desire to other objects. Western literature often imitates at a distance the saint's life's tendency toward sublimation. In his diptych of "bachelor" novels—*Le Cousin Pons* and *Le Curé de Tours*—Honoré de Balzac regularly employs sexual metaphors to suggest that Pons and Birotteau have a more than natural love of their possessions. As confirmed bachelors, Pons the collector and Birotteau the priest have transferred to objects incapable of returning their affection the feelings that under "normal" circumstances would have been bestowed on a woman, thus assuring the continued applicability of the subject/object dichotomy. Whereas the reasons for the sublimation of Balzac's bachelors are only hinted at, an entire generation of romantic heroes abandons sexuality out of a more or less overt fear of contamination by its dark, incestuous, overtones. François René de Chateaubriand's René, Mary Shelley's Frankenstein, Stendhal's Octave (*Armance*), Balzac's Louis Lambert, and Flaubert's Frédéric Moreau all sublimate their sexual desire in favor of transcendent goals unrelated to such base matters as sexuality. Like adultery, chastity is a method of going beyond normal marriage, of overcoming banality in favor of a particularizing voyage into unknown territory.

If dual-focus narrative serves to protect society and its laws, identifying them as cosmos and opposing them to chaos, single-focus texts regularly begin with an incursion into the chaotic world of non-value, the only place where individuality can be discovered and defined. The dual-focus system perpetuates the cultural canon, through exclusion or reduction of those who oppose it, whereas single-focus strategies promote development and preservation of the individual. This fundamental shift reorients the text's imaginative geography. Dual-focus texts emphasize boundaries separating mutually exclusive worlds. Whether natural (the river Jordan isolating the Promised Land from all else, the Pyrenees splitting Charlemagne's France from the land of the Saracens) or man-made (city walls, army stockades, family compounds), these boundaries oppose land cleared for human dwelling to unconquered chaos. Dual-focus pastoral inverts the pattern by transferring to the city the labyrinth metaphor once associated with wilderness. The dangers of the forest and the desert are now found in the low life of the city, where criminals and prostitutes take the place of beasts, ogres, devils, barbarians, and pagans.

Cosmos walled in and protected from chaos—such is the geographical constant of dual-focus narrative. To break through the barrier dividing the two worlds requires immense energy and unconventional purpose. Such energy and purpose are precisely what single-focus desire provides. Originally located within the warm womb of cosmos (family, court, city, laws), the protagonist's first movement involves a plunge into the unknown, motivated precisely by the fact that it is unknown. As in Dante's *Divine Comedy*, single-focus protagonists begin the adventures that make their tale worth telling by entering into a "selva oscura," a dark wood to which they would bring light. Each single-focus subgenre derives its thematics from the specificity of its particular chaos. Obeying real historical considerations, the saint's chaos takes the form of the desert. Inspired to live a more holy life, early confessor saints like Anthony and Paul of Thebes (as opposed to martyr saints, whose stories appear earlier and are invariably dual-focus), are represented by Athanasius and Jerome as quite literally walking out into the desert from the cities of northern Egypt. Other saints imitate their love of desert places. Sulpicius Severus's Martin seeks out the caves surrounding Tours. Benedict, so Gregory informs us, first abandons his family in favor of Subiaco, then his monastery in favor of a narrow cave nearby. Bede's Cuthbert finds solitude on the edge of his monastery, then greater seclusion still on the island of Lindisfarne. Felix recounts Guthlac's departure for the marshes of Crowland. Brendan and others in the Irish *imram* tradition set out across uncharted seas (*The Voyage of Brendan*). In these cases and hundreds of others, the man of God shuns established values. His search for ever-greater isolation corresponds to a desire for increased exceptionality and individuality, albeit in the service of God.

The saint's radical revision of established value structures offers an especially clear view of single-focus economics. Dual-focus narrative operates according to a zero-sum system. Since the division into inside/outside, us/not-us is based on diametrical opposition between the two groups, one marked as positive and the other negative, the sum of the opponents' values must always be zero: the elect's positive value balancing the damned's negative value. The geometry of the equal-arm balance assures this inverted equivalence and its nil sum. Martyrs' lives (*passiones*) work according to this principle, with the Romans' negative value balanced by the Christians' positive value. The *vita* abandons this closed universe in favor of a new principle, that of gradation and its implied variable-sum game (Altman 1975). When Anthony leaves the city and its materialism, he does so without utterly condemning it; in fact, he gives away his money to the poor, suggesting that money does indeed represent some sort of value. Instead of simply reversing the accepted opposition of civilization's plus value to the desert's minus value (as the martyr saints do in destroying pagan idols), Anthony ushers in a new set of assumptions whereby life appears as a perpetual striving toward greater value. Money and the city are not bad; they are simply not as good as a solitary life of devotion to God.

This gradational approach appears most clearly in the myriad lives wherein the individual reaches eremitic status in two separate stages. First, he retires from society to a monastery, a movement that we might characterize as +/++, as opposed to the typical dual-focus+/−balancing. Once in the monastery, however, Benedict or Cuthbert soon continues his search for ultimate value by separating himself from the community in favor of solitary confinement. This second movement, opposing the hermit to the monk, says nothing pejorative about the monk's status but identifies the anchorite as having increased his value by choosing the more difficult life. We must schematize this movement as ++/+++, because the saint has achieved still greater virtue than he established by his original departure from society.

With the secularization of the single-focus form, the gradational value structure is retained, not only in pious texts like John Bunyan's *Pilgrim's Progress* and William Langland's *Piers Plowman* (with its clear delineation of value into good, better, and best categories), but also in picaresque tales of increasing success and stability from *Lazarillo de Tormes* to Alain René Lesage's *Gil Blas de Santillane*. With the rise of the novel, the gradational value structure is further reinforced by a tendency toward economic stocktaking of the protagonist's position in society, a development especially visible in the novels of Daniel Defoe and Pierre Marivaux. While the ledgers of Robinson Crusoe have become legendary, those of Moll Flanders are even more to the point here, for at the end of every episode Moll counts her coins, conning us into adopting her own monetary set of values. Through repeated financial and social evaluations of their current situation, Marivaux's upstart peasants,

Marianne (*La Vie de Marianne*) and Jacob (*Le Paysan parvenu*), consistently emphasize traditional single-focus gradational values. Gone is the dual-focus willingness simply to oppose good to bad. Here value is like a bank account—there is never so much that more cannot be added. Yet, as picaresque and psychological protagonists quickly discover, the fact that value can be increased implies that value can be reduced as well. Leaving one situation for another, investing one's money in a cargo of uncertain worth, trading country calm for city bedlam—all such attempts at increasing value involve investments that are speculative at best, entailing the risk of losing goods, capital, value, and self.

If the saint's trials take place in the desert, the romance knight sets out into an unmapped wasteland. Just as the hermit's progression depends on a double separation and individualization—from society to cloister, then from monastery to anchorite life—so romance progresses through two stages. The would-be knight, whether Wolfram von Eschenbach's Parzival or Stephen Crane's Henry Fleming (*The Red Badge of Courage*), must first leave home in search of something more glorious than the familial fireside. Acceptance by the group, however, is no more conclusive in the medieval court than in a modern war novel like Erich Maria Remarque's *All Quiet on the Western Front*. In order to achieve further individuation, the protagonist must abandon his community. When the Green Knight appears at Arthur's court in the anonymous *Sir Gawain and the Green Knight*, Gawain takes the opportunity to prove his own worth independently of the court's established values. To his uncle Arthur he claims:

> Bot for as much as ye ar myn em I am only to prayse;
> No bounté bot your blod I in my bodé knowe. (1974:vv. 355–56)

Praise deriving from lineage is insufficient for the romance knight. In *The Song of Roland*, Charlemagne is content to derive his power from God, from his Christian category, but Chrétien de Troyes's Yvain will not be satisfied until he confronts the mysterious Knight of the Magic Fountain. The medieval epic presents a job to be done, a society to be secured, but romance has other designs, for it is caught up in the individual's desire to assert himself, to challenge the unknown in search of that which never was discovered by any knight before him—his own personal identity.

The quest for identity that informs medieval romance also invests the psychological novel. An important inversion has taken place, however, between these two incarnations of single-focus narrative. The saint's life and the romance can conveniently be read as reactions to a dual-focus world in which the city or the court is seen as cosmos, while its surroundings are regarded suspiciously because of their potentially chaotic nature. Within this dual-focus epic configuration, protective of the civilized agglomeration, value adheres to those who defend the castle from the forces of evil without. The saint and the knight challenge the very dichotomy on which this system is based by searching for value alone, outside the walls, in the Egyptian desert or the forest of Brocéliande. In a later period when courts and cities have grown to a point where they no longer need fear for their own existence, dual-focus narrative reverses its field and identifies with the pastoral values now fast on their way to extinction. The unknown is no longer called wasteland, desert, or chaos, but "utopia"—nowhere. It is now positively valued and specifically opposed to the city's degradation and sin. The Renaissance pastoral, the Enlightenment utopia, the Romantic serial novel, the Hollywood myth—all are taken in hand by dual-focus pastoral's antiurban dichotomy.

It is in such an atmosphere that the single-focus novel develops. Dual-focus epic opposed the known to the unknown, marking the former as positive, the latter as negative. The thirteenth-century French knight could establish his identity by setting off into the unknown defined by twelfth-century epic, but the novelistic hero finds that the unknown has already been usurped by utopias, romances, and fantastic tales. His only alternative is to sally forth into the realm of the real. Renaissance pastoral was still thriving when Lazarillo set out to make his living as a blind man's boy, or even when Cervantes' Rinconete and Cortadillo ran away to Toledo, satisfying the reader's curiosity along with the youths' desire. Lesage's Gil Blas, Marivaux's parvenu peasant Jacob, Defoe's Moll Flanders, Fielding's Tom Jones, Balzac's Rastignac and Lucien de Rubempré, Stendhal's Julien Sorel, Flaubert's Frédéric Moreau, Dickens's David Copperfield, Zola's Gervaise Macquart, Dreiser's Sister Carrie, and countless others begin their lives in the country only to seek the city when youth's desire calls. The saint's life and romance were based on an epic known/unknown disjunction, so both saint and knight met not the beasts of nature but the monsters of the unknown: demons, talking animals, ogres, giants. The novel sends its heroes into a swarming city defined by the ideal/ real dichotomy, so their tests are modeled on the very real evils that gave the city its bad reputation: criminals, prostitutes, swindlers, drunkards. The protagonists must thread their way through a maze, but in the first model, where the known is reserved for the proprietors of value, both the hero's pathways and the skills used to navigate them successfully must take on the characteristics of the fantastic, while in the second model the heroine's problems and solutions must reflect everyday reality.

Though they originally took shape to respond to specific historically conditioned dual-focus configurations, these two complementary single-focus approaches metamorphose rapidly in the modern world, providing cinema and the popular novel with some of their most persistent subgenres. The romance city-to-country plot, for example, is regularly reincarnated in what have come to be called "road films." Like the romance or saint's life, the road film begins with a discovery that established values are inadequate. Born of this recognition is a desire to hit the road, whether on a bike (Dennis Hopper's *Easy Rider*), in a car (Arthur Penn's *Bonnie and Clyde*), or an airplane (M. Antonioni's *Zabriskie Point*). The modern woman's version begins as the woman collects her things but leaves her ring on the table, exchanging it for the keys to the family station wagon, creating an ironic image of her situation: she is free, but only to take the dog to the vet, do the grocery shopping, pick up the kids, and deliver them to their scout meetings. Only in the product of the society that she loathes, in the symbol of her enslavement to that society, can woman then set out in search of the Magic Fountain (Francis Ford Coppola's *The Rain People* here standing for an increasingly large class of films).

Complementing the road film, with its implied cult of the countryside, we find the song of the city par excellence, the detective story. Dual-focus detective tales exist, firmly entrenched in the Dick Tracy tradition of Manichaean strife, thereby reiterating the clichés of a Romantic serial novel like Eugène Sue's *Mystères de Paris*, where the hero's clairvoyant sleuthing derives from his generalized perfection and immaculate representation of Good. True detective novels, however, feature a renegade detective—C. Auguste Dupin (Poe, *Murders in the Rue Morgue*), Sherlock Holmes (Doyle, *Adventures of Sherlock Holmes*), Sam Spade (Dashiell Hammett, *The Maltese Falcon*), Inspector Maigret (Georges Simenon, *Le Commissaire Maigret*)—a complex individual in the Vidocq (*Les Mémoires de Vidocq*) tradition, more intent on proving his own mettle and retaining his independence than on simply solving crimes. It is the panache of Sherlock's solutions that delights us, not the petty fact that he happens to have solved a crime through them. We react to Edgar Allan Poe's "The Gold Bug" exactly as we do to his mystery/detective stories, yet the only crime in "The Gold Bug" is a hypothetical one, discovered quite by accident and alluded to only briefly. Our joy in reading this story comes from the clever solution of the cryptogram—the maze is unraveled, the chaos of symbols at last forming a coherent message. In just this way the detective reduces the city to an aspect of his own personality.

All single-focus narrative implies, in a certain sense, a departure into the unknown. Romance space opposes court to wasteland, but the dichotomy disappears as the knight proves his ability to cross the forest, to refrain from temptation, and eventually to recycle all that was once perceived as waste. In like manner, scientific space divides the known from the unknown, but single-focus texts bridge that gap as soon as the scientist's Promethean desires are born. Faust's overreaching leads him into a wasteland where religious, psychological, and sensual knowledge is both more complete and less orthodox than in the stable, conventional world that he leaves behind. Mary Shelley's Victor Frankenstein, like the narrator in the novel's epistolary frame, undertakes a voyage of discovery into the scientific unknown. Frankenstein is Promethean not only in his desire to create a human being without the assistance of his own creator but also in his relationship to the novel's paternity. It is only through his desire that the story exists at all. Dual-focus texts operate like rituals, independent of the participants, for their categories can be actualized by any placeholder, but single-focus stories owe their very existence to individuals who usurp the text's following-pattern through their desire. Even the intrusive narrator of Balzac's *La Recherche de l'absolu* appears to derive his story from his character's search for an absolute, and not vice versa. Adam was created by God, but he is re-created by his own desire for knowledge.

A short excursus on the Adam story is apropos here, for the single-focus meaning of this essential myth gathers and emblemizes many aspects of single-focus narrative. The balance of Genesis may represent a dual-focus origin myth, but the Adam and Eve story can properly be read as a single-focus account of the birth of desire, repeatedly retold within single-focus texts.

Until the episode of the forbidden fruit, man's purpose is described in strikingly simple fashion: "Be fruitful and multiply, and fill the earth and subdue it; and have dominion over the fish of the sea and over the birds of the air and over every living thing that moves upon the earth" (1:28). Such an exhortation defines man in familiar categorical terms, with sex and social stature providing the only operative parameters.

The story of the tree of the knowledge of good and evil breaks from this external categorical definition, a fact reflected in the names accorded at different points in the action to the two human characters. Before the transgression, the term 'adham (from ground= 'adhamah) is a collective singular, referring to man in general (2:17); only later will Adam become a proper name designating a particular man, a distinguishable individual (4:25, 5:1–3). Woman, before the fall, is simply 'ishshah (2:23), that is, "out of man" (= ish); not until the forbidden fruit has been tasted is she given her own name of Eve (3:20). Naming is an important aspect of single-focus beginnings because the desire to name oneself is tantamount to recognition that both patronymic and paternal values provide insufficient individuation. As a mark of his prowess, Chrétien's Yvain earns the title of "Chevalier au Lion"; Gawain wants to establish the worth of his own name independently of his lineage; Quijada must change his name to Quixote before setting out on his quest (Cervantes, *Don Quixote*); James Gatz heralds his new life by taking the name Gatsby.

Adam and Eve gain more than new names through their transaction, however. As in *The Scarlet Letter*, a value speculation (risking secure, established values in order to maximize value), leads to an affirmation of the importance of *spec*-ulation, of point of view: "She took of its fruit and ate; and she also gave some to her husband, and he ate. Then the eyes of both were opened, and they knew that they were naked" (3:6–7). Nothing has changed in the outer world; Eden is still Eden, Man and Woman are still Man and Woman. But their action creates an inner world, where being depends on seeing, where the subject/object relationship is all important. This discovery of inner life evidently teaches them that words are not in a simple one-to-one correspondence to reality, because Adam's response presumes ulterior motives in God's first question. When God says "Where are you?" Adam hears an accusation and a threat. Instead of answering God's question directly, Adam substitutes a narrative about his own perceptions and his own motivation:

"I heard the sound of thee in the garden, and I was afraid, because I was naked; and I hid myself" (3:10). Just as the serpent capitalized on Eve's desire to make her follow his argument, so Adam's newfound individuality motivates this causal statement. The cause-and-effect arrangement of single-focus narrative depends on the stringing together of similar pronouns the way Adam does in his first speech: "I heard . . . I was afraid . . . I was naked . . . I hid." God reacts just as Adam did. Adam heard God's "Where are you?" as an effect that must have a cause (anger, he thought). God hears Adam's speech in the same manner; he seeks to understand why Adam might speak in just that way: "Who told you that you were naked? Have you eaten of the tree of which I commanded you not to eat?" (3:11). And so on until the entire deed has been elucidated. This doubling of action is characteristic of the single-focus mode as a whole. Genesis 3 reads like a detective story, the narration of the crime giving way to an interrogation in which the evidence is made, through a series of cause-and-effect deductions, to reveal the author and motivation of the crime.

The only thing that permits God to solve the crime is Adam's guilt. Were Adam able to disguise that, he could easily cover up all the evidence. This he cannot do, however, for the fruit conveys the twin attributes of the single-focus mentality: consciousness *and* conscience. Along with freedom of choice and knowledge of good and evil, Man gains the anxiety born of that knowledge. Before the fall, "the man and his wife were both naked, and were not ashamed" (2:25), but once Man's independence from God is asserted, concern for the wholeness and righteousness of the ego immediately follows. Adam's knowledge conveys individuality but also self-deprecation and self-incrimination. Now he himself must decide whether or not he is guilty, whence his anxiety. Before the fall there was no ego, just as there could be no differentiation between superego and id; after the fall, human desire for individuation causes the split and the attendant inner complexity. Eve recognizes this complexity when she affirms that "the serpent beguiled me, and I ate" (3:13). How could Eve be beguiled if there were no distance between the voice of her id and that of her superego? The notion of guile makes sense only after this split.

Perhaps the most interesting aspect of the Eden story involves a reversal in the relationship between God and man. Genesis 1 represents God's style as performative and his language as creative: "And God said, 'Let there be light,' and there was light" (1:3). God names a category, and the universe daily reenacts that category. This is the very heart of the dual-focus ritual use of language. When Longus identifies Daphnis as a boy and Chloe as a girl, those categories are not inconsequential. We expect the characters to respond to this performative use of language ("And Longus said, 'Let there be characters'; male and female he created them. And Longus blessed them and said to them, 'Be fruitful and multiply.'"). Man's transgression changes all that. Now God's discourse ("Where are you?" "Who told you that you were naked?") depends on his creature's action. Once, God created man and laid the ground rules for his conduct; now God must ask questions in order to establish the motivations underlying Adam's action. Single-focus narrators follow protagonists like voyeurs, desirous of ever-more information about eccentric individuals. This is precisely the position into which Adam has forced God. Before, it was "'Let there be light,' and there was light"; now an instantaneous performative has given way to a time-bound cause-and-effect interrogative: "And they knew that they were naked. . . . 'Who told you that you were naked?'" Adam is now the perpetrator of his own acts, the creator of his own self, the author of his own text. He has thus merited his own personal name and instituted a new type of discourse independent of and opposed to God's categories.

Models and Motives

In dual-focus narratives, the law is the ultimate arbiter of access to the text. Those who fail to respect the law are eventually evicted from textual space, just as exile constitutes the ultimate punishment in the dual-focus community. Single-focus narratives reverse this situation, according textual space to individuals who break the law, violate a taboo, or flout accepted custom—in short, to "misfits," as Nancy Armstrong (2005:27–28) aptly terms the exceptional individuals highlighted by the developing novel. Instead of reproducing dual-focus cyclical plots, emphasizing representative cases, single-focus texts exhibit a markedly linear character. Starting from a known point of departure, normally figured by an existing dual-focus society or situation, the single-focus protagonist sets off into the unknown, meets with extraordinary adventures, and hurries on toward an unknown destiny. Whereas a centripetal pull brings dual-focus narrative ever back to a famililar center, the centrifugal drive of single-focus narrative assures continuous investigation of the unknown. While the birth of desire assures liberation from the circle's well-known contours, thus initiating the single-focus text, the remainder of the protagonist's tale describes a trajectory that is anything but ritually predictable.

Dual-focus texts build cyclical plots around increasingly rapid alternation between the two foci, culminating in direct confrontation. The freedom accorded to—indeed, stolen by—the single-focus protagonist requires a fundamentally different strategy. Here the basic building block of the plot is not confrontation but choice. Whereas the operative concepts of dual-focus plotting may be expressed as the spatially conceived trio of this side, that side, and confrontation, single-focus texts turn on a temporal triad organized around a moment of decision: preparation, choice, and evaluation. For the romance hero, the decision may be as physical as which road to take; psychological novel choices stress the protagonist's internal self-evaluation; the detective novel turns on logical deductions. Within each basic moment of the single-focus progression, certain characteristic attitudes regularly reappear.

For the character who views the moment of decision as an opportunity, the period of prospection is marked by dreaming, planning, or plotting. For these self-assured characters, the moment of decision itself is marked by exaltation, by full and open expression of the self, as when Hester Prynne celebrates removal of her scarlet letter by letting down her hair, accompanied by a sudden bursting forth of the sun. With the period of retrospection comes an expression of self-satisfaction, of boasting, of glorying in previous decisions—expressed in the detective novel by the sleuth's self-satisfied account of the deductions that led to the successful conclusion of the case. For characters who view a decision with fear and trembling, however, this tripartite progression looks different indeed. The period of prospection is marked by insecurity and hesitation, such as that exhibited throughout the sentimental education of Flaubert's Frédéric Moreau. The moment of decision brings the anxiety defined by Kierkegaard as "the dizziness of freedom" (1980:61), a trademark of the existential novel. For protagonists lacking self-assurance, the period of retrospection is spent in regret, like that following Henry's first battles in *The Red Badge of Courage* or La Princesse de Clèves's initial demonstrations of love for Nemours. Additional interest can be produced by radical changes in self-assurance, such as the pastor's transformed tone after he has reread his diary in André Gide's *La Symphonie pastorale* or the revolution in Julien's character at the end of Stendhal's *Le Rouge et le noir*.

Products of their own desire, single-focus protagonists owe their very textual existence to the liberty that they have taken with society's customs and laws. Even real individuals follow this rule. Saints inspire stories only because they radically break with accepted values and practice. The pamphlets and ballads that were instrumental in the development of the novel in England invariably tell the story of a crime, meant to be sold on the day of the criminal's hanging. In civil life, crime leads to punishment, but in textual life it is the crime that guarantees a place in the narrative, a text of one's own. Freedom from the law may be prerequisite for admission into single-focus narrative, but freedom comes at a price. Anthony is tortured by demons, Yvain is nearly beheaded by a giant, Lazarillo almost starves to death, Moll Flanders marries her own brother, Emma Bovary is driven by debt to suicide, Gide's immoralist loses all desire to live. Playing by definition a lonely role, single-focus protagonists are forever exiled from the conformity of the dual-focus community. But in the characters around them they invariably find models and motives for action. However important the single-focus protagonist may be for initiating the text, for providing the extra/ordinary decisions that make the story worth telling, the tale remains incomplete without the characters who influence and inform the protagonist's behavior.

How do secondary characters fit into the single-focus pattern? What do we make of the role of the devil in the Adam and Eve story? How do we handle novels with several salient characters, like Balzac's *Père Goriot?* Who is the main character of Homer's *Odyssey*, and how does he relate to the others? If *The Odyssey* is simply the story of Odysseus, why do we follow his son for four full books before the hero of the Trojan war finally takes over the narrative? On the other hand, if this is Telemachus's narrative, why is he abandoned for ten long books while we follow his father's fate? Are the first four books an expanded introduction and Telemachus a secondary character? Or is the tale of Odysseus a simple included story meant to divert us from the relatively sparse central plot of Telemachus's growth to manhood?

Support for both options comes from the distinguished literary reinterpretation of this classic. If some periods have rewritten the story of the wandering Ithacan, stressing his exemplary, dual-focus, heroic qualities, others have made the account of his son's growth into the very type of the education of youth (especially in the wake of François Fénelon's neoclassical treatise titled *Télémaque*). Neither of these readings can be either totally rejected or wholly accepted without doing serious violence to the text, however. By its interest and themes, as well as its metaphors and following-pattern, *The Odyssey* is fundamentally the story of two men, one thought dead and the other not yet fully living. The plot must bring two heroes to life, to full enjoyment of that which is theirs. Like *Madame Bovary*, *The Odyssey* provides two separate protagonists, granting each in turn the individuality of the single-focus hero. A clearer understanding of the relationship between the two will help explain why Homer yokes their stories together, making *The Odyssey* the story of two men and their relationship rather than that of a single individual.

From the very beginning, the stories of Penelope's husband and son are mingled. Athene pleads eloquently to Zeus for Odysseus's return home, but her first action is to "go to Ithaca to instil a little more spirit into Odysseus' son" (Homer 1946:27), as if the father's return were to depend on the son's courage. Our first view of Telemachus is hardly encouraging on that score, for he is "dreaming of how his noble father might come back from out of the blue, drive all these gallants pell-mell from the house, and so regain his royal honours and reign over his own once more" (28). Far from depending on Telemachus's courage, Odysseus's prospective homecoming actually inhibits Telemachus: as long as the son maintains a vague hope that his father may return, he retains the privilege of doing nothing, dreaming about Odysseus's return rather than asserting his own rights. Only sure knowledge of his father's death would make Telemachus lord of his house, forcing him to master his own fate instead of relying on his absent father. Or so it appears.

Athene arouses Telemachus from his lethargy by calling on far deeper feelings than those of simple succession. "Are you really Odysseus' son?" (30), she queries, implying that there is more to paternity than a simple physical relationship. When she assures Telemachus that his father will soon return, he suddenly realizes that he may shortly be called on by Odysseus to account for his behavior. Now "full of spirit and daring" (33), Telemachus realizes that his unseemly behavior will be looked on as that of a child who is not a fit son for one so great as Odysseus. The effect of Athene's exhortations is immediate—Odysseus's son claims to be master of the house and takes his father's seat as he calls an assembly of the suitors. From that moment on, every one of Telemachus's actions is defined by his relationship to his father, by his role of apprentice to his father's model. When he goes looking for Odysseus, he is clearly searching for Odysseus-like qualities within himself as much as he is seeking his father. To be Odysseus's son means to inherit his manly vigor, Athene suggests—one who is the true son of Odysseus will have no trouble finding him.

Not until father and son are reunited, however, do we realize the full human content of Athene's questioning of Telemachus's paternity. Odysseus has never seen his son as a young man and thus has no way of knowing whether the youth who claims to be his son actually is. "If you really are my son and have our blood in your veins," says Odysseus, emphasizing once more that Telemachus has yet to prove that he is worthy of being called the son of Odysseus, "see that not a soul hears that Odysseus is back" (253). Shortly, Telemachus will prove his mettle, and in precisely the terms suggested by Athene in the first book: "I have learnt to use my brains by now and to know right from wrong," claims Telemachus; "my childhood is a thing of the past" (312). He then proceeds to put such pressure on his father's bow "that he might well have strung it yet, if Odysseus had not put an end to his attempts with a shake of the head" (319). Telemachus has finally succeeded in emulating his famous father.

If *The Odyssey* is the story of the old man finally returning home, it is also the story of the young man who leaves home in search of himself. Throughout, Odysseus serves Telemachus as a model, from long before they meet to the day their work is done. Only when Telemachus has succeeded in imitating his father, thus finally becoming his true son, can the text end. The reason for the presence of two "central" characters is now clear: the story of Telemachus's progression toward a distant goal can be understood only if we can see how difficult a goal his father's courage represents. Odysseus's role as model must be expanded to display not only his courage and ingenuity but also his son's emulation and ultimate acquisition of that same courage and ingenuity. *The Odyssey* thus builds on a standard single-focus pattern—the apprentice imitating the master—but the role of master is expanded so far that he outshines the youthful apprentice. When we read *The Odyssey* as a single-focus text built around Telemachus's attempt to imitate the difficult model provided by his famous father, we are better able to account for the differing development of the two men than if we take Odysseus as protagonist of the text that traditionally bears his name. While Odysseus varies little from beginning to end, Telemachus develops from a child into a man during the course of the text.

The *Odyssey* joins other single-focus narratives in celebrating the accession of youth to maturity. Where dual-focus texts typically commemorate the replacement of one generation by the next, the single-focus approach stresses the successful emulation by one generation of its model in the previous generation. The *Odyssey* offers an account of apprenticeship, dramatizing the passing of knowledge from one age to the next. In Vergil's *Aeneid*, Ascanius's relationship to his father Aeneas is totally different, emphasizing only a slot to be filled. Throughout *The Aeneid* we fear that one master of the Trojans will be exchanged for another, knowing full well that Ascanius need not resemble his father in order to replace him in his military and administrative functions. In *The Odyssey* we watch the word "master" go through a series of mutations. At the outset, Telemachus must fulfill the functions of master of the house—greeting and feeding Athene, for example—but he is in no way master of himself; at the end, with Odysseus's return, Telemachus loses all claim to be master of the house, but he is now master of himself and his fate, and thus paradoxically ready to become master of the house.

The *Odyssey* is an instructive text, indeed, for it clearly reveals the type of logic presiding over single-focus texts. Dual-focus secondary characters commonly differ from heroes and villains only in degree, not in kind. With the exception of the middleman, every character is aligned with one camp or the other. Not every character receives the same amount of attention, but in terms of structural significance, every character holds the same fundamental position. To read a text as single-focus, however, is to interpret all secondary characters according to the function they occupy in the protagonist's story. Even Odysseus must be considered secondary when measured by the basic standards of single-focus narration: choice and change. A hero of *The Iliad*, Odysseus embodies the fundamental role that single-focus texts reserve for the heroes and villains of previous dual-focus texts—that of model, either negative or positive, for the neophyte anxious to break out of childlike dependence and into the freedom of adulthood.

Like Odysseus, the devil always seems to be on his way home from a dual-focus affair of epic stature. We are so accustomed to the Manichaean tradition where the devil is an independent source of evil, a worthy adversary for a benevolent God, that it is hard to imagine what function the devil or his agents might have outside their familiar dual-focus environment. The Adam and Eve story reveals just how important a role the forces of evil may play in single-focus narrative. It may seem strange to read the tale of Adam and Eve as a single-focus text centering on the human pair, when such an obvious dual-focus interpretation is available: God and the devil are locked in combat over the human soul. Indeed, this reading matches the dual-focus approach to the Old Testament commonly taken by medieval iconography, popular mythology, and earlier chapters of this book. It is inappropriate for the Adam and Eve story, however, for two essential reasons. The first concerns the rhetorical flow of the story, its following-pattern, and its thematic emphases. We never alternate between God and the serpent; instead, we follow the human couple, suggesting that their actions and reactions constitute the tale's meaning. In addition, Eden's serpent derives his force not from some independent Manichaean power source (like the primitive dragon, the early medieval pagan gods, or comic-strip villains) but from the desire of the characters themselves. He brings that desire out into the open, catalyzing their actions, but without their curiosity he can do nothing. The serpent is not an independent principle but a projection of human longings. He must be treated as a function of human desire, not as constituting a separate focus.

The dual-focus devil in his many incarnations is an independent power principle opposing the hero or group from without. Whereas the dual-focus devil is a barrier, a hindrance, an immobile force, the single-focus devil is a tempter, a far more ambiguous figure who can at best influence the protagonist's decisions. The primary Old Testament meaning of the verb *satan* is persecution by hindering free forward movement. This description perfectly fits Israelite foes from the Amalekites to Ahasuerus. The New Testament presents the devil in a different light. Christ's only confrontation with the devil occurs during the traditional forty days and forty nights in the desert. Matthew 4:8–10 recounts the third temptation in this way:

> Again, the devil took him to a very high mountain, and showed him all the kingdoms of the world and the glory of them; and he said to him, "All these I will give you, if you will fall down and worship me." Then Jesus said to him, "Begone, Satan! for it is written, 'You shall worship the Lord your God and him only shall you serve.'"

This passage stands out for its mildness. Earlier Near Eastern tradition would have had the cultural hero battle the sea monster, destroy the enemy giant, or desecrate the altars to Baal. This Satan, however, requires no such force, for he exerts none himself. In fact, any astute reader will quickly infer that he has none to exercise or bestow. If he can really give Jesus all the kingdoms of the world, then he could just as well take them for himself. Jesus has the power, not Satan. The tempter's role is not to exert power but to divert the protagonist's attention from his chosen object, to bring unconscious desires to the surface and to capitalize on them. In order to have power in single-focus texts, the devil must derive it from the very characters he tempts.

Western single-focus narrative may be conveniently divided into those texts where the devil's plea is rejected and another, more interesting, class where acceptance of Satan's offer sets the plot in motion. In the former class, we find texts modeled on Jesus' example, such as the lives of saints from Anthony onward. In most of these texts the original impetus for the narrative is provided by a departure from society and its values. The devil's plea is rejected as proof that the hermit's commitment is total, that he is no longer susceptible to worldly pleasures. Because this devil offers the opportunity not for greater individuation but for a return to commonality, his plea must be rejected. Adam's serpent, on the other hand, represents differentiation, departure, and transcendence. Promethean heroes, in a line stretching from Adam to Theophilus and Faust, all accept the devil's offer, which promises to fulfill desires while assuring individuality. Far from fleeing the world, these heroes commonly begin their career by defiantly entering a world of mixed values, of uncertain morals, of risky but potentially lucrative endeavors.

The economics of transactions with the devil deserve a word here. Whenever such transactions are undertaken, they take on the character of speculation. The protagonist enjoys value A, or "morality" (peace, innocence, virtue); the tempter arrives and offers value B, or "reward" (rank, knowledge, money, or simply a new definition of morality). For this offer to become operative, the protagonist must desire B, whence the importance of desire for setting the single-focus system in motion. Once the devil's offer is accepted, the protagonist gains B, but what of A? According to a popular medieval legend (as recorded, for example, by Rutebeuf in his *Miracle de Théophile*),

Theophilus's contract with Satan sets the soul as the cost of reward, but such a simple-minded barter could hardly delight the confirmed speculator. The birth of desire corresponds to a discovery that all value is not here, *hic et nunc*, within one's category. Greater value may be available elsewhere. But with the discovery that value can be increased goes the risk that value will instead be decreased, for the first step toward greater value—willing abandonment of one's own category and its built-in morality value—may also lead to a loss of value. Once the support of the family, the group, the category, has been lost, all certainty disappears. The gradational system characteristic of single-focus speculation thus features none of the cut-and-dried, once-and-for-all alliances of the dual-focus diametrical system. Dual-focus texts permanently position the individual, vis-à-vis value, from the start. In single-focus situations, speculation never stops. At every point there is a path that leads forward, as well as one that represents a falling back.

The single-focus open-ended system thus produces a radically new myth of personality. The dual-focus arrangement locates value clearly and inalterably, requiring characters either to accept that location or lose their place within the system. Individual personality has little place here. Since each character is expected to replicate the basic aspects of his or her category, individual variations are treated as nothing more than "accidental" differences. The single-focus approach, on the other hand, depends on a cluster of four closely related characteristics:

1. Postulation of unlimited value
2. Birth of desire for increased value
3. Attempted maximization of value through speculation
4. Continual necessity of choice in order to assure profitable speculation

Gone are the certainty of dual-focus belonging and the simplicity of dual-focus decisions. Personality is instead governed by an impulse to maximize personal value, while protecting against risk and its accompanying anxiety. To gather rewards without foregoing morality—such is the hallmark of single-focus psychology. A forward look and a backward look, never the present. Dual-focus texts take place in the present, for past and future are nothing but aspects of the everlasting now, the static category, the timeless dimension of space.

Though the single-focus protagonist is in one sense a direct descendant of the dual-focus middleman, hesitating between competing values, single-focus characters are rarely content simply to abandon one set of values in favor of another. Single-focus speculation implies the desire to retain morality while maximizing reward or, in the case of the saint, to regain reward after having walked away from the world where it is the norm. Were the saint to abandon society's rewards entirely, we would perceive him as simply setting up an alternative locus of value. His morality would be opposed to society's reward, just as the martyrs' virtue contrasts with the Romans' riches or Lazarus's poverty-cum-salvation is opposed to Dives's riches-cum-damnation (Luke 16:19–31). The key to the single-focus *vita*, however, is that the saint's slow ascent toward God restores the power and rewards that he seemed to have abandoned when he left the world. The difficulty of profiting from such a risky speculation is revealed by the fact that it takes miraculous events to assure the saint's reward. Is Cuthbert hungry? An eagle appears to provide his supper. Is Benedict thirsty? A rock brings forth water. Is one of his associates in danger of drowning? God grants Benedict the power to perform a miracle in order to save him. When money is short, a purse is provided; when a storm threatens, a simple gesture quiets it; when old age finally takes its toll, the saint's dead body remains incorrupt. When miracles are in short supply, the marvel of point of view must suffice: morality is reward enough because the saint has learned to endure fasting and pain.

Subjectivity's sleight of hand proves even more useful in the novel. Having abandoned morality in favor of reward, the protagonist may conveniently grow blind to the value of morality or the fact that it has in fact been lost. In his first amorous episode, Jacob de la Vallée, Marivaux's parvenu peasant, refuses to compromise his morality. Jacob is rewarded handsomely for marrying Geneviève, but only on the understanding that he will permit his wife to become the master's mistress. "Wasn't it Adam's apple come back just for me?" Jacob asks, recalling the last three letters of his proposed bride's name. Yet Jacob has no heart of stone. After refusing this first temptation, he soon succumbs to others—salvaging his pride by dissimulating their immorality. As he rises in society, reaping reward after reward, he covers his moral nakedness with a veil of rhetorical language designed to convince the reader that his speculation has been successful, that he has won his rewards without having to pay with the currency of morality. Unable to have both morality and reward, Jacob compensates for the loss of morality through point of view, through *spec*-ulation. Rhetoric thus becomes the device whereby the protagonist's speculation succeeds. To paraphrase François de La Rochefoucauld, his rhetoric is the homage that reward pays to morality.

Miracle stories and unreliable narrators thus fulfill similar roles in the same system. Each represents a method of transmuting an even one-for-one trade (morality for reward or vice versa) into a profitable speculation. Each produces "immaculate conception" of the newly gained value, without tarnishing or abandoning the old. We have no more evidence of miraculous events than of Jacob's virtue—in both cases only words—yet both, if they convince the reader, assure the success of the protagonist's speculation. The ultimate result of this system is a Machiavellian utilitarianism, wherein the end justifies the means, the reward restoring in the eyes of the public the morality abandoned along the way. The following passage from *The Prince* could, with only minor changes, have been pronounced by Balzac's archfiend, Vautrin, to Rastignac, *Le Père Goriot*'s quintessential young-man-on-the-brink-of-life:

> Everyone sees what you appear to be, few touch what you are; and those few do not dare oppose the opinions of the many who have the majesty of the state defending them; and with regard to the actions of all men, and especially with princes where there is no court of appeal, we must look at the final result. Let a prince, then, conquer and maintain the state; his methods will always be judged honorable and they will be praised by all; because the ordinary people are always taken by the appearance and the outcome of a thing; and in the world there is nothing but ordinary people; and there is no room for the few while the many have a place to lean on. (Machiavelli 1964:149)

The option of morality or reward is thus not a simple choice but a complex game inviting players to devise a strategy whereby, in choosing one value they will not be required to abandon the other.

In *The Odyssey*, one character serves as an embodiment of the values that another is called to adopt. Balzac's *Le Père Goriot* offers two models—Vautrin representing the pleasures of reward, Goriot figuring the sanctity of morality. Both aspire to a successful speculation, employing open allegiance to one value in the hopes of gaining the other as well. Under the influence of the title, generations of readers recall *Le Père Goriot* as the story of an old man who carries fatherly love to suicidal lengths. Often compared with Shakespeare's *King Lear* for its repeated evocations of filial insensitivity, *Le Père Goriot* is given by some as the very type of Balzacian characterization, old Goriot embodying the novelist's tendency to conjure up monomaniacal characters whose traits surpass and mythify the real world of their epoch.

The following-pattern of *Le Père Goriot*, however, tells quite another story. The entire exposition, excruciatingly long and detailed, seems specifically charged with disguising the novel's true subject. As the narrator tours Madame Vauquer's boarding house, each character is described at length. No character stands out as the novel's subject or organizing principle, though the mysterious Vautrin and the retired pasta merchant Goriot do attract our attention. But as the exposition ends, it is Rastignac—the young student recently returned from the provinces with renewed ambition—who captures the narrator's interest. From this point on, we leave the aspiring law student only once. While several scenes provide Balzac with the opportunity to describe social gatherings of every sort, it is always with Rastignac that we arrive, always with Rastignac that we leave.

What does Rastignac have that the others don't? Why is he the book's *fil conducteur* and our guide to Paris society? Simply because Rastignac shares with the author the ability to observe society. He alone serves as the subject of knowledge (collecting and disseminating knowledge) as well as the object of knowledge (about whom something is known). Time and again, it is Rastignac who discovers a salient detail about the residents of the Pension Vauquer. Our knowledge of Paris society is repeatedly gained through Rastignac. Plot organization also concentrates attention on the young provincial. For all other characters, the story's November 1819 beginning is an unmemorable point on an unbroken and continuous time line. For Rastignac, however, that date represents the beginning of his Paris adventures, the starting gate for his ambition. Other characters enter into the plot, but only through Rastignac and his activities can the plot be adequately traced or represented. The novel's following-pattern clearly identifies its single-focus affinities and the narrative importance accorded to Eugène de Rastignac.

But if Rastignac is designated by the following-pattern and his own perspicacity as the novel's protagonist, then what role, structurally speaking, must we accord to the figures of Vautrin and Goriot, who loom large in every reader's memory of Balzac's novel? Constantly tempting Rastignac with respectability built on ill-gotten gains, Vautrin combines the attributes of Machiavelli's Prince and Goethe's Mephistopheles (indeed, Balzac's novel contains many direct echoes of *Faust*, albeit it on a realistic register, including the duels that result in the deaths of Margaret's and Victorine Taillefer's brothers). Vautrin's evaluation of the quagmire metaphor present throughout the novel could not be clearer. As Rastignac learns on his very first outing, it is difficult to navigate the muddy streets of Paris without being splashed with mud. Says Vautrin of the Parisian cesspool: "If it dirties your carriage as you pass, you're respectable. If it dirties your feet, you're a rogue" (Balzac 1965b:51). To come up in the world, the master-criminal implies, is to rise above bourgeois morality, and that can be accomplished only by those rich enough to ride by carriage, thus protecting riding coat and reputation alike. Madame de Beauséant, Rastignac's worldly cousin, carries the carriage image a step further: "Look on men and women simply as post-horses," she says, "and leave them behind as soon as they're exhausted. In that way you'll reach your goal" (82). Yet Madame de Beauséant is herself likened to a horse. Soon left behind by her own coachman, she amply demonstrates the risks involved in this Machiavellian system: when she loses her position in society, she is treated as if she had lost her morality as well.

Whereas "Papa" Vautrin tempts Rastignac with his get-rich-quick schemes (gain morality by maximizing reward), Goriot holds out the example of saintly self-sacrifice. The one serves as treasurer for criminals' ill-gotten gains; the other gives away his hard-earned gold, devoting himself selflessly to his daughters in the expectation that they will care for him in his old age (gain reward by maximizing morality). Constituting Scylla and Charibdis in the Odyssey metaphor developed throughout *Le Père Goriot*, Vautrin and Goriot serve as constant models for the young Rastignac, who must steer a course between them in order to reach his proposed goals. Rastignac does indeed sail by, for he adopts neither Vautrin's diabolical schemes nor Goriot's virtuous passivity. In Balzac's mythology, Rastignac is the one stable element, the one major character who is never caught up in the whirlpool of his desires or thrown on the rocks of misfortune.

But what permits Rastignac to navigate the straits without abandoning either his quest for reward or his slim hold on morality? He solves his problems through the same point of view that Marivaux used to assure the success of

Jacob's speculation in *Le Paysan parvenu*. *Le Père Goriot* is not narrated by Rastignac, however, so he cannot control the narration as tightly as Jacob. What Marivaux accomplishes through unreliable narration Balzac must achieve through the composition of a character who operates like his predecessor's rhetoric. Rastignac must retain his ambition at all times but talk, instead, about his concern for moral integrity. He must learn to make a show of compassion for Goriot just as he is abandoning him on his deathbed. In short, he must create a personality mask just as Jacob relied on a mask built out of rhetorical style. Let him borrow all his sister's savings, but if he wishes the virtue as well as the money, he must learn to regret her sacrifice out loud. Rastignac may have refused the devil's compact, but Balzac has to turn him into something approaching a hypocrite in order to secure his speculation.

Like *The Odyssey*, *Le Père Goriot* is appropriately read as the single-focus tale of a young man in search of a father. If Homer's text provides a single father figure, Balzac's novel furnishes a pair of memorable models. Throughout the single-focus tradition, secondary characters concretize the protagonist's potential paths. In *The Divine Comedy*, as in *Le Père Goriot*, much of the interest derives from the mysterious happenings to which the protagonist is witness. Yet far from representing a simple compendium of literary and real life characters, Dante's text, like Balzac's, always sets these visions in the service of the hero, providing positive and negative models that Dante the pilgrim must either imitate or avoid before he can proceed. In the same manner, Augustine's *Confessions* implicitly oppose the example of his pious mother to that of his worldly father. Wherever we turn in the single-focus world, protagonists are surrounded in their quest by models of behavior against which we readers regularly measure their conduct.

How the single-focus protagonist handles the twin necessities of morality and reward (along with their embodiment in models like Goriot and Vautrin) constitutes a fundamental question in single-focus narrative. Dual-focus tales serve to illustrate the triumph of the group that constitutes its audience. Even when historical factors force the narrator's side into temporary defeat (as in the martyr legends, *The Song of Roland*, the Negro spiritual, or Irish song), postulation of apocalyptic victory guarantees eventual domination. Dual-focus narrative cannot afford to admit defeat because of its role as defender of culture and perpetuator of society. Imagined victories, supernatural aid, and apocalyptic triumphs all collude to salvage that which history has erased. Single-focus narrative operates according to a similar principle, but where the dual-focus system protects categories, laws, and groups, single-focus texts guard individual egos against rupture. Single-focus protagonists have so much invested in their choices—which represent their desires and their individuality—that they cannot admit failure. They must adjust the facts, their interpretation, or the locus of values in order to assure the survival of their psyche, now understood as separate, individualized, and (from the point of view of the protagonist) valuable independently of categories, laws, and groups. Such tampering with the facts does not always go unpunished. If Rastignac achieves full socialization by accommodating his views to the reality of the situation, his contemporary Julien Sorel (in Stendhal's *The Red and the Black*) eventually self-destructs out of recognition of the hypocrisy involved in his too great accommodation to the world's values.

We can thus identify two typical results of the single-focus individuation process. "Reconciled" protagonists are progressively attuned to their limitations, having successfully negotiated the relationship between personal desire and the world's strictures. Henceforth equally at home in the realms of morality and reward, they have accepted a compromise between the two. This is the situation of many saints (who often return to the world as bishops), of Chrétien's Yvain and Erec (who at last learn to reconcile the twin demands of court and marriage), of Gawain (who, through his encounter with the Green Knight, experiences the Christian duality of man's glory and sin), of Moll Flanders (who rapidly abandons use values in favor of exchange values), of Henry Fleming (who earns his Red Badge of Courage), of Rubashov (the hero of Arthur Koestler's *Darkness at Noon*, who convinces himself that the Communist Party's mission is more important than his truthfulness), and of countless other heroes who adopt the precepts of Machiavelli's *Prince*.

The romantic hero(ine), in contrast, rejects a life not big enough to contain both morality and reward. Goethe's Werther cannot simultaneously maintain his respect for Lotte and become her sexual partner, so he kills himself. Faced with a similar conflict between purity and profanation, Flaubert's Frédéric Moreau simply avoids the problem, as does Chateaubriand's René. Frankenstein, Julien Sorel, and Emma Bovary all sacrifice their lives rather than abandon their aspirations. They retain the profound disappointment of goals unachieved, power unconquered, dreams unrealized.

These romantics retain to the breaking point their dream of becoming as gods. Their novels can end only with rupture from the world that has proven so inhospitable. They are truly what Georg Lukács (1963) and Lucien Goldmann (1964) have labeled "problematic heroes."

The romantic hero(ine) cannot make peace with the world, as René Girard has shown (1961), because his or her desire is mediated by a previous literary figure whose unreal perfection constitutes an unimitatable model, an unattainable goal. In the larger perspective of the single-focus mode we recognize Girard's mediator (Amadis for Quixote, Napoleon for Julien Sorel, Virginie and the Paris myth for Emma Bovary) as only one among a large class of figures who serve to catalyze the protagonist's desire. We have already examined the workings of one of these catalysts, the tempter, who offers new rewards. The mediator plays precisely the same role, though in a more indirect fashion. Athanasius asserts that Anthony leaves home because he has heard about Jesus' life and Christian precepts; Hilarion and Augustine (according to Jerome and Possidius) commence their spiritual careers in imitation of the stories told about Anthony. Parzival's vision of knights in shining armor, followed by the kindling of his desire to become one of their number, stands as a fit emblem of romance mediation.

Yvain demonstrates the process of triangular desire still more clearly. Chrétien's poem begins with a story designed to demonstrate what a man must do to gain individuality and win respect. At the outset, Yvain listens to Calogrenant's tale of bewitched forests and enchanted castles, of magic fountains and difficult tests. What Yvain hears is an admission of defeat on the part of Calogrenant, who undertook the adventure but could not carry it through to successful completion. What Yvain sees, however, is reorientation of the court around the storyteller, instead of its titular head, Arthur. Calogrenant's tale thus serves Yvain as an object lesson in the value of individuation. Only those who have undertaken unusual feats can capture the court's attention, whether or not they have accomplished them successfully. Calogrenant's story is part of Yvain's poem because it serves as the goad and the model for his desire. In much the same fashion, Telemachus seeks a new identity only under the influence of his father's model, forced on the young man by Athene, who understands fully the concept of triangular desire. Implicitly, all single-focus texts both begin and end with a story like that told by Calogrenant. The proper result of every single-focus adventure is the tale of the adventure, a legacy left by the single-focus protagonist to motivate other prospective single-focus protagonists. The end of one text thus serves as the logical beginning for another.

The Red Badge of Courage modernizes the concept of mediation by identifying the enormous influence of the yellow press. Long accustomed to the morality of home and mother, Henry Fleming now yearns to take part in "one of those great affairs of the earth" that he has read about in the "pages of the past." Despairing of ever "witnessing a Greeklike struggle," Henry's ideas of war come directly from the most exciting battle literature of the nineteenth century—the newspaper:

> He had burned several times to enlist. Tales of great movements shook the land. They might not be distinctly Homeric, but there seemed to be much glory in them. He had read of marches, sieges, conflicts, and he had longed to see it all. His busy mind had drawn for him large pictures extravagant in color, lurid with breathless deeds. (Crane 1960:117)

Intrigued by art's power to widen the angle of vision, to produce "large pictures" where the human eye sees only isolated details, Henry longs not for the battle but for the singer's tale of the battle, not for the ambiguous thrill of a closer look but for the vantage point of a Zeus on Olympus—or an editor in the copy room. For a while his mother's protests stay him:

> At last, however, he had made firm rebellion against this yellow light thrown upon the color of his ambitions. The newspapers, the gossip of the village, his own picturings, had aroused him to an uncheckable degree. They were in truth fighting finely down there. Almost every day the newspapers printed accounts of a decisive victory. (118)

Unaware that the yellow light is thrown by the press, not his mother, Henry remains blissfully oblivious to such obvious contradictions as daily reports of decisive victory. Rushing headlong into his dreams, Henry discovers that the view from the road is not quite what he had expected. More than the story of Henry's slow and winding trip to courage, *The Red Badge* is a tale of weaning, not from the breast or the bottle but from the equally temporary support of triangular mediation. Like Collins in Crane's short story, "A Mystery of Heroism," Henry must enter a world where deeds more or less good are done by men more or less moral—no perfection, no heroes devoid of flaws, only uncertainty and compromise.

Whatever the original source of the protagonist's desire, a rapid monetary return often takes the place of the tempter or mediator figure. Robinson Crusoe's second voyage is undertaken haphazardly, without any final decision as to whether he should return home according to his parents' wishes or set out to sea in order to make his fortune, yet the profit that he reaps convinces him more thoroughly than any third party that the life of the sea is for him. "This voyage made me both a sailor and a merchant," he relates, "for I brought home 5 pounds 9 ounces of gold dust for my adventure, which yielded me in London at my return almost 300£, and this fill'd me with those aspiring thoughts which have since so compleated my ruin" (Defoe 1945:15). Much the same situation obtains in Marivaux's *Le Paysan parvenu*, where Jacob receives monetary incentive to deploy his considerable masculine charms even before recognizing their existence. Like Eden's serpent, Paris and its easy money soon corrupt the provincial peasant, defining his new morality rather than rewarding his natural honesty and openness, as he would have us believe.

A still more fascinating and unexpected use of money as catalyst informs the twelfth-century Spanish *Poem of the Cid* (*Cantar de mio Cid*). Don Rodrigo's revolt against King Alfonso culminates in the Cid's exile, connecting this text to the French medieval epic cycle known as the "cycle des barons révoltés." From the very outset, however, it is not Rodrigo's wounded honor that is stressed but his impoverished condition. On the one hand, he is characterized by his lack of money ("Gone is my gold and all my silver"); on the other, he systematically reduces his allies' motivations to a monetary level ("Martín Antolínez, you are a hardy lance! / If I live, I will double your pay"; stanza 6). Some two hundred lines are devoted to the trick that the Cid plays on the Jews of Burgos in order to obtain enough money to begin his campaign. His prayers would seem more appropriate for Benjamin Franklin's *Autobiography* or a heavy laborer on the Alaska pipeline:

I pray to God our Father in heaven
that you who for me have left home and possessions,

before I die, may receive from me some gain;
that all you lose now twofold may be returned. (*Poem* 1963:18)

Whatever originally motivated Rodrigo's actions, his continued progress is measured by a single parameter: profit. Just as Emma Bovary is lured farther and farther from the standards of Yonville-l'Abbaye, so the Cid pushes on, like some crusty forty-niner, following the call of demon gold. "Ah, knights, I must tell you the truth," he says; "one would grow poor staying in one place always; / tomorrow in the morning let us move on" (54). Many similar pronouncements suggest that the Cid's entire life force has been invested in his outsized love of money. Releasing his prisoner, the Count of Barcelona, Rodrigo stresses the immense booty that he and his men have taken from the field of battle: "I need it for my men, who share my pauperdom," says the Cid, perhaps fooling the Count but certainly not the reader. "We keep alive by taking from you and from others," admits Rodrigo (62). The *sententia* that sums up the Cid's single-focus quest is found in no previous dual-focus epic, from *The Iliad* to *The Song of Roland*. Only a lord who has been exiled from national, categorical power would turn his attention so visibly to the twin processes of individuation and estate building; only a nouveau riche like Cid Ruy Díaz could subscribe to the dictum that "who serves a good lord lives always in luxury" (45).

The father figure, the tempter, the mediator, the quick profit—four categories of single-focus models to which we may now add a fifth and final class, the teacher. Dual-focus narrative has its judges, its sages, its interpreters of the law, but their word is final and incontrovertible, codified and specific, whereas the single-focus teacher deals in precepts and ambiguous sayings, simple indications that are neither final nor binding. Just as the serpent's power derives from human desire (unlike the power of the dual-focus devil, who incarnates an independent source of evil), so the teacher (as opposed to the giver of the law) relies on the protagonist's choices. The Old Testament stresses establishment of and respect for the law. The New Testament reserves a parallel place for the parable, the new form of Christ's teachings. The Christian experiences Christ not as a giver of law but as a pointer, indicating an ambiguous path that is narrow and difficult but singularly lacking in specificity. To choose a line of conduct, the believer must read his own experience into the biblical text, whether he is Augustine hearing in the garden the famous words from *Confessions* VIII ("Tolle, legge"—"Take, read"), the late medieval mystic striving to understand the teachings of Thomas à Kempis's *Imitation of Christ*, a fictitious cleric like Zola's Father Mouret, or Gide's diary-writing pastor.

Two texts that stand out for their literary figuration of pointing are also distinguished by their pictorial representation. By introducing the figure of the teacher as mediator between the protagonist and specific *exempla* of virtues or vices, John Climacus's *Climax* (also called *The Ladder of Perfection*) and Dante's *Divina Commedia* provide a fascinating single-focus alternative to the dual-focus approach used by Prudentius's *Psychomachia*. Illustrations of Prudentius's fourth-century text remain largely the same through the twelfth century: either Virtues and Vices appear as statically confronted warriors or the Virtue adopts a dominant position, with her foot on the corresponding Vice. Whatever the setup, the difference in characterization between the two warriors carries a clear message. The iconography of John's *Climax* radically alters this system (J. R. Martin 1954). In Vatican cod. gr. 394, for example, each illustration presents three figures: the student (a monk poised to climb a rung higher on the Ladder of Virtue), the lesson (the Virtue or Vice to be adopted or shunned), and the teacher (the author, who stands between them, pointing out the Virtue or Vice to the monk). Whereas *Psychomachia* illustrations derive largely from Old Testament dual-focus types (e.g., David and Goliath) and Roman martial sculpture, *Climax* iconography reproduces the New Testament arrangement whereby Christ teaches his disciples by pointing to the daily life examples that surround them. In accordance with this model, both Virtues and Vices are portrayed as real men and women, the ambiguity of their identity underlining the importance of the student's ability to see beyond their surface features.

The lesson thus loses its autonomy, no longer existing independently of the teacher and student. Furthermore, the elements are no longer related by metaphor (where Virtue and Vice represent parallel but diametrically opposed notions) but by metonymy, the pointing finger implying continuity through eye and mind as well. The switch from metaphor to metonymy is directly related to the lesson's loss of autonomy, for it is the presence of the lesson in the student's and teacher's mind that assures the connection between the elements. *In their mind*—an essential concept, for the pointing relationship necessarily implies a thinking consciousness, absent from earlier Virtue/Vice representations. In the dual-focus system, whether portrayed in *Psychomachia* iconography, the Utrecht Psalter, or illustrations for the Old Testament, *The Aeneid,* or *The Song of Roland,* judgment takes place at a level beyond and above the text. The text's constitutive duality can be resolved only by intervention of the gods or by their agent, the narrator. In *Climax* iconography, later psalters (including Vatican cod. gr. 1927, where David is constantly portrayed as pointing to exemplary wickedness), illustrations of *The Divine Comedy* (where Vergil and Beatrice are shown pointing out examples, not symbols, of Virtue and Vice), and in countless later single-focus texts, individuals do their own judging, constantly evaluating the moral or monetary value of ambiguous individuals or events. The text no longer depends on static confrontation of clearly marked opposite values, with measurement of the differences between values supplying textual meaning, but on the student's perception and ability to understand and carry out the teacher's precepts.

The text is not complete without some indication of the student's reaction to the lesson. *Climax* iconography regularly portrays the monk's successful learning in the form of a ladder, with the monk climbing one step in each episode. This alternation between lesson and learning, the two linked by a following-pattern emphasizing the monk-student, gives *Climax* iconography its distinctive single-focus character. The contents page reinforces this pattern, for in most *Climax* manuscripts the chapters are listed in order from the bottom to the top of the page, each chapter number and title inserted into one rung of the ladder that provides the page's pictorial framework. Movement through the text thus corresponds to ascension of the ladder, the monk-student and the reader together progressing metonymically from ground level to the heavenly realm above.

Twice-Told Tales

The Odyssey first engages our sympathies for young Telemachus, before unveiling the fabulous adventures of his famous father. The overall effect of this technique is to subordinate, structurally, Odysseus's activities to his son's search. I call this process "bracketing," where one person's story is inserted into and subordinated to another's. By mathematical convention, or in printed prose, bracketed material has a double status: it carries both its own independent meaning and a secondary signification. The same holds true throughout the history of single-focus narrative. One of the major markers separating the Renaissance story collection from the nascent novel is the importance accorded to listening. The included stories of *La Princesse de Clèves* may serve as separable tales, like the seventy-two entries in Marguerite de Navarre's *L'Heptaméron*, but they also measure the reactions and illuminate the destiny of the protagonist who listens to them. What Madame de Lafayette accomplishes with oral narratives and listening, her eighteenth-century heirs achieve with written texts and reading. Packed with letters from one character to another, *Pride and Prejudice* reveals its eighteenth-century roots. No matter who has written them, no matter the recipient, Elizabeth is always present to read and evaluate the book's many letters. Darcy's letter to Elizabeth, though it reveals not only his feelings toward her but his personal history as well, is not sensed by the reader primarily as an account of Darcy's life, but as evidence of Elizabeth's mistaken evaluation of her future husband. Here, as elsewhere in the single-focus tradition, attention given to a secondary character broadens the story's scope and deepens the reader's interest yet in the text's overall strategy serves only to bring the reader's attention back once again to the protagonist.

In the cinema, several techniques have evolved to concentrate interest on a protagonist who must regularly give up the screen to other characters. Most of these techniques involve the use of the protagonist's eyes or ears to subordinate one shot to another. When a character looks offscreen, the next image is conventionally accepted as the character's view. It thus loses its independence and becomes bracketed within the character's story. Dissolves introducing a dream sequence (or other imaginary scene) serve a like purpose. Even more common is the shot/reverse-shot sequence, in which one character is presented as viewed by another. This alternation between following the protagonist and following what the protagonist is following is part of a general single-focus tendency for protagonists to take on the role of secondary narrator.

The single-focus protagonist's penchant for usurping the place of the author is especially evident when the protagonist takes responsibility for building the text's events into a coherent story. In many ways, the subject matter of detective novels would seem to make them perfect candidates for dual-focus treatment. Often pitting a master criminal against a master detective, many detective novels thrive on a Manichaean worldview and its familiar black-and-white characters. Take Eugène Sue's *Les Mystères de Paris*, a Dick Tracy comic strip, or an early television crime show. Here justice is achieved by the action of an oh-so-moral and equally astute representative of law and order. We are squarely in the dual-focus world, alternately following good guys and bad guys, aware all along of which is which, of where the right lies and where the wrong. With the single-focus detective tale, from Poe on, no such assurance seems possible. The detective is not simply a representative of the law, designated to outwit or outfight his counterpart. He is also the only one with clear vision, able to separate the innocent from the guilty (a role formerly reserved for the dual-focus judge/narrator), and reconstitute the story that inculpates the one and exonerates the other. This reconstruction of the story carries an enormous weight in single-focus detective stories. From Dupin to Holmes and Maigret to Columbo, single-focus detective tales commonly end with a first-person narration in which the detective recapitulates his own process of thinking and thus the truth about the crime.

As the detective novel amply demonstrates, single-focus narrative is particularly attuned to the ordering of events and thus to the dimension of time. Just as dual-focus narrative uses the medium of space, measuring one two-dimensional area against another, single-focus narrative models time, basing its own linear structure on the irreversible, unidimensional nature of time. In the dual-focus universe, time is sensed only to be annulled. Years bring no changes but the ever-renewed cycle of the seasons. Centuries reveal no progress but the never-ending replacement of one generation by another. Clocks and calendars are invariably mentioned in dual-focus texts only in order to highlight the moment when the two foci will meet (e.g., the incessant clock inserts preceding D. W. Griffith's last-minute rescues). When a single-focus character pulls out a clock or a calendar, however, an entirely different structure is engaged. For months, Emma Bovary keeps her private record of the time lapsed since her visit to the Vaubyessard ball. With each passing week, with each month of added distance from her sole contact with a real milieu corresponding to her romantic readings, Emma slips one step further toward the provincial despair that will eventually claim her life. Time represents the distance between two Emmas: a dreamlike past experience on one hand and daily reality on the other. Wherever time is evoked in single-focus narrative, it serves to measure the gap between two moments in a protagonist's life, two states in a progression, two points on a line whose trajectory defines the text in question.

The time line that undergirds single-focus narratives is typically doubled by a physical embodiment that often takes the form of a journey (whether the literal wanderings of voyagers, the spiritual path of a Dante, or the psychological vagaries of the Bildungsroman). In order to turn the undifferentiated flow of time into a system capable of producing meaning, single-focus narrative resorts to a wide variety of techniques designed to pair moments whose significance surfaces only in their comparison. The most characteristic involves the use of a "moral mirror": the protagonist's memory triggered by an event in the present, he/she recalls a corresponding moment in the past, then compares the two. On the verge of leaving the Pension Vauquer to share a sumptuous apartment with his mistress, Rastignac consults his moral mirror: "He found that he looked so different from the Rastignac who had come to Paris the year before that, observing himself by an effect of moral optics, he wondered at that moment whether he really looked like himself" (Balzac 1965b:288). In these few lines we learn worlds about the way in which single-focus characters are conceived. Without the dimension of time, Rastignac is nothing, for his fundamental characteristic is the ability to change, to become a different character. However much he may utter the expression "himself," we know that there is no such fixed category, for the novel is constructed precisely to show the development of one self into another, to reveal the nonexistence of the unchanging base that dual-focus texts take for granted.

It is instructive to compare this typically single-focus use of the mirror—as if Narcissus always saw his former self when he gazed in the water—with the characteristic dual-focus mirror. In Honoré d'Urfé's *L'Astrée*, the fountain in the middle of the forest has magic properties. Instead of reflecting the person looking into the fountain, the mirror reveals that person's true love, both ideal complement and perfect partner. The pastoral practice of amoebic verse embodies the dual-focus mirror in literary form. Each male verse is mirrored by a female verse, with changes in only those aspects that male/female difference requires. This flaw in the mirror—the matching of a male verse to its female counterpart—recapitulates the sexual difference on which the text's duality is based. A similar effect rules over dual-focus epic, where formulaic verses (such as those that stress the similarities between Charlemagne and Baligant only to highlight their differences) and symmetrical images (as in the shootout showdown of a Hollywood western) capitalize on the similarity between foes to better isolate and play up the differences between them.

Perhaps the most common mirroring device in single-focus narrative involves the use of a recurrent place or motif to serve a measuring function, drawing attention to the physical, moral, or psychological distance traveled since the last similar scene. In Chrétien's *Yvain*, for example, the magic fountain is visited by the title character four times. Each visit stands out as a milepost in Yvain's career, offering an opportunity to measure his development since the previous visit. When Yvain first comes to the fountain, he is only acting out a scenario, imitating his cousin Calogrenant. Shortly afterward, he returns, this time to defend the woman with whom he has fallen in love. The third visit shows definite progress, for it represents the first time since his madness that Yvain has remembered his wife and his marriage responsibilities. Not until his last visit to the fountain does he show any initiative, forcing Laudine to take him back by using the fountain's marvelous powers to create a perpetual storm in her kingdom. The comparisons facilitated by the fountain thus demonstrate how Yvain's youthful boldness has been turned into mature responsibility.

Another common method of measuring the protagonist's change (especially in the nineteenth-century realist novel) is the cumulative metaphor. In Balzac's *Grandeur et décadence de César Birotteau*, the merchant's acceptance of the Cross of the Legion of Honor is treated as a veritable crucifixion. Tracing the perfumer's trajectory from ambition to apotheosis, from bankruptcy to death, this extended developmental metaphor provides a framework for the protagonist's progress, at the same time constantly suggesting the probable outcome of the affair. The cumulative nature of the metaphor has the function of further concentrating interest on the central character. When the magistrates who restore Birotteau's right to do business are likened to the angels who rolled the stone away, this figure functions less as a description of the magistrates than as commentary on Birotteau's situation. Each new extension of the figure sends us back to the central character.

In *Le Père Goriot*, Rastignac is the active component of two extended metaphors: one regarding a young man's need to acquire a carriage in order to keep from being spattered by mud; the other likening Rastignac to Telemachus in search of his famous father. The moral and physical overtones of these figures dominate the novel's imagery, focusing attention on the protagonist even when it is women who are termed "post-horses" or when Goriot and Vautrin are compared with Scylla and Charibdis. Zola's *La Faute de l'abbé Mouret* lays enormous emphasis on a developmental metaphor likening Mouret to Adam, for, like Adam, Mouret will be expelled from a paradise of fresh fruit and free love. In *L'Assommoir*, Zola makes much of the objects surrounding Gervaise. Too simple to understand or express the changes taking place in her own life, Gervaise dwells in an atmosphere charged with meaning. The gutter in the Rue de la Goutte d'Or, for example, changes color to match the laundress's fate. So sensitive does the reader become to Zola's use of Gervaise's surroundings to reflect her past and predict her future that it becomes increasingly difficult to read a description of objects, buildings, or characters without seeing it as a commentary on Gervaise's life. Wherever we turn, the created world returns us to the protagonist. How surprising to find in one of the key texts of naturalism one of the basic tenets of romanticism, for what is Zola's technique if not an extension of the pathetic fallacy, the system that reads the natural world as an expression of the character's feelings?

It is instructive to compare pathetic fallacy—along with other extended metaphors built around the protagonist's development—with epic simile. As all readers of *The Odyssey* will remember, the dawn is "rosy-fingered" and Odysseus is "much-enduring." In keeping with dual-focus tradition, each object and character is defined by a fundamental, inalterable attribute. If Aeneas is "long-suffering," it is not because of some transitory condition but because of the patient courage that constitutes his very character. Epic similes immobilize a character. Far from evoking developmental capacities, they suggest that the gods created these people and objects once and for all, in this particular way and in no other, whereas pathetic fallacy and extended metaphor offer opportunities to measure changes in the protagonist's situation.

The developmental tendency of the single-focus mode appears most clearly through altered repetition. With moral mirrors, repeated scenes, reiterated locations, or developmental metaphors, the general strategy is the same: a subsequent moment, through formal similarity and/or thematic echoes, recalls an earlier moment, the difference between the two constituting the transformation that gives single-focus narrative its reason for being and its basic meaning. By combining elements of similarity (which attract attention and induce comparison) with elements of difference (which permit the reader to discover change and thus meaning), altered repetition provides both the rhetorical and structural building blocks of single-focus narrative.

Considered from a distance, all single-focus texts look alike. A character leaves familiar shores and accepted mores out of a desire for higher values, thereby attracting the narrator's and reader's attention. Faced in the course of time with numerous choices, the protagonist creates himself or herself anew. Here and there throughout the text, echoes of past experiences recall to the reader (and often to the protagonist as well) the distance covered by the protagonist. Single-focus texts are built around retrospective moments which, by their ability to measure change, lend meaning to the text (and the life of the protagonist). Laid out along a time line, these clear representations of present, past, and the distance separating the two provide a strong framework to which the other aspects of single-focus narrative are easily attached.

If single-focus meaning is based on the difference between paired moments in the life of the protagonist, single-focus presentational strategy regularly depends on another kind of pairing. Where dual-focus narrative thrives on parallel presentation of similar events, single-focus texts systematically follow an event with its interpretation. *Pride and Prejudice*, for example, slowly works into a regular alternation between group scenes and Elizabeth's reaction to their content. Dialogue permits Austen to cover a broad range of topics apropos of a large group of characters; internal views of Elizabeth's reactions facilitate identification while providing continuity between seemingly unrelated scenes. Evaluating each conversation with Elizabeth, readers increasingly regard each new statement from her point of view, thereby broadening the range of reader experiences without compromising the sense that Elizabeth is indeed the novel's central character.

It is interesting to compare this typically nineteenth-century technique of alternation between scene and summary, narrator and character, with the technique of a similar author writing under the effect of a strong theatrical influence. Madame de Lafayette's *La Princesse de Clèves* is heavily marked by the techniques of classical theater, especially by the practices of her contemporary Jean Racine, well known for his alternation between scenes confronting major characters and scenes restricted to a single major character alone or in private discussion with a confidant(e). True to the practice of her period, which reserves dialogue for the theater and dedicates the novel to impersonal narration, Madame de Lafayette eschews direct reporting of dialogue, preferring to alternate between a public scene showing Madame de Clèves in action and a private scene entirely devoted to her heroine's evaluation of the preceding public event.

This constant alternation between event and interpretation, action and contemplation, is wholeheartedly adopted by the eighteenth-century novel, which rapidly makes the necessary accommodations to first-person narration. The memoir novel characteristically alternates between an adventure story that might as well be narrated in the third person and the protagonist's evaluation of the adventures recalled. The epistolary novel microminiaturizes this alternation, often combining in a single letter the narration of events with commentary appropriate to the recipient of the letter in question. Indeed, the "squeezing" of both event and interpretation into a single scene or sentence is an increasingly frequent occurrence in the history of single-focus narrative. Madame de Lafayette's *Zaïde* regularly constructs sentences melding the protagonist's reactions to the unknown woman of his dreams with the facts that he has been able to glean about her. Readers are constantly called on to split sentences in two, separating Consalve's objective observations from his subjective conclusions. In the following representative passage I have italicized Consalve's reactions and interpretations:

> *He was surprised* to find such symmetrical features and such a delicate face; *he stared with astonishment* at the beauty of her mouth and the whiteness of her neck; *indeed, he was so charmed* by this beautiful foreigner *that he was nearly convinced she was not a mortal.* (de Lafayette 1961b:43)

This interweaving of reporting and reaction grows along with the novel to the point where the latter half of the nineteenth century gives over much of its narrative energy to devising methods for further merging the language of events with that of interpretation. Free indirect style, as perfected by Flaubert and Zola, makes it possible to combine both concerns in the same words, thus assuring a permanent bond between event and interpretation. What the French perfected as a stylistic trait becomes for Henry James a veritable principle of narrative construction, with each bit of information filtered through the eyes and mind of an idiosyncratic protagonist.

At the root of this tradition lies a fundamental single-focus attitude toward language. In Edgar Allan Poe's short story "The Gold Bug," a parchment provides the directions for finding a buried treasure. Before becoming a treasure map, however, this parchment had first revealed only a senseless sequence of letters and a death's head. Indeed, before the cryptogram appeared, the parchment had been taken by Legrand to be no more than a dirty blank sheet. For there to be a story here, for a treasure to appear out of the ground, a very basic change has to come about in Legrand's attitude toward the parchment. At first the parchment is only an appropriate place to sketch the scarabeus that Legrand has found. So far there is no story. Only when Legrand's visitor suggests that the scarabeus looks like a death's head does Legrand begin to change his attitude toward the parchment. Once he recognizes that the dirty sheet before him is capable of signifying, Legrand becomes like an insane man, sealing himself off from the outside world and following clue after clue like Holmes on the moor. His discovery that the parchment is not just a fact of nature but conceals an authored message, a message possibly written by Captain Kidd, unlocks a new world of meaning for Legrand. Before, the parchment was taken simply to *exist*; now, it is understood to *signify*. Every mark on the parchment becomes a potential sign, every sign a potential message, every message a potential treasure. On this assumption the story hinges.

All single-focus texts operate in roughly the same fashion. Only when the *facts* of the world are clearly taken to be *artifacts* does the world open itself to single-focus meaning. In his little book on *Robinson Crusoe*, Hugh Kenner (1968) makes much of Robinson's change in attitude once he has seen a footprint on "his" island. Before this moment the shipwrecked sailor had asked no questions of the many things he found on the island. Things are just there; they are part of the landscape. Created by God, they excite no suspicion regarding their authorship. Once Robinson sees the imprint of a human foot, however, every rock, every tree, every animal becomes a potential sign of human presence. Utterly transformed, things that once were just *things*, referring only to themselves, now become *signs*, always pointing to an author and thus to potential danger. The things themselves, of course, have not changed in the process. The sea is still the sea, but now it is constantly scanned for evidence of a hostile invasion. The sand remains unchanged, but for Robinson it has now become a potential bearer of evidence that men have passed this way. Even Robinson's musket shots and cooking fires change meaning, for they now risk exposing Robinson to his potential enemies. From constant concern with survival and daily organization, the narrative turns to Robinson's preparation for a future confrontation with the savages of whom he has seen repeated evidence.

Before he saw the human footprint, Robinson took all things to be *facts*. From that point on, things become signs of authorship, or *artifacts*. Facts point only to their own existence, artifacts always imply the logical progression that led to their existence. Facts are simply there: they carry no message, they call for no interpretation. Artifacts, in contrast, can always be made to divulge a meaning, a hidden signification. But they must be interpreted in order to come to life. The quintessential single-focus attitude toward the world is an artifactual one, a sense that things are not as they seem, that meaning lies beneath the surface, that only active interpretation can reveal the truth about things. Single-focus protagonists thus make a full-time job out of the simple process of reinterpreting the world before them. In fact, it is the specificity of a personal interpretation that lends each single-focus character individuality and thus the right to regulate the narrative. Reading the artifacts is what single-focus narrative is all about. It is thus hardly surprising that two of the most important and representative single-focus genres should be built around characters whose sole concern is to read the artifacts.

"Murder mysteries," Pauline Kael is reported to have said, "are apt to end with a confession." Indeed, we might say that the confession and the detective story are part and parcel of the same artifactual text. Whether it is the detective or the criminal who tells the story, the progression and the effect are the same: once the facts are laid out, they are turned into artifacts by the one person who knows how to interpret them, and finally the true story is revealed. Thus all confessions, like all detective novels, tell the same story twice—once to lay out the facts, and a second time to lay bare their meaning. How this process works in the tale of confession is made strikingly clear by the text that lies at the root of all other confessional tales, Augustine's *Confessions*.

If many single-focus texts represent what R. W. B. Lewis calls "denitia-tion" (1978:346), the separation of the individual from a preestablished norm or group, Augustine constructs his story in the form of a double denitiation, the garden conversion of chapter eight balancing the pear stealing of chapter two. In order to place himself above God—like Adam—Augustine wantonly disregards the law by stealing pears. This departure from the straight and narrow is matched by the later garden experience that calls Augustine away from the dissolute life into which he had fallen. "Tolle, legge," a voice says—take this and read. Opening the Bible, Augustine finds a new path available to him, the path leading to his decision to record these confessions. By progressing through *perversion* to *conversion*, Augustine changes the meaning of his religion. Instead of remaining subservient to his Creator, Augustine places himself in a situation where he can now recognize his sin, thus not only glorifying God but at the same time establishing his own indi-viduality.

The confession itself constitutes the spiritual exercise called for by the conversion. Recognition of sin creates a new desire—this time for God—causing the Christian to desire purgation, a radical emptying of past failings out of the body's vessel. Like the detective novel, the confession records both the commission of the crime and its undoing, for to admit the perversion is to accomplish the conversion. Here, as throughout the single-focus tradition, meaning derives from interpretation rather than action alone. Augustine's text transmutes actions into words, just as the detective counteracts the crime by reconstructing the fable, turning action into story. Again we see the immense importance of point-of-view concerns to single-focus narrative, for the action of perversion (as its etymology implies) involves turning away from God, but the confession of perversion signifies conversion—turning back toward God. This shift moves us from the realm of fact into artifact. Words not only designate events but also point simultaneously to a motiva-tion for describing those events.

If his *Confessions* recount the story of Augustine's life, they are also the account of his attempt to come to terms with the nature of evil. Constantly seeking to explain evil differently from the archetypically dual-focus system of the Manichaeans, Augustine finally finds a solution in the perversion/conversion format underlying his confessions. The problem, succinctly stated, is this. Experience teaches us that there is evil in the world, yet the

Bible and the church tell us that God is good, so God cannot be held responsible for the existence of evil. Nevertheless, evil exists. The Manichaeans explain this situation by positing an evil principle—separate from and opposed to God—responsible for the presence of evil in the world. As a Christian, Augustine refuses this solution, because it denies God's omnipotence. Where, then, does evil come from? Augustine confects a strikingly single-focus alternative to the Manichaeans' dual-focus approach. Humans may be made in God's image, Augustine recognizes, but they are free to act according to their own desires. It is in this freedom that Augustine discovers the source of evil. Refusing the static dual-focus approach, Augustine redistributes value along a linear path, defining evil not as an essence but as a *direction*: to move away from God is evil, to come closer to God is good. Man is thus solely responsible for the presence of evil in the world, through a tendency to turn away from God. We now see the importance of Augustine's story of his own perversion, for it is only through his wicked itinerary that Augustine eventually discovers the importance of turning back toward God (thereby respecting the etymology of the term "conversion").

The Manichaean solution involves confrontation of two mutually exclusive spaces. This configuration provides no room for individual human beings, whereas Augustine makes the penitent sinner the source of both evil and good. God remains the source of all life, but evil and good appear as a function of the individual's itinerary. When humans move away from God (perversion), they create evil, but when they move back toward God (conversion), they produce good. Like the innumerable confessional texts that they inspired, Augustine's *Confessions* infuse the story of perversion with the spirit of the conversion, thus making a change in attitude rather than a change of activity responsible for transmutation of evil into good. For Augustine, all men and women begin with God, thus producing a memory of previous happiness sufficient to inspire a subsequent desire for God—and thus a reinterpretation of previous perversion.

Augustine's artifactual reading of his own past, recognizing a motley array of actions and thoughts as evidence of the sinner's search for God, is matched by the artifactual reading of the detective, who demonstrates the systematic nature of the case's givens, thus preparing the thief's confession, ready to be signed at the end of the story. In Poe's "Purloined Letter," Dupin interprets the room where the letter is hidden, making it come alive with authorship, inducing it to speak with the voice of the minister who carried off the letter. To the bumbling police inspector, the notepad by the phone reveals nothing but empty sheets. Sprinkling a substance on the pad, the detective magically produces an impression, the trace of a conversation. Prowess at artifactual reading is repeatedly emphasized by juxtaposing the detective's version with another, pedestrian, attempt. In Arthur Conan Doyle's "A Case of Identity," Holmes asks Watson for a description of the woman who has just presented her case. Though competent and accurate, Watson's description is neutral and declarative, never deductive and artifactual like the one Holmes later provides. Throughout Doyle's fiction this technique holds: Holmes's explanations always stand out in contrast to the uninspired versions that they supplant (commonly those of the client, Watson, or some police supernumerary). Poe works in a similar manner, using an uncomprehending foil for the extraordinary deductive capacities of Dupin or Legrand. In more recent private detective tales, the official police commonly play the role of inadequate interpreters.

The need for a mistaken, incomplete, or simply uninterpreted version of the story—for which the detective will provide the proper reading—regularly leads the detective novel to present two complete versions of the events surrounding the murder. Or perhaps I should say that a first version relates the events *surrounding* the murder (an array of facts, lacking order), while a second version relates the events *leading up to* the murder (a reasoned, linear, account). John Guillermin's 1978 film version of Agatha Christie's *Death on the Nile* presents two full series of images, each purporting to relate the events of the crime. The first represents an objective view of the facts but fails to connect them in a meaningful manner. When juxtaposed with Hercule Poirot's artifactual reading, however, the first version suddenly appears unenlightened rather than objective. The detective's voiceover in the second version reveals the clever deductions that lend brio and truth to his interpretation.

Like his fellow detectives, Poirot is something of an eccentric. From Dupin and Holmes to Rockford and Columbo by way of Spade and Marlowe, detectives are marked by a slightly antisocial and even vaguely suspicious nature. Indeed, if detectives are often confused with criminals, it is because their behavior is every bit as idiosyncratic as the criminals' conduct. It is this secret harmony between the detective and the criminal mind that makes it possible for detectives to complete their investigations successfully. The police regularly fail to discover the criminal because their law-and-order methods simply do not correspond with the lawless logic of the outlaw. Detectives can easily put themselves in the skin of a criminal, because they think like a murderer. According to the genre's first master detective, Poe's C. Auguste Dupin, the detective's success depends on his ability to achieve "*thorough* identification" with his opponent ("The Purloined Letter"; 1981c:463). "The analyst throws himself into the spirit of his opponent," says Poe, or he loses all chance of victory ("Murders in the Rue Morgue"; 1981b:379).

Here we see just how radically the single-focus detective tale differs from its cousin the cops-and-robbers story. Based on confrontation between two similarly organized teams, each vying for supremacy in a limited arena, the cops-and-robbers story commonly develops along familiar dual-focus lines, with regular alternation between the two groups and with a hero distinguished by righteousness rather than an ability to identify with the enemy. The dual-focus version of criminal justice has flourished in the popular media. Comic strips have devised one supercop after another, from the archetypal Dick Tracy and Superman to Batman, the Avenger, and many another protector of the law. Television as well has by and large eschewed the single-focus approach to crime detection, preferring the more physical and clearcut dual-focus approach. It takes a Peter Falk (Columbo) or a James Garner (Rockford) to make something attractive out of the single-focus detective's mental prowess, while the chases and shootouts of the dual-focus version depend far less on versatile acting. In truth, the single-focus detective story need not even have a criminal present, for the only criminal who counts is the one created by the mind of the detective as he gives order to a series of seemingly unconnected events. In a sense, the detective must always play the murderer's role as well as his own.

"I will now play Oedipus to the Rattleborough enigma," begins the narrator of Poe's "Thou Art the Man" (1981d:471)—Oedipus, the master detective, he who solved the riddle, he who protected his society from the Sphinx, simultaneously bringing shame and destruction on the community. So thorough is the detective's identification with the lawless opponent that behind every detective story there lurks the vague sense that the detective is only solving his own crimes, that the detective is so good at identifying with the criminal because he *is* that criminal. Like a good detective, Oedipus reads the evidence, following every clue until he has eventually fully composed a confession—his own. The poetic justice of the affair can be seized only when we realize that Oedipus's self-blinding echoes Adam and Eve's desire to have their eyes opened, to see with the eyes of a god. The two great single-focus myths thus complete each other, for Oedipus the detective always wants to know too much, always seeks to know that which it is unhealthy to know. This is why the detective is never a normal member of the regular police—from Dupin to Holmes, from Spade to Serpico, the detective always represents pride, the desire to know more, to surpass normal human (i.e., police) force. The detective's overweening pride (he is always sure of his ability to surpass the police) must therefore be punished. Oedipus paid for his own pride and desire; more recent detectives simply transfer the confession to the captured criminal, the detective and the criminal being the only characters to believe the same version of the crime.

Tales told twice—such is the content of single-focus texts. The official version of the facts is rewritten by the detective. The adventure version of the story is reinterpreted as sin by the confessor. The Bildungsroman hero is forever looking back and recalling the past as the present rewrites that past through a series of altered repetitions. Ironic nineteenth-century novels pair the protagonist's limited view with the insights of an infinitely more perceptive narrator. The mechanisms driving this system are nowhere more visible than in the psychological novel. As Jean Rousset has pointed out, de Lafayette's Princesse de Clèves forever alternates between action and contemplation, between a scene in society and a private scene involving self-analysis (1964:21). Under the influence of imitators like Richardson, this rhythm provided a prototype for centuries of psychological novels. Building a new model for literary characters around public/private and outer/inner dichotomies, de Lafayette at the same time consecrates a new method of reiterating the same story. When Madame de Clèves falls in love with the Duc de Nemours, her public conduct changes radically, so much so that her solitary moments are consistently devoted to analysis of her public actions. After each new encounter, Madame de Clèves scurries back to her apartment—to her mind—to consider the meaning of her actions. The mechanism underlying the system may best be understood in the following manner:

1. Madame de Clèves *encodes* her love in public activities.
2. In private, she *decodes* her public actions as signs of her love.

Before she has heard her mother's stories of court intrigue, before she has herself fallen in love, Madame de Clèves takes every event at face value. After her fall, however, she sees every action (including her own) as an artifact, a sign to be interpreted, a mark of her own motivations. Like Adam, whose fall turned a world where bodies and meanings are never veiled into a new world of signs and sham, Madame de Clèves remains haunted by the fear that others will discover what she has found in the mirror of her own actions. Of course, her worry comes too late, for the reader—that arch-decoder—has long read her actions and discovered her secrets.

Besides its evident connections to the artifactual reading strategy of the confessional tale and the detective story, the encoding/decoding process recalls the narcissistic, oedipal context of single-focus narrative as a whole. Consider Elizabeth, upon receiving Darcy's self-justifying letter at the midpoint of *Pride and Prejudice*. Her reactions lead to a total reevaluation of the events of the first half of the novel. In the space of a couple of pages we review Wickham's claims, Jane's enamourment, and Bingley's departure, not to mention Elizabeth's condemnation of Darcy, whom she now finds fully justified. Yet the emphasis is not on the apparent change in Darcy, the object of her musings, but on the clear change that she senses in herself, as subject of her evaluations. After a period of careful comparison of her current opinions to her past conclusions, Elizabeth returns to her own situation and to the psychological state that led to her conclusions. Darcy and Wickham become mirrors for her own position, markers of her own faults:

She grew absolutely ashamed of herself.—Of neither Darcy nor Wickham could she think, without feeling that she had been blind, partial, prejudiced, absurd.

"How despicably have I acted!" she cried.—"I, who have prided myself on my discernment!—I, who have valued myself on my abilities! who have often disdained the generous candour of my sister, and gratified my vanity, in useless or blameable distrust.—How humiliating is this discovery!—Yet, how just a humiliation!—Had I been in love, I could not have been more wretchedly blind.

But vanity, not love, has been my folly.—Pleased with the preference of one, and offended by the neglect of the other, on the very beginning of our acquaintance, I have courted prepossession and ignorance, and driven reason away, where either were concerned. Till this moment, I never knew myself." (Austen 1966:143–44)

Like Madame de Clèves, Elizabeth is constantly brought back to herself by consideration of others. The secondary characters of single-focus narrative—model, tempter, teacher—mirror and reveal the central character. With *Pride and Prejudice*, we discover that any event, however unrelated to the protagonist it may seem, can be made to bring the heroine back to herself.

The characteristic single-focus method of producing meaning involves paired segments related by altered repetition and located along a linear, chronological sequence. Single-focus authors are thus confronted by the ever-present danger that significant connections between events will be masked by the considerable temporal and textual distance separating them. Many single-focus texts therefore deploy techniques specifically designed to bring together in textual space events that are quite distant in terms of diegetic time. In the confessional tale the (sinful) past and (penitent) present are perpetually juxtaposed through a judicious combination of action and narration. Stories of past events are thus separated from current reactions by no more than a few words. The detective novel similarly intertwines the crime story (featuring the criminal as actor) with the solution story (starring the detective as narrator). Psychological novels use a remembered past and projected future to maintain a double temporal framework. Secondary characters figure a hypothetical future, investing the present with future possibilities, just as the past constantly wells up within the present, giving it depth and meaning. More than just a chronological, linear tale, marked by temporally separated altered repetitions, single-focus narrative also labors mightily to invest single moments with the depth of multiple time frames.

Modes of Identification

Within the single-focus tradition the process of reading occupies a position of special importance. Detectives read the world for clues, penitent

Christians read their own past for signs of sin, young ladies in love read their behavior in order to discover the state of their affections. Dual-focus narrative makes of the book—and by extension the world—a sacred object, open for all to see, from generation to generation the same, but the single-focus system predicates the protagonist's individuality on prowess at reading the world. From a public activity where the god-given, factual nature of the world is taken for granted, reading becomes a private process where every phenomenon, taken as artifact, can be made to divulge the conditions and motivation of its creation. But what of the reader of single-focus texts? How is this external reader positioned with respect to the reading process within the text?

The role of storytelling within single-focus narrative provides a convenient introduction to the process of single-focus reading. Consider the typical medieval narrative image sequence recounting the life of a saint. Common for centuries, these sequences are found on reliquaries and many other sacred objects. Typically, all but one of the scenes relate the saint's life and miracles. The final scene, however, differs significantly, for it reveals not the saint's life as such but a text—in the form of relics, a shrine, or a pictorial sequence—made from and recalling that life. This pattern holds sway throughout the single-focus tradition: a series of events leads, in a final moment, to their sedimentation as text, a recollection of the actions and thoughts of the protagonist, and thus a monument consecrating and recalling the protagonist's individuality. What the saint's life accomplishes with a relic and an admiring public converted by the saint's example, the romance handles through an account of adventure offered to the court or the knights gathered around the Round Table. When Chrétien's Erec (*Érec et Énide*) returns, victorious, from the Joie de la Cour adventure, he celebrates his victory over uxoriousness by telling his tale, thus reorienting the court around his own story. Instead of deriving his renown from the Round Table, Erec reverses the relationship, now covering Arthur's court with the glory represented by the account of his own success. The final moment in a complete adventure is not, as Joseph Campbell (1956) would have it, the return of the triumphant hero but the telling of his story. For the successful completion of an adventure confers on the protagonist the right to authorship.

Even with the least Promethean of protagonists, the ability to generate a story marks elevation to a higher sphere. When the blind man's beggar boy

Lazarillo finally reaches the stage where he is able to compose a preface filled with literary references, when he can recount with humor the various stages of his eventful life, it is quite clear that he has reached a new plateau, that of the lettered man. In a period marked by the popularity of story collections, it is only with texts like *Lazarillo de Tormes*, where included stories or first-person accounts become specifically tied to the destiny of the protagonist, that the novel (and with it single-focus narration) firmly takes hold. As long as included stories are not clearly justified as narrated by characters who have won the right to recount their own stories, then we remain in the late Renaissance "country inn" subgenre, no doubt an important ancestor of the novel, but still too diffuse and unintegrated to take full advantage of the single-focus system. Numerous early texts bend the included story to single-focus ends. In Madame de Lafayette's *Zaïde*, for example, the protagonist Consalve spends a major portion of the novel soliciting stories regarding the origins of his beloved Zaïde and the man pictured in the portrait she reveres, only to find out in the final story that the man pictured is himself. As the circle is completed, we discover that Consalve has for two hundred pages been in search of himself and that his search has resulted in this surprisingly modern novel, published in 1670. Throughout the eighteenth century, preference for first-person narration—as memoirs, diaries, or letters—simplifies the process of tying the story's narration to its narrated material. The need to justify narration of one's memoirs becomes a major thematic motif, generating preface after preface dedicated to the single-focus practice of transmuting character into author.

With the nineteenth century, Promethean longings are transferred to the personality or profession of the protagonist. For many a Romantic hero or heroine, the ultimate consecration is to turn their thoughts or feelings into stories. The realist novel offers characters whose inquisitive nature makes them capable, like Rastignac, of collecting the material necessary for elaborating a story—a race of characters that evolves quite naturally into the detective. Flaubert inaugurates a new period in the development of single-focus storytelling. With characters diminishing in intelligence as the century wears on, producing lower lights like Emma Bovary and Gervaise Macquart, the probability of Romantic overreaching lessens accordingly, yet Emma and Gervaise hardly lack ambition to create their own stories. In this context, free indirect style proves astonishingly effective, allowing Flaubert and Zola to assign much of the narration to their heroines, without abandoning realistic presentation. The point-of-view experiments often identified with Henry James (but in fact far more widely practiced) represent the zenith of the single-focus tendency to transfer narrational duties to the character who has merited the position of protagonist.

Corresponding with the single-focus protagonist's tendency to become a teller of tales is the frequency with which single-focus protagonists derive individuality from their interpretation of others' stories. Perhaps the simplest version of this procedure is the initial tale inspiring the young protagonist to enter the world in a particular way. Brendan yearns to experience the marvels recounted by Barinthus; Yvain dreams of holding the court's attention as Calogrenant does while telling his story; Henry Fleming longs to imitate the heroism reported by his local newspaper. Often, the protagonist gains inspiration from another text: the Bible in Augustine's *Confessions* and many a lesser pious text; chivalric romances in *Don Quixote*; or even the protagonist's own writings, as in Gide's *La Symphonie pastorale*.

Symbolic of all such attempts, in terms of method as well as content, is Poe's landmark story, "The Gold Bug," where a cryptogram is made to divulge a tale of buried treasure. So it is throughout the single-focus tradition: apparently unrelated facts are transformed by the protagonist into a map of hidden treasure—the protagonist's personality. In the wake of Poe's stories of mystery and intrigue come not only a spate of cryptogram stories but also the entire genre of detective fiction, devoted from the start to glorifying the process of reading: reading secret documents, reading faces, reading evidence, reading the world. Methodologically speaking, we find surprising models for the reading process championed by the detective novel: on the one hand, the self-analysis of the psychological novel (Madame de Clèves or Elizabeth Bennet analyzing their own actions in order to discover the state of their emotions); on the other, the careful letter-reading that characterizes epistolary novels from Gabriel de Guilleragues's *Les Lettres portugaises* to Choderlos de Laclos's *Les Liaisons dangereuses*.

The type of reading that characterizes single-focus internal readers offers important clues about the role reserved for external readers. The Gospels provide a particularly apt example. Among the teachings of Jesus, none is more pervasive and characteristic than his insistence on individual participation in the process of deciding what is right. Eschewing the Old Testament tendency to promulgate a large number of very specific laws, Jesus speaks instead in parables, microminiaturized stories that imply rather than state, always leaving to the reader the freedom and responsibility for interpretation. Defining his followers from the start as readers and interpreters (a process furthered by reformers throughout the history of the church), Jesus constantly insists on the reader's participatory status. More than simply absorbing the text, the reader must attempt to understand it, must come to decisions regarding it, must comment on it. In short, as Matthew 15:10 clearly states, "not what goes into the mouth defiles a man, but what comes out of the mouth." Dietary laws and other legal restrictions must be replaced by personal convictions. This new system is reinforced by Jesus' insistence on the importance of virtues and sins that remain invisible to the casual observer, for they are not to be found in tangible actions.

In response to the Old Testament's restrictive Commandments, Jesus offers the Beatitudes, stressing qualities of the spirit rather than prohibitions of the flesh. Where the Old Testament prohibits murder, Jesus warns against anger (Matthew 5:21–22). Where the seventh Commandment outlaws the act of adultery, Jesus stresses the mental state of lust (Matthew 5:27–28). His systematic reinterpretation of Jewish law lays enormous weight on intent, on emotion, on spiritual concerns—in short, on aspects of life that are hidden from the outsider. No longer justified by adherence to a fixed set of legal codes, individuals must be judged according to their inner lives. No one, not even we ourselves, can judge our value on the basis of externals. In coming to terms with our own actions and thoughts, we thus remain as much outsiders to ourselves as we do to others. Only by reading and interpreting our actions and thoughts can we discover our true intentions, our true values. A new myth of personality is thus born. The model of personal organization fostered by Jesus and his teachings includes an observer as well as an actor—someone to judge actions and thoughts as well as someone to perpetrate them.

The system popularized by Christianity pervades single-focus narrative. Stressing internal states, this system constantly asks individuals to discern, among the data collected by their senses, patterns implying a particular kind of meaning. Whereas the dual-focus *Ephesian Tale* (Xenophon) simply states that Habrocomes loves Anthia, Madame de Clèves must repeatedly analyze in private her previous public behavior in order to find out what she thinks and feels. *The Scarlet Letter* constitutes, from beginning to end, an elegant demonstration of the inadequacy of public judgment to the question of personal destiny. Gide's novelette trilogy—*L'Immoraliste, La Porte étroite, La Symphonie pastorale*—repeatedly demonstrates the difficulties of knowing a human being, even when that being is oneself. The process of analysis is necessary, for without it the narrative cannot reach the level at which the single-focus system locates knowledge and value.

A special weight is thus put on the process of reading, for internal and external readers alike. Single-focus reading is not a direct mode of knowledge, where one individual absorbs another's truths, but a creative process wherein raw words and brute facts are transformed into meaningful patterns or justified evaluations. Patterns and values are not located on the same level as facts and words, so the reader's intervention is needed to assure passage from one level to another. Each evaluation, each interpretation, is thus invested with a particular reader's personality. Every time we read and interpret we are constituting ourselves. Augustine discovers and expresses his religion by reading his own past. The personalities of Marivaux's Marianne and Samuel Richardson's Pamela and Clarissa are created by and through their interpretation of the society around them. Gervaise Macquart is indistinguishable from her (mis)understanding of those whom she daily encounters. As single-focus readers, we are constantly thrust into a position where we cannot avoid expressing—indeed, creating—our personality through the conclusions we reach about the text's raw words and brute facts. Regularly faced with ambiguous characters and unreliable narrators, as well as undefined mixes of character and narrator responsibility for specific remarks, single-focus readers find themselves unable to read in the transparent manner appropriate to the dual-focus text. We have to work at making the facts speak, even if, like Doyle's Watson, we are ultimately embarrassed by our paltry results. The text calls us to read, offers examples of how to read, then frees us to invest our reading with our own particular personalities.

Single-focus texts belong to protagonists who remain on the margins of accepted practice or law. By stepping beyond traditional limits, single-focus protagonists attain the exceptional status that makes them fit objects of interest for author, narrator, and reader alike. The tenth chapter of Bede's *Life of Saint Cuthbert* provides an elegant demonstration of the mind-set necessary for collecting tales of the exceptional. While visiting Coldingham, Cuthbert leaves his bed in the dead of night. Now this is not common behavior, so it arouses the curiosity of one of the young monks, who follows Cuthbert down to the sea. There he witnesses a quite unexpected scene: after standing for hours in the deep water, praying constantly, Cuthbert is dried off and warmed up by otters. The young monk, expecting something of a more scurrilous nature, confesses his presumption and promises not to reveal the purpose of the saint's nightly vigils. Eventually, however, he must have told his story, for otherwise it would not have reached Bede, whose avidity for exceptional events has made it possible to compile an account of Cuthbert's life.

This simple tale presents a powerful figure for the composition and reading of single-focus narrative. Many other events no doubt took place on that same night in Coldingham, but we hear of none of those, for none was sufficiently abnormal to warrant narration. Cuthbert's actions, on the other hand, are in every way unusual and thus arouse the eventual narrator's curiosity, without which Cuthbert's affair with the otters would never have been known. The paradox in this tale lies in the fact that the young monk, curious about Cuthbert's exceptional actions, himself acts in an extraordinary way by leaving his bed in the middle of the night. If Cuthbert is the paradigmatic single-focus protagonist, distancing himself from the identity of his group, the young monk is the paradigmatic single-focus reader, transformed into a voyeur through pure curiosity. The saint's activities are *mira*-culous, the romance knight's adventures are *spec*-tacular. All single-focus protagonists owe their very existence to the fact that their actions deserve to be seen, that their stories deserve to be told. Exhibitionist and voyeur, the protagonist and reader thus form an interdependent couple, locked together by one's need to be seen, the other's desire to see.

Already in classical times we find this protagonist/reader symbiosis projected into the text as a theme or plot device. When young Telemachus sets out in search of his famous father, he is regaled at every stop by a story of his father's prowess. The son's task is to seek, so the father must be worthy of being sought—and thus a fit subject for tales of adventure. If *The Odyssey* prefigures the numerous texts where relatively passive protagonists serve as repositories of knowledge, as the convenient ear justifying a tale (especially from the late Renaissance to the eighteenth century), Lucius Apuleius's *Metamorphoses or the Golden Ass* provides the paradigm for the many single-focus texts built around the prying eyes of an actively curious narrator.

Anxious to witness the marvels of Thessaly, preternaturally curious about the practice of witchcraft, Apuleius's hero, Lucius, suddenly finds himself transformed into an ass—and thus able to observe in secret the enchantments of the provinces where he takes us. Centuries later, the nascent novel multiplies experiments with strange and wonderful narrators endowed with privileged or unusual vision. Jonathan Swift's *Gulliver's Travels* and Voltaire's "Micromégas" employ this technique to philosophical and political ends, while Lesage's *Le Diable boîteux* (where Asmodeus's X-ray vision permits him to see through house tops) and Claude de Crébillon's *Le Sopha* (which relates the memoirs of a sofa) prefer to titillate. Others use similar techniques to support fantastic tales or frankly pornographic accounts.

As Victor Shklovsky (1973) has shown in the case of Don Quixote—a button-brained eccentric born out of the necessity to fit material from many different traditions and genres into a single story—formal concerns often play an important role in generating specific character types. So it is with the tendency to turn single-focus protagonists into voyeurs, eavesdroppers, or detectives, for the dependence of single-focus narrative on a single pair of eyes would be severely limiting were those eyes not accorded special powers. Examples of this process include characters like Marivaux's Jacob or Balzac's Rastignac, who listen at doors, increasing the amount of information available through the central character. From *Lazarillo de Tormes* to Louis-Ferdinand Céline's *Journey to the End of the Night*, the picaresque novel engages our interest by the quality and variety of the protagonist's perception. The travel motif equips another set of characters with the oversized eyes and ears characteristic of single-focus narrative. Medieval texts like *The Voyage of Brendan* already follow this pattern, but it is with the age of discovery that the voyage motif comes into its own. Seventeenth-century nonfiction travel accounts soon give rise to eighteenth-century philosophical treatises like Montesquieu's *Lettres persanes* or nineteenth-century tales of Romantic exile like Chateaubriand's *René* and *Atala*.

The nineteenth-century novel as a whole devotes extraordinary technical energy to reconciling realistic limitations on vision with the need to carry desire into ever more forbidden arenas. Realist novels often combine protagonist mobility (providing access to unusual scenes) with protagonist insensitivity (stressing narrative irony, the reader recognizing the protagonist's limitations). The French novel in particular is rife with examples of this type of personage (Julien Sorel, Emma Bovary, Gervaise Macquart). With Henry James the attraction of the limited point of view reaches its height, in the international psychological fashion of *The Portrait of a Lady*, the spine-chilling suspense of *The Turn of the Screw*, or the morbid naïveté of *What Maisie Knew*. Modern diary novels carry this process a step farther, featuring lonely, unhappy protagonists who, incapable of contact with others, become the object of their own gaze (Bonaventura's *Die Nachtwachen des Bonaventura*, Kierkegaard's *The Diary of a Seducer*, Sartre's *La Nausée*, Dostoevsky's *Notes from the Underground*, Hesse's *Steppenwolf,* Svevo's *La Coscienza di Zeno*).

Perhaps more striking still is single-focus narrative's capacity to derive energy from revisionist versions of history. Starting with Wace's twelfth-century *Roman de Brut*, the ferment that gave rise to medieval romance developed out of renewed attempts to discover the unknown byways of European history. The rise of the novel in seventeenth-century France owes a still more overt debt to historical voyeurism, for the *histoire secrète* and the *nouvelle historique* are overtly constructed as behind-the-scenes versions of what really happened in history, often concentrating on the amorous motivations of kings and queens reputed to have made decisions for reasons of state alone. The English and French memoir tradition similarly provides privileged information about well-known historical figures. A century later, under the influence of Walter Scott, the novel once again found new inspiration in historical subjects, thanks to protagonists' ability to reveal details to which academic or traditional history had failed to provide access. From Scott's *Waverly* to Prosper Mérimée's *Chronique du règne de Charles IX* and Alfred de Vigny's *Cinq-Mars*, the typical protagonist of a nineteenth-century historical novel is a young man with acute vision.

Curiosity is thus a fundamental component of single-focus syntax, on the part of the protagonist as well as that of the reader. Yet, as we all know, curiosity killed the cat. The dangers of curiosity have been regularly chronicled by writers of fiction and protectors of moral order. With Lucius's transformation into an ass standing as a fit symbol, the price of man's curious nature has been posted by texts as diverse as the various versions of the Pandora's Box myth, the "Curioso impertinente" novella embedded in *Don Quixote*, and nineteenth-century fascination with scientific overreaching. The most celebrated critique of curiosity is contained in a letter from Saint Bernard of Clairvaux to William of Thierry, at the outset of the twelfth century, the first important period of widespread adoption of single-focus norms. Railing against the Benedictine art of his time, Bernard is careful to specify that his attack on *curiositas* does not cover all religious art, nor even all representational art, for where the categories and values of Christian doctrine are respected, church decoration is fully in accord with the church's mission. What he does fear are carvings that divert attention from Christian symbolism, stressing instead pagan, secular, or purely aesthetic aspects. Bernard is well aware that innate human curiosity gravitates to unusual, unreligious details that fascinate precisely because they escape from the restrictions of doctrine. As Bernard sees it, Christian art requires a studied effort to avoid appealing to people as accidents of nature, to constitute them fully as defined by their Christian categories:

> Beautiful pictures, varied sculptures, both adorned with gold, beautiful and precious cloths, beautiful weavings of varied colour, beautiful and precious windows, sapphire glass, gold-embroidered copes and chasubles, golden and jewelled chalices, gold letters in books: all these are not required for practical needs, but for the concupiscence of the eyes. (Schapiro 1977:7)

For Bernard, the problem lies not with overtly secular arts and texts, but with beautiful objects that pander to human curiosity in the name of the church.

A similar problem presides over early development of the novel. Vilified for its lack of a classical model, the novel at first justified its existence as a moral guide. Preface after preface during the novel's formative period claims an intent to delight and instruct simultaneously. Consider the following frontispiece from one of the myriad crime story pamphlets that influenced the joint rise of the novel and single-focus narration in Elizabethan England:

> Sundrye strange and inhumaine Murthers, lately committed. The first of a Father that hired a man to kill three of his children. . . . Wherein is described the odiousnesse of murther, with the vengeance which God inflicteth on murtherers (Marshburn and Velie 1973: frontispiece)

Along with assurance of crimes strange and inhumane—a juicy topic indeed—we are promised a moral tale specifically identifying and castigating the sins of the protagonist. Moralizing not only eases a potentially objectionable text past the societal (and personal) censor, it actually advertises the immorality that lures the curious single-focus reader. Books "banned in Boston" sell best. The pamphlet, ballad, and early novel build such censorship into their own structure by announcing from the outset that they will present immoral actions.

The overtly immoral content of early novels corresponds to a convenient change in their physical size and social deployment. During the first half of the seventeenth century in France, the dual-focus pastorals of a d'Urfé or Scudéry, meant to be read to a group, were printed in large quarto or octavo volumes (8 inches by 10 inches or larger). When these multiple-volume behemoths gave way during the latter half of the century to the single-focus texts of Du Plaisir, Saint-Réal, and de Lafayette, the new stories were systematically produced in a pocket-sized duodecimo or 16mo format (4 inches by 6 inches or smaller). For the reader of these novels, now alone in her room, each short novel provides both moral teaching and temptation—in short, a new opportunity to follow her curiosity into the unknown.

The structure of single-focus narratives is predicated on continuation of the curiosity that first brought the reader to the text. Fostered largely through hypothetical visions of the future—hopes, dreams, fears, and other aspects of the narrative level that Roland Barthes (1970) has dubbed the "hermeneutic" code—the single-focus reader's dedication to reading always depends on curiosity about a veiled future. The uncertain future of romance or adventure novels typically involves the outcome of a physical combat. We continue to read psychological or philosophical novels in order to know what decisions will be made. The detective novel engages our interest by the promise of a solution for the crime. This investment in the future goes a long way toward explaining why the end looms so large in single-focus texts and why so much of what precedes is specifically end-oriented. In the dual-focus system, where the end is by and large known from the start, the process of reading takes on the character of ritual repetition, with each segment of the text recapitulating the whole, and each dual-focus text recalling familiar legal, moral, and economic codes. Single-focus readers, quite to the contrary, are forever projected forward toward an unknown or, rather, toward one more in a long series of unknowns, this one made to seem most important of all by the rhetoric of the text's hermeneutic code.

The effect of continued investment of curiosity regarding the destiny of the protagonist is to bind the reader irreversibly to that destiny. While we must view the protagonist from without, we nevertheless imaginatively adopt the protagonist's position when evaluating story data. When we learn of the machinations surrounding Balzac's César Birotteau, we automatically evaluate them from his vantage point, even though we are privy to far more information than poor César. Each action, each thought, each deed projects us into a hypothetical future regarding the Parisian merchant's chances of receiving the Legion of Honor and paying back his debts. However distant we remain from César, however severely we judge his actions, however ironically we view his hopes and fears, our interest in the protagonist's future nevertheless binds us to him. No wonder, for the reader's decision to continue reading always constitutes an investment of desire. Once that desire has been fixed on the protagonist, the protagonist becomes an extension of the reader's own self, an indirect method of self-expression, a figure for the reader's own identity. Like the single-focus protagonist, the single-focus reader enters into a speculation with each new investment. Never knowing ahead of time what kind of return to expect, the reader nevertheless expects that narrative contracts will be kept and that interest will be maintained.

On one side, then, are the traditional techniques of the hermeneutic code, enjoining us to care about and thus identify with the hero(ine)'s destiny: consistent following of the protagonist, subordination of all information to the protagonist's trajectory, positing of a problem intimately tied to the protagonist, hypothesis of numerous potential solutions to this central problem, alternation between endangerment and safety of the protagonist. These familiar techniques, often accompanied by the creation of a particularly engaging central character, infallibly lure the reader into sharing the protagonist's vision—that is, looking *with* the protagonist rather than simply looking *at* the protagonist, measuring the world against the protagonist's desires instead of just measuring the protagonist against the world. With this identification comes a tendency to redefine every aspect of the plot in terms of its effect on the protagonist, along with a penchant to believe the protagonist, a willingness to take the protagonist as the text's ultimate author.

At the same time, however, an entirely different set of indicators suggests a radically divergent type of identification on the reader's part. Forever involved in a value speculation, the central character must go to great lengths to achieve success. Thus constantly given to exaggeration, to stretching the truth, to flights of rhetorical fancy, and even to outright lies ("fabulation," we might say—it is not for nothing that single-focus protagonists insist on personally assuring the narrational function), single-focus protagonists are inferior informants who repay our confidence poorly indeed. While the characteristic techniques of the hermeneutic code induce reader identification with the protagonist, the protagonist's own behavior often belies the reader's confidence. Like Machiavelli's Prince, single-focus protagonists require allegiance, not love; support rather than sympathy. In first-person narration, as critics since Wayne Booth (1961) have carefully documented, rare is the narrator who fully deserves the reader's confidence. Where sins of commission are avoided, there remain the clever omissions exemplified by Marivaux's Jacob, whose bland account of success in society steers clear of aspects that might be seen as compromising. Third-person narration might seem to protect the protagonist against such accusations, the narrator taking responsibility for the narration, but this assumption neglects the tendency of single-focus narrative to attribute major narrational responsibility to the protagonist, even in stories where the focal character does not do the telling.

Pride and Prejudice offers an especially clear example of the characteristically contradictory identification signals emitted by single-focus texts. Organized around Elizabeth Bennet's growth into a mature woman capable of understanding her own mistakes and thus the particularity of her own character, *Pride and Prejudice* alternately relates Elizabeth's decisions and her modifications of those decisions. On no single character in the novel do her opinions remain unchanged throughout. We readers are consequently obliged to do some fancy footwork in order to maintain comfortable identification with Elizabeth. As much as her first decision to spurn a would-be husband fosters increased identification with Elizabeth (for Collins's inflated sense of self-satisfaction clearly renders him unacceptable for such a sensitive and humble woman), her refusals of Wickham and Darcy, on contradictory grounds, increase our doubts about her ability to evaluate situations correctly. Eventually, Elizabeth's soul-searching in response to Darcy's long letter sets her onto a more reasonable course, dissolving the contradiction between our identification and our suspicion of her decisions. In the meantime, the novel has gained its life and assured its readership by the long middle section, during which Elizabeth retains our sympathy and remains the object of our identification, all the while giving us reason to doubt her conclusions and thus her right to occupy the narrational role.

Novel after single-focus novel simultaneously fosters two, seemingly contradictory, modes of participation: identification and suspicion, the latter often appearing through narratorial irony. Consider Stendhal's *Le Rouge et le noir* and its engaging hero, Julien Sorel. Few novels provide more motivation for identification. Yet seldom, as Victor Brombert has demonstrated (1954), does a narrator have more fun at the expense of a character. As much as identification is essential to appreciating the novel, suspicion and irony are needed to understand its complexity. Who can fail to appreciate the youthful idealism of Werther, Wilhelm Meister, Waverly, or Frédéric Moreau? Yet who would take their conclusions, pronouncements, and dreams at face value? The genius of single-focus narrative is to assure constant oscillation between identification and suspicion, irony, or judgment. Readers alternate between a participatory present, sharing the protagonist's position, and a retrospective stance permitting recognition of the central character's foibles. Each single-focus reader's individuality derives from a particular fashion of negotiating this double identification and the dialectic it engenders.

This dialectic is heavily conditioned by the factual/artifactual opposition. If dual-focus characters commonly take the world and language as givens, never suspecting them of masking the truth, of producing rhetorical effects, single-focus characters develop their full complexity only when they begin to interrogate the world for concealed messages. Dual-focus characters recognize symbolic effects, but only single-focus characters regularly question the fundamental transparency of words and things, thereby generating a problem of significant proportions for single-focus readers. When a character produces an interpretation of the facts set forth in the text, are we to read this reading factually or artifactually? We have every reason to take the interpretation at face value: we have followed the protagonist from belief to suspicion; we have participated in the process whereby a deeper truth was made to emerge from a series of seemingly superficial givens; and we have been convinced by the protagonist's newfound sincerity, self-knowledge, or acumen. At first, Elizabeth believes Wickham's account of his past, blindly condemning Darcy and remaining in the factual mode of reading characteristic of dual-focus narrative, where words offer a transparent view of the truth. Yet Elizabeth soon reconsiders her hasty conclusions. With Darcy's letter in hand, she analyzes anew the facts of the case, this time measuring motives as she goes. A new conclusion emerges: indirect evidence is more useful in reckoning the truth than the self-serving pronouncements of the perfidious Wickham. The reader, at this point, would be hard put to disagree with Elizabeth's conclusions.

Yet there remains something incongruous about the reader's *factual* reading of Elizabeth's *artifactual* conclusions. Out of this incongruity a second reading is generated, based on identification with Elizabeth's method, not her conclusions. Taking appropriate distance from this marriageable young woman, we suspect that multiple motivations may underlie her change of heart. When at first she refused Wickham and Collins and vilified Darcy, no one around her had yet been married—is her change of heart unrelated to the example of her friends and sisters? When she first concluded that Darcy was unworthy, she had not yet seen his country manor—does the splendor of Pemberley have no effect on the provincial lass? When she first condemned Darcy, she had neither been courted by him nor had she a rival for his hand—does competition from Lady Catherine de Bourgh and her daughter not influence the proud Elizabeth? Once we engage an artifactual reading of Elizabeth's behavior, of her own artifactual reading process, a vast arena for interpretation opens up, revealing a multiplicity of possible Elizabeths. When her reading of Darcy's letter causes her to exclaim, "Had I been in love, I could not have been more wretchedly blind. But vanity, not love, has been my folly" (Austen 1966:144), we are rightly suspicious of a conclusion that conceals as many of Elizabeth's emotions as it reveals. Suddenly Elizabeth becomes a character of far more potential depth, a complex individual with whom we can readily identify but whom we would as lief interrogate and interpret.

What I have called "identification" involves factual acceptance of the protagonist's artifactual reading activity. What I have termed "suspicion" depends on adoption of an artifactual reading process with regard to the protagonist. The characteristic single-focus dialectic of identification derives from a structured alternation between these two positions. To be sure, not all single-focus texts present the same opportunities for this dialectic.

Some tales create such complete sympathy for the protagonist that only the most cantankerous reader could expect anything but total sincerity and accuracy. Others provide reading matter for young people (like the biographies of famous men and women that occupied my youth) but take limited advantage of the complexities implicit in the single-focus form. By negating the potential insufficiencies of the protagonist, they deprive us of a major component of single-focus reading pleasure. Many modern novels present ample justification for reader suspicion but give readers little cause for the identification without which the suspicion rings hollow (e.g., the line of novels inaugurated by Dostoevsky's *Notes from the Underground* and perpetuated by Hesse's *Steppenwolf,* Albert Camus's *The Fall,* and Svevo's *La Coscienza di Zeno*).

The most successful single-focus texts, the ones that are reread for generations, simultaneously inspire confidence and suspicion, identification and distance. Perhaps this is why medieval romances have retained their popularity over the centuries while saints' lives have led only a cloistered existence. Who can doubt a saint? For that matter, who can fully identify with one? What intrigues us about Tristan, Lancelot, and Gawain is the complex nature of their motivation. Opened up to multiple interpretations, their motives play a role in the reader's own establishment of individuality.

Consider the development of the detective novel since Poe and Doyle. Though C. Auguste Dupin and Sherlock Holmes are solitary, impenetrable figures, nothing in their comportment permits us to suspect their motives in solving crimes. Whenever Hammett's Sam Spade or Mickey Spillane's Mike Hammer works a case, however, we get the uneasy feeling that his crime-solving activities are motivated by some dark secret in his own background, that he solves crimes more out of a personal grudge than a sense of justice. Spade and Hammer are fascinating because of the suspicion they instill—at the very moment they are drawing us in to greater identification. The more the process of crime solution is overdetermined, motivated out of personal and legal commitments, the more the reader enters into the full single-focus identification dialectic.

The process by which single-focus readers adopt artifactual reading methods elucidates the difference between reader positioning in dual-focus and single-focus texts. In dual-focus narrative, the notion of interchangeability, of potential substitution, reigns over the text. If a commander dies on the field of battle, another individual may be—must be—substituted. Charlemagne, Roland, and a simple foot-soldier differ only in degree, not in kind, for all belong to the category out of which *The Song of Roland* is generated: Christianity. All who share the same focus are potentially interchangeable, while all who are on opposite sides of the text's paradigmatic bar are utterly unsubstitutable (the impossibility of substituting pagans for Christians or men for women providing the underlying logic of texts like *The Song of Roland* and *Daphnis and Chloe*). The process of substitution rapidly overflows the text itself, encompassing wider and wider audiences, eventually including readers and listeners in the circle of potential substitutions. The typical dual-focus relationship to the text's characters is thus a metaphorical one, with readers experiencing the text from the position of those characters for whom they are substitutable.

In single-focus texts, to the contrary, readers spy on protagonists while they are spying on someone else, judge protagonists while they are judging someone else, "read" protagonists while they too are engaged in reading. In other words, while dual-focus reading coincides with the character's experience, single-focus readers are attached to the text as one more in a series (e.g., as a current Christian in the line of Jesus-Anthony-Hilarion-Benedict-Gregory . . . , each imitating the previous link in an unbroken chain of metonymic relationships stretching all the way to today). Instead of reliving adventures, fitting into a prescribed mold and fully identifying with the hero, as in the dual-focus scheme, single-focus readers experience protagonists as models to be interpreted, as sources of our own individuality. In the text, the protagonist's role is to view the surrounding world, but in the reading process, the protagonist shifts roles to become the object viewed and evaluated by the reader. This process, which lies at the heart of single-focus reading practices, may be called the "metonymic shift," for it involves a shift in identification that occurs according to the sliding, contiguous pattern commonly identified with metonymy.

The history of Western drama, as chronicled by Karl Young (1933), provides a particularly significant example of the metonymic shift. In the chancel drama generally taken by historians as the simplest (and by extension—though the conclusion does not necessarily follow—the earliest) medieval ancestor of modern theater, the three Marys come to the tomb in search of the crucified Jesus. "Whom do you seek?" the angels say to them.

"Jesus Christ who was crucified," they respond, to which the angels retort: "He is no longer here. He is resurrected." In subsequent versions, this kernel is rounded out with additional material, including the encounter between the Marys and the apostles Peter and John, who ask the same question as the Marys had earlier addressed to the angels.

One could hardly imagine a simpler story, yet in terms of the Christian contribution to single-focus thematics and technique, the "Quem quaeritis" drama (so called by its first Latin words, meaning "Whom do you seek?") reveals manifold and far-reaching ramifications. The first regards the new approach to theophany present in the Gospels. Where the Old Testament promised flesh-and-blood presence (e.g., Exodus 19:11, "the Lord will come down upon Mount Sinai in the sight of all the people"), provided visible signs (e.g., the burning bush of Exodus 3), and called its God "Being" (JHWH), the New Testament has nothing but an empty tomb to offer. Far from producing Jesus, the Christian theophany reveals nothing but an absence. But along with that absence it provides an interpreter. "He is no longer here," the angels say. And then they continue, asserting, "He is resurrected." Between these two lines stands the entire logical system on which Christianity and single-focus narrative alike are founded: an absence is not just a lack of presence but a vacuum inviting the reader to create a presence through interpretation. The empty tomb is not a fact, but an artifact, an invitation to interpretation, a summons to signification.

Chancel drama portrays this exhortation particularly well. In the initial scene, the Marys expect to find Jesus dead, but the angels have already concluded that the absence of a dead man here means the presence of a living being elsewhere. As such, the angels serve as models for the hesitant Marys. Seconds later, all hesitation gone, the Marys encounter two disciples intent on discovering the fate of their Master. This time it is the Marys who take on the role of the angels, convincing Peter and John that their Master is risen. Subsequent scenes generated by this pattern implicitly represent the good news (i.e., interpretation) reported by Peter and John to two more disciples, and so on, all the way to the present audience, final link in the chain of faith begun by the Marys at the tomb. With each shift, students become teachers, those who were sure of death become convinced of life, and doubters confronted by an assertion now find themselves asserting.

Christian theophanies take place in the heart, the only place where the text's absence can be made into a presence. In place of Judaism's ever-present laws, Jesus stresses parables, lacking a universally applicable conclusion. Christians remain responsible for providing an interpretation, for inserting their own beliefs into the empty tomb. Following this logic to its conclusion, Protestant reformers refused to recognize any marker, other than belief, of a Christian's justification. Says Martin Luther: "It is clear, then, that a Christian has all that he needs in faith and needs no works to justify him; and if he has no need of works, he has no need of the law" (1960:284). If all that is needed is faith, we might add to this passage from the *Treatise on Christian Liberty*, then no one else can say whether or not a Christian is justified, for no one else can possibly know the state of an individual's faith. Fundamentally single-focus in orientation, the Protestant Reformation had an enormous effect in bringing single-focus modes of thought to counterreformers and independent thinkers like Montaigne, Descartes, and Pascal. It also brought important innovations that contributed heavily to the development of the novel: the importance of the individual, a tendency toward internalization, and emphasis on the practice of solitary reading.

The Single-Focus System

Because they fit more neatly into the causally connected, beginning-middle-and-end model that has long dominated definitions of narrative, single-focus strategies are better known than their dual-focus counterparts. In order to find substantial clusters of dual-focus texts, we have to visit the relatively distant traditions of Greek pastoral, Christian martyrs' lives, and the medieval epic or culturally disenfranchised forms like serial novels, comic strips, and genre films, whereas single-focus texts are readily found in the more familiar modes of biography, confession, romance, and novels of many sorts—psychological, memoir, realist, naturalist, detective. Though single-focus narratives vary enormously in terms of subject matter, style, and structure, the single-focus approach is readily recognizable through the following shared traits:

- A following-pattern that concentrates on a single individual
- Predominance of metonymic modulations as a method of circulating between the protagonist and the supporting cast
- A text generated by the protagonist's desire, often expressed through a departure into previously unexplored territory, behavior, or thought
- A narrator attracted by a main character capable of satisfying the reader's curiosity through unusual qualities, surprising activities, or culturally unacceptable practices
- Protagonists endowed with Promethean aspirations to self-creation, sometimes to the point of usurping the narrator's position
- A text characterized by gradational oppositions and speculations associated with a variable-sum economic system
- Secondary characters who serve as models for the protagonist, often taking the form of father figure, tempter, mediator, or teacher
- Altered repetition that gives both reader and protagonist ample opportunity to measure the protagonist's progress, through moral mirrors, repeated scenes, reiterated locations, or developmental metaphors
- A text typically alternating between presentation of an event and evaluation or interpretation of that event
- Tales that are twice-told—as perversion and conversion, action and evaluation, murder and solution, encoding and decoding
- A narrative that concentrates on the past and the future, thereby stressing what Barthes calls the "hermeneutic code"
- Values that depend on private and personal questions (motivation, intention, thought), always subject to interpretation
- Protagonists who are constructed as a combination of actor and observer and thus alternate between the roles of viewer and viewed object
- Readers who typically shuttle between confidence and suspicion, identification and observation, factual and artifactual reading strategies

If dual-focus narrative presents a timeless conflict over fixed values and limited resources, single-focus texts view the world as a limitless domain where enterprising individuals can discover and exploit new values. As such, single-focus narrative is particularly well suited to expanding societies and confident cultures. In order to assure their fate, dual-focus characters have only to follow rules that are apparent to all. For the single-focus protagonist, to the contrary, everything is done at a certain risk. In order to gain the right to play for enormous potential rewards—whether financial, moral, or otherwise—single-focus characters must expose themselves to a very real potential for substantial losses. Where the fate of dual-focus characters is typically reported by an Olympian narrator whose knowledge is unimpeachable, single-focus destinies are judged by limited narrators and readers who must base their conclusions on scant and sometimes slanted information. Single-focus values always depend on intentions rather than on completed actions, thereby placing a premium on interpretation—and therefore on rhetoric designed to skew that interpretation. Although dual-focus readers are a confident lot, knowing exactly where value lies and how to evaluate individual characters, single-focus readers must typically develop a level of suspicion unknown in the dual-focus world. Reading single-focus texts is thus a complex affair, involving the same kind of speculation and lack of certainty that characterizes single-focus protagonists and their attempts to make sense of the world and create their position in it.

SIX Pieter Bruegel, or the Space of Multiplicity

I n the preceding chapters of this book I introduce a wide variety of narrative examples—not only verbal texts like epics, novels, and sacred history but also image-based and multimedia examples including comic strips, television programs, and films. Here I continue this broadening impulse, employing the graphic works of Pieter Bruegel as an initial example of multiple-focus narrative. Two short analyses of artworks organized according to dual-focus and single-focus narrative principles provide a useful context for this treatment.

The twelfth-century tympanum on the western façade of the basilica at Conques, in southwestern France on the pilgrimage route to Santiago de Compostela, is one of the masterpieces of Romanesque art (fig. 6.1). Haunting and complex, this enormous stone composition of over a hundred human, diabolical, and angelic figures has received the attention of many scholars (Altman 1977, Schapiro 1977, Bonne 1984). A schematic analysis of the Conques tympanum will help explain how dual-focus images work.

Pilgrims entering the church square are immediately struck by a balanced arrangement. Instead of seeing individual faces or bodies, viewers initially grasp a geographic schema like that represented in figure 6.2. This impression is reinforced by a closer view, which breaks the large areas into numerous smaller sections, still in equilibrium across a central, vertical axis of symmetry. The two "mansions" in the lower register exemplify a typical dual-focus treatment. Dominated by figures looking straight out at the viewer, each roofed area achieves a certain stability thanks to the existence of its opposite

FIGURE 6.1 Tympanum of the abbey church of Conques (Courtesy of Scala/Art Resource, New York)

number. The presence of a balancing counterpart guarantees that each mansion constitutes a significant unit of the image as a whole. We may contemplate specific points within the devil's kitchen on the right or the individual faces of the elect in the bosom of Abraham on the left, but we always do so in the context of the broader balance between the two mansions.

Eye movement from one area to another is made difficult by the presence of thick lines, separating each area from its neighbors. This tendency toward compartmentalization—along with a persistent habit of using lines as boundaries—characterizes not only Romanesque art as a whole but also dual-focus images in general. The lines in the lower register go nowhere, instead dividing space into smaller and smaller pieces without ever pointing to another space. The roof structures, stretching as they do from border to border, never invite us to move along the line that they constitute. Instead, they lead us to sense the tension between symmetrical areas. The arches that paradoxically seem to imprison the elect are made of lines that begin at the

FIGURE 6.2 Initial Gestalt of the Conques tympanum

bottom margin, rise to the roof, then fall again to the base—each arch utterly in equilibrium, never vectorizing the line of which it is made.

The posture of the major figures reinforces the area-oriented nature of the carefully outlined mansions. Looking straight out at the viewer, both Abraham (lower left center) and the devil (lower right center) arrest our gaze, hold it front and center, making us provide the energy to move left or right, up or down. This characteristically Romanesque hieratic pose is reiterated in the central figure of Christ, who, like many another celestial figure ensconced in a mandorla, appears completely separate from the turmoil surrounding him. Even the heavenly procession includes figures who look straight out at the viewer, thus tempering the seeming vectorization of the processional line toward the upper center. A certain amount of progression is allowed, indicated by the slight turning of certain procession figures toward the Christ and by the attitude of the latter's arms, as if he were "directing traffic"—as Meyer Schapiro (1977) has put it—but that linearity is everywhere tempered by compartmentalization, frontality, and other area-oriented techniques. The pilgrims' progress is substantially retarded by the frontally presented angels with their balanced banners, dominating the entire procession.

That profiles should be far more common on the diabolical side of the composition suggests that the dual-focus tendency toward compartmentalization, frontality, and area orientation coincides with the early medieval Christian ideal of stasis, atemporality, and immutability as a model for eternal repose. The use of faces presented in profile to lead the viewer's eyes from one point to another is virtually nonexistent in the tympanum's heavenly regions, but profiles are regularly used in hell to shunt our gaze from one horror to another. However, this circuit of eye-leading is regularly aborted by compartment boundaries and frontal figures, thus limiting the potential range of diabolical linearity (into which are paradoxically drawn the devil's closest opponents—the militant angels to the right of Christ and the doorkeeper at bottom center—as if by too close contact with the nether world).

This schematic analysis highlights certain characteristic tendencies of dual-focus images. By and large, space is compartmentalized into autonomous areas, hierarchically balanced but securely walled in and thus sealed off from effects of, or defections to, any other area. Frontally presented characters and rhythmically conceived dead-end lines serve to anchor the gaze within each area. Lines rarely lead *from* one point *to* another but, instead, serve as boundaries between areas, not only marking one area off from another but also implicitly opposing each area to its neighbor. Even when lines are vectorized, as in the case of processions or the rare faces seen in profile, numerous devices are available to reduce the effects of this linearity. The heavily compartmentalized nature of dual-focus images, like that of dual-focus literature, puts a premium on the rare spots where a crossing of boundaries takes place, where the activities of different areas come into a seemingly promiscuous contact.

How radically different is the system underlying a Renaissance painting like Hugo van der Goes's rendition of the Nativity (1476), which serves as the central panel of the Portinari altarpiece (fig. 6.3). Where the Conques tympanum uses geometrical figures as stable areas, van der Goes's composition follows the common perspective solution of conceiving the world as a series of concentric lines, all marked by a strong centripetal sense of movement toward the vanishing point. This new world is built like a cone into which we look from the large end, with every sign of perspective construction

FIGURE 6.3 Hugo van der Goes, *Nativity* (central panel of the Portinari altarpiece) (Courtesy of Scala/Art Resource, New York)

drawing us farther and farther inside. Of all perspective markers, the strongest and most obvious—those that most clearly vectorize our viewing—are straight lines parallel to our gaze, pointing directly at the vanishing point. The van der Goes *Nativity* provides numerous lines of this sort, both left and right of the central Virgin. The radial arrangement of these lines leads our gaze unfailingly toward the enraptured face of the new mother, whence it is directed by her eyes toward the babe beneath. The vectorized linearity of perspective serves the painting's overall centrality, but only by means of a relay through the Virgin mother, creating for her a special place on the route that leads inexorably to the Christ child.

Face after face is turned toward the babe, doubling the indirect perspective route through Mary's gaze by a more psychologically inspired linearity. No truly frontal position arrests our movement toward Jesus. Even the angels in the upper central background, forced by their location to square their shoulders toward the viewer, avoid the sense of frontality by looking down, pulling our gaze away from them and toward the center of the circle of gazes. The choice of vantage point effectively avoids any possible balancing of areas, as might have occurred if, say, the angels on either side of Mary had been at her height and of her size. As it is, the relative size and placement of these angels reinforce the centralizing line-based perspective system instead of establishing an independent, area-reinforcing equilibrium. Perhaps the most striking aspect of this painting, in contrast to the Conques tympanum, is the radically different role played by the angels. At Conques, frontal positions and balanced composition assure the eternal stasis of these heavenly beings. Van der Goes, on the contrary, makes his angels all eyes. Like curious adolescents, they peer down from above, concentrating our attention on the Christ child.

Compared with the Conques Last Judgment, the van der Goes *Nativity* depends heavily on linear eye-leading, not only through perspective lines and facial direction but also by hand positioning and color contrast. Here lines serve not so much to separate areas as to lead from one point to another. The areas that are defined, often by color (e.g., in the vast expanses of uniform-color fabric), are rapidly resolved into vectorized linear shapes (e.g., the pointing hands of Joseph, Mary, the shepherds, and numerous angels). Most fascinating in the development of this kind of single-focus image is the establishment of a series of relays connecting each part of the image to the single center of the babe. Though certain portions of the image take us directly to the Christ child, others bring us through Mary to her son, thus elevating the Virgin to a syntactic role not unlike that played by John the Baptist for Christ and by Jesus for God the Father ("No one comes to the Father but by me"). Whereas dual-focus images often dwell on the boundary where area collides with area, single-focus compositions turn on the potentially ambiguous effect of those who lead to the center, for the painting's vectorizers may easily interest us more than the surprisingly lifeless point located at the apex of our vision.

For all the studied centrality of the Portinari altarpiece, viewers eventually discover that the interior space box of the stable does not cover the painting's full rectangle. On the upper right there remain openings to another world, to other characters—openings that seem to pull us away from the fully centralized world of Mary, the babe, and their admirers. Where do these chinks in the space box's armor take us? What happens when the viewer chances to escape from the world set in perspective? Is there yet another possible organization of space? Answers to these questions may be found in the work of Pieter Bruegel, whose paintings, drawings, and engravings provide an object lesson in the workings of multiple-focus narrative.

Born between 1525 and 1530, Bruegel's active career began in the early 1550s and continued until his death in 1569. Before the late 1550s, Bruegel devoted nearly the entirety of his creative activity to drawings destined for engraving and publication by his employer, the Antwerp publisher Jerome (Hieronymus) Cock. Largely devoted to Alpine landscapes, to new creations in the style of Hieronymus Bosch (the most popular Flemish artist of the previous generation), and to traditional religious topics (such as the Virtues and Vices, to which Bruegel devoted fifteen major drawings between 1556 and 1559), these graphic works brought a certain notoriety to the Antwerp draughtsman Pieter Brueghel, who in 1558 dropped the *h* from his name (it would be restored, along with reversal of the *u* and *e*, by Pieter's two painter sons Pieter and Jan Breughel), and began the series of masterful paintings for which he has remained famous ever since. An understanding of Bruegel's principles of composition and their evolution will provide an illuminating introduction to the problems of multiple-focus narrative. In particular, Bruegel's conception of space—in his drawings as well as his paintings—exemplifies the important differences separating multiple-focus images from their single-focus and dual-focus counterparts.

Before addressing the works of Bruegel, however, we must resolve a thorny methodological problem. In chapter 1, I insist that both "characters" and "actions," as used in defining narrative, are complex entities, technical terms quite different from the "actors" and "activities" that are often evoked in definitions or analyses of narrative texts. Quoting Borges on the frustrations of Funes the Memorius, I suggest that characters are produced when a viewer resolves Funes's apparent contradiction of the dog at three fourteen (seen from the side) and the dog at three fifteen (seen from the front) by recognizing the two images as representing the same character. Because it requires two separate views, this definition of character poses a problem for treatment of single narrative images. Neither the Conques tympanum nor the van der Goes *Nativity*—nor, for that matter, any of Bruegel's compositions—offers multiple views of the same character. What then justifies treatment of these pictorial texts as narrative? More problematic still, none of these examples adheres to a strict notion of following, as defined in the opening chapter. Instead of clearly following characters, these compositions offer single images of separate actors.

Pictorial texts force us to reconsider the strict definition of narrative offered above. On the question of following, we must recognize that individual graphic texts—whether drawn, painted, sculpted, or photographed—regularly take advantage of what we might call the "zero degree of following." Without offering the multiple views normally required for following, these graphic texts offer snapshots apparently taken from the middle of a sequence involving following. Though they do not show the multiple views usually involved in the process of following, the single view that they do show is readily taken—by those with a sufficient level of narrative drive—as implying the full following process. Unless we accept this zero degree of following as sufficient to define narrative, then we are bound to forego any possible insights into narrative that single-image graphic texts might offer.

A similar stretching regarding the notion of character is required to take advantage of the lessons that instantaneous images might bring to our study of narrative. Funes is bothered by application of the same name ("dog") to two successive images—demonstrably different at the graphic level, but the same in terms of character name. Bruegel's images may not offer successive images of the *same* character, but by providing simultaneous images of multiple characters they successfully activate the character-oriented aspects of each individual actor. To make narrative sense of Bruegel's compositions, we must recognize the possibility that characters can be formed by comparison of separate parts of the same image, just as they can be constituted by comparison of multiple successive images. Only by stretching our definition can we assure coverage of all types of narrative.

The Hole in the Center

With a simplicity and graphic clarity no longer available in the major paintings, Bruegel's drawings (and the engravings made from them) offer a particularly transparent version of the techniques operative throughout his oeuvre. The so-called Large Landscapes were published by Jerome Cock between 1555 and 1558. Probably drawing on the sketches that he made in the Alps on his way to Italy at the outset of the decade, Bruegel systematically employs an extreme high-angle vantage point from which he dominates an immense vista. Most of the landscapes include human figures, who narrativize space while fragmenting nature, creating tension by dividing the landscape. The process is especially apparent in three of the best-known Large Landscapes: *Saint Jerome in the Desert, Penitent Mary Magdalene* (fig. 6.4), and *The Cunning Bird Catcher*. In all three compositions, the lower right-hand corner is reserved for the diminutive title figure, looking outward and separated from the landscape by a strong diagonal produced by a steep drop-off. In addition to a title character who remains oblivious to the splendor of the scene behind, each composition includes several smaller figures who turn their backs to us and move toward the margins of the drawing, destabilizing the frame.

The landscape itself here becomes an almost inert space whose characteristics—in terms of the composition's narrative dynamics—constitute no more than simple filler. Instead of drawing us into the scene, outward-facing characters (as well as roads, rivers, and other lines) direct our attention away from the landscape. Systematically hiding their faces, Bruegel's characters never allow our gaze to settle on them. As vectorizers of space, they project our attention elsewhere, usually outside the frame. Bruegel's early compositions thus produce a fundamentally unbalancing effect. The upper left landscape draws our attention by its size and relative uniformity, as well as by the horizon line or mountain chain capping it. But the characters—the title figures nestled in the lower right-hand corner, as well as other smaller characters—lead our attention away from the majestic landscape. Midway between landscape and title character runs a line—path, river, hill. Far from simply separating character from area, thereby setting up a balanced structure with one weighed against the other, the line is set in motion by people and animals moving away from us, pushing our gaze toward the upper right-hand corner. The self-sufficiency of a lovely landscape is undermined by this vectorizing, centrifugal use of the diagonal. The imbalance of the composition, with its fragmentation of the viewer's attention, has an unnerving effect. We remain unable to image the drawing as a whole, to constitute visually any unity or hierarchy, to restore a center in terms of either interest or space.

Another one of the Large Landscapes, *Alpine Landscape with Deep Valley* (fig. 6.5), confirms these principles in an interesting fashion. Built in many ways like the three early drawings mentioned above, this landscape lacks the back-to-the-center title character in the lower right-hand corner, but it bounds a similarly majestic landscape with the familiar lower-right short diagonal. Where all three of the other drawings place the river valley on the left-hand border, however, *Alpine Landscape* centers the river, affording space for full treatment of the left bank. It is as if *Alpine Landscape* were simply a reworking of familiar materials, presenting the same view as the other three drawings, but with a slight pan left, taking us away from the figures of Jerome, Mary Magdalene, and the Bird-Catcher and toward the opposite bank of the river. Though the title characters of the other three drawings disappear from *Alpine Landscape*, their function remains. The entire drawing is covered with figures moving toward the margins. On the right, we are pushed out of the frame by the pack donkeys following the path "off-screen." On the left, a hunt propels our gaze away from the central river and its embankment. We follow the mounted hunters trailing the hounds who are fast on the heels of a stag only one bound away from the safety of off-screen space.

As with the three drawings discussed earlier, here paths and lines serve to isolate the central landscape area while propelling the viewer away from that area. In like manner, the minuscule characters, from the recognizable pack animals to the stick-figure hunters and hounds, engage in directional activities that orient the viewer's attention away from the central rushing stream and toward—indeed, beyond—the margins of the composition. It is perhaps worth noting that sixteenth-century engravers often added small characters

FIGURE 6.4 *Penitent Mary Magdalene*, engraving by Johannes and Lucas van Doetechum after a drawing by Pieter Bruegel (Courtesy of the Board of Trustees, National Gallery of Art, Washington, D.C. [Rosenwald Collection])

to otherwise narratively inert drawings. In this case, however, the human figures engraved by Johannes and Lucas van Doetechum, already appear in Bruegel's original drawing, preserved by the Louvre. By the late 1550s, Bruegel had already discovered the usefulness of human figures to narrativize and fragment space.

The overall effect of this technique is to leave a hole in the center of the drawing. What more picturesque landscape than a deep valley, with its fast-flowing stream, sharp banks, and steep cliffs? What more unified scene than a deep valley, enclosed on both sides by mountain peaks and stony escarpments? In short, what more centered subject than a deep valley? Yet, characteristically, Bruegel turns this valley—to paraphrase a famous paraphrase—into a subject to be drawn and quartered. Like some medieval torturer, Bruegel submits the valley to a destructive fragmentation. Horses and hounds, hunters and pack animals—even the geese in the sky above—all conspire to pull apart the darkened valley, to draw the viewer's attention away from the apparent subject of the drawing. The landscape area is thus sacrificed to the vectorizing, narrativizing influence of line and point, path and character.

Bruegel's tendency to devalue the center, to pull our attention away from the area of traditional interest, is nowhere more obvious than in the crowded, high-angle, small-figure compositions of his middle years. Typically representing a feast day in a crowded town square, these compositions often manifest a paradoxical dependence on the wheel metaphor to explain their decentered structure. The center of *The Fair at Hoboken* (fig. 6.6), for example, is occupied by two carts positioned at right angles one to the other. Dominating this central composition is an enormous wheel, echoed in other partially visible wheels, the circular openings of the canvas cart coverings, and the circular cages (or demijohns) carried on one of the carts. Throughout the engraving, this circular motif is repeated: in the barrel top and bowls at lower left, in the dance on the left-hand square, in the enclosure surrounding the upper centrally located church, in the procession occupying the upper-right square, and in many other details. *The Fair at Hoboken* thus initially appears as a unified series of circles echoing the central wheel.

Yet radiating out from the foremost wheel are the harness poles of the two carts, undermining the harmony and unity of the wheel as a centering

FIGURE 6.5 *Alpine Landscape with Deep Valley*, engraving by Johannes and Lucas van Doetechum after a drawing by Pieter Bruegel (Courtesy of Collections artistiques de l'Université de Liège [Belgium])

metaphor. While one pole constitutes the engraving's basic upper-left/lower-right axis, the other forms the composition's lower-left/upper-right axis. The carts and their wheels may be dead center, the poles seem to say, but there is no interest in this center. Only by radiating out from the center do we come to the varied characters and activities that make *The Fair at Hoboken* worthwhile. The central carts offer not only the wheel metaphor as an interpretive principle but also its deconstruction via the double diagonal represented by the cart poles.

At the hub there is nothing of interest. The only major mid-1560s paintings with a centered subject—the two 1563 versions of *The Tower of Babel*—ironically represent the moment when, according to Genesis 11, humanity "was dispersed all over the earth." Far from focusing on the center, Bruegel's compositions typically project attention outward, as in the striking composition of three dreamers positioned like spokes around the central tree in *The Land of Cockaigne* (1567) or the hauntingly eccentric arrangement of *The Census at Bethlehem* (1566), *The Massacre of the Innocents* (1566), and *The Adoration of the Magi in the Snow* (1567). This "spoke construction," with its constant dependence on what I call the "double diagonal," contributes heavily to Bruegel's genius for achieving a "hole at the center" as a compositional device. Operative throughout his work, this tendency may best be understood as functioning in three interdependent domains.

Space

Like all of Bruegel's high-angle town square compositions, the 1559–1560 *Children's Games* (fig. 6.7) draws our attention to numerous small figures filling the foreground. Our gaze is initially imprisoned within the triangle composed by the dominant straight lines delimiting the foreground: on the left, the façade of a shop and its continuation in a colorful fence; on the right, the long beam (used as a bench/table) that grows out of Bruegel's signature in the lower right-hand corner. Like the pavement of a Quattrocento Italian interior, these dominant straight lines serve to concentrate viewer attention on their central intersection, at the apex of the triangle they form.

Instead of leading the viewer to a unifying religious or civic personality, however, the converging lines of *Children's Games* lead only to an empty

FIGURE 6.6 *The Fair at Hoboken*, engraving by Franz Hogenberg after a drawing by Pieter Bruegel (Courtesy of the Board of Trustees, National Gallery of Art, Washington, D.C. [Rosenwald Collection])

public building, a lifeless hulk which, like many others placed by Bruegel in upper-central locations, serves to fragment space. Indeed, it is only with the dead end of the darkened door and the lifeless building behind that we discover the treachery of the converging lines issuing from the lower corners. The shop and the fence on the left are clearly constructed according to the rules of single-point perspective. They thus project the viewer's attention toward a vanishing point located higher up within the frame. At first glance, the beam on the lower right appears to obey the same principles. The object is clearly rectilinear; its sides apparently meet at right angles (as is appropriate for a carefully hewn beam). Therefore its long dimension must be parallel to the viewer's gaze, pointing toward the same vanishing point as the lines issuing from the lower left-hand corner. According to this analysis, then, the central triangle not only recalls the space box or pavement arrangement of Quattrocento perspective, it actually reproduces that configuration, with the apex of the triangle apparently constituting the vanishing point. Inspection of the entire painting reveals that this interpretation is patently false, however, for all other perspective markers point toward the town hall or church at the extreme end of the street leading into the upper right-hand corner.

Children's Games depends on a trap that constitutes—like many of Bruegel's compositions—a more or less overt deconstruction of the principles of perspective. According to the compositional methods dominant at the time of Bruegel's education, a painting's margins are given over to a series of concentric lines defining a unified perspective space. A figured floor or pavement pushes the viewer's attention toward the upper center, while a regularly constructed ceiling or series of architectural details propels the viewer toward the same central location, this time from above. The central portion of the painting valorizes the edges by justifying the attention concentrated there. Typically providing a well-known figure where the rays converge (Virgin, Christ, saint) or a pair of figures flanking the imaginary center (Arnolfini and wife, annunciatory angel and Mary, baby Jesus and admirers), the Renaissance painting establishes a perfect symbiosis between what might be called the inside and the outside of the space box. The outside directs the attention to a point on the inside justifying that attention. A complete version of this arrangement would take account of the rays arriving from all angles, as in figure 6.8. The overall effect may be conveniently summarized as in figure 6.9.

FIGURE 6.7 Pieter Bruegel, *Children's Games* (Courtesy of Erich Lessing/Art Resource, New York)

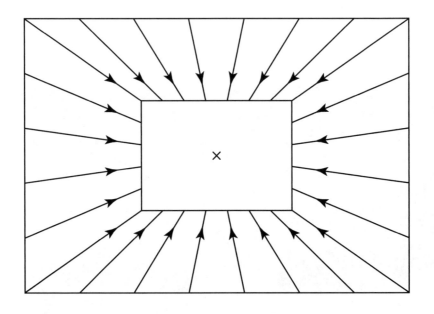

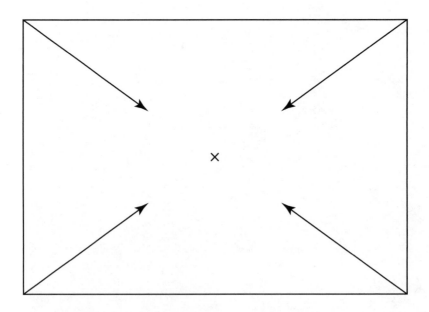

FIGURE 6.8 *(above)* Centripetal rays of the Renaissance space box
FIGURE 6.9 *(below)* Summary version of space box centripetal rays

However they may rework this configuration, the hundreds of variations devised throughout the period all begin with it. Indeed, Bruegel does so as well, for his *Children's Games* cheats on perspective not in order to deny it but in order to pervert it by recalling it. Without the table/bench in the lower right-hand corner, *Children's Games* would have an eccentric but nonetheless traditional perspective structure (as in fig. 6.10), with the upper right-hand vanishing point already used for *Flemish Proverbs* (1559) and *Combat between Carnival and Lent* (1559). According to this version, the "center" would be displaced, but the traditional perspective method of construction would remain unchanged. As modified by the false perspective lines of the lower right-hand beam, however, the composition takes on an entirely different aspect. An initial movement directs the viewer's attention to the foreground, only to push it upward toward the apex of the space box's lower triangle, as evidenced in figure 6.11. At this point in the traditional composition, two devices hold us at the center. On the one hand, the upper triangle's push toward the center balances the effect of the lower triangle, thus arresting upward movement and immobilizing interest at the center, as in figure 6.12. On the other hand, the subject matter provides an independent reason for holding our gaze at the center (e.g., by placing near the convergence point a recognizable character known for playing a central role in other narratives).

Now, this is precisely what does not happen in *Children's Games*. Instead of the Virgin at the center, there is a vacuum, a hole that deceives all our expectations, thus freeing our gaze to respond to other invitations. Once foiled at the center, we either follow the numerous perspective markers toward the distant vanishing point in the upper right or heed the call of the open space to the left, a perspectiveless realm that provides an equally acceptable, if less geometric, sense of escape. Paradoxically, we have reconstituted the diagonals that constitute the armature of perspective technique. But instead of pulling us in toward the center, the upper diagonals push us out. The overall configuration clearly depends on familiar perspective techniques, but with a strategic reversal at the center. Instead of confirming the meaning of the diagonals, Bruegel's center refutes their importance, adopting them as exit routes rather than as entrances (fig. 6.13).

As in *Alpine Landscape with Deep Valley*, here the center is hollowed out in favor of the margins (which abound with cut-off characters drawing our attention ever outward). From the high-angle landscapes of his early career

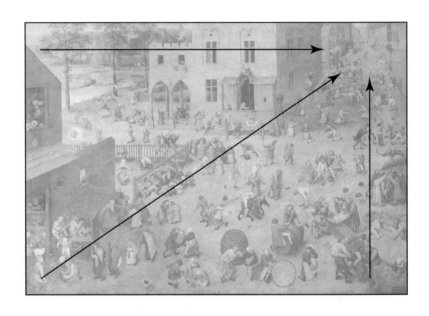

FIGURE 6.10 *(above)* Upper right-hand vanishing point of *Children's Games*

FIGURE 6.11 *(below)* Centripetal push of the lower half of *Children's Games*

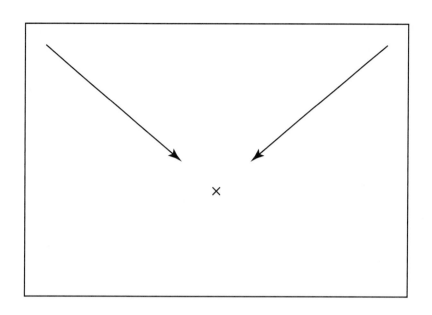

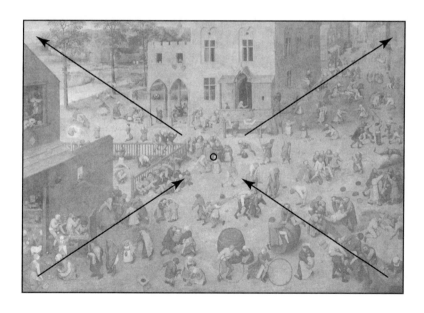

FIGURE 6.12 *(above)* Traditional upper half centripetal push
FIGURE 6.13 *(below)* Lower centripetal push and upper centrifugal push of
Children's Games

(where the central landscape is devalued in favor of outward-bound paths or outward-facing characters), to the town-square paintings and drawings of his middle period (where a major building occupying the upper center splits city space in two, thus creating two upper diagonals to drain viewers' attention away from the center), Pieter Bruegel uses the double diagonal to striking advantage, undermining perspective principles to ensure perpetual recirculation of viewer attention. The traditional approach allows viewers to enter the painting only once. Influenced by the perspective system of centered diagonals, viewers are inevitably guided toward the central area, which, by its prestige, has the power to hold the gaze permanently. Constantly propelling us away from the center, Bruegel instead brings us close to, and eventually over, the edge. Once outside, we inexorably return, each time describing a new path through the city maze, each time attending to a new set of characters.

Celebrity

Paintings are too often dealt with as if they were made up solely of pigment. As physical object, a painting consists of chemical substances recognizable as paint. As text, however, a painting is vastly more complex. The physical object exists alone, whereas the text implies a viewer who contributes perception and knowledge. This is especially true of narrative painting, for in order to evoke narrative with a minimum of investment, paintings often refer directly—by title or convention—to preexisting narratives, stories that must be known to the viewer in order for the painting in question to achieve its full meaning. Besides representing a single moment in time, narrative images often extend backward and forward by reference to a previously constituted story and tradition. To people unfamiliar with the tradition, a painting of a dozen or so men gathered around a table lacks the sense of urgency and impending finality available to viewers who recognize a rendition of the Last Supper. Paint it is, then, and the forms constituted by the paint, but the painting also calls on knowledge that the viewer brings to the painting and that the painter often names in the title lest the paint itself not suffice.

Thanks to a poem by W. H. Auden (1945) and an article by Bertolt Brecht (1964), one of Bruegel's earliest paintings has become well known in the English-speaking world. Though the date and authenticity of the two extant versions are contested by some scholars, the 1558 *Landscape with the Fall of Icarus* (fig. 6.14) represents a fascinating variation on the techniques operative in the Large Landscapes published by Cock over the preceding three years. The characteristic short diagonal (here separating off a small area on the lower left, rather than the even smaller lower right area reserved for Jerome, Magdalene, and the Bird-Catcher in the Large Landscapes) divides the composition in two. On the lower center left, a farmer plows the land into the most stylized furrows before Grant Wood, seemingly modeled on the folds of his own cloak. Characteristically, his gaze is directed at the ground as he follows his horse out of the frame. He is doubled by a shepherd leaning on his staff and gazing out of the frame to the left. The area to the right and above the diagonal represents a typical Bruegel seascape: palatial residences, splendid ports, and jagged peaks surround a calm bay covered with ships of all sizes and shapes.

In turning their backs on this majestic vista, peasant and shepherd refuse to contemplate not only a noteworthy seascape but also the drama of a drowning man whose position marks him as having fallen headfirst from a great height. Just as the Large Landscapes went out of their way to undermine the landscape areas of the series' title, so *The Fall of Icarus* undermines the title area, the realm of a subject sufficiently well known to unify an entire painting by itself. Exactly reversing the familiar system whereby a well-known central figure reinforces and justifies the focusing effect of perspective lines, *The Fall of Icarus* instead plays up the striking difference separating viewers of the painting (who know the title of the painting) from the characters within (who ignore the name of their experience).

One of the most obvious effects of Renaissance perspective painting was to bind together, artificially, the experience of viewer and character. Just as shepherds and magi are drawn by the strength of their own fascination to observe the baby in the manger, so are we induced, in part by their gaze, to view the babe. In so doing, we all—shepherds, magi, and present-day viewers alike—reproduce the centralizing effect of perspective's centripetal rays. Viewer activity reiterates not only character activity but the painting's formal basis as well, thus assuring the perspective system's familiar projection of the spectator into the position and point of view of the painter. If there is one thing we can be sure about in most Renaissance painting, it is the fundamental similarity of the knowledge available to character and viewer. Shepherds, magi, and townspeople alike share with the viewer the sense that this particular birth is an event of universal significance. The title of Bruegel's painting—*The Fall of Icarus*—is the one piece of knowledge that the painter can be sure of passing on to the viewer, yet this is precisely the one piece of information to which the painting's characters are oblivious. Just as the Large Landscapes constitute a treatise on the subservience of area to the vectorizing effect of point and line, and *Children's Games* further illustrates the centrifugal potential of the line, over against perspective's traditional centripetal use, *The Fall of Icarus* demonstrates the importance of not conflating character and viewer. The painting is designed to preclude viewer identification with the characters. The fact that we know and they don't makes us forever distinct and disjunct.

Several critics have remarked that Bruegel is not a painter of faces. Even among his medium-to-large-size figures, many turn their backs to the viewer or have their faces hidden (by hats, jugs, hands, other characters, or, in a seeming send-up of the entire practice, beekeepers' masks). This remark needs to be set in an appropriate context. Rarely willing to turn the human visage into an area for careful and final attention, Bruegel prefers instead to treat the face as a vector, a single spot unworthy of attention in itself but carrying a directional influence that clearly tells the viewer where to look next. It is thus less important to note that Bruegel's characters often have their back turned *to the spectator* (this is the comment we might expect from scholars interested in the Renaissance concern to revive the face both as window to the soul and as reflector of social class, mental activity, and personal individuality) than it is to note just how commonly Bruegel's characters turn their backs *on the center*. Of over two dozen characters in the 1565 *Hay Making*, only the three rakers in the foreground reveal their faces in full. One of these, the young woman in the middle, looks directly out at the spectator. Her eye contact with the viewer only reinforces the strange composition by which Bruegel has balanced three rakers with visible faces, moving off toward the left, against three porters whose baskets hide their faces, moving off toward the right: in the middle, nothing. Split apart by the two trios, the painting degenerates into a series of separate vignettes, with no possibility of pictorial unification.

When the characters in *The Fall of Icarus* turn their backs on the pair of legs disappearing into the sea, their action grows out of more than just a lack of knowledge of this particular myth or a need to attend to more practical duties. In relation to the spectator, a further connection is developed. In *Children's*

FIGURE 6.14 Pieter Bruegel, Landscape with the Fall of Icarus (Courtesy of Scala/Art Resource, New York)

Games, an insidious use of the principles of perspective draws the viewer's attention to the center of the painting only the better to fan out the gaze, assuring multiple different viewings with diverse reentry points. Exactly the same process occurs in *The Fall of Icarus*, with the reader's knowledge of previous narratives taking the place of the linear aspects of perspective technique. Each painting insists that the viewer reach a certain point in the viewing process (the "center" in *Games*; the disappearing legs in *Fall*), independently of the many other activities taking place throughout. Yet once we have reached the point pressed on us by perspective technique or by the naming of the painting, we are not allowed to stay there, for just as *Games* drives us away by the very means of perspective (flight to the horizon, open spaces, vanishing points), so *Fall* lures us away from the title character by the characterological resources implicit in the myth itself. Following the activity of the farmer, the gaze of the shepherd, or the frantic attempts of the seamen in the ship on the lower right to contend with the rising wind, our gaze necessarily radiates out from the apparent center provided by the title. If the title provides a focal point, it is not to summarize the painting (as we have the habit of expecting) but to furnish a starting point that will inevitably be left behind, undermined by the painting's centrifugal structure. Instead of unifying the painting around the title character, Bruegel invites us to follow several characters separately and sequentially.

Implicit throughout Bruegel's career, what we might call the "Icarus effect" constitutes the very subject of numerous paintings. *The Suicide of Saul* (1562) and *The Conversion of Saint Paul* (1567) employ similar mountainous landscapes to subordinate the historic event associated with the title character to the military hordes around them, while *Christ Carrying the Cross* (1564), *The Census in Bethlehem* (1566), and *The Adoration of the Magi in the Snow* (1567) all northernize and banalize the events of Christ's life to the point where we are hard put to locate the title event. And even when we find it, we are immediately led away to explore the far corners and least historical characters of the painting.

Style

Why is the hole at the center? Why does Bruegel depend so heavily on the short diagonal, joining the bottom center to left or right margin? Why do his characters turn their backs not only to the viewer but to each other as well? As tempted as one might be to answer these questions in a strictly historical manner, an additional factor must be invoked. To be sure, Bruegel is one of the great innovators of the late Renaissance. It is hard not to think of him in conjunction with Erasmus, Rabelais, Sir Thomas More, and Luther. Innovators all, these adventuresome sages changed the world not by pure invention but by criticizing existing systems. So Bruegel, who by attacking the conventions of perspective freed the space of painting from Italian tyranny. Read this way, the hole in the center, the short diagonal, and the back-to-the-center position are all simply inversions of perspective conventions. The hole appears at the very place of fullness, the short diagonal cuts across and thus undermines the lower rays of perspective construction, and refusal to use characters' eyes to assure con/centration of spectator attention reverses a familiar habit.

Though every one of these claims is true, the retrospective historical mode in which they are framed robs them of their specificity and, in particular, dissimulates the full mechanism of their deployment. To fully understand Bruegel's strategy, we must reintroduce the spectator into the system. To be sure, Bruegel's devices produce (or at least echo) historical change. More important, they are integrated into his works in such a way as to engage the historical spectator, who reads change not just as difference but as foiled expectation, as failed investment, as unexpected deception. The hole in the center, the short diagonal, and the prominent back are more than new practices—they are inversions of old practices and, as such, specific breaches of contract with the viewer. In other words, Bruegel's techniques "work" only on those who know and expect the concentric conventions of mature Renaissance perspective. Denial—and thus recognition—of convention are at the heart of the Bruegel experience. Here, as with Brecht or the Russian formalists, estrangement and defamiliarization can take place only by contrast with the familiar.

The dynamics of celebrity confirm this hypothesis. There can be no "Icarus effect" for the spectator who knows nothing of the Greek legend. Not only must we know the story, but we must also be convinced that it is a tale of universal importance, familiar to all. Otherwise the attitude of the painting's other characters would carry no meaning—they would be no more than workers going about their business. Yet they are more than that. They are workers going about their business at a time when we, with our knowledge, expect that they might well be doing something else—paying attention to the legendary event taking place right under their noses. From hole in the center to Icarus effect there is no more than a change of register. Both depend not on the viewer's careful delineation of the connections between elements of the painting but on recognition of the connections that are lacking—those we expect to find but do not.

In the realm of style, Bruegel takes this method one surprising step further. Time and again the artist implants within the bounds of one of his compositions an example of the very style he is diverging from, as if to recall not only his precedents but his competitors as well. This "style clash" dates from 1556–1557 and a sequence of drawings clearly inspired by Hieronymus Bosch, including *The Ass at School* and *The Temptation of Saint Anthony*, as well as the series of Virtues and Vices. Bosch provides an important model here, for in spite of his popular reputation as creator of composite beings and unreal spaces, Bosch was also a distinguished religious painter who regularly introduced fragments of his "straight" style into his "twisted" canvases. Thus in the left-hand panel of *The Garden of Earthly Delights* (c. 1500), devoted to Paradise, we find mixed in with composite animals and fanciful trees a Christ or God figure whose flowing robes might have been equally at home on one of the donor figures of his traditionally composed *Epiphany* (c. 1510) triptych.

When Bruegel renewed contact with his Boschian heritage in 1562, he rediscovered the structural potential of the "style clash" device. Starting with a trio of works directly inspired by Bosch, Bruegel experimented with increasingly striking contrasts. *Mad Meg* (1562) intersperses realistic renditions of armor, weapons, and cloth with a horrific array of Boschian creations. *The Fall of the Rebel Angels* (1562) accentuates to a shocking degree a conventional stylistic difference—the disparity between the heavenly form and color of angels and the relatively drab rendering of their earthly charges. *The Triumph of Death* (1562) saves the lower left and right corners for regal apparel and earthly sumptuousness, all the more surprising in this vision of darkness and death. The drawings of the *Fall of the Magician* (1564) and *Saint James and Hermogenes* (1565) continue this Boschian strain, providing a single figure whose style stands out in contrast to the unearthly beings around him.

More interesting, however, are the five major paintings from 1564 to 1567 that extend the shock of contrasting styles to works that owe nothing to Bosch. The 1564 *Christ Carrying the Cross* (fig. 6.15) represents, for most of its

FIGURE 6.15 Pieter Bruegel, Jesus Carrying the Cross or The Way to Calvary (Courtesy of Erich Lessing/Art Resource, New York)

considerable expanse, the very type of "domestification" of a traditional scene. Horses with sumptuous saddles ride side by side with nags sporting nothing but a sackcloth; tight peasant breeches complement the flowing cloaks sported by the king's militia; fun-seekers share the scene with the few who sense the horror and suffering of the occasion. So far, the only contrast is between objects, not styles. In the lower right-hand corner, however, separated from the masses by a familiar short diagonal, we find the women in Christ's life mourning his fate. Their long robes—and especially the yards and yards of material (the shroud?) clutched by the woman on the left—are treated after the manner of Rogier van der Weyden (e.g., *The Deposition* [1435]). The timeless repose that characterizes this corner is in striking contrast to the curiosity-driven movement of the procession behind.

A similar contrast marks the central portion of *The Adoration of the Magi* (1564), where the baby and the mother alone (along with the fabric of the Magi's robes—but not their faces) escape the mean realism of all other faces and spaces. In like manner, the title figure of *The Woman Taken in Adultery* (1565) stands out from the crowd of Pharisees not only by virtue of her sex and demeanor but also through the technical means deployed in delineating her angelic expression and carriage. With *The Sermon of Saint John the Baptist* (1566) it is the choice of foreground colors and fabrics that shocks. Although all the distant characters wear traditional, flatly treated, and somber colors, the larger foreground figures come straight from some oriental bazaar. The next year the mannerism of late Renaissance foreshortening stands out in *The Conversion of Saint Paul* (1567), where the horses in the right foreground recall Uccello, Mantegna, and Pollaiuolo.

Why imbed a few square feet of van der Weyden drapery or Uccello horses in a painting largely treated otherwise? Is this simply a case of the well-known notion of artistic influence? I think not, for the regularity of Bruegel's recourse to stylistic contrasts, either in the mode of Bosch or according to his own broader approach, suggests a more deliberate, structured use of the style clash phenomenon. First, the contrast between recognizable styles reminds us that we are dealing with a painting of a scene and not with the scene itself. Neither the hieratic qualities of a van Eyck, nor the imagination of a Bosch, nor even the hyperrealistic efforts of later painters can alone point to a painting's constructed nature. Achieving the necessary level of reflexivity requires the composite nature of Bruegel's style clash technique, helped along by numerous devices (centrifugal structure, truncated characters, off-screen gazes) drawing attention to the margins: that is, to the fact that, unlike the real world, the painting has limits. Second, the style clash phenomenon clearly fragments the painting's psychological space, rendering implausible the likelihood of suturing together through stylistic unity an exploded space where not even traditional notions of celebrity suffice to assure harmony of response.

The practice of confronting contrasting styles derives not just from the hazards of historical influence. It is instead part of an overall strategy of decentering, of centerlessness. As such, it is part and parcel of the process that Mikhail Bakhtin terms "novelization," whereby traditional forms "become dialogized, permeated with laughter, irony, humor, elements of self-parody and finally . . . an indeterminacy, a certain semantic openendedness, a living contact with unfinished, still evolving contemporary reality" (1981:7). Supreme representative, along with Rabelais, of the carnivalizing style that so permeates and energizes the late Renaissance, Bruegel leaves untouched little that was sacred to his predecessors. Exploding space, undermining the celebrity of familiar tales, calling attention to the value of his own rough-and-tumble realism by contrasting it to other, radically different styles, Pieter Bruegel sets for the viewer a peculiarly Renaissance problem: Now that the old beliefs have been abolished, must we give in to the fragmentation of the new world? Or is there unity to be found in the fragmented universe that survives the overthrow of the old?

Thematic Resolution

Though Pieter Bruegel is in every way a Renaissance artist, much of his work can be understood only by reference to late medieval models. In particular, Bruegel's early career is heavily marked by works in the allegorizing tradition common at the time throughout Europe, especially in popular or folkloric imagery. Drawing heavily on late medieval examples, Angus Fletcher characterizes allegory as depending primarily on "the use of encapsulated units within a larger frame so as to produce a studied discontinuity within the whole" (1964:369). According to Fletcher, this technique leads allegorical artists to conceive their works as a series of independent vignettes "placed on the picture plane without any clear location in depth" (87).

From 1556 to 1560, nearly the entirety of Bruegel's production reveals the encapsulated units, discontinuity, and disdain of careful spatial construction characteristic of fifteenth-century and sixteenth-century popular allegorical images. The works most obviously deriving from this tradition are the two extended series that Bruegel drew for Jerome Cock: *The Seven Cardinal Vices* (1556–1557) and *The Seven Cardinal Virtues* (1559–1560). In the same vein are a series of individual drawings, all more or less indebted to the tradition of Hieronymus Bosch: *The Temptation of Saint Anthony* (1556), *Big Fish Eat Little Fish* (1556), *The Ass at School* (1556), *The Last Judgment* (1558), and *The Witch of Malleghem* (1559). While neither moralizing nor allegorizing in the strict sense, Bruegel's first trio of painted masterpieces (*Flemish Proverbs, Combat between Carnival and Lent, Children's Games*) deserve to be seen in this same allegorical light, for they, too, are more attentive to the elaboration of a series of independent, discontinuous units than to the careful construction of a unified space. After 1560 only *Mad Meg* (1562), *Dulle Griet* (1561–1562), and *The Triumph of Death* (1562) clearly perpetuate this approach.

The technique to which Bruegel falls heir, as a Renaissance popular illustrator, is fully apparent in his drawing of *Prudentia*, dated 1559 and very probably the last work that the artist signed as "Brueghel" (though by the time the engraving reproduced in figure 6.16 was completed, he would be identified as "Bruegel"). Carrying a coffin, wearing a sieve on her head, and gazing into a mirror, Prudence is surrounded by myriad examples of prudential virtue. A woman puts out a fire before it spreads, a sick man is attended by both a doctor and a priest, and a merchant salts away his gold while a youth inserts a coin in his bank. The farm women put up meat for the winter, the hired hands bring in potatoes, and the farmer stores firewood. A house is repaired before the weather turns bad.

Drawings like this one are a pleasure to describe because they so clearly match the structure of verbal language: to this part of the picture corresponds one phrase, to that part corresponds another, and so on. Each independent section is made to be perceived and mentally processed separately. A certain amount of visual overlapping creates a minimal sense of spatial unity, but there is never any doubt about the type of relation existing between contiguous objects. The women salting pork represent one narrative unit, and

FIGURE 6.16 *Prudentia*, engraving attributed to Philip Galle after a drawing by Pieter Bruegel (Courtesy of the Board of Trustees, National Gallery of Art, Washington, D.C. [Rosenwald Collection])

the farmhands carrying potatoes constitute another. Each group is independently engaged in an activity representing the title virtue.

The overall composition is handled in the manner of fresco painting, where each day a certain area is covered with lime, the excess being removed at day's end. Fresco painters endeavor to end the day at a seam that will dissimulate differences in color and masonry from one day to the next. The daily units of wall covering and composition thus coincide. Each part of the wall is typically conceived as an individual unit, with clear outlines and only incidental overarching spatial relationships. The building on the left in *Prudentia* is clearly configured in this self-contained manner. Its distinct outlines separate it from the distant shores, the river behind, and the ladders on which Prudence herself stands. Bruegel's challenge is to fit functionally separable parts together in such a way that they will not seem completely separate. He eventually succeeds in front of the building by overlapping the woman and the scene behind (even though her front yard fire hardly seems spatially appropriate), but he fails on the top and side, where the building appears cut off from the rest of the composition. By and large, the overlapping is so minimal that each encapsulated unit remains fundamentally independent of its surroundings. Rather than being spatially unified, the composition is held together by the viewer's mental activity of recognizing various examples of prudence.

The popular allegorical tradition dominant throughout the first decade of Bruegel's career thus joins centrifugal composition, the Icarus effect, and the style clash technique in diminishing spatial unity and prohibiting spatial resolution. A bizarre work of 1558 provides an unusual opportunity to seize the method by which viewers were expected to make sense of Bruegel's "isolated image" compositions. We are fortunate to possess both Bruegel's original drawing (fig. 6.17) of *Elck* or *Everyman* (in the British Museum) and the engraving published by Cock in 1558 (fig. 6.18).

This enigmatic representation of the human condition reveals a bearded, bespectacled man stepping over an oversized orb, in order to inspect with the aid of a lantern the piled-up objects strewn about. On the other side of the pile, two other men rummage through basket and bag in search of we know not what. Behind them two small figures with similar lanterns walk about an army camp in the direction of a modest church. Still another figure—this one a dead ringer for the first, with identical hat, hair, glasses, beard, and

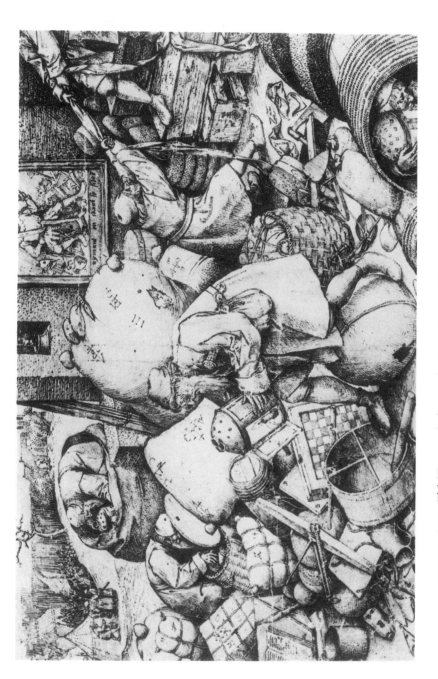

FIGURE 6.17 *Elck* (*Everyman*), drawing by Pieter Bruegel (Courtesy of British Museum)

lantern—inspects the inside of a barrel in the left foreground. Behind him two bearded men dressed exactly like the first engage in a tug of war over a long, narrow piece of material. On the wall next to them a commedia dell'arte character in a poster or painting observes himself in a mirror, accompanied by the inscription: "Niema(n)t en kent he(m) selv(en)" ("Nobody knows himself"). A direct quote from the Flemish poem accompanying the engraving (and which the drawing may well have been commissioned to illustrate), this inscription is accompanied in the engraving (but not in the drawing), by the first lines of the Latin version of the poem, "Nemo non" ("Nobody . . ."), inscribed on one of the sacks immediately behind the central figure. Here is the French version of the poem (slightly modernized for understanding's sake), along with an English translation:

Sur le monde un chacun par tout recherche,	In the world everyone seeks all about,
Et en toutes choses soi-même veut trouver.	And everywhere looks to find himself.
Vu qu'un chacun donc toujours se cherche,	Since everyone always seeks himself out,
Pourrait quelqu'un bien perdu demeurer?	Could anyone possibly remain lost?
Un chacun pour le plus long tire aussi,	Everyone tries to get the longer piece,
L'un par haut et l'autre par bas s'efforce.	One pulling up and the other down.
Nul se connaît soi-même presque en ce monde ici:	Nobody recognizes himself in this world;
Ce bien noté s'émerveiller est force.	This fact is indeed a cause for wonder.

Commonly known by the first word of the Flemish version of the poem, *Elck* (literally "each one" or, by extension, "everyman"), the engraving takes some liberties with the original drawing. In particular, the engraver took upon himself to identify the characters whose enigmatic activities fill up the frame. On the hem of each character's cloak (or on the ground beneath the characters on the upper right) we find the identifying inscription "ELCK."

FIGURE 6.18 *Elck* (*Everyman*), engraving by Pieter van der Heyden after a drawing by Pieter Bruegel (Courtesy of the Board of Trustees, National Gallery of Art, Washington, D.C. [Rosenwald Collection])

The engraver's interpretive gesture says worlds about the type of reading required by Bruegel's composition. Seen by itself, without "ELCK" nametags or the poem appended to the engraving, the drawing appears to the casual viewer to represent eight unrelated individuals engaged in activities that are both separate and inexplicable. The careful viewer may notice the close resemblance among many of the figures, as well as the repeated motif of the lantern, but no amount of attention or acuity will divulge the hidden connection between the bearded lantern holders and the pictured saltimbanque contemplating his own image in the mirror. Nor is there any explanation for the cloth-tuggers.

The engraving provides the solution. Multiple individuals engaged in differing occupations are given the same name, as if they were not, in fact, separate characters. What justifies this leveling, this "Elck effect"? One pulls up: *the name on his hem identifies him as Elck*. One pulls down: *his hem identifies him as Elck*. One wears glasses: *Elck*. Another doesn't: *still Elck*. One character is hidden inside a barrel, his hem invisible, his anonymity seemingly assured: *still he is Elck to us*, for we have discovered the principle that lies behind the Elck effect. Bruegel's strategy requires us to take characters who are not the same when represented in space and to raise them to a higher level of generalization, converting them into the same "Everyone" (*elck, chacun*), or its inverse, "Nobody" (*niemant, nemo, nul*). This is the "Elck effect," and the name on the hem is its consecration.

That the Elck effect involves a special relationship between visual and linguistic representation is confirmed by the effect's origin in allegorical images. Recall, for an instant, *Prudentia*. Viewing this engraving involves the intertwined processes of dissecting the composition into separate encapsulated units and providing those units with a dual identity. At one level we locate the individual characteristics of each unit (salting pork, banking money, storing potatoes). At another level—without which the picture would lose its primary, allegorical sense—each individual unit is identified by its higher-level-of-generalization "hem" name: Prudence. This is how allegory works. Knowledge of the hem name facilitates division into constituent units, which, in turn, provides confirmation of the hem name. The name of the composition is inscribed at the bottom center, directly beneath the feet of the title character: "Prudentia." In the engraving representing "Temperance," the Virtue's name is literally inscribed on the hem of her robe, thus revealing quite clearly the source for similar treatment in *Elck*.

The naming of an allegorical composition (or other similarly constructed work) constitutes a short cut to interpretation, an immediate identification of the hem name to be allotted to diverse individuals. Most obvious in the allegorical tradition, this approach is also operative in Bruegel's early separate-unit paintings, especially *Flemish Proverbs* and *Children's Games*—which make no sense at all until the hem name of each individual unit is provided by the overall title of each painting. The same system operates throughout the long multiple-focus literary tradition. In chapter 7, I show how novels as diverse as Leo Tolstoy's *War and Peace*, Émile Zola's *La Terre*, D. H. Lawrence's *Women in Love*, André Gide's *Les Faux-monnayeurs*, and André Malraux's *La Condition humaine* predispose the reader to a regular process of hem-naming: of raising multiple individual characters to a higher level of generalization, where they represent a category implied by the title.

The Elck effect, with its tendency toward hem-naming and attention to higher levels of generalization, constitutes a necessary analytical response to Bruegel's characteristically decentered space. Single-focus images like the Portinari *Nativity* construct a unified, centered space, with the possibility of final repose for the viewer's eye. Intellectual unity is not needed, for unity is provided directly to the senses. Bruegel's technique requires something quite different. We are pushed out of Alpine landscapes left and right, top and bottom. We are forbidden by internal boundaries to connect Virtues or Vices. Eccentric eye-leading prevents us from imaging separate areas of the large paintings as parts of a single, coherent unit. We are never allowed to imagine the experience of characters within the paintings as matching in any way our own, thus increasing distance and frustrating identification. Even the potential role of stylistic unity as a comfortable resting place is time and again denied.

By rejecting the satisfaction of visual unity, Bruegel pushes us toward nonvisual organization of narrative space. Thematic resolution provides this nonvisual satisfaction not only in *Elck* but also in numerous compositions that work according to the same principles. Fragmentation of space, the hole in the center, and the stabilizing influence of the Elck effect thus prove related, for it is through interpretation of the fragments, at a higher level of generalization, that thematic resolution compensates for the hole at the center. Pieter Bruegel offers fair warning of a new kind of narrative, where the modes of identification associated with the single-focus and dual-focus systems no longer hold.

The Tilted Plane

Bruegel's approach to composition changed decisively during the painter's last years. Instead of the high-angle point of view from which the early works are conceived, we find instead an eye-level approach. Whereas the earlier technique produces scores of smallish characters, stacked up one above the other, no one figure blocking more than a small proportion of the one located behind (for in this system *behind* is figured by *above*), the revised technique generates a smaller number of large foreground characters, partially obliterating the small-to-medium-size figures behind them (for here *behind* is figured by *behind*). While the elements of this new approach can be seen as early as 1565, the full system does not reach fruition until 1567–1568, with the completion of the drawing *Summer* and two large paintings now located in Vienna: *Peasant Dance* and *Peasant Wedding.* To understand the new style, we must backtrack a decade to the era of Bruegel's first major paintings.

In 1558, Bruegel painted a series of medallions representing Flemish proverbs. Framed together during the seventeenth century as a single composition, these twelve individual vignettes, now known as *Twelve Flemish Proverbs* (fig. 6.19), constitute a fascinating study for the 1559 *Flemish Proverbs*, which packs well over one hundred proverbs into a single composition. While others consider the earlier work interesting primarily as a stylistic model for its more famous successor, I am intrigued by the clues that the individual medallions provide regarding the theoretical source for Bruegel's early style.

As originally conceived by Bruegel, each proverb is a separate entity, worthy of independent representation. As such, the scale of each of the twelve vignettes is nearly identical. The characters are depicted as if they existed not in space but only in the artist's mind; the painter's relationship to his material is thus more mental than physical. The question of point of view never enters into the global conception of this artwork, for the objects to be represented exist first in the artist's imagination and only then before his eyes. This approach owes an obvious debt to allegorical representation. As

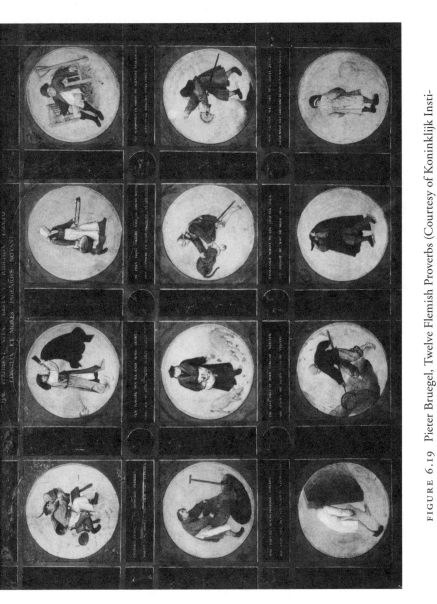

FIGURE 6.19 Pieter Bruegel, Twelve Flemish Proverbs (Courtesy of Koninklijk Instituut voor het Kunstpatriotrimonium/Institut Royal du Patrimoine Artistique [KIKIRPA], Brussels [Belgium])

concepts, Virtues and Vices exist only in the imagination. The work of illustrating them is first a mental task and only thereafter a visual one. This is why, in Bruegel's allegorical drawings, as well as in the contemporary paintings devoted to Flemish proverbs, the representation of individually recognizable units takes precedence over the construction of coherent space. The relationship between the units is originally and primarily conceptual—the very process of fitting them into a single space is by nature awkward, for it works at cross-purposes to the painting's announced conceptual topic.

To reduce the awkwardness of fitting conceptually conceived units into a visually oriented space, Bruegel at first adopted a solution requiring the least possible divergence from the physical arrangement associated with pure conception. In their purely conceptual existence, proverbs appear as in a list, as in a layout like that of the seventeenth-century mounting of *Twelve Flemish Proverbs*. They cannot help existing in some sort of space, but that space is at the very limit of not being a space. It is non-space, neutral space, space without an observer. Growing out of a conceptual approach, with the spaceless space of a list, a layout, or a chart, Bruegel's early work follows contemporary mapmaking in choosing visual conventions that suggest the conceptual while nevertheless creating visually coherent space.

Now, Renaissance maps are not fully conceptual. Like Michel Étienne Turgot's well-known eighteenth-century map of Paris, they commonly adopt a physical point of view in order to represent geographical space. A province or city is not depicted from straight above as in modern cartography but as it might be seen from an appropriately located mountaintop. Towns thus appear as clusters of buildings seen from one side rather than from above. Mountain chains are indicated not by the color differences or altitude indications of modern topographical maps but by an outline of the peaks as they might be seen from one side. Rivers and seas sport boats seen in profile. In this way, the conceptual and visual aspects of charting are reconciled.

Friend of cartographers, employee of an important map publisher, Bruegel was undoubtedly influenced by the bird's-eye views of contemporary mapmaking. However, the important point is not simply that Bruegel may have been influenced by this or that mapmaking style but that he found in current approaches to cartography a stylistic correlative to his own, conceptually oriented, approach. Within this framework we can understand to what extent the early career of Pieter Bruegel is of a piece. At first glance, the Alpine drawings of the Large Landscapes seem to have little to do with the Virtue and Vice series, which, in turn, offer few obvious parallels with the artist's early painted masterpieces, but we easily see that all three draw on a well-defined system stressing an elevated point of view, discrete units located one above the other, and a strongly conceptual notion of compositional unity.

How, then, may we consider the large-figure compositions of the late 1560s? For many critics, this new style constitutes a radical departure from the previous small-figure approach. I suggest, instead, that the large-figure style continues the movement visible in the earlier allegorical mode. Just as the visual representation of a conceptual concern produces what we might term a "lowering of perspective" (from the overhead vantage point of the chart or layout to the high-angle point of view of, say, *Children's Games*), so the viewpoint of the late masterpieces offers continued tilting of the plane. Figures 6.20 to 6.22 offer a schematic representation of this progressive lowering of perspective, as if the viewer were moving from the cheap seats high up in a theater to the first balcony and finally to the orchestra.

More is at stake here, however, than the simple formal convenience of presenting an artist's development as a coherent progression. What is really at issue is the procedure that we use to interpret artwork of the sort represented by Bruegel in his later period. I am less interested in the historical precedents of the artist's later work than I am concerned to describe the meaning-making system on which those later masterpieces depend, thereby revealing the conceptual framework latent in them. In claiming that Bruegel's development is primarily not a change but a process of tilting, I am asserting that his later, seemingly realistic works call for the same conceptual readings that we apply to the allegorical works of the early period. To understand why this is so, we must turn to a careful analysis of Bruegel's style in his last years.

In Bruegel's *Peasant Wedding Dance* (1566; held in the Detroit Institute of Arts), as well as in a contemporary engraving that treats a similar subject, we find a strange mixture of old and new styles: the foreground figures are large, but the angle is so high and the perspective so skewed that even the background figures (e.g., the bride in the engraving) are over one-half the size of the large foreground figures. In addition, the high angle piles the figures up so that the characters' heads are stacked up one atop the other throughout the upper two-thirds of the composition. In the Detroit painting, the horizon line is located within inches of the painting's top margin, while the engraving piles the

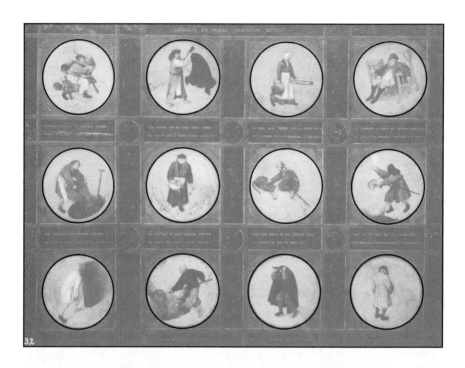

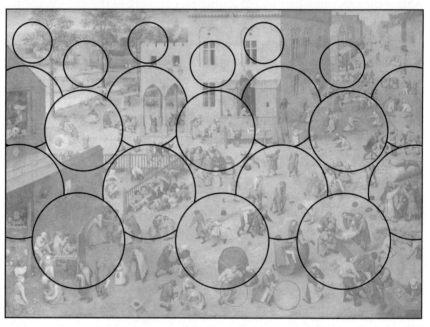

FIGURE 6.20 *(above)* Top view, with separate vignettes
FIGURE 6.21 *(below)* High-angle view, with minimal overlapping

FIGURE 6.22 Eye-level view, with extreme overlapping

heads up all the way to—and past—the top. This is a "large-figure" work in name only. While it certainly differs from *Flemish Proverbs* and *Children's Games*, it retains the major compositional attributes of these early paintings.

The Vienna-held *Peasant Dance* (1567) offers an entirely new approach (fig. 6.23). Every head (save the miniature woman and child in the lower left-hand corner) is located within a single narrow band just above the center of this striking composition. Though forty-five inches high, the painting crams some three dozen heads into a vertical space of less than nine inches. Nearly all the action is thus concentrated in a strikingly restricted space where background heads often peer out between middle-distance and foreground heads. There is a consequent loss of activity in the bottom and top registers of the composition, but this reduction of interest in the very areas where earlier Bruegel compositions excel is strongly compensated by renewed interest in the horizon height—precisely the area that Bruegel had traditionally left empty.

From left to right, the foreground couples of the Vienna *Peasant Dance*—individual units like those of the allegorical compositions—extend almost uninterrupted from left to right margin, covering nearly every bit of space. Every bit of foreground space, that is. Yet, in this case, the activity hardly stays in the foreground, for each couple defines a space-in-depth that leads us inexorably into the background, toward further activities. Between the pair on the left with outstretched arms we see another couple at the same table, while behind them are two lovers kissing. Additional dancers fill in the space between the bagpipers and the highsteppers: a couple frames a pair of background heads, which, in turn, frame yet another pair of heads. The far right-hand couple defines a space that seems at first to have little to do with Bruegel's previous compositions. Between the two large heads a second couple dances in the middleground; between the heads of the foreground and middleground couples appear the heads of merrymakers located in a first background plane, while beneath the raised arms of the middleground dancers we glimpse the head of a woman in the deep background conversing with other fairgoers.

Where once Bruegel would have used the human head to project us off into the distance, outside the margins of his composition, now he employs the human head to frame other human heads, pushing our attention into the hole between heads, where another pair are ready to draw us still farther, eventually projecting us off into the distance, but this time the distance may be found within the frame itself. Whereas Bruegel once multiplied points of entrance into the painting by sending the viewer outside the frame a maximum number of times, now he multiplies centers of interest and new approaches to the painting by providing numerous "dead-ends in depth," individual areas of concentration, from which it is not possible through normal methods of eye-leading to reach another area. An in-and-out movement still dominates, but the earlier technique sent us in and out of the frame, whereas here we go in and out of the distance built into the space of the frame. Greater realism results, but the strategy is not fundamentally different.

Why fill up the middleground and background with figures, when these distant characters must be given expressionless faces or even faceless bodies? Here we begin to understand Bruegel's use of the tilted plane. When the artist wanted to symbolize Prudence, he covered the space of a high-angle composition with examples of Prudence, inviting the viewer to hem-name each character, thereby conceptually unifying the composition. Having mentally identified each character by the hem name "Prudence," the viewer

FIGURE 6.23 Pieter Bruegel, *Peasant Dance* (Courtesy of Erich Lessing/Art Resource, New York)

then becomes free to flit from example to example, guided by the conceptual ties linking the composition's spatially isolated units. A decade later, Bruegel employed his new rotated-plane technique to represent *Summer* (fig. 6.24). Once again, the heads constitute a restricted line across the center of the composition, with the large-scale foreground pair framing a middleground pair who, in turn, frame . . . and so forth and so on. While one refreshes himself, another cuts the wheat, others gather it, and still others carry it to the barn. At the same time, the vegetable and fruit brigade perform their duties, while in the distance a second crew doubles the entire process and a third crew tackles the follow-up straw collection duty.

This is not a portrait of a man drinking from a jug (sporting one of the few examples in Western art of a foreshortened codpiece!), nor is it a traditional landscape. Instead, it is a multiple-focus composition whose subject, as the title makes clear, is the season of "Summer." Each actor in summer's traditional final act—the wheat harvest—is implicitly marked with the hem name of "Summer." All these individual activities, taken together and understood not in their specificity but in their collective generality, make up the season known as "Summer," just as another set of activities defines the notion of "Prudence," and still another group of festivities together constitute a "Peasant Dance" in all its generality and permanence. The final unity always depends on the concept named on the hem—the generalizing level that reduces seemingly diverse individuals to a common category.

Compare this approach to single-focus composition strategies, which place a group of figures, all more or less in the same plane, in front of a narratively insignificant background, either an architectural element as in Piero della Francesca's *Brera Altarpiece* (1472–1474) and Andrea Mantegna's *San Zeno Altarpiece* (1457–1459), or a neutral or symbolic landscape, as in Piero della Francesca's *Resurrection* (1459) and Leonardo da Vinci's *Annunciation* (1472–1473). Narratively speaking (and often visually as well), these single-focus backgrounds are out of focus. In fact, the very notion of "*back*ground" reveals the constitutive single-focus strategy: in order to focus attention on a single plane or individual, others are demoted to out-of-focus status. Bruegel's multiple-focus system, to the contrary, rejects the notion of a second-rate background, insisting instead on sharp focus throughout the composition's multiple planes-in-depth.

Iulius, Augustus, nec non et Iunius Aestas .   Frugiferas arus fert Aestas torrida meßeis .

AESTAS

FIGURE 6.24 *Summer*, engraving by Pieter van der Heyden after a drawing by Pieter Bruegel (Courtesy of the Board of Trustees, National Gallery of Art, Washington, D.C. [Rosenwald Collection])

Prefiguring cinema's development of deep-focus photography, Bruegel's deep-focus technique has many advantages. In particular, it facilitates a full spatialization of the conceptual units underlying his compositions. Whereas the pieces of *Prudentia* remain only pieces, never providing visual satisfaction but only conceptual rewards, the pieces of *Summer* and *Peasant Dance* constitute a spatial reality that cooperates with conceptual concerns rather than fighting them. Having exploded the canvas horizontally and vertically, Bruegel needed only to valorize the depth dimension in order fully to exploit the multiplex nature of his space. His innovations provide striking new solutions to numerous complex problems, and with them a first example of the uses of narrative multiplicity.

W hen a text follows several different characters, I speak of "multiple-focus narrative." Many multiple-focus narratives involve multiple plots. In fact, British theater's tendency toward multiple plots (as compared with French classical theater's spare unity-of-action style) is primarily responsible for much important writing about texts that attend to several different characters (Empson 1950, Dryden 1965, Levin 1971). But it is important not to confuse multiple-plot texts with the more general approach of multiple-focus narration. Whereas all multiple-plot texts are by definition multiple-focus, many multiple-focus narratives are organized around a single plot. Indeed, the level and type of a text's multiplicity is one of the main topics addressed by critics considering the broad questions related to multiplot novels (e.g., Maatje 1964, Garrett 1980, Bakhtin 1981,). While in this chapter I consider many texts with multiple plots, my primary concern is the more general question of multiple-focus narration.

Characterized by a following-pattern that attends to several separate characters, multiple-focus narratives offer many opportunities for interpretation through the dual-focus or single-focus approaches presented in the preceding chapters. It is even tempting to consider that all narrative texts can be treated as a combination of single-focus and dual-focus modes. Books that recount the stories of multiple, apparently unrelated, individuals—like Thornton Wilder's *The Bridge of San Luis Rey* and John Hersey's *Hiroshima*—might easily be configured as a combination of individual single-focus tales. However diverse the cast of characters followed in Charles Dickens's *Nicholas Nickleby* and *Oliver Twist*, many readers are likely to reduce that multiplicity to manageable proportions, either by organizing the novel's material around the title character or by treating each new episode and character as part of a familiar dual-focus replacement operations sequence. The separate sections of D. W. Griffith's *Intolerance* are so obviously composed of self-contained dual-focus stories that they were eventually distributed as separate films.

Indeed, it is not uncommon for a text that clearly operates according to dual-focus or single-focus principles to begin with a section characterized by multiple-focus following, or vice versa. Though Honoré de Balzac's *Le Père Goriot* and Jane Austen's *Pride and Prejudice* eventually leave little doubt as to their single-focus identity, they both commence by introducing many different characters, apparently inviting readers to interpret the text according to multiple-focus standards. While both novels settle rapidly into a single-focus configuration, others take much longer to resolve a multiple-focus following-pattern into a familiar single-focus or dual-focus arrangement or to shift from an apparently single-focus arrangement to a multiple-focus following-pattern. Gustave Flaubert's *Madame Bovary* follows Charles for several chapters before definitively settling on Emma. George Eliot's *Middlemarch* follows Dorothea for ten full chapters before spinning out to fuller treatment of provincial life and its actors. Many a Grail romance begins by following a single knight before unexpectedly expanding the following-pattern to several others.

In one sense, the writing and reading of multiple-focus narratives is like tightrope walking—great care is needed to avoid falling off the multiple-focus high wire into the safety nets provided by single-focus and dual-focus traditions. Though they may employ familiar constitutive units, the most interesting multiple-focus texts develop important new types of meaning, beyond the single-focus and dual-focus strategies analyzed in the preceding chapters. Not only do the formal aspects of multiple-focus texts differ from the patterns displayed by their single-focus and dual-focus counterparts, but also multiple-focus spectators are positioned in a radically new manner. From the complexity of its typical following-pattern to the implied critique of dual-focus and single-focus organization that it presents, the multiple-focus mode offers a separate approach to narrative construction and meaning.

Multiple-focus texts thrive on discontinuity, forcing characters and readers alike to devise novel methods of deriving meaning from apparently unrelated fragments. This process is especially salient in medieval Grail romances.

Illegitimate Narration

At a key moment of Chrétien de Troyes's *Le Roman de Perceval*, the handsome and courageous knight Gawain is accused of having killed his host's father. Outnumbered, far from the protection of Arthur's court, Gawain appears doomed, condemned to a fight to the death with the dead man's son. In extremis, however, he is offered an alternative: if within a year's time he can bring back the bleeding lance that pierced Christ's side, then he will be set free. His life in danger, Gawain dismisses his servants and sets out alone to find the bleeding lance. Suddenly the narrator interjects:

> Neither of them nor of their sadness
> Do I have any further desire to speak.
> Of Sir Gawain the tale
> Has no more to say at all
> But starts in on Perceval. (1959:vv. 6212–16)

For three hundred verses we follow Perceval through a memory loss, five years of wandering, and a religious lesson from a hermit, who turns out to be the young knight's uncle. Having promised to join the hermit in two days of penitence, Perceval takes communion on Easter Sunday. Then:

> Of Perceval no longer
> Does the tale speak here;
> Instead you will have first heard
> Much about Sir Gawain
> Before you hear me tell of him again. (1959:vv. 6514–18)

"The tale," as Chrétien puts it, would appear to have a mind of its own. Previously, Chrétien had always held his tale firmly in check. In *Cligés* he had followed the familiar dual-focus practice of alternating between two separated lovers. In *Yvain* he had contributed to nascent single-focus technique by sticking with the title character throughout, even when temporary madness strips him of mind, speech, and clothes alike. Yet in *Perceval*, the title character is regularly forced to relinquish control over the following-pattern. So unconventional is this procedure that the narrator refuses to take responsibility for the poem's repeated ruptures. Narrative discontinuity must be blamed on "the tale" itself.

The difference between this narrative disruption and its single-focus and dual-focus counterparts is striking. The metaphoric modulations that characterize dual-focus narrative immediately identify the grounds justifying their existence. "Meanwhile," "in a similar situation," "no less confused," and dozens of other formulas are employed to stress, from the outset, the logic uniting successive following-units. Even when no descriptive term identifies the connection between one following-unit and the next, grammatical or formal parallelism eases the transition, for the two foci always provide an invisible symmetrical armature for the unfolding of the tale. Though told in time, dual-focus narrative constantly relies on its fundamentally spatial structure to domesticate the apparent multiplicity of its following-pattern. As we flit about the Mediterranean in the Alexandrian romance—from lover to pirate to loved one to rival—we always know immediately where to place each new following-unit. Every apparent multiplicity is instantaneously reduced by the dual-focus structure to a new version of a familiar duality.

The metonymic modulations of single-focus narrative involve a similar reduction. Though *Pride and Prejudice* brings numerous characters into contact with Elizabeth Bennet, some of whom are followed momentarily or described in detail, we regularly connect each of them to Elizabeth's experience and evaluate them from her point of view. Similarly, secondary characters and eccentric following-units in Madame de Lafayette's *La Princesse de Clèves*, Daniel Defoe's *Moll Flanders*, Pierre de Marivaux's *La Vie de Marianne*, Nathaniel Hawthorne's *The Scarlet Letter*, and Henry James's *Portrait of a Lady* are all subordinated to the life of the heroine by a reader predisposed by the single-focus following-pattern to weigh each new following-unit in terms of its ability to shed light on the one character without whom the others would have no reason for being.

The fashion begun by Chrétien's *Perceval* wreaks havoc with the comfortable habits developed by readers of dual-focus and single-focus texts. Metonymic and metaphoric modulations provide immediate justification for their existence, along with grounds for unification of preceding and succeeding following-units (thus exerting a settling influence, which reinforces the reader's comfortably unified identity), but hyperbolic modulations actively deny familiar expectations. Take the case of *La Quête du Graal* (*La Queste del Saint-Graal*), the most important of the many thirteenth-century prose imitations and continuations of Chrétien's Grail romance. After having successfully concluded numerous adventures and resisted various temptations, Perceval is sent off into the unknown on a mysterious boat. "Fear not," he is told, "for wherever you may go God will be with you. Soon you will see Bohort and Galahad, the companions you are longing to meet again" (1965:154). Setting out onto uncharted seas, Perceval is promised exciting adventures, divine protection, and the fulfillment of his desires. Far from permitting us to follow Perceval's adventures, however, the narrator abruptly yanks us away from the pure-hearted seafarer, about whom "the tale ceases to speak," transferring us instead to the worldly Lancelot. Numerous encounters later, Lancelot finds himself in mortal combat with a knight in black armor, who has risen out of the sea. His horse slain under him, Lancelot is backed up to a cliff, closed in on three sides: behind him the rocks, to one side the sea, to the other a dense forest. While Lancelot resorts to the ultimate hope of prayer, the reader trembles for the knight's life, but the narrator blithely announces that "here the tale leaves Lancelot and returns to Gawain" (183). Every one of our expectations, conditioned by single-focus and dual-focus narrative, is frustrated by the multiple-focus technique of hyperbolic modulation.

The logic underlying hyperbolic modulation is nowhere more clearly explained than in André Gide's *The Counterfeiters* (*Les Faux-monnayeurs*), which is doubled by the author's journal of the novel's creation. Throughout the novel, Gide systematically refuses to follow plot developments to their logical conclusion, preferring to leave a character or conflict rather than take a chance on letting traditional concerns usurp the reader's interest. "Never take advantage of acquired momentum," says Gide in the *Journal des Faux-monnayeurs* (1932: vol. 13, p. 50), thus enunciating a fundamental rule of multiple-focus composition. Like Gide's most active novelistic characters—Lafcadio in *Lafcadio's Adventures* (*Les Caves du Vatican*) and Bernard in *The Counterfeiters*—each new segment, each successive following-unit must be an *enfant naturel*, an illegitimate child. Although single-focus and dual-focus texts allow each segment to give legitimate birth to its successor, multiple-focus texts thrive on illegitimacy and its guarantee of a new start, a freshness unavailable to the legitimate heir.

Of course, the social status of the bastard is hardly a comfortable one. Never was anyone introduced as "the illegitimate son of so-and-so," conventional morality requiring dissimulation of a state that falls outside of socially approved practices. The same situation exists in narrative, where hyperbolic modulation is perpetually branded with the stigma of social unacceptability. Medieval authors often blame discontinuity on a previously existing tale, thereby absolving the narrator of switching characters in mid-action. Modern authors take advantage of the implied disclaimer contained in a stretch of white space separating one following-unit from the next. The need to justify hyperbolic modulation by inserting white spaces in the text led Lodovico Ariosto to divide *Orlando furioso* into almost five thousand stanzas. In a similar manner, the prose romances of the late Renaissance used the license provided by white space to authorize inclusion of a wide variety of written forms: not only do we hop from character to character and from continent to continent, but also we flit regularly from straight narration to included stories, letters, poems, tomb inscriptions, legal manuals, and what-have-you.

The ultimate consecration of white space as justification for hyperbolic modulation came, surprisingly, in the quarrel over Pierre Corneille's controversial theatrical masterpiece, *Le Cid*. In the public debate over the type of *liaisons* (connections between scenes) that should be allowed, a conservative view rapidly prevailed. According to this dominant opinion, the baroque practice of locating successive scenes in diverse places with different characters must be abandoned. Successive scenes must assure continuity by the continued presence of at least one actor. Between one act and the next, however, a complete change of actors may be tolerated. As consecrated by the 1640s in plays by Mairet and Corneille, French classical dramatic theory prescribed what I have called metonymic modulations between scenes but allowed metaphoric or hyperbolic modulations between acts. By the century's end, this logic had been transferred to the question of chapter divisions within the novel.

Only with late-nineteenth-century multiple-focus narrative, however, would white space between chapters begin to play its full role. Throughout the eighteenth and nineteenth centuries, chapter divisions corresponded more often to the passage of time than to a radical change of character or plot line. Dividing their texts into ten or fifteen chapters gave novelists a desirable organizational aid, but it hardly provided the cover necessary for a major campaign of hyperbolic modulations. Consider the change in chapter allocation that accompanied Émile Zola's conversion to multiple-focus organization. His early single-focus novels (*Son Excellence Eugène Rougon*, *L'Assommoir*, *Nana*) average only a dozen chapters; his later multiple-focus efforts explode into a multitude of short fragments (e.g., forty chapters for *Germinal* and thirty for *La Terre*), each generally justifying a new hyperbolic modulation. It takes D. H. Lawrence thirty-one chapters to wind through the interlaced multiple plots of *Women in Love*, while John Hersey's *Hiroshima* follows André Malraux's practice in *La Condition humaine* of supplementing chapter divisions by the liberal use of white space to separate sections dealing with different characters. Whether in the allegorical drawings of Pieter Bruegel, the plates of Denis Diderot's *Encyclopédie ou dictionnaire raisonné des sciences, des arts et des métiers*, or the eccentric following-patterns of Tolstoy's *War and Peace* and Gide's *Counterfeiters*, a little bit of white space serves to justify juxtapositions that would otherwise have been deemed inappropriate.

Carnivalization

Pick a day, any day. Whom did you see all day? Chances are they were people like you: people who live on the same block, work in the same office, go to the same church, shop in the same store. Day in, day out, we see the same people. Not the exact same people, but the same sort of people, the ones who share our schedules and lifestyles. The nightshift factory worker drinks coffee with other nightshift factory workers, not with dayshift policemen. The farmer stops to discuss the weather with another farmer, not with a longshoreman. The kindergarten mom waits for her five-year-old alongside other parents with small children. Only rarely are we thrust into regular contact with others unlike us.

We do encounter a limited amount of difference whenever we use public transportation, but it usually takes an emergency, interrupting the normal pace of life, to radically change our regular pattern of contacts with people like us. Carnivals are designed to produce a similar effect. Engineered to attract people of all types by staging strange and unknown experiences, carnivals invite people of diverse backgrounds, occupations, and classes to live the experience of difference. If the carnival is any event, any place, any time when the "normal" tendency to stick to one's own kind may be "normally" transgressed, then multiple-focus texts constitute the ultimate in narrative carnivalization. Constantly choosing special circumstances favoring juxtaposition—not of opposites (the heart of dual-focus narrative) but of apparently unrelated individuals—multiple-focus texts offer a variety rarely seen in their single-focus or dual-focus counterparts.

Several devices are regularly deployed in favor of this variety. Renaissance narrative reveals a predilection for minimally motivated story collections (Boccaccio's *The Decameron*, Geoffrey Chaucer's *The Canterbury Tales*, the anonymous *Les Cent nouvelles nouvelles*, and Marguerite de Navarre's *L'Heptaméron*). Early modern novels often use the "Spanish Inn" strategy to lend realism to texts by including diverse characters and their stories (Miguel de Cervantes's *Don Quixote*, Paul Scarron's *Le Roman comique*, Henry Fielding's *Joseph Andrews*). To justify the promiscuous mixing of populations, later multiple-focus texts employ crowd scenes (Victor Hugo's *Notre-Dame de Paris*), wars (Leo Tolstoy's *War and Peace*), general strikes (Zola's *Germinal*), revolutions (Malraux's *La Condition humaine*), or a breach in the normal physical order of events (Wilder's *The Bridge of San Luis Rey*). Hollywood catastrophe films guarantee variety by concentrating on public spaces during natural disasters and similar events (George Seaton's *Airport*, John Guillermin's *The Towering Inferno*, Mark Robson's *Earthquake*, and dozens of look-alikes). One of the most frequent devices for assuring the carnivalesque mixing of classes, professions, and sexes involves the emergency status provoked by a plague (*The Decameron*, Albert Camus's *La Peste*) or a nuclear attack (John Hersey's *Hiroshima*, Nicholas Meyer's *The Day After*). Mikhail Bakhtin provides many more examples in his groundbreaking study of carnivalization, *Rabelais and His World* (1968).

Consistently, multiple-focus texts posit a level of unity beyond that of single individuals. Often, a public event is used to justify a multiple-focus following-pattern, with each individual providing only one piece of a mosaic that is of necessity transindividual in nature. Victor Hugo's first major novel, *Notre-Dame de Paris*, begins with an evocation of festivities at the Paris Palais de Justice on January 6, 1482. After a first chapter devoted to a general description of the crowd waiting to watch a mystery play, a second, entitled "Pierre Gringoire," concentrates on the author's difficulty in getting his play under way. The remaining four chapters in this first book take their titles from the major figures of the novel's plot who are followed in turn: "Monsieur le Cardinal," "Maître Jacques Coppenole," "Quasimodo," and "Esmeralda." The chapter units thus mirror the multiple-focus following-pattern, but the first book as a whole comes to a close only when the event is itself complete. Hugo's method of dividing his novel into books and chapters (like the chapter/fragment approach chosen by many twentieth-century multiple-focus authors) reveals the fundamental structural duality operative throughout the multiple-focus tradition: while one level is regulated by the following-pattern, with its characteristic discontinuity and multiplicity, a higher level unifies that multiplicity around an event or theme of a broader nature.

The master of multiple-focus narration in the service of a major event is, of course, Leo Tolstoy. Book 2 of *War and Peace*, for example, provides a multiple-character, multiple-location look at Napoleon's Russian campaign of 1805. We follow numerous major characters, both historical and fictional. Each one of the sixteen individual chapters is unified by attention to a single individual. Between chapters, however, there is rarely any direct connection. We flit from camp to camp and from character to character through the seeming sole justification provided by the events that constitute the campaign of 1805. As a result, the reader is constantly challenged to read on two radically different levels: that of character and that of event. Tolstoy's treatment of the skirmish at Schön Grabern, which ends book 2, typifies multiple-focus handling of events. In the chapters preceding the battle, we follow aide-de-camp Prince Andrew Bolkónski to the Austrian court, where in rapid succession we visit the Austrian Minister of War, Bolkónski's friend Bilíbin, Hippolyte Kurágin and his effete friends, and the Emperor Francis.

After draining all he possibly can from following Prince Andrew, Tolstoy abandons him for bigger game. First concentrating on the desperate position of the Russian commander in chief, Kutúzov, Tolstoy then details the un-orthodox attempts of the French advance guard commander, Murat, finally quoting at length a letter from Napoleon censuring Murat's initiatives. When Bolkónski is assigned to a fighting division under the command of General Bagratión, Tolstoy uses him as an introduction to the artillery brigade com-manded by Túshin, the forces deployed along the front lines, and even an uneasy conversation between Dólokhov and a French grenadier. Having prepared us for the battle with half-a-dozen views of every level—from em-peror to simple soldier—Tolstoy devotes four further chapters to the thick of the battle itself. If at first we observe both Túshin's artillery regiment and Bagratión's decision-making through Prince Andrew's eyes, we soon are in-vited by a white space on the page to view instead the rout of the right flank and the flight of young Nicholas Rostóv. After a closeup of Dólokhov's hero-ism and an extended view of the breakup of the artillery regiment, Tolstoy brings all the major actors of the battle together for a sort of postmortem: Bolkónski, Bagratión, Túshin, Rostóv.

Halfway through the next book, Prince Andrew Bolkónski and the young Nicholas Rostóv are confronted over their respective roles at Schön Grabern and, implicitly, over the type of account that best represents the battle. Giv-ing in to his familiarity with conventional accounts of military heroism, Nicholas has just given a standard first-person account of the events, the kind that would attract Henry Fleming (in Stephen Crane's *The Red Badge of Courage*) into active Civil War duty:

> His hearers expected a story of how beside himself and all aflame with excite-ment, he had flown like a storm at the square, cut his way in, slashed right and left, how his saber had tasted flesh and he had fallen exhausted, and so on. And so he told them all that. (Tolstoy 1966:260)

A few seconds later, infused with his borrowed heroism, Nicholas flies up at Prince Andrew, for whom such battlefield accounts are only so many "stories":

> "Yes, many stories! But our stories are the stories of men who have been under the enemy's fire! Our stories have some weight, not like the stories of those fel-lows on the staff who get rewards without doing anything!" (261)

Prince Andrew may have a general idea of how silly Nicholas's evaluation is, but only the reader (who has witnessed the behavior under fire of both men) understands the full degree of the young soldier's hypocrisy. Constantly drawing attention to the manner in which his tales are narrated—not only through his characters' discussions but also by means of his own massive commentary, particularly toward the end of the novel—Tolstoy regularly emphasizes his refusal of traditional single-focus and dual-focus accounts of war. Seen from every possible angle, each battle is not just a moment in the development of an individual (as it is, say, in *The Red Badge of Courage*), nor is it simply one more archetypically determined episode in an eternal struggle between Us and the Enemy (as in *The Song of Roland*). Instead, Tolstoy's battles constitute independent events, existing through, but nevertheless beyond and above, the characters who live them.

If the typical single-focus battle account is largely linear and one-dimensional in nature, stressing the lines tying every event to the protagonist, and if dual-focus wars tend to be two-dimensional, built on tension within a flat area, Tolstoy's multiple-focus approach succeeds in adding a third dimension, thereby offering a full sense of the volume of events. Single-focus technique constantly pulls the reader back to the camera constituted by the main character. All possible interest is located on the line linking the protagonist to the objects of his or her vision. Rarely allowed to stray from that vector, the reader concentrates on moving back and forth from war to warrior. The dual-focus approach sets out a compartmentalized space, dominated by conflicting areas that keep the reader on the surface of the text, fitting all data into symmetrical areas that rarely exploit the notion of depth. With multiple-focus technique, we find a studied attempt to provide that depth. Battles never appear out of nowhere but are prepared in terms of time as well as space. We know who has done what, where, and why. A map is often needed to help us connect the individual fragments that are all we will be given. Instead of being directly narrated, the battle must be pieced together by the reader, through reference to a series of following-units, each affording a different angle, a different play of light and shadow, and so a different view of the battle's reality. The event in all its volume takes on a meaning and an existence of its own, one to which only the reader can claim full access.

What is true of battles has been equally true of similar historical events since the mid-nineteenth-century revival of the multiple-focus form. Clearly linked to the rise of journalism, multiple-focus texts share both journalism's attempt to get to the bottom of any given event, no matter how many different reporters it might take, and journalism's recourse to the editor figure as final arbiter of the organization of individual accounts. Whereas single-focus and dual-focus authors are usually presented as creators, the multiple-focus author is often styled as the editor of preexisting material. An art of juxtaposition rather than invention, multiple-focus narration does not need to create the materials from which it is built. Whether the raw material of individual multiple-focus following-units is traditional (Grail romances), narrated by someone other than the principal narrator (story collections, "Spanish Inn" novels), written by someone other than the principal narrator (multiple-writer epistolary novels), historical (the late-nineteenth-century novel), derived from stock footage (historical documentary films), assembled from existing fragments of reality (cubism), or made up of interviews (newspaper articles), this raw material gains its specifically multiple-focus sense only when integrated by an editor into a coherent—albeit interlaced—narrative.

It is no accident that multiple-focus texts often have a documentary "feel." From Zola's naturalistic essays on mining, peasant life, and urban squalor, through the postwar documentary impulse of Hersey's *Hiroshima* and Italian neorealism (or, for that matter, American neorealism in such films as William Wyler's *The Best Years of Our Lives*), to the success of docudramas like *The Day After*, multiple-focus narrative seems incapable of renewing itself without a constant return to the wellspring of history—not what actually happened, but an event or set of events with the depth, complexity, and volume of a historical incident. Even a nondocumentary novel like Gide's *The Counterfeiters* regularly claims to be reporting independently existing real activities, thereby maintaining a richness and a thickness that surpass the ability of any single account—or even multiple accounts—to represent them. Like Chrétien in *Perceval* and Hugo in *Notre-Dame de Paris*, Gide constantly deploys the familiar device of refusing to take responsibility for the actions of his own characters, on the grounds that they are not characters but real beings, who enjoy the independence and carry the responsibility of real beings.

One of the surprising effects of multiple-focus narrative's documentary penchant is a strong tendency away from storytelling altogether. This pattern can be seen at its purest in the corporate report. Since the goal is not to trace the rise and fall of any individual but to document the state of a particular corporation, the following-pattern chosen is typically multiple-focus in nature. The report moves from one division to another in an effort to define the state of the abstract entity constituted by the corporation. While an anecdote here or there may be appropriate, the ultimate goal is clearly not narrative in nature, at least not in the traditional sense of the term.

Multiple-focus literature is only slightly less susceptible to this antinarrative impulse. Beginning with the late-medieval allegorical tendency to reduce the narrative interlace of Grail romances to a symbolic, moralizing framework, multiple-focus literary texts have developed numerous techniques for undermining the intrinsic narrative interest of their component following-units. From *The Decameron* to *The Heptameron* and from *Don Quixote* to Diderot's *Jacques le fataliste et son maître*, Renaissance and early modern texts typically provide a social or philosophical context, inviting a static reinterpretation of the included tale's dynamic narrative. Nineteenth-century multiple-focus novels often sidetrack narrative interest through authorial commentary. Balzac and Zola may concentrate most of their direct philosophizing and politicking in their critical texts, but other authors fill their novels with commentary designed to generalize the case of an individual character, thus lifting a seemingly single-focus or dual-focus fragment out of its local narrative context and placing it in a broader social, political, or philosophical framework. The novels of Hugo, Eugène Sue, Dickens, and Tolstoy depend on constant narratorial intervention and redefinition for their overall thematic effect.

While Romantic novelists are relatively comfortable interrupting their stories to comment on their meaning, naturalist and modern authors typically dissimulate their interventions. Early in *La Terre*, Zola has Jean read to an attentive rural audience the generalizing saga of "Jacques Bonhomme," the archetypal peasant, thereby concentrating reader interest on the representative quality of his peasant characters. Other novelists create a "sage" character, an individual whose age and experience has produced sufficient wisdom to help readers understand the thematic value of the other characters' lives. Sometimes representing the voice of the ages, like old Gisors in Malraux's *Man's Fate* (*La Condition humaine*), at other times the figure of the sage provides an autobiographical outlet for a thoughtful author (Birkin in

Lawrence's *Women in Love*). May the gullible reader beware, however, for this technique is eminently susceptible to ironic reversal, as in the case of Gide's Edouard, whose seeming position as the author's mouthpiece in *The Counterfeiters* is constantly undermined by the ridiculous nature of his pompous pronouncements.

Multiplicity as Critique

Historically as well as theoretically, one of the most important products of multiple-focus carnivalization is the creation of multiple-focus texts out of independent single-focus or dual-focus segments that take on a new existence once they have been inserted into a larger context. The multiple-focus nature of Spanish Inn episodes (which often occur in texts otherwise organized according to single-focus principles) depends on the inclusion of numerous independent stories which, told by different individuals, have no apparent unity of plot, theme, or tone. The Renaissance story collection gains its complexity from the multivalence of individual stories. However we may interpret any individual tale in *The Decameron* or *The Heptameron*, juxtaposition of that tale to other tales told on the same day (or other tales told by the same storyteller) forces us to build a new interpretive framework, separate from the strategy used for reading individual tales. Half a millennium later, the theoretical writings of nineteenth-century France's most important novelists (Balzac's "Avant-propos" to *La Comédie humaine*, Zola's treatise on *Le Roman expérimental*) would insist on a multiple-focus reading of their own, primarily single-focus, novels.

In their wake came two generations of novelists who built their multiple-focus texts out of traditionally narrated adventures of successive generations of the same or related families (Thomas Mann's *Buddenbrooks*, John Galsworthy's *The Forsyte Saga*, Roger Martin du Gard's *Les Thibault*, Jules Romains's *Les Hommes de bonne volonté*, Anthony Trollope's Barsetshire novels). In the film world, the tendency to build multiple-focus texts out of narratively unrelated single-focus or dual-focus blocks reached its zenith quite early with D. W. Griffith's quadripartite *Intolerance* (1916), parts of which were actually distributed independently as separate films. Today, documentary filmmakers regularly build footage from several different sources, representing multiple individuals, into a single multiple-focus composition.

The possibility of constructing a multiple-focus text out of several single-focus or dual-focus texts reminds us that multiplicity of focus may even be a question solely of the reader's interests. The chained single-focus tales of a young man and his exemplary father (*The Odyssey*) or the embedded single-focus treatments of a man and the woman who ruins his life (*Madame Bovary*) can also be read in multiple-focus terms. The critic who reads *Madame Bovary* as a portrait of contemporary country life featuring several representative rural figures (a common reading at the turn of the century, when France was still under the spell of naturalism's multiple-focus tendencies) is simply reading Flaubert's novel as a multiple-focus text, just as the critic who stresses the portrait of provincial bourgeois life in *Pride and Prejudice* sacrifices Elizabeth Bennet's single-focus story to a multiple-focus version of Austen's novel.

Many texts invite a single-focus or dual-focus reading, only to undermine that reading in favor of a multiple-focus alternative. Victorian fiction offers many novels whose titles apparently promise single-focus fare but whose multihundred pages provide strong justification for multiple-focus reading (e.g., Dickens's *Little Dorrit* and *Nicholas Nickleby*, Eliot's *Daniel Deronda*, Thomas Hardy's *Tess of the D'Urbervilles*, William Thackeray's *History of Pendennis*). Indeed, several critics have suggested that Victorian novels are best understood in terms of a structured relationship between narrow personal accounts and broad panoramas of society, between individual and social explanations of behavior—which is to say, between single-focus and multiple-focus approaches (Eagleton 1976, Garrett 1980, Armstrong 2005). If Tolstoy actively offers an opportunity for dual-focus reading of Russian history (the Napoleon-Alexander approach), as well as multiple separate single-focus readings (focusing on Andrew Bolkónski, Pierre Bezúkhov, Nicholas Rostóv, and especially General Kutúzov), it is only in order to critique them all the more effectively. Similarly, *Notre-Dame de Paris* and *Man's Fate* offer various dual-focus and single-focus lures, the better to hook us eventually on a multiple-focus overview. The same technique is regularly deployed by Italian neorealist filmmakers.

Just as the single-focus mode, both historically and theoretically, operates as an implicit commentary on dual-focus narrative, so multiple-focus texts often critique the single-focus units out of which they typically arise. Positing a dual-focus universe as implied context, single-focus narrative gains its energy from the protagonist's refusal of conventional values and consequent departure into an unknown world that dual-focus narratives had previously identified with non-being. Single-focus protagonists thus make new meaning out of the very realm that dual-focus tradition treats as meaningless. A similar process takes place in the multiple-focus mode, which—again historically as well as theoretically—operates as a specific critique of the single-focus approach.

In the hands of Chrétien de Troyes, late-twelfth-century romance constitutes one of the first high points of single-focus narrative. Characters like Lancelot and Yvain hold not only our uninterrupted attention but that of the narrator as well. The story appears to depend on the decisions and actions of the individual who remains at the focal point throughout. But Chrétien's last work, *Le roman de Perceval ou le conte du Graal*, systematically undermines individual characters' ability to organize the tale. Even the great Gawain can be unceremoniously dumped with no more than a curt "I don't feel like talking about his entourage any more, and anyhow the tale stops speaking about him here" (1959:vv. 6213–15). Where *Lancelot* and *Yvain* were organized around their title characters and extolled personal qualities, *Perceval* flits from Perceval to Gawain and back, thoroughly compromising identification and interest. By substantially increasing the number of characters followed, subsequent Grail romances magnify this disdain for individual characters and their qualities. Using interlaced adventures to concentrate attention on such specifically Christian virtues and doctrines as virginity and the celibacy of the priesthood, these romances successfully direct interest away from individual prowess and toward doctrinaire moralism. Knights seeking the Grail can no longer expect to succeed on the basis of their own prowess but must adhere to a new source of power to be found in Christian virtue, which becomes the true subject of the Grail romance.

In many ways, the development of multiple-focus narration in the nineteenth century follows a similar pattern. Under the influence of Sir Walter Scott's *Waverley*, the historical novel—and, on a broader scale, the novel in general—began its nineteenth-century career as a largely single-focus affair. Despite occasional experiments to the contrary, the Romantic worldview remains resolutely individualistic. Only with Thackeray, Tolstoy, and Zola does a single-focus view of history and contemporary social reality give way to a multiple-focus approach aimed specifically at critiquing and replacing the individualism and psychological orientation of the single-focus mode. As in the Grail romances, Tolstoy dwells on individuals identified by their titles (emperor, general, commander) as the heroes of previous narratives. These are characters who may be expected to make and enforce decisions, thereby changing the course of history. Yet the Russian author demonstrates how these very characters are unable to control their own fates, owing both their successes and their failures to forces beyond their power. From this standpoint, Jean Renoir's *La Règle du jeu* (*Rules of the Game*) resembles *War and Peace* to a striking degree. However independent the characters may appear to themselves, however convinced they may be of their ability to control their own fates, however important their individual stories may seem to the construction of the text—our view of multiple couples and classes reveals the extent to which social behavior is in fact controlled by factors beyond the reach of any particular individual.

The public quarrel over interpretation of Émile Zola's *L'Assommoir* offers an especially pertinent example of multiple-focus ability to contest and invalidate familiar single-focus principles. The changes that Zola made while composing *L'Assommoir* speak volumes about the inadequacy of single-focus technique for Zola's naturalist project. Already known for his 1867 single-focus study, *Thérèse Raquin*, Zola makes quite clear in the 1868 "Notes générales sur la nature de l'oeuvre" that he expects to continue the biographical approach in his Rougon-Macquart series. Citing Stendhal's single-focus protagonist Julien Sorel as a model, Zola firmly states his intention to build his novels around exceptional individuals (1967c:V,1743). The first novels of the Rougon-Macquart series carry out this plan to the letter. Concentrating on characters like the promiscuous priest of *La Faute de l'abbé Mouret* or the ambitious politician of *Son Excellence Eugène Rougon*, Zola was sure to attract public interest while remaining within the bounds of familiar single-focus technique.

For several years, Zola remained insensitive to implicit contradictions between his novelistic technique and his theoretical program. Each novel offers readers the opportunity to follow a single exceptional individual, to experience the world as he or she sees it, to participate in his or her desires and decisions. Though Zola the theoretician expected readers to find a social component in his writing, readers easily concluded that individual decision-making is what makes the world go round. As leader of the naturalists, Zola repeatedly described his novels as engaged critiques of the deleterious effect of various environmental and hereditary defects. Without the narratorial intervention that permits authors like Hugo, Sue, and Eliot to guarantee that their readers will not miss the point, however, Zola found that his novelistic technique did not always lead his readers where he wanted. Not until the summer of 1876 did this theory/practice contradiction come to a head. Chapters 1 through 6 of *L'Assommoir* had caused an enormous amount of commotion, not just because of Zola's decision to infuse this working-class novel with less than noble working-class language but also because of the negative judgments that readers understood Zola to be making about his main character, Gervaise Macquart, the provincial girl who falls on rough times in the big city.

Zola set out to write a treatise about the ill effects of alcohol on the working class ("L'Assommoir" is the name of the neighborhood bar, built around a still). What readers saw, however, is the conventional story of a naïve, small-town girl who at first hoists herself up by her bootstraps, taking in washing and saving money until she can afford to open her own laundry, but who then tries to live above her means and subsequently loses everything—shop, apartment, husband, self-respect. Easily read as a personal tragedy, the first half of *L'Assommoir* was enough to convince many readers that the locus of responsibility for the characters' personal problems must be sought only in their individual decisions. With only two-thirds of his novel completed, and publication due to resume immediately, Zola was so frustrated by public reaction that in July he ceased writing altogether. By the time he returned to his desk in September, he had solved his compositional crisis and come to terms with his readers' reactions. During the summer of 1876, Zola learned that single-focus technique was inadequate to his social commentary aspirations and that only multiple-focus presentation could assure the desired reading of his novel.

Responding to Albert Millaud's public attacks on the novel, on September 9, 1876, Zola outlined the message that he sought to make visible in the completed novel:

If you insist on knowing the lesson which, on its own, will arise from *L'Assommoir*, I will formulate it in approximately these terms: provide moral instruction for workers, free them from the misery in which they live, fight the crowding and promiscuity of ghettos where the air is thick and foul, and especially wipe out drunkenness, which decimates the working classes by killing the body and the mind. (Zola 1928:49:455)

Implying that the ultimate message of his novel depends on the as yet unpublished final chapters, Zola invites us to take a closer look at the portions of *L'Assommoir* composed after his July crisis. Careful inspection of the final four chapters suggests a growing desire on Zola's part to decentralize the novel in order to generalize his message. Far from simply continuing the single-focus form and thematics of the first two-thirds of *L'Assommoir*, the last part calls into question the conclusions of the first. Not only does it generalize Gervaise's situation, it also depsychologizes her in order to convince readers that her conduct can be explained only by something other than personal motivation.

Three distinct but related methods help to remove the dénouement of *L'Assommoir* from the single-focus realm of the psychological. First, Zola diverts the typical psychological novel linear plot, blurring causality, stressing survival and repeated daily action, and eventually molding the plot into something of a cyclical nature. Once Gervaise has returned to Lantier's bed and thus sealed her doom, the narrative style, like the wallpaper in the laundry, begins to lose its color. The only real events remaining are the deaths of Coupeau and his mother; Gervaise is reduced to "the single pleasure of eating three meals a day" (Zola 1967a:II,642). The imperfect therefore begins to drive out the preterit as dominant tense. Decisions are replaced by accumulations. The whole concept of causality is questioned as events begin to organize themselves in spirals—the progression is there, perhaps, but you have to squint to see it. When Nana first runs away it is an event, a morally reprehensible action that even her parents are quick to condemn. When she disappears again, however, her parents rapidly get used to the new situation. A page later, Nana is back once more, but in less than ten lines she is gone yet again. Then, within two lines, she has flown the coop and straggled back one more time. Now, however, Zola destroys the specificity of the action through use of the imperfect. In the following passage, note how the first three preterits, describing instantaneous action, are transformed into habitual imperfects through the clever transitional device of a preterit designating repeated action (*continua*):

> Elle *reçut* une rossée, naturellement; puis, elle *tomba* goulûment sur un morceau de pain dur, et *s'endormit*, éreintée, avec une dernière bouchée aux dents. Alors, ce train-train *continua*. Quand la petite se *sentait* un peu requinquée, elle *s'évaporait* un matin. Ni vu ni connu! l'oiseau *était parti*. Et des semaines, des mois *s'écoulaient,* elle *semblait* perdue lorsqu'elle *reparaissait* tout d'un coup, sans jamais dire d'où elle *arrivait*. (1967a:II,743; my italics)

> She *got* a beating, naturally; then she *dove* into a crust of bread and *fell* asleep, exhausted, with the last mouthful between her teeth. This routine *continued*. Whenever she *would feel* a bit perked up, she *would evaporate* one morning. Out of sight, out of mind, the bird *was gone*. Sometimes months *would go by*, she *would seem* lost when she suddenly *would show up* again, never saying where she *was coming* from.

The linearity of the plot rapidly disappears into passages like this. At the beginning of the novel, Gervaise's problems were caused by poor decisions, like her insistence that Coupeau convalesce from his fall at home rather than at the hospital; now the narrative is removed from the realm of decisions entirely and transferred instead to time's dehumanizing tendency to wear people down, both physically and morally.

Second, the degradation of Gervaise and her family is increasingly associated with the parallel problems experienced by others in their milieu, as the following-pattern becomes less rigidly concentrated on Gervaise. One day, when Coupeau claims to have been working, Gervaise decides to ambush him at the pay office, thus assuring her share of the pay. To her surprise, she is not alone, for there are other wives who have the same problem. Even when Gervaise turns to prostitution, seemingly the ultimate degradation, she is but one in a long line of ladies of the night. Is it any wonder that Gervaise learns to excuse her actions by pointing out that she is not alone? Wasn't it natural for her to go with Lantier? Hadn't she known him when she was fourteen? And, anyhow, the Rue de la Goutte d'or isn't so clean itself, with Madame

Vigouroux rolling in the coal from dawn to dusk and the grocer's wife making it with her brother-in-law, not to mention that tight little old watchmaker who carries on with his daughter. Where once Gervaise's firm decisions differentiated her from her neighbors, now she is made to blend in with those around her, sliding imperceptibly from the exceptional character around whom Zola once planned to build the Rougon-Macquart series to the representative character born of his new swerve toward multiple-focus technique.

Third, traditional notions about individual accountability are challenged, as responsibility for actions is increasingly redirected from the individual toward the group. This change is heralded by a slow but insistent evolution in point of view. During the early parts of the novel we are constantly aware of Gervaise's projected future, her hopes, her evaluation of the people and activities around her. As the novel progresses, however, our interior views of Gervaise become less frequent and less detailed. A shift in the following-pattern requires Gervaise to share her central spot in the narrative with the other characters, thereby losing the right to our exclusive attention. In addition, the center of Gervaise's being has moved progressively lower—from heart and mind to bowels and belly. In a parallel development, Zola's free indirect style deserts Gervaise for a far more generalized point of view. Instead of her thoughts, as Brian Nicholas has pointed out (1962:10), it is the local gossip that we get in free indirect discourse form. With this shift in point of view comes a change in value systems: from a deadline-conscious individualistic work ethic to a nearly atemporal communitarian approach where everyone always has time to sit and chat. Where wrong decisions or defective morals would once have been blamed for characters' failures, now individual responsibility is replaced by social explanations.

Looking back on his novel shortly after its 1877 publication in book form, Zola once more sought to get the monkey of personal responsibility off his back. Writing to the director of the magazine that had published the first half of the novel, Zola insisted that he had planned every step of his characters' fall in such a way as "to show that the environment and alcohol are the two great disorganizers, beyond the individual will of the characters." Gervaise and Coupeau must be seen as passive objects and nothing more. "As for Nana, she is a product. I wanted my drama complete. I needed a good-for-nothing child in the family. She is the daughter of alcoholics, she undergoes the fatality of misery and vice. . . . Consult the statistics, and you'll see whether I'm lying" (1928:vol. 49, p. 469). Following multiple-focus logic, Zola introduces characters on social and thematic grounds instead of choosing them because of an attractive personality or the importance of the decisions they must make. Nana is necessary in order to broaden the syndrome to yet another generation, thus further refuting the single-focus reading that would make characters fully responsible for their own fate.

"Consult the statistics," Zola urges, at the dawn of the age of sociology. Zola is here describing his literary technique as well. "I have created and arranged my characters in such a way as to incarnate in them the different varieties of the Parisian worker," he affirms in the same letter, suggesting that his novel is composed in such a way as to provide the reader-sociologist with all the requisite data for proper analysis. Only with his abandonment of strictly single-focus organization in the final one-third of the novel, however, does Zola's true purpose become apparent. To emphasize the statistical thematics of sociology, Zola seems to have learned during the *Assommoir* experience, the novel must become statistical and sociological in its form as well. Only multiple-focus technique could accomplish his thematic purposes. In the years to come, Zola's most important novels would be built from beginning to end according to multiple-focus principles. Whenever the leader of the naturalist school decided to use the novel as a vessel for sociological study or social commentary—as in *La Terre* and *Germinal*—he would remain faithful to the techniques of multiple-focus narrative.

How Did We Get Here from There?

Discontinuous, fragmented, resisting consistent reader identification, multiple-focus narrative requires a mode of reading different from that of dual-focus and single-focus narrative. From the Grail romances to Victorian novels and from Bruegel to cubism, multiple-focus texts set familiar pieces into unexpected patterns, calling into question the comfortable habits of readers and viewers alike. The multiple-focus romances that dominated Western European narrative from the thirteenth century to the Renaissance offer interesting insights into the new mode of reading required by multiple-focus texts. In single-focus romances, a strict code of conduct specified appropriate forms of action for the romance knight. The knight who refused to lend succor to a damsel in distress could expect castigation on the part of reader and narrator alike. In multiple-focus Grail romances, however, variations from the knightly code of conduct constitute only minor sins, paling before the great fault, the one that returns again and again, from text to text the same. The cardinal sin in the Grail romances involves not the knight's role as actor in the world but his responsibility to question the world. The knight's greatest failing is inability to inquire about the unknown, to locate the ineffable: in short, to ask the Grail questions. That this new emphasis on the mystic, the symbolic, and the thematic should accompany a change in narrative technique is no accident, for if multiple-focus narrative exists at all it is in order to ask questions that the two other modes are unable to articulate.

Time and again in multiple-focus texts we find ourselves transported by the narrator from one character to another. We were hearing about Perceval, then suddenly the tale switches to Gawain. We were following Andrew Bolkónski when, with no more warning than a little white space on the page, we find ourselves following Nicholas Rostóv. This hyperbolic modulation invites us regularly to ask, "How did we get here from there?" and thus, implicitly, "What justifies juxtaposition of these particular following-units?" In this way, multiple-focus readers systematically stretch beyond the action-oriented and character-oriented questions of single-focus and dual-focus narrative. Regularly deprived of familiar identification patterns, multiple-focus readers are forced by hyperbolic modulation into positions where they will be encouraged to ask the "Grail" questions, the questions that reach beyond the familiar character and plot surface of the text and into the thematic regions beyond.

One important method of inducing readers to ask questions of a far-reaching nature is to undermine the star system on which single-focus and dual-focus narrative typically repose. However much we may associate the star system with Hollywood, stardom existed long before the moving pictures. Consider the fate of poor Lancelot, legendary romance hero, when his latest adventures were included in the thirteenth-century prose romance, *La Queste del Saint Graal.* Far from being treated like a star, he is allowed to fall fast asleep when he sees the Holy Grail—a sin that is rapidly tied to his lascivious sexual conduct. Lancelot is used here as sucker bait. We know his reputation as the era's consummate sex symbol, so we follow him with the interest accorded to a star. His inability to ask the Grail questions, however, transfers our investment from Lancelot to the Grail itself. What is it? What does it mean? What kind of a knight does one have to be in order to ask the right questions? Just as Zola had to downplay Gervaise's role in order to make a more general point, so the author of *La Queste del Saint Graal* must abandon Lancelot in order to further his chastity-oriented program, eventually inducing readers to recognize in the Grail an unspoiled vessel symbolizing chastity.

The inability of the star to ask the right questions in the Grail romances is matched in Bruegel's compositions by an absolute unwillingness to set characters in a hierarchy. Mary and Joseph must wait their turn to be counted just like all the rest. Each proverb and each children's game is on a level with all the others. Even in the mature large-figure paintings, a system of eye-leading assures democratized attention to all. This refusal to emphasize particular individuals, to create a spatial and narrative center, becomes a basic tenet of twentieth-century multiple-focus narrative. As in the ensemble acting style popularized by the touring Meiningen Players in Germany and André Antoine's Théâtre Libre in Paris, the multiple-focus novel systematically refuses to let a single individual take over the following-pattern. Even with characters who hold an apparently dominant position—like Dorothea Brooke for the first ten chapters of *Middlemarch* or the novelist Edouard in Gide's *Counterfeiters*—the course of circumstances quickly undermines their authority, robbing them of the central position to which they were apparently destined.

A further hindrance to familiar identification patterns may be found in the multiple-focus dependence on intersecting plots. In a typical single-focus scene, we observe numerous characters from a vantage point that is easy for us to discover and occupy. No matter who is speaking or acting, we evaluate each contribution from the standpoint of the protagonist, even during the limited periods when someone else is being followed. Little confusion is likely—except at the start, before a specific individual has been identified as the protagonist (e.g., during the description of the Pension Vauquer at the beginning of *Le Père Goriot*). Multiple-focus narrative radically revises this configuration. Because the multiple-focus system refuses to take advantage of momentum—treating every new following-unit not as the sanctioned continuation of its predecessor but as an illegitimate child—multiple-focus texts begin again and again. Sometimes they seem made up of nothing but repeated beginnings.

Showing a marked preference for group scenes, often including several characters who have been followed independently, multiple-focus narrative causes significant problems for the reader. When, in book 3 of *War and Peace*, Nicholas Rostóv lauds the role of the fighting men in the Schön Grabern skirmish, at the same time castigating the staff officers for their inaction, we are hard put to know whether this statement is to be registered as part of young Rostóv's Bildungsroman (the story of his personal development) or whether it is told as a test for Prince Andrew Bolkónski, who listens imperturbably, refusing to take offense in spite of the opinions that our recent close following of Prince Andrew give us the right to attribute to him. Because we have followed both men separately during Tolstoy's rendition of the 1805 campaign, we experience the scene between Rostóv and Bolkónski from both sides simultaneously. As readers, we are just as fragmented in our identification tendencies as is Tolstoy's following-pattern.

What the modernist novel accomplishes through interlaced plots built around a multiple-focus following-pattern, the cinema sometimes achieves through the technique of deep-focus cinematography. Until the late 1930s, film mise-en-scène and editing were heavily indebted to proscenium theater. Important characters were stressed by placing them in sharp focus against a background that, lacking interest and focus, served only to concentrate attention on foreground activity. How different is the system employed by Jean Renoir in *La Règle du jeu*. Upon their arrival at the country mansion where the bulk of the film's action takes place, the film's extremely diverse cast assembles in the entrance hall to welcome the guest of honor, André Jurieu, a Lindbergh look-alike who has just flown the Atlantic solo, only to be snubbed by the countess for whom he all too publicly undertook his exploit. As the camera focuses on the countess attempting to explain (away) her part in the aviator's flight, we note two other faces, perfectly in focus even though they are not located in the foreground: the countess's husband and her friend Octave (Jurieu's other rival for the countess's affection). In a single shot, Renoir brings together four separate lines, combining an extraordinary economy of expression with a complex invitation to multiple viewings, for only the most experienced viewer will succeed in seeing all four characters at once on first viewing. Most spectators will focus on one character one time and another the next, thus multiplying the possible permutations of the following-pattern without varying the basic multiple-focus system.

Later in the same film, we find deep-focus technique serving another common multiple-focus function. While the masters have been squabbling over the mistress, the servants have been fighting over her maid. One of the evident tasks of this film is to reduce diverse classes to a single, human, common denominator. Throughout the film, we have been alternating between the classes and the sexes. Only when the interlaced paths cross, in a series of deep-focus shots that always give us more than one squabbling trio at a time, are we forced to consider one plot in terms of the other, one following-unit in terms of another. Since the paths of Jurieu, the count, and the countess constantly cross the paths of Schumacher the game warden, Marceau the poacher, and Lise the countess's maid, it becomes harder and harder for the spectator to avoid asking the Grail questions about these two trios. Who are they? What do they represent? Why are we constantly seeing them together? Why do they keep doing similar things?

William Wyler's postwar masterpiece *The Best Years of Our Lives* also uses deep-focus cinematography to force comparisons among the three interlaced plots around which the film is built. Unrelated by anything but the coincidence that brought them home in the same airplane, three diverse servicemen are followed separately and apparently independently. Halfway through the film they run into each other at Butch's Place, where Gregg Toland's extraordinary camera work juxtaposes them in a single image. The three will not be seen together again until the final scene, where Toland once again deploys the resources of deep-focus cinematography to connect them. While one serviceman's marriage occupies the foreground, a deep-focus image reveals the other two in the background. The Grail questions cannot be avoided: Why these three? What do they have in common? What is it that brings them together here in this image, this story?

Hem-Naming

Single-focus and dual-focus narratives encourage readers to ask questions located at the level of the narrative. The answers to these questions are also located at the level of the narrative. Question: What will happen to Jesus?

Answer: He dies and is resurrected. Question: With whom will Fred be paired? Answer: With Ginger. The Grail questions induced by multiple-focus texts always extend beyond the level of the narrative, however. They call for answers that cannot be furnished by narrative action alone. The narrator's own commentary may provide the requisite answers, extending, as it often does, far beyond the events of the narrative itself. More often, however, readers themselves must postulate and inhabit a level beyond that of narrative action in order to satisfy their multiple-focus desires.

To make sense, the separate parts of multiple-focus texts must be made to signify in similar terms. At first, Malraux's *Man's Fate* appears to be only a disjointed account of revolutionary activity. It begins to develop the thematic resolution characteristic of multiple-focus narrative only when the common humanity of the various participants comes to the fore, only when each of the activities presented can be fitted into a thematic framework common to all the actors. Compilation of the multiple stories of D. W. Griffith's *Intolerance* into a single film appears unjustified until their common thematic basis becomes evident. Just as the individual characters of Bruegel's drawing *Elck* lack a reason for being brought together in this particular composition until the engraving inscribes the same name—Everyman—on the hem of each one's garment, so all characters and activities must go through a process of hem-naming in order to fulfill the promise of multiple-focus texts. Often, the hem name is immediately provided by the work's title. Think, for example of the multiple-focus effect achieved from the very start by the choice of titles like "Children's Games," "The Counterfeiters," "The Human Condition," or even "The Big Calves" (Fellini's early film *I Vitelloni,* the story of five overgrown children, each failing to find a meaning in life).

Just as the interlacing of Grail romances forces attention away from simple questions of knightly prowess and toward the more ethereal question of Christian virtue, so multiple-focus texts regularly employ the technique of juxtaposition to transcend their lowly materials. Nowhere has this process been more precisely described than in the considerable literature surrounding the cubist movement in art and poetry. As the poet Guillaume Apollinaire says in his 1913 essay on cubist painters: "What separates cubism from all previous painting is that cubism is not an art of imitation but an art of conception" (1965:56). The montage strategy of cubism, like the interlace approach of multiple-focus literature, strives to reach beyond visual perception and narrative resolution. Early-twentieth-century avant-garde artists refused to be satisfied with a specific view of an object, instead replacing vision with conception as the artist's fundamental mode. The artist does not paint an object itself but instead suggests that object in "all its essentials, even those hidden by optical perspective," as Paul Klee put it in 1902 (1945:443). "In order to achieve maximum strength," asserted the poet Pierre Reverdy a quarter-century later, "an image must grow out of the spontaneous juxtaposition of two extremely diverse objects whose connection can be seized *by the mind alone*" (1927:34; his italics). Art must force us to step beyond familiar methods of perceiving the world. "If the senses totally approve the image," says Reverdy in the same passage, "they kill it for the mind." Our uneasiness with cubist works is thus accounted for and valorized: only by frustrating the senses can a work of art force lazy consumers to become active participants, thus freeing them to discover new relationships, new realms.

No longer able to count on vision as a unique method of knowing, the spectator, like the artist, must develop a new type of understanding, such as that recommended in 1912 by Maurice Raynal, one of the most important early theorists of cubism:

> We never, in fact, see an object in all its dimensions at once. Therefore what has to be done is to fill in a gap in our seeing. Conception gives us this means. Conception makes us aware of objects we would not be able to see. "I cannot *see* a chiliagon [a 1,000-sided figure]," said Bossuet, "but I can conceive it perfectly well." When I think of a book, I do not perceive it in any particular dimension but in all of them at once. And so, if the painter succeeds in rendering the object in all its dimensions, he achieves a work of method which is of a higher order than one painted according to the visual dimensions only. (Raynal 1966:95)

Like multiple-focus literary narratives, cubism constitutes not only an alternative to previous approaches but also a specific critique of their ground for being. As Raynal succinctly states, "In painting, if one wishes to approach truth, one must concentrate only on the conceptions of the objects, for these alone are created without the aid of those inexhaustible sources of error, the senses" (96). For the cubist, the senses exist only to provide material for conceptual activity (just as multiple-focus literature uses single-focus or dual-focus passages as a means of leading the reader past identification to the questioning activity particular to multiple-focus narrative).

How early-twentieth-century art movements sought to achieve the conceptualization of art is admirably explained by Gino Severini in his "Futurist Manifesto 1913." Insisting throughout that a painting's "subject matter, when its effect is considered, sacrifices its integrity, and therefore its integral quantities, in order to develop to the utmost its qualitative continuities" (1973:123), Severini offers a specific example of a particular "qualitative continuity":

> In this way certain forms and colours expressing the sensations of noise, sound, smell, heat, speed, etc., connected with the experience of an *ocean liner*, can express by *plastic analogy* the same sensations evoked in us by a very different reality—the *Galeries Lafayette* [a prominent Paris department store].
>
> The experience *ocean liner* is thus linked to the experience *Galeries Lafayette* (and every experience is linked to its specific but diverse correlative) by its *qualitative radiations* which permeate the universe on the electrical waves of our sensibility.
>
> This is a complex form of realism which *totally* destroys the integrity of the subject-matter—henceforth taken by us only at its *greatest vitality*, which can be expressed thus:
>
> *Galeries Lafayette= ocean liner*
>
> The abstract colours and forms that we portray belong to the Universe outside time and space. (121–22)

If dual-focus narrative models space and single-focus texts develop in time, the multiple-focus form seeks out the *tertium quid* of conception. This it does by juxtaposing objects, characters, or narrative segments that possess what Severini calls the same "qualitative radiations." What would be the subject of a painting in which the Galeries Lafayette and an ocean liner are placed side by side? To be sure, neither the ocean liner nor the Galeries Lafayette. Instead, it is the shared qualities of the two objects that garner our attention, that provide the ultimate answer to our inevitable question: "How did we get here from there?"

While futurists were setting department stores next to ocean liners, while cubists and surrealists were heeding the call by Isidore Lucien Ducasse (Comte de Lautréamont) to juxtapose an umbrella and a sewing machine on an operating table, while Sergei Eisenstein was developing his theories of montage, D. H. Lawrence was interweaving the stories of four characters in *Women in Love*. Instead of perpetuating familiar single-focus strategies, Lawrence's novel—like many other symbolic novels of the same period—is less interested in characters than in states. Anxious to define certain basic concepts like being and existence, Lawrence has his characters enact themes rather than make choices, thereby compromising character individuality. Because the story must be put to conceptual purposes, narrative exists only to be superseded. Updating the Grail romances like so many other modern multiple-focus novels, *Women in Love* challenges the reader to reestablish the secret connections among Birkin, Ursula, Gerald, and Gudrun. Yet Birkin insists that no common ground can possibly justify comparing one person to another: "One man isn't any better than another, not because they are equal, but because they are intrinsically *other*, that there is no term of comparison" (1960:97). As the novel weaves on, however, Birkin and friends continually provide us with the very terms of comparison whose existence he has denied, so we are hardly surprised to hear Birkin affirm that there are only "two great ideas, two great streams of activity remaining" (296).

According to Lawrence's spokesman, all people act and react "involuntarily according to a few great laws" (296). The highly charged language with which Lawrence typically infuses his writing has already revealed the secret of those two great laws: on the one side, the sensual, proud, and electric; on the other, the sensuous, conceited, and mechanical. Again and again, Gerald is identified with industrial mechanisms, to the point where Lawrence terms him "the God of the machine" (220), while the relationship between Ursula and Birkin brings to them "a rich new circuit, a new current of passional electric energy" (305), a source of power that is "deeper, further in mystery than the phallic source" (306). "Nothing that comes from the deep, passional soul is bad" (viii), says Lawrence in the preface to *Women in Love*. Indeed, the entire book appears as an attempt to create a space for the author's beloved passional soul. Like *La Queste del Saint Graal*, which uses the mystic notion of the Holy Grail to champion male virginity, so Lawrence attempts to reach beyond accepted social practices toward a mystic state that can only be hinted at, that can be suggested only by the indirect methods of multiple-focus narrative.

To induce readers to discover the common denominators necessary to make sense of multiple-focus characters and plots, particularly good use has been made of narratorial intervention, parallel scenes between otherwise unrelated characters, and narrative metaphor. Eugène Sue's *Les Mystères de Paris* is one of the earliest and most successful of nineteenth-century serial novels combining dual-focus and multiple-focus techniques. Modulating back and forth from Rodolphe and his angelic legion of do-gooders on the one side to La Chouette, Bras-Rouge, Jacques Ferrand, and their criminal comrades on the other, *Les Mystères de Paris* also provides a constant interlace of seemingly unrelated plot motifs, all of which ineluctably cross at the high points of the narrative. In between, we are regularly privy to Sue's reflections on his narrative strategies. Three-quarters of the way through the novel, for example, Sue chooses to give us a close look at the menagerie of inmates condemned to do time in La Force prison. Because this interlude contributes nothing to the book's dominant dual-focus narrative, hardly touching on the story's main characters, Sue provides an explanation of his strategy:

> I may perhaps then be excused for having grouped around the prisoners who are already well-known characters in this story a number of secondary characters, designed to activate, to give relief to certain critical ideas, and to complete this initiation into prison life. (1963:679)

Like Victor Hugo in *Notre-Dame de Paris* and *Les Misérables*, Sue turns to narratorial intervention to make sure that his interlaced tale will be understood on his terms—in this case, the terms of a social reformer more interested in the common causes of his characters' misery than in the specificity of their individual destinies.

In their concern to guarantee that separate characters will be understood according to the same general parameters, multiple-focus authors regularly create parallels tying one character to another. Take, for example, the voyeuristic tendencies of the Frollo family in *Notre-Dame de Paris*. Jealous to the point of homicide, older brother Claude secretly watches the young dandy Phoebus make love to the gypsy princess Esmeralda until he can stand it no longer. Shortly afterward, younger brother Jehan hides under a table and observes while Claude debates the principles of alchemy with other philosophers. The shared voyeuristic position of the Frollo brothers in these two scenes serves to bind permanently together the two master plots of Hugo's novel—alchemy and love. Parallel scenes like these encourage readers to resolve differences between characters at a higher level of generalization. Instead of experiencing a novel as separate interlaced stories of characters connected only by chance meetings or plot wrinkles, we begin to reformulate the text as a coherent landscape, unified by the hem-naming process.

Consider the efffect of the following parallels (chosen among many) on *War and Peace*:

- Pierre Bezúkhov believes that everyone sees him falling in love with Hélène, just as Nicholas Rostóv is sure that everybody can see his fear upon entering a battle.
- The dissolution of Andrew Bolkónski's marriage is timed to correspond with the celebration of Pierre's marriage.
- While Borís is openly attempting to profit from the social advantages of military rank, Pierre consciously puts Masonic brotherhood above social status.
- To Pierre's Masonic conversion corresponds Andrew's newfound communion with nature and his decision to modernize his serfs.

In addition, nearly every character is characterized according to his or her particular belief in a different version of the notion of fate: Mary Bolkónski in providence, Pierre Bezúkhov in a Masonic God, Andrew Bolkónski in nature, Nicholas Rostóv in Alexander, and so forth. While Tolstoy is not one to hammer home the social or symbolic import of his parallels, like Sue, Hugo, and the author of *La Queste del Saint Graal*, these parallels nevertheless pull us out of straightforward character or plot concerns and launch us into a realm more commonly inhabited by narratorial intervention—a world of questions and answers that lie beyond the limits of the narrative as such.

A similar process presides over the organization of many Victorian novels. Combining multiple plot lines, they must deploy many different devices to bring the various parts of the novel together, both globally and locally. George Eliot's enormous *Middlemarch* offers a particularly clear example of this process. Based on two originally separate projects (a story about Dorothea Brooke and a study of provincial life), Eliot's novel reflects in its structure this combination of single-focus and multiple-focus origins. Beginning with ten chapters about Dorothea, *Middlemarch* eventually spins out to a much broader following-pattern involving many different characters. Underlying the novel's at times apparently random organization are several important parallels. As Peter Garrett points out:

> [Eliot's decision to join the two projects] seems to have arisen from a recognition of similarities between Dorothea and Lydgate, and the reader reenacts this perception as he compares these two stories of idealistic aspirations frustrated by social restrictions and mistaken marriages. From Book 2 onward, we are prompted to pursue this kind of reading by book titles that direct us to compare "Three Love Problems" or "Two Temptations" and to find multiple applications for rubrics such as "Old and Young" or "The Dead Hand." (1980:142)

Though *Middlemarch* may be one of the novels excoriated by Henry James as a "large loose baggy monster" (1934:84), it clearly offers many principles of unification across an extremely diverse following-pattern.

One of the most interesting and successful of multiple-focus hem-naming techniques involves the use of metaphor to establish connections between realms once deemed separate or whose relationship was not previously obvious. Shuttling between military scenes and views of daily life away from the front, *War and Peace* confects a common language to bring the two domains together, repeatedly using battlefield metaphors to describe the salon and images of the hunt to describe battle scenes. Attributing to his military characters emotions normally encountered in the boudoir, Tolstoy also develops extended parallels between social and military hierarchies. Though the cast of *War and Peace* is large and varied, our ability to detect hidden connections among the characters helps provide unity to Tolstoy's novel. Similar methods are used by Hugo in *Notre-Dame de Paris*. Through the ever-present spider/fly metaphor, with its graphic extension into the domain of webs and concentric circles, every character is defined by reference to the problem of fate. In *Nostromo*, Joseph Conrad brings together the cast of thousands through a pattern of symbols built around the silver of the mine (Schwartz 1994:704–5).

Realm-tying metaphors are especially popular among authors concerned to avoid overt narratorial intervention. Malraux never editorializes about the unifying principle of *Man's Fate*, leaving that task instead to his opium-smoking sage, Gisors:

"It is very rare for a man to be able to put up with—how shall I say?—his human condition . . ."

He thought of one of Kyo's ideas: whatever cause men are willing to die for tends, however confusedly, to justify this condition by lending it dignity: Christianity for the slave, nation for the citizen, communism for the worker. [. . .]

"Intoxication is the rule for everyone: this country has opium, Islam has hashish, the West has women . . . Maybe love is the main means that Westerners use to free themselves from their human condition . . ."

Beneath these words flowed a murky counter-current of half-hidden figures: Tchen and murder, Clappique and his craziness, Katow and the revolution, May and love, himself and opium . . . Only Kyo seemed to him to resist these domains. (1946:185)

Providing us with a single parameter according to which all the characters may be understood—the way in which they give sense to or escape their humanity—Gisors offers a fully conceptual manner of integrating the various following-units of Malraux's classic.

At the same time, the book's figurative language concretizes Gisor's interpretation. "To submit, for a woman," claims Ferral, "to possess, for a man, are the only two methods of understanding available to human beings" (98). Accordingly, the one action that each character values above all others is treated as his or her sex act. Tchen reaches heights of ecstasy only when contemplating his own death (123); not surprisingly, he labels those who have not yet committed murder "virgins" (50). He refuses to leave the suicide-murder of Chiang-Kai-Shek to anyone else, "because I don't like the women I love to be screwed by others" (124). We are told that Clappique embraces gambling as one might a prostitute (193–98). Kyo's woman is the revolution itself. Now nine months pregnant, "she would either give birth or die" (121). As for Ferral, "he never slept with anyone but himself, but his narcissism depended on his not being alone" (188). Character after character submits to the same metaphor, thereby revealing his or her particular response to the challenge of the human condition.

The champion of the realm-tying metaphor is certainly Émile Zola, whose naturalist theories forced him to forego the intervention of a strong narrator like that employed by Tolstoy and Hugo. The way Zola uses figurative language in *La Terre*, for example, is quite instructive. From the very first chapter, in which Françoise helps a bull to mount her cow, *La Terre* is the story of sexual coupling, not only among farm animals but also within the other realms that characterize the novel's rural universe. The farm world is systematically defined by a mythic identification between the sowing of seeds and "coitus with the earth," as Zola so indelicately puts it. The business world is largely restricted to the extended treatment afforded to the Charles family brothel. Family life is reduced to "la culbute" ("taking a tumble"), a deliciously ambiguous term that Zola sometimes uses to evoke sexual pleasure and at other times deploys to refer to death. Relationships between generations, between male and female, client and proprietor, farmer and earth are all brought back to the same basic verity, the same fundamental human activity. Sex, eating, and other simple pastimes are regularly employed as metaphors to link a broad spectrum of activities. More than any other novelist, perhaps, Zola knows how to make grist for his multiple-focus mill through the use of a single master metaphor.

Zola is also adept at combining metaphorical language with his characters' actions in order to link various realms and characters. When every imaginable sort of power is redefined in terms of *Germinal's* eating metaphor, a relatively static product results. The book becomes almost allegorical in its tendency to reduce all activity to the same hem name. Contrast to that process the description of old man Fouan's kids at the beginning of *La Terre*, as they dicker to lower the pension they will owe their father. The children bargain, Zola tells us, "with the bad faith of peasants buying a pig" (1967b:28). This early in the novel, the pig comparison passes for a simple descriptive device. Zola makes us wait some 140 pages to discover the full meaning of the metaphor, as Fouan's son actually dickers for a pig. Instead of exhausting itself in its first, descriptive, use, the metaphor takes on a second life, reversing its field, as it were. Now the process of buying a pig seems colored by the previous metaphor. Peasants buy pigs, this reversal implies, with the bad faith of greedy children out to cheat their aged parents.

Right in the middle of the pig-bargaining process, a similar scene involving a cow gives further life to the dickering metaphor. Just as he had driven a hard bargain for the pig, so Buteau drives the price down on the cow that Lise covets. As Zola makes abundantly clear, this bargaining scene constitutes a displaced form of courtship, a fact recalled later when Buteau courts

Lise "as if he were still bargaining for the cow" (172). To no one's surprise, the new wife gives birth at the same time as the new cow (243–56), for in the mythic world of Zola's master metaphors, the two females are one and the same. Every possible peasant activity is seen as a function of every other activity, for the subject of the novel is not any individual destiny but the effects of the Earth itself on the people that inhabit it.

Intentional Accidents

Because hyperbolic modulation repeatedly induces multiple-focus readers to ask "How did we get here from there?," the process of hem-naming that provides each text's thematic resolution often dwells on questions of causality. Is the movement from one narrative segment to another dictated by tradition, by chance, or by design? Is the flow of the text caused by narrator decisions or by character actions? Why do things happen as they do? And why are they reported in this particular manner? Replete with chance meetings, multiple explanations of single incidents, and reflections on the reasons for historical events, multiple-focus texts challenge readers to rethink familiar notions of causality. Victor Hugo announces ceremoniously in the preface to *Notre-Dame de Paris* that his book is about fate. Leo Tolstoy peppers *War and Peace* with divergent explanations of the failure of Napoleon's Russian campaign. Thornton Wilder sandwiches *The Bridge of San Luis Rey* between chapters titled "Perhaps an Accident" and "Perhaps an Intention." Multiple-focus narrative cries out for special attention to questions of causality.

The Bridge of San Luis Rey explains one chance meeting with another. The collapse of the great bridge brings death to five people crossing it by chance. "Why did this happen to *those* five," the author asks. Presented as an answer to that simple question, Wilder's book is organized as a series of single-focus sections. Following, in turn, each of the characters who died, moving from one to another through the familiar expedient of chapter divisions, we develop a sense of the compartmentalized nature of their lives, which seem so totally separate that we do indeed wonder why a similar fate was reserved for these particular characters. Soon, a plan begins to emerge. While the paths of the main characters never cross until they plunge to their deaths together, we learn that their lives centered around two characters who did not die on the bridge—a talented but faithless singer, the Perichole, and a nun with the heart of a loving mother, Madre María del Pilar. Not until the very end of the novel do we learn that the lives of these two characters have crossed, that the Perichole has been so touched by the death of her loved ones and the fact that she alone was saved, that she has begun to work for the poor and the sick in Madre María's convent. This encounter, which at an earlier point in the novel might have seemed solely the result of chance, is explained by Madre María in totally different terms. "Learn at last that anywhere you may expect grace," she says of the fall of the bridge (Wilder 1927:231).

The search for a hidden pattern to explain seemingly random occurrences dominates many a multiple-focus text. John Hersey's *Hiroshima* adopts many of Wilder's strategies. Beginning with the introduction of six people who survived the atomic blast at Hiroshima, the author immediately invites speculation in a manner reminiscent of *The Bridge of San Luis Rey*: "A hundred thousand people were killed by the atomic bomb, and these six were among the survivors. They still wonder why they lived when so many others died" (Hersey 1946:4). Writing two decades after Wilder, Hersey increases the compartmentalization of his characters by narrating still shorter segments of their lives—one after the other, always in the same order, always with the same coldness of observation. When the paths of three of the six characters meet in Asano Park, however, we sense a change. Up to this point we have experienced each of the stories as a separate single-focus tale. Now that the interlaced accounts have crossed, it is the relationships among the characters that come to the fore. As the effects of the bomb slowly wear off, we wonder how Hersey will exploit these relationships and whether they will eventually lend meaning to this modern disaster. In February 1946, Miss Toshiko Sasaki, still infected and despondent, is visited by one of her fellow survivors, Father Kleinsorge. In one of the book's very few direct-address passages, she recalls the theme evoked at the outset:

She asked bluntly, "If your God is so good and kind, how can he let people suffer like this?" She made a gesture which took in her shrunken leg, the other patients in her room, and Hiroshima as a whole. "My child," Father Kleinsorge said, "man is not now in the condition God intended. He has fallen from grace through sin." And he went on to explain all the reasons for everything. (1946:109)

Not all readers will be reassured by Father Kleinsorge's explanation of "all the reasons for everything," but for Miss Sasaki, his explanation brings new strength, a rapid cure, and an eventual conversion to Catholicism. Here, as in *Bridge*, order can be detected behind the chaos of life, proving that even the most horrible disasters are truly acts of God.

What difference does it make that Wilder and Hersey chose a multiple-focus approach? On the surface of things, a single-focus approach would appear more appropriate. Wilder could have followed the Perichole throughout her eventful life, ending with the typical single-focus conclusion of conversion. Hersey could have concentrated on the story of Toshiko Sasaki, following her from sin and the bomb to cure and conversion. The problem with these solutions is that they lay overmuch emphasis on individual action, always a potential single-focus trap. Casting a story in the single-focus mold tends to concentrate attention on the protagonist's choices and on the individual attitudes and decisions underlying them. Whether the pattern chosen is sin and repentance, a change in goals, or finding oneself, single-focus concentration on the protagonist tends to dissimulate the role of the agent of change—even when that agent is the very hand of God.

To undermine familiar single-focus causal explanations, multiple-focus authors regularly offer a variety of possible causes. In the preface to *Notre-Dame de Paris*, Victor Hugo concentrates our attention on causal concerns by telling us that his book is about fate—in capital letters and written in Greek, if you please. The novel's very first scene takes place in the Palais de Justice, which, as Hugo explains, is described only because it no longer existed in 1831. Having been burned down earlier, it was thus unknown to the reader. Why was it burned down? That depends on whether you prefer (a) a historical explanation, passing through Ravaillac's assassination of Henri IV; (b) an astronomical approach, replete with falling star; or (c) the verse-maker's theory:

dame Justice,	lady Justice
Pour avoir mangé trop d'épice,	Having eaten too much spice,
Se mit tout le palais en feu.	Lit the entire palace on fire.

Whatever we may think of this triple explanation—"political, physical, poetic"—we understand that it is the fire of 1618 that has forced the author to describe the Palais de Justice. "Which proves this novel truth," opines Hugo, "that great events cause unexpected results" (1963:244).

As we move through Hugo's novel, we are constantly subjected to unexpected and seemingly arbitrary comments on causal concerns. We would hardly expect the common activity of following a character to elicit philosophical commentary, yet Pierre Gringoire's decision to follow the young gypsy girl Esmeralda through the streets of Paris is treated as "a voluntary abdication of his free will" and as "a mixture of devil-may-care independence and blind obedience, a sort of intermediary between slavery and freedom" (265). Nearly every occurrence is redefined in terms of its possible causes. The pitiful recluse Gudule, for example, has concluded from the fact that gypsies stole her baby that all gypsies are dangerous. The reader follows another line of reasoning, concluding that if Gudule's daughter was carried off sixteen years ago by a band of gypsies she must now be a girl in her late teens and probably thought to be a gypsy herself. Gudule's mistaken hypothesis is proven wrong only when she is finally united with her daughter. This reunion becomes, in turn, a new link in the chain of causality, for Esmeralda was convinced that she would eventually find her mother only if she retained her purity, and she has preserved that only at the expense of the freedom offered to her by Claude Frollo. She retains her purity, therefore she finds her mother. "But is such a story believable?" asks Gudule ironically, drawing our attention once again to the ridiculousness of what human beings call "causes."

Again and again, Hugo presses the reader to concentrate on problems of causality. One day, by "coincidence," Claude Frollo leans on a manuscript of Honorius of Autun's *De Praedestinatione et liber arbitrio*, while he reads his only printed book, *Glossa in epistolas D. Pauli*. The irony of the juxtaposition of these two books is clear only when we remember the central doctrine enunciated in Paul's letters—that of the paradoxical "freedom through bondage"—the same type of freedom acted out by Pierre Gringoire as he followed Esmeralda through the streets many pages earlier. Causal paradoxes remain part of Hugo's arsenal throughout *Notre-Dame de Paris*. When Jacques Charmolue raises his hand to save a fly attacked by a spider, Claude Frollo tells him to "let fate have its way" (Hugo 1963:336). The irony of the mysterious priest's notion of fate, which can succeed only with his help, is apparent to all but Claude. Later playing the part of the spider, Claude holds

Esmeralda in his clutches. Finally trapped in his web, "she sensed that destiny is an irresistible force" (401). And yet she resists him, foiling destiny and forcing Claude to redefine his notion of fate. We think we understand the workings of destiny, yet Hugo's paradoxes serve to convince us that fate is beyond the grasp of a single human being. This kind of philosophical equivocation, where fate is redefined to fit the situation, remains a favorite motif of multiple-focus authors.

In *Lafcadio's Adventures*, André Gide attributes precisely the same kind of inside-out reasoning to Lafcadio, who prefers to let the roll of a die determine his actions: " 'If I roll a six,' he said to himself as he pulled out the die, 'I'll get off the train!' He rolled a five. 'I'll get off anyway' " (1958a:831). When Lafcadio turns to pick up his suitcase, however, it has disappeared; he finally spots it being carried away, but when he tries to give chase he is stopped by the sight of Amédée's jacket. "Too bad for the suitcase!" he decides. "The die spelled it out: I shouldn't get off here" (832). Is Lafcadio remaining on the train out of obedience to the roll of the die? because of his own free will? or because of the presence of Amédée's jacket, a reminder of the murder he has just committed? We are not meant to know, but we do realize that Lafcadio has no more idea of what it is to commit an act without motivation than Brother Juniper does of the reasons for the fall of the Bridge of San Luis Rey, in which he thought he saw both "the wicked visited by destruction and the good called early to Heaven" (Wilder 1927:219).

In *Notre-Dame de Paris*, Hugo establishes a multiple-focus tradition by using court decisions to further concentrate attention on problems of causality. First we see Quasimodo's trial for having attempted to abduct Esmeralda. When the hunchback is punished, he assumes it is for having committed a crime, "which when you come right down to it was hardly the case, since he was punished only for being deaf and for having been sentenced by a deaf judge" (1963:320). Shortly afterward, Esmeralda is accused of resorting to sorcery in the near-fatal stabbing of her lover Phoebus. The ultimate proof of this contention is that a dry leaf has been substituted for the gold coin with which Phoebus paid for the room where she was stabbed, but we have seen that a flesh-and-blood boy actually made the substitution. In spite of such "conclusive" proof, Esmeralda refuses to confess her alleged crime until she is subjected to the limb-tearing torture of the rack, where the innocent girl finally admits her "guilt." "Justice has finally been done!" says Jacques Charmolue, this time perfectly happy to see the fly crushed (345). All that remains is for the local gossips to try the poor gypsy girl: " 'Say there, is it true that she refused a confessor?' 'That's what they say.' 'I told you she was a pagan!' " (358). Had the multiple-focus following-pattern not permitted us to see the scene in which Claude Frollo tries to seduce Esmeralda under the guise of confessing her, we could not understand the irony and horror of the gossips' syllogism.

The events leading to Esmeralda's death demonstrate the impossibility of isolating individual causes. She is condemned to death for killing a man who did not die and whom she loved; he was stabbed only because he had to borrow money from Claude Frollo to pay for a room. The gypsy girl is at first saved by Quasimodo, whom she fears, but the hunchback thinks that the vagrants who come to help her want to harm her. The king thinks that the beggars are angry because Esmeralda has not yet been hanged, but he is sick and so decides to have both the girl and the vagrants hanged. Claude Frollo and Pierre Gringoire save Esmeralda, but because she refuses to satisfy his desires Pierre leaves her with Claude, who has no more success with her than Pierre, and so leaves her with Gudule. Gudule is her mother, but she is powerless to save the hidden Esmeralda when she cries out to the passing Phoebus, the one whose "death" began this merry-go-round. In the end we see Esmeralda trapped by her love. She dies not, as we expect, because of those who hate her but in spite of them.

The case of Esmeralda is like that of the legendary battle: for want of a nail a shoe was lost, for want of a shoe a horse was lost, for want of a horse a rider was lost, for want of a rider a battle was lost, for want of a battle the war was lost. One approach to multiple-focus narration involves following, in turn, the negligent blacksmith, the inobservant stableboy, the unsuspecting rider, and his surprised commander in order to end up with the opposing king, whose conclusion that the war was won by his superior strategy only we can properly judge. Multiple-focus narration is the form of the little people, the insignificant individuals whose role can be appreciated only when their combined contributions are allowed to outweigh that of the king, emperor, or general. The simple national and individual explanations of dual-focus and single-focus writing are rejected in favor of a more complex view of the causes underlying events.

Without a full view of every link in the causal chain, the final event either looks like a coincidence or is apparently explained by what turn out to be mistaken interpretations. Thus Edouard, Gide's novelist in *The Counterfeiters*, is baffled by the death of little Boris and refuses to insert it into his novel on the grounds that it "lacks sufficient motivation" (1958b:1246). The reader, however, enjoys a privileged position that even Edouard, with his novelist's eye, does not share. Because we have followed all the characters, we are able to piece together the whole story, from nail and horse to rider and battle. We eventually note the inadequacy of Madame Sophroniska's Freudian approach (the quintessential single-focus explanatory principle) to explain Boris's basic instability. His final action results from a normal desire to belong and is not at all a suicide, as Edouard assumes.

Throughout *The Counterfeiters* our privileged position has been brought home to us by the special emphasis placed on characters who manage to combine the information of a number of other characters. After Bernard has heard Olivier's story about Vincent, and read Edouard's journal entry about Laura, he senses that he is the only one to have combined the two stories—along with the reader, of course. The same overview is apparently achieved by Pauline Molinier when her own suspicions are added to her husband's hunches about certain stolen letters. This time, however, we have known for quite a while that her son Georges took the letters. We learn now, if we had not realized it previously, that we readers and not Edouard are the omniscient ones. We alone can draw conclusions based on observation of a given event from several different points of view. The reader is the only one who can attribute a cause to Boris's death, the seemingly unmotivated event that closes Gide's novel, but which Edouard refuses to include in his.

Making sense of a seemingly unmotivated act is also the task allotted to readers of Gide's other long narrative, *Lafcadio's Adventures*. The first character followed in this bizarre work (which Gide refused to characterize as a novel) is Anthime Armand-Dubois, Freemason, and one of the stock types of multiple-focus fiction. Like his brother-in-law Julius, like Edouard in *The Counterfeiters*, like Claude Frollo in *Notre-Dame de Paris*, Anthime is a scientist confronted by facts that cannot be explained by his system. If he turns from cruel experimentation to devout prayer, it is because he has been forced to revise his opinions about causality. At the end of book 1, however, we leave Anthime. As so often happens in multiple-focus works, the seeming arbitrariness of interlaced narration leads us to wonder whether there isn't a hidden principle at work. Our questioning is only reinforced by Lafcadio's surprise murder of Amédée. This much-publicized "gratuitous act," along with Lafcadio's reflections, continues to focus our attention on questions of causality, even after Protos has mistakenly been incarcerated for Lafcadio's crime.

Single-focus crimes are typically solved by reconstruction of the criminal's motivation. Lafcadio's act is an exemplary multiple-focus crime because it lacks the kind of motivation typically associated with single-focus narrative. To the reader privy to Lafcadio's every thought and action, numerous indirect "motivations" appear. To Lafcadio, however, his act appears totally gratuitous, according to "that psychological law," formulated by Tolstoy apropos of *War and Peace*, "which compels a man who commits actions under the greatest compulsion, to supply in his imagination a whole series of retrospective reflections to prove his freedom to himself" (1966:1374). As in *The Counterfeiters*, only we readers are in a position to connect the book's many events. We are the only ones who understand the strange series of events that place Amédée and Lafcadio in the same railway car and who know Lafcadio's past well enough to realize what bizarre effects Lafcadio's various "uncles" (particularly Wladi, of whom he has just been dreaming) have had on him. If the gratuity of Lafcadio's act remains uncertain, however, one thing is sure: we cannot sojourn long in Gide's multiple-focus universe without concentrating our interpretive energy on questions of causality.

The same is true—in spades—of Tolstoy's *War and Peace*. Again and again, in short paragraphs or chapter-long commentary, the Russian master focuses our attention on causal concerns. He does so to undermine the very notion of causality, in the traditional single-focus sense of the term. For Tolstoy, causal explanations depend for their validity on the free will of the individuals acting; yet, as he shows through repeated analyses, the characters of history are deluded in asserting their own free will: "It is true that we are not conscious of our dependence, but by admitting our free will we arrive at absurdity, while by admitting our dependence on the external world, on time, and on cause, we arrive at laws" (1966:1351). As Tolstoy asserts in the novel's final words, it is necessary "to renounce a freedom that does not exist, and to recognize a dependence of which we are not conscious" (1351).

How closely this conclusion is tied to the choice of multiple-focus technique we can see from the numerous metaphors that Tolstoy draws from the science of mechanics. To undermine the notion of a soldier's free will, for example, Tolstoy offers the following logic: "If many simultaneously and variously directed forces act on a given body, the direction of its motion cannot coincide with any one of those forces, but will always be a mean—what in mechanics is represented by the diagonal of a parallelogram of forces" (1109). In other words, if we want to know why an action happened in a particular way, we cannot concentrate only on the apparent agent of the action, for the action is in fact not initiated by that individual. Nor, for that matter, can we expect to find a single direct line of actions leading up to and causing the one in question, for motion is caused by a multitude of forces, whose vectors must be known and combined for the resultant motion to be understood. What Tolstoy describes as the parallelogram of forces in mechanics corresponds directly to multiple-focus technique in narrative.

The Reader as Alchemist

Readers of multiple-focus texts can hardly be said to have an easy time of it. Every time a narrator interrupts a moving story to tell me that "the tale now abandons so-and-so in favor of what's his name," I get the vague feeling that I'm being had. What's more, the narrator knows perfectly well that he's aggravating me—otherwise, why would he systematically blame tradition for his unexpected hyperbolic modulations? I react similarly to the self-satisfied hopscotch of Hugo, Gide, and Luis Buñuel. Where I enjoyed the constant complicitous winks of the single-focus narrator, enlisting my sympathy for (or laughter at) the protagonist, the antics of the multiple-focus barker leave me cold, for I just can't shake the feeling that the son of a gun is laughing at *me* every time he frustrates my desires. Instead of inviting me to become part of a privileged circle, sitting in judgment over someone else, multiple-focus narrators always seem to summon everyone else to laugh at me, to celebrate my inability to control the narrative. Even those narrators who don't flaunt their power and my weakness leave me wondering about their novels. Along with Henry James, I keep asking myself what such "large loose baggy monsters" might actually mean (1934:84).

Reading dual-focus and single-focus narrative, I always feel at home—whether it is the group-based home of dual-focus texts or the single-focus identification with an individual. Coming to multiple-focus narrative with expectations developed in another world, I sense the new form as a loss, a lack, a diversion from the expected path. Trained to expect coherence and to respect legitimacy, I can't feel at home in the multiple-focus world of illegitimate narration. Instead, I constantly find myself in the state of homelessness that constitutes the multiple-focus reader's fundamental condition. However homeless multiple-focus texts may make me feel, they also offer new experiences, forcing me to see anew and to engage familiar objects and situations with renewed interest and attention. Where traditional materials once produced only traditional reactions, they now signify in new ways.

To make sense of multiple-focus texts, we must always step beyond the language in which they are couched. Only by discovering a common denominator among characters and activities are we able to stitch together the studiedly separate strands of the multiple-focus fabric. To each period of intense multiple-focus activity thus corresponds a particular type of the ineffable, a domain lying beyond the familiar world of the senses. The disparate characters and equally varied activities of the Grail romances are brought together thematically in the realm of the spiritual—invisible, otherworldly, beyond direct human perception, beyond direct representation by dual-focus and single-focus narrative. The allegorical mode of the late Middle Ages and Renaissance reaches beyond the senses by concentrating on abstract qualities. Prudence is no longer a typically dual-focus construction, represented (as in early medieval practice) by a lone female figure. In Bruegel's drawing, Prudence becomes a quality rather than a character: an abstraction to be constructed on the basis of the examples portrayed.

In the late nineteenth century, multiple-focus narrative is regularly employed to stretch beyond the visible toward a sociological level of abstraction that reveals greater truth than the separate physical observations out of which it is built. Zola's peasants are carefully studied and minutely drawn, but no reader would seriously maintain that Zola's genius stems from his ability to depict individual peasants, any more than Bruegel deserves accolades for his representation of individual faces. Instead, Zola's multiple-focus fresco permits us to construct a generalized view of the peasantry and its passionate devotion to Mother Earth. In like manner, the philosophical novel joins cubism in turning narrative material into mental matter, always pushing the reader away from a traditional construction of the story toward a new kind of synthesis.

As long as the novel remains in the multiple-focus mode, it continues to seek new types of knowledge, new methods of knowing that cannot be represented directly. I remember as a Boy Scout being asked to chart a tree in the middle of a field. The problem was that we weren't allowed to enter the field. First I had to locate on the map a position on one side of the field. Then I sighted through the tree to a spot on the other side of the field. After drawing a line between these two points I repeated the process on the remaining sides of the field, producing a line that crossed the first line right where the tree stood. Multiple-focus texts invert this process. Instead of asking the Boy Scout to map the tree, they provide a set of story lines in relation to which a given point must be constructed. Because the point is always located outside the area defined by the text's narrative, it can be located only through triangulation and hem-naming.

The principles of inquiry at work in this Boy Scout exercise are strikingly similar to those regularly invoked by multiple-focus texts. We must follow individual characters, but we always do so with a certain degree of indifference, knowing that none of them individually represents the text's object. Instead, we find ourselves tracing our own paths through the text, based on those of the characters but independent nonetheless, as we become full partners in the process of charting the text's forbidden spaces, the realms (spiritual, allegorical, sociological, philosophical) where the senses prove insufficient. Attention to precharted character paths, so salient at the start, is progressively replaced by active mapping of thematic intersections. Multiple-focus reading involves a process of rewriting, a tripartite procedure that engages the reader intellectually instead of (or in addition to) provoking identification:

1. The reader begins by following each character in turn, identifying with some more than others, fitting each piece into an overall outline of the story presented.
2. As the text advances, the reader reorders the narrative material according to an increasing number of thematic intersections, suggested by metaphoric ties, conceptual parallelism, or narratorial intervention.

3. Fixing on common traits or themes that bring characters and events together, the reader radically redefines the text, now seeing new characters and actions in terms of their ability to concretize conceptual categories. Once this hem-naming stage has been reached, characters and actions lose their autonomy, now being read for what they represent in thematic terms more than for what they are or do.

During the overall process of multiple-focus reading, readers are thus weaned from single-focus and dual-focus reading strategies, with their characteristic modes of identification, in favor of a new self-consciousness and a new liberty.

It often happens that the early chapters of multiple-focus texts are read according to single-focus or dual-focus standards. For many readers, this traditional mode of identification may last throughout the text. *Les Mystères de Paris* can hardly fail to begin for most readers as a dual-focus text. As it proceeds, some readers will continue to read it that way, while others will follow Sue's commentary down a multiple-focus path. *War and Peace* and *Man's Fate* remain fundamentally single-focus experiences for readers who, for whatever reason, find themselves intrigued by the fate of a single character. Films that follow several representative characters (such as those that concentrate on an army platoon or the victims of a natural disaster) often produce the same result, especially for viewers with a strong tendency toward personal identification with one of the film's exemplary characters.

The process whereby readers begin to discover thematic intersections in multiple-focus narratives is among the most poorly understood in novelistic theory. Most criticism of multiple-focus texts has been formulated apropos of nineteenth-century or twentieth-century social or philosophical novels. Seeking the overall meaning of each text, critics rarely treat the construction of meaning as a process, instead taking the novel as a synchronic whole, fully known to the critic and available to the memory in a single Gestalt. Yet the process of reading multiple-focus narrative involves the excitement of apprenticeship to new modes of knowledge. The reader's slowly acquired willingness to wrench traditional following-units out of their narrative context and realign them in new ways constitutes a characteristic aspect of multiple-focus narrative.

If the margins of my dual-focus texts are filled with comments noting the relationship between the two foci ("same language used for other side," "parallel to her sleepless night on page x"), and the notes in my single-focus texts constantly refer to earlier moments in the life of the protagonist ("note change since previous occurrence," "reversal of her earlier reaction"), the margins of my multiple-focus novels are systematically covered—and increasingly so as each novel progresses—with references to metaphoric or thematic motifs that tie together otherwise disparate sections ("same metaphor used for Tchen and Ferral—see pp. y and z," "this evocation of the social rules vs. sincere expression motif ties the Schumacher-Lise-Marceau trio to the Count-Countess-pilot trio"). As we move through the text, increased attention to these thematic intersections progressively undermines our interest in the text's narrative investment, eventually transferring our primary attention from the Chinese Revolution to the human condition and from two specific women to the very meaning of life and love.

Though at times frustrated by a lack of clear road signs, multiple-focus readers commonly gain significant pleasure from the heady liberty offered by multiple-focus texts. Convinced that they are breaking new ground each time they recognize a new thematic intersection, readers experience the excitement of the explorer, the inventor, indeed the alchemist. Turning mean narrative into the most noble of substances, multiple-focus readers become increasingly captivated by the search for the fifth essence, the quintessential conceptual pattern that gives meaning to the entire narrative universe. Where dual-focus narrative typically dispenses meaning from the narrator's world above, and the single-focus form regularly puts the keys to meaning in the hands of the protagonist, multiple-focus narrative gives the reader a strong sense of playing God, of finding the formula capable of transforming not lead to gold but story to theme, a more noble alchemy yet.

The Multiple-Focus System

Because it has never previously been identified and analyzed as such, multiple-focus narrative has received relatively little attention. Though the separate traditions of the Grail romance, allegory, the generational novel, and the philosophical novel share many strategies, inability to connect their common narrative techniques has kept critics from discovering the fundamental building blocks of the multiple-focus narrative system. As I demonstrate in this chapter, multiple-focus texts deploy the following characteristics:

- A following-pattern that attends, in turn, to several different characters
- Hyperbolic modulation between successive following-units, typically justified by tradition or the aleatory nature of real life and marked by the use of white space, chapter divisions, or other separation devices
- Presentation of separate sections as preexisting, whether borrowed from tradition, written accounts, documentary footage, or reality itself
- Use of single-focus and dual-focus constitutive units only the better to critique single-focus and dual-focus modes of understanding
- Dependence on plot devices justifying contact among diverse characters (crowd scenes, carnivals, wars, natural disasters, etc.)
- Presentation of multiple separate views of the same event, thereby lending depth, volume, and complexity, while contesting simplistic explanations of the event
- Recourse to narratorial commentary, parallel scenes between otherwise unrelated characters, and realm-tying metaphors to assure multiple-focus interpretation of segments that might otherwise appear to call for a single-focus or dual-focus reading
- Readers who, discomfited by hyperbolic modulation, evince curiosity about connections between following-units, thereby elevating questions of causality into a theme of choice
- Use of the process of hem-naming (i.e., defining disparate characters and actions according to a common denominator) to make the separate parts cohere and signify in a uniquely multiple-focus manner
- A tendency toward conceptual interpretation, sometimes to the point of abandoning the domain of narrative altogether
- Signification that works like a mosaic and its tesserae: the separate following-units of multiple-focus narrative eventually signify as a whole something quite different from what they represent individually

Over the course of the centuries, the dominant multiple-focus conceptual connections have been spiritual (Middle Ages), allegorical (late Middle Ages and Renaissance), sociological (late nineteenth century), and philosophical (twentieth century). Even though multiple-focus narrative has had a less-continuous history than its single-focus and dual-focus counterparts, multiple-focus texts have been sufficiently numerous to establish a strong tradition.

One question raised by this treatment of multiple-focus narrative regards the relationship between multiple-focus texts and their single-focus and dual-focus counterparts. Because multiple-focus texts depend heavily on single-focus and dual-focus components, they at times may seem to invite readers to reduce multiple-focus diversity and complexity to a relatively straightforward single-focus or dual-focus interpretation. Yet the most challenging multiple-focus texts, those that take the fullest advantage of multiple-focus resources, systematically make meaning through the total-izing strategies of hem-naming and conceptual resolution. This tendency to resolve a multiple-focus following-pattern into a single-focus or dual-focus framework may be more than a localized phenomenon. In one sense, all texts begin with what at first looks like multiplicity. Though it can easily appear as a composite, dependent on single-focus and dual-focus compo-nents, or as a latecomer, dependent on the prior existence of dual-focus and single-focus texts, multiple-focus narration may also be understood as a master mode, containing and explaining all others.

EIGHT   Theoretical Conclusion

T he body of this book has been devoted to two complementary methods of considering narrative texts. The *rhetorical approach* concentrates on the fluid relationship between reader and text that is created by the following-pattern. Constitutive of narrative itself, the process of following (along with its attendant panoply of modulations) positions the reader in a specific relationship to the characters and their actions. The study of following thus represents a necessary initial step in the understanding of narrative meaning. Limited to the bounds of a single text, the rhetorical approach is usefully complemented by a *typological approach*, which acknowledges the existence of common organizational and signifying practices—single-focus, dual-focus, and multiple-focus modes—across a large corpus of narrative texts. Recognizing in any given text the play of diverse typological traditions, we are better able to understand not only how individual texts signify but also how entire narrative traditions take on meaning. In this theoretical conclusion, I consider a third way of understanding narrative texts, the *transformational approach*, and show how it interacts with rhetorical and typological approaches to constitute a fully formed model of narrative reading.

Mapping

The process of reading may be conveniently broken down into two separate operations. For every reader, the experience of a text includes a chronological unfolding, word after word, image after image, scene after scene. This prospective view of the text is largely guided by the narrator's decisions. We circulate among characters and places, not according to our own interests but according to an itinerary fixed by the narrator. The process of following determines our progress through the text, in the process dividing the narrative into constitutive segments. We read a novel word by word and sentence by sentence. We watch a film frame by frame and shot by shot. Each form has its own particular base language that we must experience prospectively, piece by piece.

What permits treatment of diverse forms according to the same fundamental method is their shared narrativity, stemming from a common tendency to complement their base language with divisions defined by following (a process which, as outlined in chapter 1, assumes the constitution of "characters," as well as a particular relationship between a "narrator" and those characters). To understand narrative, we must reserve an important place for the Pied-Piper-like action of following, with its characteristic division of the text into following-units, connected in turn by modulations. In this system, modulations play an important role, for they serve to mark the arrival of a new unit, thereby reinforcing the successive unfolding of the text. The articulative function of modulations also serves to define the pairs of units that characterize our prospective experience of the text. Each following-unit, as it appears, is tied to the previous one, reinforcing a chainlike perception of the text, where each link gains its meaning from attachment to its neighbors.

If it is inaugurated by the process of "following," the act of reading also involves a tendency toward "mapping." The process of following keeps our attention constantly riveted on current experiences—with a thought toward those to come—but the techniques that contribute to the constitution of a narrative map all require a large measure of retrospection. Calling on our memory of the text at hand, as well as our prior experience of other texts, the process of mapping involves the reader in a perpetual return to the past, and a constant attempt to define the present in terms of that past, permitting eventual understanding of the present. Whereas the rhetorical dimension of narrative texts depends heavily on the narrator/character relationship, narrative mapping is primarily dependent on character/action considerations. It is to this aspect of the narrative text that we now turn.

How do we make meaning? Through what channels does the process of understanding flow? Which analytical techniques best utilize the mind's methods of apprehending reality? In describing the act of reading, it is appropriate, I suggest, to recognize two different types of mental activity. The component of reading that I have labeled "following" is heavily marked by the linguistic nature of the text. We read words and sentences one after the other, making sense of them according to the rules of a language that we already know. We need no special terminology to describe this aspect of reading, for the text itself constantly provides all the terms necessary. In the Grail romances we read lines like "The story now leaves them and returns to the Good Knight." What resources do we need to understand this statement? Only those of language itself. We need to know about antecedents and pronouns in order to understand the term "them," about epithets and attributes to identify the "Good Knight" as Galahad. Our analytical terminology for dealing with this phase of reading can be borrowed, by and large, from the vocabulary developed for describing the text's base language—whether English or Old French, moving or still images, paint or celluloid.

The process of mapping, however, involves other concerns entirely. In terms of language, as well as following, there is little difference between Henry's entry into battle at the end of *The Red Badge of Courage* and John Wayne's archetypal role in one western after another. When we map these skirmishes, however, they produce radically different meanings. For young Henry to gather up his courage and enter the battle like a man, he must overcome his earlier fears, master himself, and exit permanently from childhood. Our opinion of his action at the end of the book is radically marked by what we have seen of him along the way. In retrospect, we might say that Crane's treatment of Henry's entry into battle is not a description of battle at all but a displaced evocation of maturation, a verbal portrait of the process of becoming a man. In terms of language and following, then, there is a battle, but in terms of mapping there is a reversal of Henry's earlier failure and thus a sketch of growth, not of death. When John Wayne faces the Indians, however, an entirely different map is drawn. Mirrored in Wayne's patience and resolve is the irresponsibility of Wayne's renegade foe, his skittish ponies, his gun-running suppliers, his bloodthirsty supporters. Unlike Henry, Wayne never had to become a man. He was born that way: strong, impassive, courageous. Although the language may from time to time resemble that used for

Henry or Galahad, the viewer maps not progression but an eternal opposition of civilization to barbarism, the same clash that once opposed David to Goliath and Aeneas to Turnus.

The process of mapping requires us to read one activity in terms of another, one character in terms of a counterpart. Following depends largely on linguistic meaning to develop its meaning; mapping, by contrast, involves a network of comparisons between diverse parts of the text, for only through sensitivity to the text's implied interconnections are we able to recognize situations where different textual meanings arise out of similar linguistic situations and so fully realize mapping's capacity for recognizing and respecting difference. It remains unclear, however, exactly how the process of mapping actually takes place, according to what principles different parts of the same text are drawn together to constitute a textual map.

Narrative makes sense largely in terms of characters and their actions. Lyric poetry may make meaning through verbal textures, evoking a state of being, an atmosphere, or a particular sensibility, but texts are understood as narrative only through systematic reference to their character/action complex. This tendency to make meaning in a particular way is exactly what we acknowledge in recognizing a text as narrative. As we devise a critical language appropriate to narrative mapping, two basic principles must then be taken into account:

1. Narrative meaning arises from character/action considerations.
2. Narrative meaning depends not on single character/action units but on relationships among units.

As we read, absorbing the author's words one after the other, we begin to map the text. But since the process of mapping is by nature relational, dependent on connections between one part of the text and another, it is by definition destructive of the text's purely linguistic existence. As Emma Bovary contemplates the shining city of Rouen from her coach toward the end of *Madame Bovary*, we marvel at the poetry of Flaubert's description, his ability to evoke Emma's desires. In narrative terms, however, we dismantle this discourse, seeing in it a Romantic pendant to Charles's mean view of the same scene when he was a student, as well as Emma's unconscious transposition of her own dreams (whose language we find here repeated and transformed). The specificity of Flaubert's language dwindles as we turn verbal patterns into narrative patterns. When we consider Emma's picture of Rouen in terms of Charles's view, it is the Romantic nature of Emma's character that stands out, but when we compare Emma's image of Rouen to her earlier dream visions, it is her diminishing hold on reality that comes to the fore.

Far from damaging Flaubert's text, this process of reduction constitutes a necessary and appropriate response to the nature of narrative. In order to map the narrative, we must be able to relate one part of the text to another; in order to relate one part of the text to another, we must be able to express both parts in terms of a common language. This common language, created by and for the mapping process, may seem to bowdlerize the verbal text (indeed, it does so to the extent that the creation of narrative meaning necessarily builds on and thus represses verbal meaning), but it is essential for the apprehension of the text's narrative structure. As key relationships are discovered in the text, a new language is formulated to serve as a common denominator of the related segments. Since a text's narrative meaning is always expressed as a series of relationships, and since these relationships must be discovered and expressed by the observer (sometimes with the help of a narrator eager to impose certain types of relationship), the mapping process necessarily involves constant repetition of the relation/reduction sequence.

This new mapping language, necessarily reductive in nature (because it can't make meaning without reducing differing linguistic phenomena to their underlying similarities), is always expressed in terms of what linguists call "cover terms," expressions whose generality permits them to refer simultaneously to two or more different phenomena. Because of their ability to identify aspects common to apparently dissimilar objects or events, cover terms have the power to reveal similarity where only difference was previously visible. With cover terms, relational and reductive qualities are inseparably linked. Critics use cover terms not simply as a matter of convenience but in recognition of the way narrative meaning is made. We note relationships between passages, then devise terminology to express the shared qualities that led us to note those relationships. The terms created via this process constitute our mapping language.

The mapping language appropriate to a text's narrative aspect always engages cover terms of a similar nature. Because narrative depends, by definition, on the character/action complex, narrative cover terms may conveniently take the form of subject/predicate summary sentences. The decision to map the narrative component of a text carries numerous limitations, however, for the very notion of narrative brings with it a heavy load of cultural baggage, including a set of implicit guidelines for the elaboration of narrative maps. The need to concentrate on character/action relationships constitutes the first such narrative servitude. The second involves the identity of the subject in the typical subject/predicate cover sentence. When, in the wake of Vladimir Propp, 1960s French structuralists set about dividing stories into their component parts, with each unit summarized by a short sentence, they quickly discovered that the same action can be summarized in several ways and that a passive summary sentence creates a totally different emphasis from an active sentence summarizing the same action. To bypass this potential reversibility of subject and predicate, the French structuralists decided to concentrate on the "agent" of each action, reasoning that the active elements of a tale are the ones that advance its action. While the tautological nature of this claim makes it, in a sense, irreproachable, such logic nevertheless begs the question of the importance of "action" to narrative structure.

Inaction is hardly an unknown narrative topic. Take, for example, Balzac's novelette *Le Curé de Tours*. Reflecting the earlier titles considered by Balzac ("La Vieille fille," "L'Abbé Troubert"), the plot involves the machinations of Sophie Gamard and her politically influential boarder, the priest Troubert, to evict and discredit another boarder, the inept abbot Birotteau. Strategically, the role of old lady Gamard is of capital importance, for she is the intermediary through whom all the book's actions must pass. The prime mover, however, is clearly Troubert, for it is his secret political influence in both Tours and Paris that causes the fight between the old maid and Birotteau and, ultimately, the latter's expulsion from Tours. Domestic strife or political intrigue—which is it? Neither, for rather than concentrating on either of these possible plots, Balzac focuses on the least active and intelligent of his characters. We never observe Gamard in the act of playing her dirty tricks on Birotteau; instead, we see the poor priest reacting to the old lady's machinations. We always learn about Troubert's influence indirectly, never by following him independently. We follow Birotteau systematically from beginning to end, always concentrating on his limited view, even when trickery and influence are located elsewhere.

When we begin to map *Le Curé de Tours*, we repeatedly connect passages concerning changes in the career or comfort of l'abbé Birotteau. The others may be the agents, but he is the one around whom the story is built. Clearly identifying Birotteau as central, the following-pattern sets rhetorical priorities for reader and critic alike. If we map Balzac's novelette in terms of the weakest character, if we chart *The Song of Roland* in terms of both Saracens and Christians, if we map *War and Peace* in terms of numerous characters, it is because the following-pattern remains our primary indicator of narrative rhetoric, our principal method of sensing emphasis. Construction of a plot around a particular following-pattern predisposes readers to notice relationships of a specific type and to draw a particular kind of narrative map.

Narrative Transformations

The retrospective process of mapping takes place at an undefined rate of speed and to an unspecified degree, depending on the text, the reader, and their cultural contexts. Popular fiction is either rapidly mapped, according to widely familiar principles, or not mapped at all (an option open to all readers, but especially characteristic of suspense-novel readers, who typically prefer the prospective aspects of the reading process). The "classics," on the other hand, never cease being mapped. Complex and multifaceted, these familiar texts are the ones that we are likely to reread throughout our lives, each time contributing anew to a partially drawn map of the text (or, in exceptional circumstances, beginning a new map according to revised principles). Some readers map consciously and conscientiously throughout their lives. Some never map. Most vary their mapping level according to cultural and personal norms, mapping Dante more than Saint Francis, Flaubert more than Dickens, film more than television, and "serious" programs more than variety shows. Whether our mapping activity is substantial or minimal, however, whether it is conscious or not, it remains governed by certain recognizable principles.

The narrative mapping process is characterized by recognition of relationships connecting specific character/action units of the text. Leading to more or less explicit reduction of the text to cover-term summary sentences expressing the noted relationships, this recognition constitutes the surveying activity on which narrative mapping depends—always a relationship, never a single isolated term. Though the textual passages whose relationship we perceive are extremely diverse, the connections that we establish correspond to a very small number of types. The formulaic language of a dual-focus text like *The Song of Roland* rapidly draws our attention to the transformational relationships connecting and separating Christians and pagans. From the paired councils that open the poem, through the paired attacks that fill up its middle sections, to the concluding paired trials of Ganelon and Bramimonde (the text's two turncoats), *Roland* juxtaposes every Christian action with a pagan version of the same action. The significant relationships noted in the process of mapping *The Song of Roland* thus regularly take the form of

| Christians hold council | $\rightarrow$ | Pagans hold council |

or

| Charlemagne fights valiantly, putting his faith in God | $\rightarrow$ | Baligant fights valiantly, relying on his possesssions |

Reductive and hollow, these cover terms nevertheless have the virtue of expressing our reasons for sensing a relationship between parts of the text. Whether we note the similar activities of entire groups or the parallel preoccupations of individuals, we find ourselves drawing together, in the mapping process, dissimilar subjects associated with similar predicates. The fundamental form of dual-focus relationships (i.e., those that lead us to experience a text as dual-focus) may thus be expressed in the following manner:

| Subject involved in a particular activity | $\rightarrow$ | Different subject involved in a similar activity |

or, to simplify,

| Character one engaged in activity one | $\rightarrow$ | Character two engaged in activity one |

or, even more simply,

| $Subject_1\ Predicate_1$ | $\rightarrow$ | $Subject_2\ Predicate_1$ |

We recognize this pattern in the familiar paired council scenes of dual-focus epic or the traditional sleepless nights of dual-focus pastoral.

But what about the case of the Charlemagne-Baligant battle, where the distant view of two foes engaged in similar activity is belied by close-ups revealing differences in their motivation and technique? If we sense the Charlemagne/Baligant relationship as especially strong, vital to the process of mapping *The Song of Roland*, it is not just because the two engage in hand-to-hand combat but also because of numerous other factors: the two hold equivalent positions in their own realms, they are shown preparing for battle in a similar manner, and they fight with equal courage and determination. In other words, an entire context of parallel formal concerns (sequence of scenes, choice of details, reiterated formulaic language) joins the similarity of the combatants' actual activities in leading readers to sense the transformational relationship that simultaneously unites and separates the two leaders. By the time Charlemagne and Baligant are differentiated according to the sources of their motivation, therefore, the reader has already long perceived the basic configuration:

Charlemagne fights valiantly   →   Baligant fights valiantly

The problem occurs when we attempt to configure the motivational distinction that eventually leads to the victory of the Christian king—Charlemagne putting his faith in God while Baligant seeks to augment his personal possessions. This is where the deceptively grammatical nature of cover-term summary sentences betrays us. At first, it would seem that the all-important difference in motivation belongs to the predicate, for each thinks and acts in a different way ("thinks" and "acts" = verbs, i.e., parts of the predicate). This is not, however, the way dual-focus narrative operates. Ever renewing the life of that familiar Latin construction, the apposition to the subject, whether with a noun ("Caesar, valiant leader of his legions") or a verb ("Caesar, having fought valiantly"), with both functioning as adjectives, the attributes of dual-focus heroes are meant to be seen as essential qualities of the confronted subjects.

Recognizing parallelism between dual-focus characters or groups, we implicitly reduce the text's complex and varied activities to more easily handled subject/predicate cover terms. In this process, predicates at the text's linguistic level are often transformed, at the mapping level, into adjectives attached to subjects. The differences thus highlighted expand and demonstrate the basic categories subtending the dual-focus world. Part and parcel of the twin processes of replacement operations and polarity adjustment, the attribution of linguistic predicates to mapping-level subjects assures the increasing specificity of the text's basic terms. From Charlemagne the Christian and Baligant the pagan, we eventually shift to an opposition between feudal fealty and self-centeredness.

The linguistic text passes through a series of transformations: individual words produce relationships, in turn mentally summarized by appropriate cover terms, which evolve as we read (or reread), only in order to be redistributed into the characteristic dual-focus form that allots to the subject all fully representative attributes. The overall process, then, looks something like this:

1. Charlemagne and Baligant are described in the flow of the text; they remain undifferentiated from the rest of the text and unrelated to each other.
2. We recognize that the actions associated with the two leaders are sufficiently similar to justify mapping their parallel activity as a form of subject substitution ($S_1P_1 \rightarrow S_2P_1$).
3. Their activities are implicitly split during the mapping process into those that are shared (these parametric activities remain part of the summary-sentence predicate) and those that differentiate the two (these differential activities become, by apposition, part of the summary-sentence subject).

In this way, the essential concerns of the dual-focus type become embedded in the transformational system that is characteristic of dual-focus narrative.

In mapping single-focus narrative, we pass through a similar set of activities, but this time we isolate narrative transformations of a different order, brought to our attention by the practice of following a single character throughout. At the beginning of *The Scarlet Letter*, we find Hester Prynne hemmed in by the heavy apparatus of Puritan justice. Weighted down by her sin, perpetually surrounded by the village gossips, Hester appears just as shackled in thought as she is bound in body. As the narrative progresses, however, we note sign after sign of Hester's liberation. She embroiders her scarlet "A," she comes to savor her sin as expressing a new and bolder morality, she lets down her hair and permits herself to speculate. The characteristic transformational relationship of *The Scarlet Letter*, and of single-focus narrative as a whole, may thus be expressed by cover terms of this type:

Hester, condemned by the law and imprisoned by the hard devices of Puritan culture, limits her freedom of mind and body	→	Hester, increasingly seen in the midst of a natural environment, lets down her hair and dares to exercise a new freedom of thought.

With numerous separate concerns rolled into one, this pair of sentences represents exactly the type of experience that single-focus mapping regularly inspires. Different categories are mixed together, multiple insights are indiscriminately combined, questions of subject and predicate or transformational type are nowhere to be found. For the after-the-fact analyst, however, the system operative here is quite clear. Expressing the changes that she is slowly undergoing, a series of related predicates is associated with Hester. Hester's stable presence provides an appropriate neutral background against which certain characteristic relationships stand out. Whereas the mapping of dual-focus texts brings us back consistently to a series of subject substitutions, with the predicate being held stable, single-focus narrative reverses the pattern:

$$\text{Subject}_1 \ \text{Predicate}_1 \quad\quad \rightarrow \quad\quad \text{Subject}_1 \ \text{Predicate}_2$$

The second predicate ("lets down her hair and dares to exercise a new freedom of thought") must be sensed as a specific transformation of the first ("limits her freedom of mind and body") in order for the mapping process to be engaged.

It is this recognition of transformation that leads us to segment the otherwise uniform and continuous single-focus text. A silent home movie of a handsome man walking down a road would probably never induce us to begin the narrative mapping process. But if the same man were to walk past an ugly beggar and give him nothing, then open his purse to a second beggar—this one handsome—not only would the narrative mapping process be very likely engaged, but the text would appear segmented into two episodes as well. Mapping and segmentation are engendered simultaneously, triggered by recognition of a transformational relationship between the first and second beggar episodes. It is not possible to establish a neat two-step process in which the critic first segments the text, then notes relationships between segments, for no meaningful narrative segments can possibly preexist the recognition of transformational relationships. Scenes, shots, or chapters may provide a preliminary segmentation, but this division based on textual presentation does not necessarily participate in the production of narrative meaning.

Like their dual-focus counterparts, single-focus texts present numerous specific difficulties in the recognition of transformation and the constitution of summary cover sentences. What, for example, do we do with the adjectival phrases expressing the striking phenomenological transfiguration of Hester's surroundings, taking her from the moral and physical hardness of the Puritan universe to the soft contours and flowing forms of the forest? And what of our changing access to the narrative voice? At the beginning so often seen from the outside, Hester increasingly takes over the narrative function, gaining through speculation the right to express her own thoughts and desires. We cannot claim that questions of figurative language, atmosphere, or narrative voice obviously "belong" to either the subject or the predicate. Again we find ourselves involuntarily guided, in the practice of transformational mapping, by typological concerns. Immediately recognizing *The Scarlet Letter* as a single-focus text, we tend very quickly to begin shunting all significant transformations toward the predicate. The relationships between the hard and the soft, the cultural and the natural, the oppressive and the liberating, are understood not as dual-focus oppositions but as a series of developments from one term to the other, seen through the drama of Hester Prynne. There may be times in reading Hawthorne's novel when we would happily chart the one against the other, sensing as we do the strong differences separating Puritan law from Hester's growing independence, but as the novel wears on we increasingly put aside the seemingly constitutive dualities in favor of Hester's changes, which ultimately constitute our high road through the novel. We quickly assimilate nearly all transformations—figurative language, atmospheric considerations, narrative voice, and many others as well—to the evolving predicates for which Hester provides a stable subject.

One might reasonably object that stressing predicate transformation in *The Scarlet Letter*, or any other single-focus text for that matter, misses the point. The character named Hester Prynne is precisely what does change in Hawthorne's novel, while the society around her retains its sterile stability. Such a claim would rest, however, on a misunderstanding of the transformational system I am presenting here. That Hester's development is summarized by a series of cover sentences all having the same subject in no way implies a lack of change on her part. On the contrary, it is the possibility of associating Hester's name as subject with this particular range and order of predicates that best expresses her specific mobility, her personal itinerary. Just as dual-focus narrative draws us into the mapping process by associating radically different subjects with the same predicate (but only in order eventually to reveal the identity of the predicates that cannot be shared by these two subjects), so single-focus narrative associates a single character with a series of activities, as a method of revealing the important modifications in that character (expressed by the impossibility of transferring certain predicates from one point in her career to another). What we are reflecting, then, when our mapping activity leads us to chart a series of predicate transformations, is not stability of character but the constant presence of that same character at the center of the following-pattern. Whereas dual-focus texts are segmented largely by modulation from focus to focus, the single-focus text is segmented by the protagonist's constant changes.

If subject substitution and predicate transformation constitute, respectively, the characteristic microrelationships of the macrotypes called dual-focus and single-focus narrative, what remains for multiple-focus narrative? The example of Bruegel's *Elck* may be instructive here. All eight characters depicted in the 1558 drawing are involved in diverse bizarre activities. Some are walking around, apparently searching for something with the help of a lantern; others are rummaging through a mound of baskets and bags; still others are engaged in a tug of war. An additional character appears in a poster, gazing at himself in a mirror and accompanied by the caption "Nobody knows himself." The engraving made from this drawing includes a poem in three languages telling us that "Every man seeks himself," but "Nobody knows himself." The engraving also adds the name "Elck" ("Everyman") to the hem of each character's garment or the ground beneath. The process of hem-naming, along with the engraving's interpretive poem, clearly identifies all of the drawing's characters as versions of the same Everyman, engaged in precisely the same activity. In other words, the drawing is built around a following-pattern that takes us from character to character and from activity to activity, a process typified by the following kind of modulation:

One character walks toward the background church	$\rightarrow$	Another character investigates a barrel's innards

This sequence is reasonably summarized as:

$$S_1P_1 \qquad \rightarrow \qquad S_2P_2$$

The engraving, on the other hand, facilitates the interpretive process, mapping the multiple-focus following-pattern in terms of a single shared activity engaged in by a series of cloned characters. The diversity of the drawing (corresponding to the process of multiple-focus following) is thus transformed into the homogeneity of the engraving (corresponding to the multiple-focus mapping process). The resultant experience looks like this

Everyman seeks himself	$\rightarrow$	Everyman seeks himself

This sequence must be summarized as follows:

$$S_1P_1 \qquad \rightarrow \qquad S_1P_1$$

The characteristic multiple-focus transformation thus turns out not to be a transformation at all but, rather, a repeated movement from one identical unit to another. Whether it is Zola producing multiple vignettes of peasant activity, Griffith interweaving diverse examples of intolerance, or Malraux rehearsing our multiple attempts to escape the human condition, the multiple-focus mode constantly calls on readers to reduce different characters and activities to the same hem-name, the same subject/predicate cover term.

Based on a process that I have elsewhere called "intratextual rewriting" (Altman 1981a), narrative mapping thus proves surprisingly economical, dependent on modest means that can be adequately expressed without complex terminology. Corresponding to the three narrative types developed throughout this book, the basic narrative transformations identified through mapping depend on strikingly simple and easily recognizable relationships.

The Transformational Matrix

The well-known Chinese proverb according to which a picture is worth a thousand words has a corollary: in order to understand literary narrative, look at pictorial narrative. The problems of the graphic world may not be identical to the problems of linguistic expression, but the insights gained from close inspection of pictorial texts often outweigh the potential dangers of comparing disparate phenomena. In 1962, the eminent medieval art historian Otto Pächt published a little book entitled *The Rise of Pictorial Narrative in Twelfth-Century England*. Concentrating on marginal manuscript illustrations, Pächt analyzes the process whereby individual, isolated images become organized into recognizable narratives with the images alone carrying a major part of the narrative weight. Instead of illustrating unrelated points in the text, Pächt's images are presented in pairs, as in figure 8.1. To understand this pair of images, we must recognize the second figure not just as a different drawing from the first, but as representing the same character in an altered position.

The hurried reader may well conclude that such belabored analyses constitute much ado about nothing. It does not take too much intelligence (and certainly no knowledge of narrative theory whatsoever) to recognize that if the first drawing is a picture of Saint Cuthbert being solicited for help, then the second represents the same saint putting out a fire. Our knowledge often gets in our way, however. The fact that we know does not tell us how we learned. Pächt's Cuthbert images exemplify an important revival of narrative composition in Western Europe, a revival that required readers to learn to recognize and interpret narrative images. What is it that they had to learn, but that we already know? What operations do we unconsciously effect without recognizing that we are doing so? As Pächt explains, the process of reviving pictorial narrative (a classical tradition suppressed by the so-called Dark Ages) involved the creation of paired images representing the same individual

FIGURE 8.1 Marginal illustration from a twelfth-century manuscript of Bede's *Life of Saint Cuthbert* (Courtesy of Bodleian Library, University College, Oxford University)

engaged in different activities. To this we may reasonably add the creation of a body of "readers" capable of recognizing the two images as representing the same character. For if the viewer assumes that the two figures represent different characters, Pächt's narrative effect is lost (or, rather, never created).

We might summarize this insight schematically in the following manner. While we recognize the Cuthbert pair as the very type of single-focus diptych analyzed above (Cuthbert is asked for help, then Cuthbert provides help, i.e., $S_1P_1 \rightarrow S_1P_2$), we now understand that an intermediary step precedes our perception of the diptych's predicate transformation. On first viewing we see two wholly different images, a frontal picture of a figure standing over a kneeling woman (S_1P_1) and then a representation of a profile figure with his hands raised toward a burning building (S_2P_2). This difference is soon reduced as we perceive similarities between the two characters (they are of the same height, wear similar clothes, and have similar facial features). Two images that once seemed entirely different now appear related by their common subject. In other words, before recognizing that the two drawings are related by predicate transformation, we must pass through a stage during which the single-focus nature of the narrative has not yet become apparent. The duration of this stage varies according to our familiarity with the written text that the illustrations accompany, our knowledge of period conventions, our visual acuity, and our level of interest. Even later, when we understand perfectly well the artist's diptych technique, we are still regularly called on (i.e., with each recognition of predicate transformation) to erase substantial differences between drawings, in order to recognize them as representing the same character engaged in different actions.

Precisely the same situation occurs in literary narrative. We must constantly take phrases that are linguistically different and recognize in them references to the same character. We do this automatically, without ever thinking about it (except at those awkward—and telling—points when character identification is not obvious). As Borges's delightfully iconoclastic character Funes the Memorius puts it, we are entirely accustomed to give the same name to "the dog at three fourteen (seen from the side)" and "the dog at three fifteen (seen from the front)." This process of reducing differences is hardly a natural one. On the contrary, it is a learned ability without which the perception of narrative as narrative would not be possible. For the cultural phenomenon that we call "narrative" has two separate but related conditions of existence. The text must produce multiple renderings of the same character (i.e., differing signs signifying the same character), and the audience must be able to recognize that different signs refer to the same character. The very existence of narrative depends on this cooperation between product and consumer in order to ensure the existence of constructs called "characters."

Though what reappears in twelfth-century illumination is not really narrative as such, but single-focus narrative, Pächt is surely right to recognize an utterly basic narrative impulse in the simple process of interpreting his Cuthbert diptychs. To recognize a character as a character requires a certain amount of narrative sophistication. Namely, it requires that we be able to pass from the original following-oriented perception, in which differences prevail ($S_1P_1 \rightarrow S_2P_2$) to a preliminary mapping-oriented perception, where certain similarities surface ($S_1P_1 \rightarrow S_1P_2$). However rapidly we may eventually reach the highly structured mapping level, we always pass through a preliminary following level, more fragmented and phenomenological.

Dual-focus narrative depends on a similar preliminary reduction, but in this case it operates on the predicate rather than on the subject. The parallel Christian and Saracen council scenes at the outset of *The Song of Roland* at first hide their connections, with Charlemagne and Marsile each handling debate in his own manner. It is only in retrospect that these initial scenes fully reveal their striking similarity (right down to the details analyzed in chapter 2). Later scenes or actions may immediately appear related (especially once the dual-focus nature of the text has become apparent), but we continue to alternate between perceiving the very real differences separating the activities of the text's two groups ($S_1P_1 \rightarrow S_2P_2$) and recognizing the subject substitution on which the text's dual-focus effect depends ($S_1P_1 \rightarrow S_2P_1$). The same remains true of every dual-focus text, however conventional or simplistic. The more complex and sophisticated the text, the longer it takes most readers to reduce the difference of the initial reading activity to the transformational relationship of the mapping process.

Where once it seemed that only multiple-focus transformations ($S_1P_1 \rightarrow S_1P_1$) differed from their related following-pattern ($S_1P_1 \rightarrow S_2P_2$), we now find a more homogeneous situation. All three types regularly present the reader with new characters in new situations. Though we eventually configure it in terms of the opposition between Christians and pagans, *The Song of Roland* begins by following, in turn, Charlemagne, Marsile, Blancandrin, and Ganelon, before settling into a clear dual-focus pattern. Hester Prynne shares the opening scene of *The Scarlet Letter* with the many onlookers who comment on her situation, just as *Pride and Prejudice* and *Le Père Goriot* set a large stage with many characters before giving the text over to the single-focus tales of Elizabeth Bennet and Eugène de Rastignac. At the start, these texts share important characteristics with multiple-focus narrative. Only through the mapping process do we ultimately discover the relationships that allow us to identify individual texts with one narrative type or another. All texts initially assault the reader with new material ($S_1P_1 \rightarrow S_2P_2$). To interpret that material narratively involves reducing utter difference to partial identity. New characters and actions must be recognized as in some sense transformations of characters and actions presented earlier.

A schematic view of this reading activity may be helpful. All narrative texts progress by the introduction of new character/action units, as in figure 8.2. As we read a dual-focus text, however, we rapidly recognize the transformational

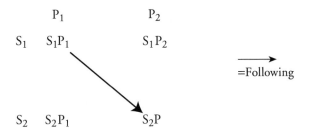

FIGURE 8.2 Introduction of new character/action units.

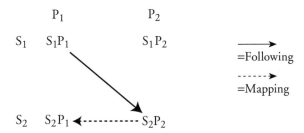

FIGURE 8.3 Dual-focus reading.

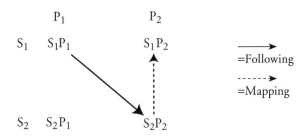

FIGURE 8.4 Single-focus reading.

relationship linking succeeding units. This recognition "tames" the text for us, bringing the radical newness of the new unit into focus (pun intended), as represented in figure 8.3. Single-focus narrative operates in the same manner, but according to a different transformational relationship, as we see in figure 8.4. The multiple-focus approach involves an even more radical reduction,

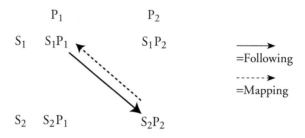

FIGURE 8.5 Multiple-focus reading.

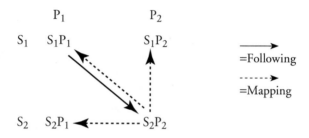

FIGURE 8.6 Master transformational matrix.

with new material revealing not just a transformational relationship, but actual identity with the original unit. This pattern may be represented as in figure 8.5. The reading process always begins with progression along the diagonal from upper left to lower right. In order to digest our reading material, however, we must break it into familiar units, suitable to feed our hunger for the known. This need is satisfied by our ability to turn each new unit into a transformed version of a previously encountered unit.

We may thus construct the master matrix represented in figure 8.6, which represents in a single diagram the various versions of the transformational process. For the sake of convenience, I have reproduced this matrix in its simplified 2×2 form, but texts are of course neither limited to, nor defined by, a single pair of units. The full form of the matrix would extend down and to the right, reproducing many times the relationships visible in the reduced version above (and in most cases combining different types of relationship). This transformational matrix helps us to see that the process of mapping is nothing more nor less than recognizing in unfamiliar material a transformed version of familiar situations.

The term "familiar," however, suggests a potential shortcoming of this analysis. Thus far, I have attended only to individual texts, stressing transformations of earlier passages in the same text. This is not the only way we make meaning, however. If some readers insist on making a new map for every text, depending heavily on the recognition of internal transformations, others borrow fully formed maps provided by preexisting type concepts. Just what is the relationship between transformational and typological approaches to narrative?

The Typological Matrix

Understanding always involves a dialectic between two activities. Whether we are listening to a new language, reading a novel, or simply visiting a historic monument, we make meaning by noting relationships between the internal parts of the "text." But in order to recognize a relationship, we must have a notion of what constitutes a relationship: we thus implicitly refer to a master list of types—derived from our experience of other texts—that is potentially appropriate to the text in question. The very fact that we have such a list in the back of our mind has a clear effect on the type of relationships we notice. Once we begin to identify a text with a particular type, we are more likely to notice the corresponding kinds of relationship within the text. Conversely, once we notice a particular kind of relationship within the text, we are more likely to identify the text with the corresponding type. Intratextual concerns alternate with intertextually derived expectations to produce a specific understanding of the text.

We must therefore modify the transformational matrix, which depends primarily on intratextual relationships, to accommodate the intertextual concerns of typological analysis. In addition to the transformational path to type recognition (constituted by the following/mapping process), we must also take into account the direct type recognition that our intertextual experience encourages us to engage in and which has the power to short-circuit the reading process. We thus recognize that each type involves two separate pathways to the same place. Dual-focus narrative may be represented as in figure 8.7. In the course of reading, we pass through the following stage (solid line), where each succeeding following-unit seemingly presents a new character and action, until such time as apparently different actions are recognized in the mapping process (dashed line) as substantially similar, thus producing the dual-focus mode's characteristic subject substitution (lower left-hand corner). Other readers may instead jump to the conclusion that the text is dual-focus; this type recognition (dotted line) takes these readers directly to the lower left-hand corner and its expectation of subject substitution within the text. In a similar manner, single-focus narrative exploits the other corner of the matrix, as represented in figure 8.8. The multiple-focus mode is somewhat more difficult to figure. As with single-focus and dual-focus narrative, the transformational method of reaching meaning is doubled by a typological method, but this time the shortcut must be figured as a round-trip voyage, as rendered in figure 8.9.

Within this "square of narrative meaning" a striking variety of complex and interrelated activities are represented—some enacted by characters, others performed by narrators, and still others realized by readers. What makes it possible to describe narrative meaning in this particularly economical fashion is the recognition that dual-focus, single-focus, and multiple-focus types are constituted by the systematic association of a particular following-pattern with a specific kind of transformation.

Schematic representations can be dangerous. While they systematize comprehension and foster understanding of relationships between texts and parts of texts, they necessarily arrest and spatialize phenomena that are hardly stable. Whereas the matrices in this conclusion reduce entire texts to individual two-term relationships, texts themselves introduce innumerable units, piled up, as it were, in depth, with no guarantee that one matrix will resemble another. Thus, in *Madame Bovary*, we sandwich numerous single-focus matrices, with their characteristic predicate transformations organized around Emma Bovary, between two small piles of similar single-focus matrices, but with predicate transformations organized around her husband Charles. In the same way, single-focus apprehension of *Women in Love* is tucked into consistent multiple-focus use of each single-focus matrix. Overall perception is thus governed not by a single matrix but by the pattern constituted by many such matrices, joined together and superimposed.

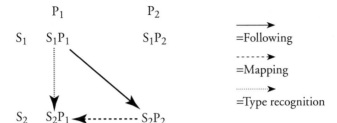

FIGURE 8.7 Dual-focus type recognition.

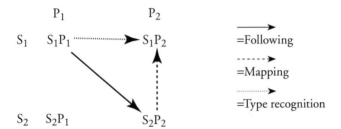

FIGURE 8.8 Single-focus type recognition.

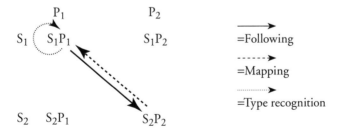

FIGURE 8.9 Multiple-focus type recognition.

Understanding individual narratives in this way—not just as instances of a type, but as a unique combination of reading principles associated with different types—permits us to recognize a host of important subtypes, depending on the way in which several different reading matrices are organized in full texts. Multiple-focus texts are often formed out of single-focus or dual-focus parts. Seemingly traditional dual-focus love stories written for a female mass market may be interwoven with the single-focus account of the woman's (supposed) liberation. Emergence of the single-focus nature of a text, as well as identification of the protagonist, may be more or less delayed, thereby prolonging the reader's freedom to attend in the meantime to other narrative possibilities, or to nonnarrative concerns. Compare the psychological interest forced on the reader by the early single-focus definition of *The Red and the Black*, *The Scarlet Letter*, and *The Red Badge of Courage*, with the availability of *Pride and Prejudice* for social analysis, because of the slowness with which Elizabeth Bennet takes over the narrative, imposing a single-focus vision on what initially seemed like a multiple-focus account of country society.

The usefulness of a method depends on its ability to isolate and appreciate not only the representative but also the unique, not just the theoretical but also the practical. In the following conclusion I propose to right, in part, the lack of balance in previous chapters. If the method presented here has any value, then it must help us discover not only abstract relationships among ideal narrative types but also real, concrete ties informing not just literary history but daily life as well.

NINE   Practical Conclusion

heories are rightly measured by two complementary criteria, pertinence and elegance. Does the proposed theory match the phenomena in question? Then it is deemed pertinent. Is the proposed theory neat, clear, and economically formulated? Then it is deemed elegant. In developing a theory of narrative based on following-patterns I have considered an additional criterion: usefulness. Can the proposed theory be easily applied to a wide range of activities? Then it is deemed useful. Here I suggest some possible uses for the theory developed in the preceding chapters. Principal areas covered include textual analysis, literary and film history, social organization, religion, and political life.

Textual Analysis

Compared with other approaches, the narrative theory presented in this volume offers an important analytical benefit. Most existing approaches to narrative stress a single aspect of textual organization. While one group attends primarily to the reader's relationship to the text (rhetorical criticism, point-of-view, and narrational approaches), other critics concentrate on internal textual connections (formalism, structuralism, and semiotics), while still others stress the large categories into which texts may be divided (archetypal and genre studies). What distinguishes the theory presented here is its ability to address all three concerns in a coordinated manner. Based on key rhetorical techniques (following and modulations) and built around typological analysis (recognition of the basic single-focus, dual-focus, and multiple-focus types), this theory also includes a key transformational component (concentrating on matched textual segments). Though these elements may be deployed separately, the theory is at its practical best only when the three approaches are combined, either simultaneously or serially. Textual analysis can only benefit from this coordinated strategy. A few examples are in order.

Stressing subject matter over presentational strategies or textual coherence, film critics treat "war movies" as a recognized type. The resources of the theory proposed here offer substantially more specificity. While battle stories might reasonably be expected to call for dual-focus treatment, careful analysis of individual texts, using all the resources at hand, leads to quite different conclusions, more nuanced and more accurate. Like *The Song of Roland*, some battle stories are built around a resolutely dual-focus following-pattern, but others, like *The Red Badge of Courage*, concentrate instead on a single character. Even these clearly affiliated texts may include contrary-to-type segments (such as the attention lavished on Roland's decisions during the attack on the rearguard), which are accessible through careful rhetorical and transformational analysis.

Perhaps more interesting still are the many battle stories that personalize the conflict by weaving an individual account into the larger conflict. Earlier, I noted important differences between John Wayne and Henry Fleming, the central character of Stephen Crane's *The Red Badge of Courage*. From film to film, Wayne seems eternally the same, whether he plays a navy commander, a cavalry captain, or a gun-totin' sheriff. Unlike Henry, he no longer needs a red badge of courage. In John Ford's *She Wore a Yellow Ribbon*, however, Wayne's humanity and his capacity for change are demonstrated through subtle treatment of his apprehension about impending retirement. Though this film may at first seem just another western, just another Wayne film—just another rote dual-focus offering—careful inspection reveals a studied interweaving of dual-focus motifs and single-focus concerns. Much of the film is given over to a clichéd clash between youthful, bloodthirsty Indians and disciplined horse soldiers under the command of the restrained, grey-haired Wayne, along with the obligatory courtship between Wayne's second-in-command and a comely eastern lass. But *She Wore a Yellow Ribbon* is also the single-focus story of Wayne's concerns about his uncertain future. Predicate transformations centering around Wayne are repeatedly interwoven with epic and pastoral subject substitutions. The theory presented here facilitates detailed analysis of the film's repeated changes of technique and focus.

Different still are the many war films that concentrate on a full platoon rather than a single individual (Tay Garnett's *Bataan*, Edward Ludwig's *The Fighting Seabees*, Sam Fuller's *The Big Red One*, Steven Spielberg's *Saving Private Ryan*). Alternately following an Italian immigrant, New York Jew, Southern farmboy, Midwesterner, African American, and other characters clearly chosen for the categories they represent, "platoon" films offer a multiple-focus view of war. The combined resources of following, transformational analysis, and typological evaluation are necessary to distinguish among these extremely varied "war films." The more mixed the text, the more beneficial this particular trio of approaches.

Because this theory deploys three separate but coordinated approaches, it provides an especially welcome resource for analyzing texts that make their meaning by blending divergent narrative strategies. Take the famous case of *Madame Bovary*'s "Comices agricoles" sequence. This justly celebrated rendition of a county fair—as observed from a quiet corner where the country nobleman Rodolphe is actively courting Emma, the rural doctor's wife who dreams of fancy dresses and far-off places—has alternately been treated as a key moment in the development of Emma's fantasies and as the very type of a modernist technique known as "spatial form" (Frank 1963). For one group of critics, the focal character Emma Bovary is the center of this scene, as she is of the rest of the novel. For another group, Flaubert's treatment of the fair is marked by its very centerlessness, by a sense of unvectored space, subordinated to no character in particular.

The theory elaborated in this book facilitates a more satisfactory treatment of the "Comices agricoles" scene. A multiple-focus incursion in what is otherwise a strongly single-focus novel, the county fair scene stands out both for its reinforcement of other peasant practices and for its status as a countertype to Emma's fondly remembered experience at the Vaubyessard ball. On the one hand, it provides grist for the mill of early critics who treated *Madame Bovary* primarily as a drab documentary of nineteenth-century rural life in France. On the other hand, it serves as a means to measure the distance separating Emma's dreams from her reality. Each individual following-unit offers multiple opportunities for transformational analysis, producing not just a single straightforward classification, or even a simple mix of two different approaches, but a structured account that explains why a scene is susceptible to multiple readings, all the while linking the scene's various parts to the diverse novel segments that they evoke and transform. To analyze a complex author like Flaubert, who always works several strains at a time, a multipartite theory like the one proposed here is clearly necessary.

Operating simultaneously on several different levels, this theory is especially well equipped to handle the contradictions, paradoxes, and slippages that characterize long and complex narratives. When Eugène Sue virtually pleads with his readers to process his story according to progressive social standards, our tripartite analysis of *Les Mystères de Paris* helps us understand why he should need to work so hard to get us to consider social questions. The novel's following-pattern and transformational relationships are all carefully aligned to stress dual-focus relationships and values. As a foreign prince with an indefensible right uppercut, the hero Rodolphe provides little grist for the social mill. Because his novel employs a resolutely dual-focus following-pattern, the only way that Sue can possibly get us to accomplish the hem-naming characteristic of multiple-focus narrative is through extensive narratorial intervention.

Émile Zola tackles a similar problem in *L'Assommoir*, but as a confirmed naturalist he must do so without the support of an obtrusive narrator. Just as *Les Mystères de Paris* fails to inspire socially conscious multiple-focus readings because of its obvious dual-focus debts, so the single-focus organization of the first two-thirds of *L'Assommoir* apparently assigns blame to the protagonist Gervaise for the very problems that Zola wants us to ascribe to broader social structures. Only through a substantial change in following-pattern and narrative transformations during the final one-third of the novel is Zola eventually able to open new multiple-focus vistas. The difficulty of inducing multiple-focus readings without resorting to narrative intervention helps us understand why authors like Lawrence and Malraux felt the need to create mouthpiece characters who are capable of assisting the narrator in hem-naming the novel's apparently diverse cast. Access to three separate analytical tools is what makes analyses like these possible.

In cinema, where sound and image are added to language, the availability of multiple approaches is even more important. One area where the present theory offers especially welcome new resources is adaptation: the combination of fine-grain analysis and broad-based type recognition makes it possible to tease out the essential differences between original and adaptation in a new and more satisfying way. Take the opening of the 1995 BBC version of Jane Austen's *Pride and Prejudice*. The novel famously begins with an apparent truism, vouched for by the narrator: "It is a truth universally acknowledged, that a single man in possession of a good fortune must be in want of a wife." The opening pages of the novel proceed to illustrate the narrator's initial statement, concentrating on no one character in particular. Before eventually homing in on Elizabeth, the following-pattern thus gives us every reason to believe that Austen's novel is a multiple-focus treatise on the generalities of country life. Director Andrew Davies handles the beginning of the 1995 BBC version in a totally different manner. Before we learn the narrator's truth about single men and their desires, before we even meet Elizabeth, we are shown Darcy and Bingley riding the English countryside while discussing a handsome manor house. Cut to Elizabeth, out walking and apparently watching the two men ride by. We then follow Elizabeth home, taking her point of view as she observes the Bennet family activities at Longbourn.

Far from inviting the multiple-focus reading that Austen offers, this initial sequence sets up two competing readings: the powerful male/female balancing of the opening shots recalls many a dual-focus beginning, while the subsequent sequence suggests a single-focus treatment of Elizabeth's story (an impression that is reinforced when Austen's opening sentence is spoken by Elizabeth in the film's next scene). The following-pattern adopted by Davies for the rest of his film reinforces this hesitation. Though the film follows Elizabeth both earlier and more overtly than the novel, thereby reinforcing the novel's single-focus tendencies, Davies' practice of cutting back and forth regularly between Darcy and Elizabeth—along with a mise-en-scène that includes Darcy in the background of countless shots of Elizabeth—pushes the film in the direction of dual-focus pastoral.

Though this is more a thumbnail sketch than a proper analysis, it should be clear that the approach facilitated by this theory attends not only to small-scale particulars—scripting, shot selection, mise-en-scène—but also to extremely broad concerns, such as the film's manipulation of the following-pattern to cue viewer reactions different from those elicited by Austen. Only by connecting the smallest intratextual details to broad intertextual categories can this analysis offer an appropriate level of specificity.

Literary and Film History

Because the theory developed in this book melds typological analysis with rhetorical and transformational components, it offers substantial resources for the historian of literature or film. In this section I provide three examples: the rise of the novel in France and England, the growing taste for metonymic modulations, and the surprising effect that theatrical versions of novels have had on film adaptations.

Attempts to describe and explain the rise of the novel typically stress realistic content, increased psychological interest, and the influence of diverse popular models. From the standpoint of the theory presented here, something quite different is taking place. The major change in narrative style between the Renaissance and the eighteenth century involves a radical reworking of the dominant following-pattern. From Lodovico Ariosto and Edmund Spenser to Paul Scarron and Madeleine de Scudéry, late Renaissance narrative is heavily marked by the interlaced following practices of multiple-focus Grail romances. These large books (in terms of physical size as well as length) routinely follow multiple characters, moving from one to another through ample use of hyperbolic modulation. During the first half of the seventeenth century, interlaced romances were so popular that multivolume French novels would appear within months across the Channel in English translations. Yet by the early eighteenth century, this mode had been almost entirely replaced by pocket-sized single-focus narratives bearing nary a trace of hyperbolic modulation. What happened to the market for these internationally renowned multiple-focus products? How did they get supplanted in the course of only a few decades?

While other theories are better equipped to deal with the realistic subject matter and popular language of the early novel, this theory is especially well suited to describe and explain the changes in narrative strategy that characterize the rise of the novel. Unrecognized as a major literary type, vilified because of its lack of a classical model, the novel remained subject, throughout the seventeenth century, to the influence of more powerful modes—especially theater. A literary debate waged during the 1630s in France would eventually play an important role in the development of the novel. Dubbed the "Quarrel of *Le Cid*," after the Corneille play that triggered the controversy, public discussion covered everything from allowable rhymes and appropriate versification to suitable subjects and proper story construction. Particular attention was given to the three "unities": unity of place, time, and action. While the first two (requiring a play's action to take place in a single location within a time frame of no more than twenty-four hours) had substantial importance for the development of neoclassical theater, they had minimal effect on the novel.

More complex and ultimately more important, the concept of unity of action eventually contributed directly to the development of new narrative strategies. At the time of the quarrel, plays and novels shared a tendency toward multiple locations, multiple plots, and multiple main characters. Successive scenes in early-seventeenth-century baroque plays commonly jump from continent to continent and back again; when one plot line flags, a new set of characters, problems, and locations is introduced. To the 1630s arbiters of taste gathered in the French Academy, these practices were anathema. Plays, they insisted, should henceforth present a single, unified plot, all of whose elements must be presented from the start. Plot development must be logical and smooth, with each scene connected to the next by the continued presence of at least one character on stage. Eventually, this emphasis on unity of action did away with the adventure scenarios of dramatists like Alexandre Hardy, leading instead to Jean Racine's characteristic alternation between a scene where a principal character acts or speaks in public and an introspective scene (with or without a confidant/e), where the same character reflects on the previous public situation.

For half a century, the precepts imposed by the Quarrel of *Le Cid* were applied primarily to the theatrical domain from which they originally sprang. The 1678 publication of Madame de Lafayette's novelette, *La Princesse de Clèves*, would change all that. Especially concerned about the use of included stories, public debate about this short novel revived interest in the notion of unity of action as a standard for literary cohesiveness. Discussion was sufficiently animated to give rise to a book-length critique of *La Princesse de Clèves* (by Jean-Baptiste-Henry du Trousset de Valincour), followed by a book-length defense (by Madame de Lafayette's advocate, Abbot Jean Antoine de Charnes). According to Valincour, novels are not unified if they include stories about secondary actions. Though the novels of the previous generation had regularly been laced with literally dozens of included stories, Valincour and his allies now sought to subject contemporary narratives to the principles previously adopted for the theater. Charnes's rebuttal defends the novel's unity, insisting that the included stories are justified because they serve to measure the protagonist's reaction. Requiring that every component be subordinated to the main character, the standard of unity of action would henceforth be directly applied to the novel. Charnes's defense of *La Princesse de Clèves* makes him one of the first important theorists of single-focus narrative—and the novel.

Within a few short years, the narrative principles developed during what we might call the "Quarrel of *La Princesse de Clèves*" would be turned into hard and fast rules by the theoreticians of the increasingly successful French novelette. In 1683, a writer known simply as Du Plaisir published a short treatise that would become a manifesto for the new generation of novelists. In the spare, clear prose of his *Sentiments sur les lettres et sur l'histoire avec des scrupules sur le style*, Du Plaisir insists on a single principal event, internally justified plot connections, and a coherent narrative structure. Abandoned forever are multiple plots, chance events, and an interventionist narrator. Heirs to a distinguished group of Renaissance scholars (Torquato Tasso, Julius Caesar Scaliger, Lodovico Castelvetro), the era's Aristotelians were quick to jump on board. For decades, René Rapin's 1674 *Réflexions sur la Poétique d'Aristote*—published in English translation before the year was out—continued to influence British literature.

Perhaps most important for the development of single-focus fiction in England was the attention that William Congreve (and other early novelists) gave to the French quarrel. As Congreve says in the preface to his *Incognita* (1692), "I resolved . . . to imitate dramatick writing, namely, in the design, contexture and result of the plot" (1930:242). Insisting that every aspect of his story is subservient to the main plot line, Congreve notes that "in a comedy [i.e., stage play] this would be called the unity of action." For well over a century, on both sides of the Channel, the novel would remain primarily a single-focus affair. Instrumental in the key neoclassical process of expanding Aristotelian theatrical standards to the novel, the Quarrel of *La Princesse de*

Clèves also underlies twentieth-century scholars' tendency to limit the category of narrative to texts that combine unity of action with a clear beginning, middle, and end.

Recognition of the novel's single-focus underpinnings offers a useful complement to views that stress the novel's development of individualism. Referring to "the autonomy of the individual as it developed in the tradition of Locke, Hume, and Smith" (2005:15), Nancy Armstrong's persuasive argument in *How Novels Think: The Limits of Individualism from 1719–1900*, suggests that the novel "was born as authors gave narrative form to this wish for a social order sufficiently elastic to accommodate individualism" (139). Armstrong's analysis comes into clearer focus—in detail and in general—when it is seen through the resources presented in this book. At the level of narrative technique, we may note that the "narrative form" that novels initially provide is precisely the mode that I have identified as single-focus. The resources that make it possible for the novel to feature the individual are those outlined here in chapter 5.

For Armstrong, the development of a literary form dedicated to presentation of protagonists who are interesting because of their individuality does not begin until such time as Locke and others were able to enunciate a new philosophy based on the autonomy of the individual. The approach presented here offers a wider understanding of the novel's connections. Before the seventeenth-century revival of single-focus narrative, two strong single-focus narrative traditions had already made their influence felt. From Augustine and hagiography to Luther and the Protestant Reformation, the Christian religion had produced a vigorous single-focus tradition, providing a strong foundation for the novelistic individual. Similarly, single-focus Arthurian romances had offered an important alternative to the dual-focus approach of early medieval epic. Championing individuals over institutions, tales of knightly prowess provided yet another model for the novel. Viewing the novel through the approach presented in this book helps us understand both the specific techniques necessary for the novel's increased attention to individuals and the broader historical context within which the novel exploits its single-focus heritage.

Careful study of following-pattern developments often offers new insight into the history of narrative. A similar situation obtains with modulations. Nineteenth-century narrative technique is heavily marked by unspoken

assumptions regarding modulation choice. While popular novelists continued to resort to metaphoric and hyperbolic modulations throughout the
nineteenth century, those with higher aspirations voluntarily restricted themselves to metonymic modulations. The reasons for this self-imposed restriction are quite clear. Revealing the active hand of a narrator, metaphoric and
hyperbolic modulations provide a poor match for the era's realistic aesthetic.
Metonymic modulations, on the other hand, seem to arise out of the narrative material itself, thereby concealing narrational activity. Nineteenth-century
novelists became increasingly adept at leading their characters to a group
scene where other characters could be momentarily featured or from which a
new character could be followed. Instead of intervening, the narrator appears to be doing nothing but observing. To keep this metonymic slant from
becoming too restrictive, authors increasingly borrowed the resources of ty-
pography, using chapter changes or white space on the page to dissimulate
hyperbolic modulations. Though the choice and manipulation of modulations has long played an essential role in the narrative art, their story has
hardly begun to be told.

Just as the choice of modulations was strongly affected by questions of
literary prestige, so the early history of cinema would be heavily influenced
by the differing status of its novelistic and theatrical sources. The split between primarily single-focus classical novels and typically dual-focus or
multiple-focus popular serials in nineteenth-century fiction is mirrored and
heightened by an even more evident split in nineteenth-century theater. On
the one side stands the "well-made play," championed by Francisque Sarcey,
Victorien Sardou, Augustin Eugène Scribe, and other students of theater history. Corresponding fairly closely to the efforts of an Austen or a Flaubert,
the well-made play followed Aristotelian principles, with particular emphasis
on the importance of unity of action—this in an era when the popular stage
was occupied by melodramas built according to principles of crosscutting
and episodic construction like those borrowed by D. W. Griffith from the
stage versions of *The Cricket on the Hearth, Enoch Arden, Ramona, Judith of
Bethulia*, and *The Clansman (The Birth of a Nation)*.

Two basic principles regarding the relationship of the novel to the
nineteenth-century and early-twentieth-century popular stage deserve mention here. First, popular dramatists tended to choose their material from existing texts whose melodramatic proclivities were quite obvious. Thus Balzac,

Dumas, Dickens, Hugo, and Zola remained their objects of choice. Second, whatever the source material, late-nineteenth-century and twentieth-century stage adaptations imprint the popular theater's own melodramatic stamp on the original.

The role of melodrama in an apparently classical narrative will be clarified by the example of one of Balzac's most durably popular novels, *Le Père Goriot*, which assures continuity, linearity, and psychological causality by focusing on the social and moral development of young Eugène de Rastignac. Following the protagonist almost exclusively from beginning to end, the narrator invites us to pay primary attention to Rastignac in his twin roles of detective and student of life. With Rastignac we discover the activities, nefarious and charitable, of his fellow boarders at the Pension Vauquer. With Rastignac we also learn about the social mores and moral dilemmas that attend life in the modern world. Viewed in this manner, *Le Père Goriot* stands as the very model of single-focus narrative.

From the picaresque episodes of a *Lazarillo de Tormes* or Alain René Lesage's *Gil Blas de Santillane* to the historical novels of Prosper Mérimée and Sir Walter Scott, from the Bildungsroman as practiced by Pierre de Marivaux and Johann Wolfgang von Goethe to the nascent modernism of Gustave Flaubert, from the *roman d'analyse* of Madame de Lafayette to the point-of-view experiments of Henry James, the pattern remains the same. Continuity is assured by consistent following of a single character along with whom we discover the surrounding world. While the protagonist's body may continue to serve the familiar adventure functions assigned to it by romance, the protagonist's mind takes on a newly expanded role. Opinions and attitudes usurp the position once reserved for actions alone. Sleuthing replaces dueling as the key to success.

When *Le Père Goriot* was adapted for the stage, however, these characteristic single-focus attributes were abandoned (Barbéris 1972). Instead of concentrating on Rastignac, the melodramatic stage version centers on Vautrin, the Mephistophelean ex-convict whose get-rich-quick schemes simultaneously horrify and intrigue his young charge, and on Goriot, the realist Lear, the spaghetti-making saint who would pair Rastignac with one of his money-hungry daughters. Contemporary novels were regularly subjected by popular theater to this type of transformation. Single-focus coming-of-age or detective stories were routinely turned into dual-focus confrontations between good and evil. While Balzac's Rastignac is the consummate single-focus character, tying scene to scene through his well-developed psychology, ever-changing throughout the course of the novel, Goriot and Vautrin seem drawn from another world, held in ritual bondage to their roles, like the blocking characters of New Comedy or, more to the point, like the antagonists of melodrama. One standing for Good and the other representing Evil, Goriot and Vautrin offer twin myths of paternity. The stage version of *Le Père Goriot* actively exploited these proclivities. Where Vautrin and Goriot had in the novel served only as models for Rastignac's conduct, on the stage they took on the directly and melodramatically opposed positions that they have retained in popular memory of the novel.

Throughout the latter half of the nineteenth century and the first quarter of the twentieth, this pattern would be repeated. Psychologically based single-focus novels were routinely turned into melodramatic dual-focus stage plays. When the young cinema industry sought to embellish its reputation by producing film versions of well-known novels, the theater provided a ready model. Instead of adapting novels directly, however, Hollywood borrowed available stage versions. Rather than emulating Robert Louis Stevenson's story of psychology and detection, several different filmmakers based their versions of *Dr. Jekyll and Mr. Hyde* on the stage play, which reinforces its dual-focus symmetry by the addition of a second female lead who is absent from Stevenson's tale. No matter how obviously a title apparently indicates that a film was borrowed from a short story or novel, a stage version is invariably the film's immediate source. The title may suggest Arthur Conan Doyle as the film's likely origin, but the 1939 *Adventures of Sherlock Holmes* (directed by Alfred L. Werker) is actually based on William Gillette's melodramatic stage play. Though a justly famous article by Sergei Eisenstein (1949) has convinced generations of scholars that Griffith's films were modeled on the novels of Charles Dickens, and that Hollywood film production in general owes a heavy debt to the nineteenth-century novel, it was actually the popular stage that influenced Griffith and his colleagues (Altman 1989).

The importance of this insight for the analysis and history of Hollywood cinema can hardly be overstated. Because Hollywood borrowed from stage versions rather than from the novel itself, and because those stage versions had recast fundamentally single-focus material in melodramatic form, early American filmmaking was heavily dual-focus in nature. Only much later would the film industry develop techniques enabling it to handle the complex psychology required for single-focus treatment of extended narratives. Once again, we find that an important historical claim is made possible only by a multipartite theory of narrative capable of recognizing essential disparities between differing versions of the "same" story.

Social Organization

As useful as the present theory may be for textual analysis and literary history, its most far-reaching contributions lie in another area entirely. Since narrative is an abstraction, a mental construct, it may easily be transferred not only from one familiar medium to another (oral story, printed tale, painting, comic strip, film) but also to the events of daily life. Though the principles of this focal theory of narrative are presented here primarily through literary examples, it is important to recognize the applicability of those principles to a far greater range of cases. Since narrative exists wherever narrative drive leads people to perceive the presence of narrative material and narrational activity, the approach developed in these pages may profitably be applied to such diverse human activities as architecture (which regiments narrative movement), religion (typically based on sacred history expressed through narrative), politics (which always involves questions of narrational control), and even the exchange of goods (which follows standards established by familiar narratives). In these cases—and many others—the analytical principles and language developed in this volume may usefully be applied.

At the end of chapter 3, I show how a tendency to develop spatial relationships at the expense of temporal sensitivity connects dual-focus narrative to the belief systems of "traditional" societies, as outlined by Mircea Eliade in *Cosmos and History: The Myth of the Eternal Return* (1959). The dualism, spatial orientation, neglect of time, and emphasis on long-term stability that characterize dual-focus narrative also find a fascinating echo in anthropologists' attempts to define the illusory phenomenon known as "peasant society." George M. Foster provides an especially clear statement:

> The model of cognitive orientation that seems to me best to account for peasant behavior is the "Image of Limited Good." By "Image of Limited Good" I mean

that broad areas of peasant behavior are patterned in such fashion as to suggest that peasants view their social, economic, and natural universes—their total environment—as one in which all of the desired things in life such as land, wealth, health, friendship and love, manliness and honor, respect and status, power and influence, security and safety, *exist in finite quantity* and *are always in short supply*, as far as the peasant is concerned. Not only do these and all other "good things" exist in finite and limited quantities, but in addition *there is no way directly within peasant power to increase the available quantities.* It is as if the obvious fact of land shortage in a densely populated area applied to all other desired things: not enough to go around. "Good," like land, is seen as inherent in nature, there to be divided and redivided, if necessary, but not to be augmented. (1965:296)

Foster goes on to show how every aspect of peasant behavior, from sibling rivalry to the use of treasure stories to account for unexplained wealth, can be derived from this model.

According to Foster, the logical consequence of this system, at least for intrasocietal transactions, is that every agreement must be bipolar and dyadic (1961). In this he parallels directly the findings of Axel Olrik on the "Epic Laws of Folk Narrative," which include the "Law of Two to a Scene" and its correlative "Law of Contrast" (1965). Foster suggests that everything in the peasant system operates according to the analogy of land, which is chronically in short supply. The spatial organization of dual-focus narrative exactly mirrors this arrangement. When "real estate" retains its original meaning—when land is the only real value—then the sum of all values remains constant. Because the amount of land available is indeed finite, the economics of a given area obey a logic known as "zero-sum." Whatever one person possesses must necessarily reduce the wealth available for another. Perhaps this is why traditional societies are so often organized according to dual-focus principles and regularly produce a preponderance of dual-focus texts.

Based on a set of presuppositions matched to constraints imposed by external factors, what Foster calls the economy of "limited good" depends on a mental state at least as much as on economic conditions. Communities operating according to the economy of limited good develop an elaborate set of self-regulatory controls designed to preclude alienation of community wealth or accumulation of private wealth. This essentially agricultural system, based on natural and historical limitation of access to real estate, measures time cyclically, assuring, for example, the complete disposal of each year's crop before the next is touched, even if that requires recourse to burning or bacchanalia. In such a society, the typically dual-focus zero-sum system governs all transactions. Not only is it assumed that the community and its enemies compete for a limited supply of land (whatever they take, we lose, and vice versa), but all internal economic interchange takes on the character of bartering (gain and loss being balanced through the barter system). The purchasing process thus takes on a ritual character, with production directly related to consumption, usually through an "on demand" system. When I need a new barrel I go to the barrel-maker and he makes me one, charging me the going rate for barrels, the cost being always roughly equivalent to the expense of time plus materials, with supply or desire having little effect. This system—partially retained in rural areas throughout the world—plays down differences among individuals of the same community, stressing instead the differences between communities.

It is instructive to note how the "limited good" arrangement is transformed with the institution of a market economy. Strictly speaking, market economies depend on the possibility of stocking produce, with the attendant practice of releasing merchandise only in favorable circumstances. Now, consider what the ability to stock the previous crop (a self-regulated as well as a naturally imposed impossibility in the "limited good" system) might mean to an economy. If the entire crop of wheat must be sold within the same limited period, then prices will be strictly dependent on the weather—no farmer's crop will be worth any more than another's, for all will be sold roughly at the same time under the same conditions. As soon as it becomes possible to stock wheat from season to season, however, two radical changes take place. The farmer (or someone storing the grain on his behalf) is now faced with decisions about the optimum moment to release the wheat onto the market. Buyers, too, must make decisions, at every point gauging the likelihood that the cost will go up or down in the future. It is not just that the law of supply and demand becomes operative with the market system: even more important in the new system is the possibility of manipulating supply—and thus demand.

For the barrel-maker, the new market economy introduces radical changes. Instead of limiting his output to making barrels on demand, the cooper now makes merchandise in advance, calculating (correctly) that many of the new system's consumers will be willing to pay a premium for a barrel that is ready when they want it (even if they have to take the "wrong" wood or size). Instead of making every barrel for a specific consumer, the cooper is now producing for a market, whose demands he must regularly estimate. Instead of fabricating products for proven needs, the barrel-maker now produces for the consumer's desires, or what he thinks those desires are or even—one day he will discover—what he can turn those desires into. Every time the cooper sits down to his task he is thus confronted by a decision: Should he maximize usefulness or marketability? These two desiderata are not always mutually exclusive, but the presence of competition from other barrel-makers (absent in the old system where societal self-regulation assured just the right number of coopers for the population) increases the need to maintain low prices and produce models that are both desired by the clientele and profitable for the cooper.

Just as producers are regularly faced with a choice between quality and profit, so consumers regularly treat the purchasing process as a complex speculation. If goods are measured as *plus* and costs as *minus*, the sum of every transaction in the world of limited good is *zero*. Goods always cost their worth, because they are worth the same to everyone. Wealth is a sign of chance or God's will (as expressed, for example, by birth). Market economies introduce an entirely different situation, where purchases are no longer paid for in direct proportion to their utility or quality, or even in proportion to the current state of the individual's desire, but according to the general state of the market. Because of the mediation of desire, you no longer "get what you pay for": the same product may differ in value for different individuals, or even for the same individual at different times. Through judicious purchases, individuals can effect transactions with a positive value, but by unenlightened spending they can end up losing value.

Each purchase constitutes a radically new experience that depends on the current state of the individual as well as that of the market. Individuals must project their future desires (because a *plus* value purchase that becomes a *minus* value purchase the next day through a change of desire is to be avoided). They must evaluate all items offered according to their own current state, judging each according to the twin criteria of desire and cost. Before the market economy, no such situation obtained. One wouldn't order slippers for work shoes, but knowing one needed work shoes one would simply order "work shoes, size 11." This was not a choice but a ritual. When something needed replacement, we did as we did the time before, as our parents and grandparents did before that. The overall needs of the community as a whole guaranteed a direct relationship between need, price, and quality, whereas, in the new system, individual differences assure an unstable market, one where each transaction remains a speculation, with value to be lost or gained depending on the individual's prowess as a purchaser.

The market economy generates massive attempts to manipulate desire, since desire is not only what sells merchandise but also the only possible benchmark on which the notion of a "successful" purchase can be based (much as, in Martin Luther's Protestant approach to religion, the individual criterion of "faith" is alone operative). In the new system, advertising fulfills the role of the single-focus model or tempter figure. Publicity points, saying "this is what you should want." Publicity plays the serpent, offering the fruit not as fruit but as object of desire. No longer considered in terms of its utility to all humans, the fruit is now evaluated in terms of its potential function in the life of an individual. Eve is there to express desire, Adam to count the expense; together they figure our twin reaction to every purchase: gain (satisfaction of desires) and loss (cost).

Single-focus medieval romances operate according to the same principle. Woman is the prize, but no longer woman as woman. In a dual-focus pastoral like Longus's *Daphnis and Chloe*, or in a traditional society, a woman is a commodity like any other. The bride price may depend on social level or even skills but not on desire, for basically a woman is seen as a woman: that is, as a human being capable of bearing children. With twelfth-century romance, something radically new enters Western culture. In conjunction with the courtly love motif, a woman becomes something more (or less) than a child-bearer. Her previous primary (reproductive) function is replaced by her ability to be attractive: that is, *desirable*. External attributes must now be brought into play, attributes that can be more easily manipulated than the inherent virtue of fertility. As with the market system, the *value + price = zero* setup is transformed. When a bride was seen solely as a child-bearer, her value to any man was the same. As an attractive individual, however, her desirability depends on the admirer or potential husband.

The multiple correspondences between the market economy and single-focus narrative practice stand out as clearly as the concordance between the economy of limited good and dual-focus principles. Producer and consumer alike, along with the single-focus protagonist and reader, can no longer depend on a time-honored, community-assured method of supplying their needs. They are instead marked by freedom and choice, along with the value speculation that accompanies them. Instead of being restricted to the limited repertory characteristic of the dual-focus system, their needs grow out of a desire to posit and maximize individual value. Replacing the old system's cyclical sense of time and the eternal return of structures, events, and values, with a clear sense of temporal progression and a tendency toward accumulation of capital, the new system emphasizes individuals' ability to modify their positions through careful management. At the same time, the market system accentuates monetary measures of value over the fixed, absolute values of the old system. This new role of money, a transferable measure of value, accompanied by a preference for secondary over essential characteristics, for desirability over utility, for quantity of sales over quality of product, encapsulates one of the most important ramifications of the market system.

The market system leads to a clear preference for exchange values over use values, along with the commodification of art forms and other values once considered outside the realm of commerce. Essence, quality, and use disappear in favor of money, quantity, and exchange. As part of this slippage from use to exchange values comes the notion that value itself has a price. Where values were once absolutes (the law, birth, virginity, allegiance), incommensurable with anything temporal or finite, value can now be measured and thus purchased. Nobility becomes a commodity to be bought or sold by ambitious individuals or enterprising governments. Religious salvation becomes an affair of pardoners and indulgences. General Motors can now calculate the value of a human life. The value of art is soon measured by price rather than by beauty.

This long detour has been necessary in order to highlight the parallels between economic and social changes in post-Renaissance Western Europe and the blossoming of single-focus narratives culminating in the triumph of the novel. The novel is born with the market economy, out of the tension between use and exchange values. For every Princesse de Clèves, who takes her own self-knowledge as a true indication of her (lack of) value, there is a Moll Flanders, who can announce "how necessary it is for all women who expect anything in the world to preserve the character of their virtue even when perhaps they may have sacrificed the thing itself" (Defoe 1964:123). Both remain caught between the two types of value, their dilemmas defined by the gap separating use and exchange. Throughout its history, the novel has gravitated toward individuals who refuse simple solutions to the dichotomy between use value and exchange value. The novel owes a heavy debt to the single-focus mode and its problematics, for the very right to become a single-focus protagonist depends on ability to incarnate the tension between the old, dual-focus values and the new values introduced by the single-focus mode.

One further analogy, this time to a geographical model, deserves to be made here. In his seminal discussion of *History in Geographic Perspective* (1971), Edward Fox distinguishes between two different types of geographical relationship: the areal (i.e., area-oriented) and the linear. Areal systems depend on self-sufficient land-based societies, where long-distance transport of goods is not economically feasible. Primarily agricultural, these communities are typically organized around central market towns through which transactions are carried out on a regular basis. In linear systems, in contrast, the possibility of transport over water makes commerce over long distances perfectly practicable. Within this second system, cities rapidly develop and trade with other, often quite distant cities rather than primarily with their areally organized hinterlands. These two systems often coexist as close neighbors (areally organized Prussia next to linear Dutch merchant cities, landlocked Paris and Burgundy just inland from port cities on the English Channel and the Atlantic Ocean), yet each develops and maintains distinctive social patterns and administrative structures. As Fox points out, the commercial societies characteristic of linear systems

> have almost always been ruled by narrow oligarchies. Policies, it is true, were fashioned by agreement, but they usually involved large sums of money, whether for defense, aggression, or investment, and were consequently made by those whose fortunes were involved. . . . In contrast, the general organization of agricultural communities has commonly been military, and their government a chain of command. Because security depended on military discipline, obedience was more important than consensus. Where commercial cities were characteristically political, agricultural societies tended to produce administrative institutions. (1971:38)

Fox goes on to hypothesize that the rise of the bourgeoisie in the commercial system, along with the importance of written documents, tends to encourage the early development of extensive and sophisticated literary production, while the traditional military character of the agricultural society tends instead to perpetuate traditional literary forms, often oral and popular in nature.

This rapid summary does little justice to Fox's argument, yet it serves to underline additional parallels between social organization and the narrative analysis presented here. The areal nature of agricultural society, its tendency to turn inward, its subordination of individuals to societal defense, and its preference for traditional literary forms embody dual-focus structure and thematics, while the linear nature of commercial society, with its emphasis on individual fortunes and personal decisions, clearly rehearses the basic organization of single-focus narrative.

Religion

The most widely distributed book in the Western world, the Bible, has heavily influenced our notions of the connection between narrative and daily life. In preceding chapters, I note the heavily dual-focus nature of Old Testament narratives, along with the strongly single-focus orientation of the Gospels and related New Testament books. This initial analysis takes on substantially more interest when it is placed in the context of established religions and the parts of the Bible that they regularly quote or on which their rituals are based. For Jews, the Hebrew Bible or Tanakh remains central to every aspect of religious life. The dual-focus tales of Exodus, Judges, Esther, and Maccabees all provide important models for a religion that depends heavily on a distinction between those who are within and those who are without. Just as these books tell stories of the separation of the world into the Israelites and their foes, so Jewish life is heavily dependent on rituals that celebrate inclusion while threatening exile for the unfaithful—the ultimate punishment in a dual-focus system. Books of history, books of law, books of wisdom and prophecy—the Hebrew Bible contains a resolutely dual-focus model for daily life.

As the founding documents of Christian doctrine, the New Testament Gospels offer a clear alternative to Jewish ritual. Organized in a fundamentally single-focus manner, the Gospels follow a single individual and stress typically single-focus values. The Old Testament emphasizes externals like completed acts, while the Gospels dwell on intention and other internal factors. For Jews, birth is all-important, whereas Jesus insists on choosing his own family (Matthew 12:46–50). Whereas Jewish dietary laws stress food restrictions, Jesus insists that "not what goes into the mouth defiles a man, but what comes out of the mouth, this defiles a man" (Matthew 15:11, Mark 7:15). Speaking in parables rather than pronouncing laws, Jesus lays a heavy responsibility on his listeners to provide their own interpretation of his words. Capped by the story of Jesus' crucifixion and resurrection, the Gospels provide model after model for a single-focus understanding of life.

What appears to be a clear split between a dual-focus Old Testament and a single-focus New Testament is contested, however, by the presence of Apocalypse at the very end of the Christian Bible. Strongly dual-focus in construction, the Revelation of John (as Apocalypse is also called) was not included in the biblical canon without a fight. Its presence in the Bible testifies to a deep-seated hesitation about the place of dual-focus narratives and values in Christian theology and life. Just as the early church felt a strong need for apocalyptic stories like the dual-focus tales of martyr saints, the high Middle Ages would introduce a fundamentally dual-focus notion into Christian theology in the figure of the Antichrist. Borrowed from an Old Testament apocalyptic passage (Daniel 7:25), the Antichrist provided a convenient opponent for Jesus, making it easy to turn New Testament single-focus passages into dual-focus narratives. Though the Gospels and the Pauline epistles provide only a few very short apocalyptic passages (e.g., Matthew 24–25 and II Thessalonians 2), and no basis at all for the Antichrist or other medieval dual-focus staples such as the Harrowing of Hell, the dual-focus nature of medieval Christianity made it virtually obligatory to furnish sufficient dual-focus material to fill Sunday sermons and cover church walls and windows. By stressing the dual-focus books of the Old Testament—along with Apocalypse—as a source for narrative illustration, and by turning the Gospels into dual-focus material by the addition of the Antichrist, medieval Christianity built a fundamentally dual-focus religion.

Fascinatingly, this tendency to bend Christianity toward dual-focus values has over the last century resurfaced among evangelical sects. While Conservative and Reform Judaism were increasingly bending toward the single-focus tendencies of liberal Christianity, Christian fundamentalists were actively pushing in a dual-focus direction. Southern Baptist hymnals regularly make Jesus into a lover and the process of conversion into a marriage. *The Watchtower* and other pamphlets distributed by Jehovah's Witnesses lay a heavy stress on apocalyptic material. Today's Christianity is clearly divided into two camps, opposed by their values and the Bible books that they stress. Where liberal Christians treat Christ as a teacher and model, evangelical Christians concentrate on his role as saviour. Fundamentalists also find a welcome model in an Old Testament God adept at separating the faithful from the faithless. The fundamentalist Bible is primarily constructed from selected Old Testament quotations (stressing the separation of the elect from their foes), Apocalypse (emphasizing future division of the world into the righteous and the sinners), and a carefully selected set of Gospel verses (accentuating the distinction between those received by Christ with open arms and those whom he rejects). Like Orthodox Judaism, fundamentalist Christianity dwells on the basic dual-focus principles of separation and distinction. The Bible championed by Protestant reformers and adopted by liberal Christians looks quite different. While it does not entirely turn its back on the Old Testament (in particular, adopting the Adam and Eve story and the Psalms, which both reveal single-focus proclivities), it concentrates heavily on Jesus' parables and the Pauline epistles. Apocalyptic material, from whichever Testament, is left almost entirely aside by this group.

Like the dual-focus texts on which it depends, evangelical Christianity deals in publicly acknowledged absolutes. One is either a "born again" Christian or not—there is no in-between. The process of "finding Christ" must be celebrated by a public event modeled on a conversion experience (like the Jewish Bar Mitzvah, which instantly transforms a Jewish youth from outsider to part of the minyan required to conduct a communal religious service). There are no gradations in the process, only a complete reversal from being "lost" to being "saved." The liberal Christian approach to the same questions draws its inspiration instead from the single-focus system. Rather than a public once-and-for-all either/or affair, religion is a personal question, dependent on individual decisions that are subject to constant modification.

Political Life

Just as religions may be understood through their commitments to differing narrative modes, so politicians typically evoke familiar narrative traditions in order to clarify their positions. While virtually any political figure might be chosen as an example, one elected official stands out for the clarity and force of his narrative commitments. Rarely has a head of state called more regularly and forthrightly on the dual-focus tradition than President George W. Bush. Already inclined by his evangelical religious training toward dual-focus formulations, Bush found in the World Trade Center attacks of September 11, 2001, all the justification he needed to increase the dual-focus nature of his rhetoric. Bush represents the world as fundamentally and permanently divided in two. On one side are the righteous, our allies. On the other side lies the "axis of evil"—Iraq, Iran, North Korea, and "terrorists" everywhere. At times, even American citizens who don't share the president's opinions would seem to be included in this group. Extending a long dual-focus tradition, these enemies are treated as a single undifferentiable block that is permanently aligned against "our" side. Conservative members of the clergy have not hesitated to declare their support for Bush's policies from the pulpit, justifying the war with Iraq by associating Saddam Hussein with the Old Testament's archetypally evil head of state King Nebuchadnezzar, whose siege and destruction of Jerusalem are reported in 2 Kings 24–25 (Marsh 2006:6). Dividing the world permanently in two, Bush and his supporters repeatedly invoke the dual-focus narrative tradition—not just its principles but even its traditional actors.

Unlike the liberal establishment, which sees the justice system as a way to guarantee individual liberties for all, the Bush government devised methods of administering justice differentially, according to the category into which it places individuals by prior judgment. While American citizens are technically guaranteed protection by the courts, those suspected of terrorism have not been allowed access to the normal justice system. When, in early 2006, a United Nations report called on the United States to close its Guantanamo Bay prison, White House spokesman Scott McClellan insisted that the prisoners cannot be released because "these are dangerous terrorists that we're talking about" (Associated Press 2006:10A). According to the Bush government, these untried prisoners would commit or contribute to acts of terror.

In other words, they have already been judged, and on that basis are denied the right to a swift trial.

While several political points deserve to be made apropos of the government's Guantanamo Bay justice system, I am more concerned here to show that the politics of George W. Bush and his government may conveniently be defined, described, and understood through the notion of dual-focus narrative. The assumptions that drive Bush's actions—and the government's prose—are determined by a set of texts and a system of narrative that are fundamentally dual-focus in nature. Not only is Bush's world permanently fixed in a we/they orientation, but also his assumptions about the unchanging nature of human character recycle familiar dual-focus epic material. Like the pagans of *The Song of Roland*, the terrorists in Bush's narratives are a known quantity, their actions entirely predictable from what is represented as their mistaken allegiance. Where once the eminently single-focus category of decisions was the government's major concern, now attention is concentrated on the fundamentally dual-focus category of borders. Whether at the level of national governments, financial investors, or personal friends, Bush clearly differentiates between an in-group and an out-group, forever separate. While this dual-focus approach has the advantage of circling the wagons and establishing a coherent community, it risks squelching the individual liberties and responsibilities on which American life has long been based.

Imaging the World

Applicable wherever humans tell stories or implicitly refer to previously told tales, the theory presented in this volume offers powerful potential for describing human activities. In this final conclusion, I suggest how the theory might be used to image and explain such varied phenomena as individual texts, literary and film history, social organization, religion, and political life. Many other domains might have been evoked. Whether the topic is literature, art, or epistemology, we regularly find a historical series that may be usefully described as developing from dual-focus through single-focus to multiple-focus. Sometimes this pattern is most visible from a distance, as in the progression of Western art from sacred to profane to analytical, or the development of dominant medieval literary modes from dual-focus epic to single-focus romance to interlaced multiple-focus romance. Sometimes the dual-/single-/multiple-focus succession may be seen in the smallest of details, as in the history of the way people have identified themselves—from a patronymic or location-based family name, to a first name or nickname based on personal accomplishment or eccentricity, to a Social Security number or location defined by GPS coordinates.

Strong internal relationships among the three narrative modes (single-focus critiquing dual-focus, multiple-focus in turn undermining single-focus) suggest that the dual-/single-/multiple-focus sequence might be considered a master key to Western culture. Certainly, the general development of dual-focus to single-focus to multiple-focus literature does indeed map clearly onto the progression from medieval culture (where people are defined by feudal or religious ties), to early modern society (establishing individual worth through Reformation, revolutions, and romanticism), to the modern world (ushered in by sociology and cubism). In spite of the general usefulness of such overviews, however, they remain all too approximate. Fortunately, the focal theory presented here offers the wherewithal to provide greater accuracy. Though we can easily see the opposition between two cities in Augustine's *City of God* as the very type of medieval dual-focus discourse, we also observe the extent to which Augustine's *Confessions* offer a way out of the dual-focus worldview, as do the many saints' lives that eventually provided a narrative model for single-focus romance. Though interlaced romance was initially developed during the thirteenth century as a multiple-focus critique of single-focus solutions, it is useful to note that the late Renaissance growth of single-focus tales (picaresque stories, *Don Quixote*, *La Princesse de Clèves*), eventually resulting in the invention of the novel, simply reversed that pattern, simultaneously critiquing and reorganizing multiple-focus material and strategies. Whatever the object or level of analysis, the approach presented in this book offers useful analytical resources.

One last foray. If medieval physics clearly grows out of dual-focus assumptions, and its Newtonian successor develops a fundamentally single-focus cause-and-effect model, then we may perhaps recognize in Einstein's famous equation $e = mc^2$ the ultimate multiple-focus hem-naming process, recognizing for the first time that energy and matter can be treated as equals. When energy and matter, action and character, are reduced to the same entity, can the end of narrative be far behind?

References

This list includes all texts referred to in chapters 1–9. A specific edition of a literary source is provided only when the source has been directly quoted. Films are listed separately at the end.

Books and Articles

Abbott, H. Porter. 2002. *The Cambridge Introduction to Narrative.* Cambridge: Cambridge University Press.

Altman, Charles F. (Rick). 1974a. "Hyperbolic Modulation in Some Modern Novels or 'How Did We Get Here From There?' " *Les Bonnes Feuilles* 3: 3–12.

———. 1974b. "Medieval Narrative vs. Modern Assumptions: Revising Inadequate Typology." *Diacritics* 4: 12–19.

———. 1975. "Two Types of Opposition and the Structure of Latin Saints' Lives." *Medievalia et Humanistica.* New Series 6: 1–11.

———. 1977. "Interpreting Romanesque Narrative: Conques and *The Roland.*" *Olifant* 5: 4–28.

———. 1981a. "Intratextual Rewriting: Textuality as Language Formation." In *The Sign in Music and Literature*, ed. Wendy Steiner, 39–51. Austin: University of Texas Press.

———. 1981b. "*The Lonely Villa* and Griffith's Paradigmatic Style." *Quarterly Review of Film Studies* 6, no. 2: 123–34.

———. 1987. *The American Film Musical.* Bloomington: Indiana University Press.

———. 1989. "Dickens, Griffith, and Film Theory Today." *South Atlantic Quarterly* 88: 321–60..

Apollinaire, Guillaume. 1965. *Les peintres cubistes*. Paris: Hermann..

Apuleius, Lucius. *Metamorphoses or the Golden Ass*.

Ariosto, Lodovico. *Orlando furioso*.

Aristotle. *Aristotle on the Art of Poetry*. 1909. Ed. and trans. Ingram Bywater. Oxford: Oxford University Press.

Armstrong, Nancy. 2005. *How Novels Think: The Limits of Individualism from 1719–1900*. New York: Columbia University Press.

Associated Press. 2006. "U.N. Chief: U.S. Should Close Prison at Guantanamo Bay." *Iowa City Press-Citizen*, 17 February, 10A.

Athanasius. *Life of Saint Anthony*.

Aucassin et Nicolette.

Auden, W. H. 1945. "Musée des Beaux Arts." In *The Collected Poetry of W. H. Auden*, 3. New York: Random House, 1945.

Augustine. 1963. *The Confessions*. Trans. R. S. Pine-Coffin. New York: Penguin.

———. *The City of God*.

Austen, Jane. 1966. *Pride and Prejudice*. Ed. Donald J. Gray. New York: Norton.

Batrachomyomachia ("Battle of the Frogs and Mice").

Bakhtin, Mikhail. 1968. *Rabelais and His World*. Cambridge: MIT Press.

———. 1981. *The Dialogic Imagination*. Austin: University of Texas Press.

Bal, Mieke. 1985. *Narratology: Introduction to the Theory of Narrative*. Trans. Christine van Boheemen. Toronto: University of Toronto Press. Translation of *E theorie van vertellen en verhalen*, 2nd rev. ed. Muiderberg: Coutinho, 1980.

Balzac, Honoré de. 1965a. "Avant-propos" to *La Comédie humaine*. Paris: Seuil. Vol. I: 51–56.

———. 1965b. *Le Père Goriot*. In *La Comédie humaine*. Paris: Seuil. Vol. II: 216–308.

———. *Les Chouans*.

———. *Le Cousin Pons*.

———. *Le Curé de Tours*.

———. *Grandeur et décadence de César Birotteau*.

———. *Illusions perdues*.

———. *Louis Lambert*.

———. *La Recherche de l'absolu*.

Barbéris, Pierre. 1972. *Le Père Goriot*. Paris: Larousse.

Barnet, Sylvan, Morton Berman, and William Burto. 1960. *The Study of Literature: A Handbook of Critical Essays and Terms*. Boston: Little, Brown.

Barthes, Roland. 1953. *Le Degré zéro de l'écriture*. Paris: Gonthier.

———. 1966. "Introduction à l'analyse structurale du récit." *Communications* 8: 1–27.

———. 1970. *S/Z.* Paris: Seuil.

Bede. *Life of Saint Cuthbert.*

Bianconi, Piero. 1967. *L'Opera completa di Bruegel.* Milan: Rizzoli.

Boccaccio. *The Decameron.*

———. *Filostrato.*

Bonaventura (Friedrich Gottlieb Wetzel?). *Die Nachtwachen des Bonaventura.*

Bonne, Jean-Claude. 1984. *L'Art roman de face et de profil: le tympan de Conques.* Paris: Le Sycomore.

Booth, Wayne. 1961. *The Rhetoric of Fiction.* Chicago: University of Chicago Press.

Borges, Jorge Luis. 1964. "Funes the Memorius." In *Labyrinths: Selected Stories and Other Writings,* ed. Donald A. Yates and James E. Irby, 59–66. New York: New Directions.

Branigan, Edward. 1992. *Narrative Comprehension and Film.* London and New York: Routledge.

Brecht, Bertolt. 1964. "Alienation Effects in the Narrative Pictures of the Elder Brueghel" ("Verfremdungseffekte in den erzählenden Bildern des älteren Brueghel"). In *Brecht on Theatre: The Development of an Aesthetic,* ed. John Willett, 157–59. New York: Hill and Wang, London: Methuen.

Brombert, Victor. 1954. *Stendhal et la voie oblique.* New Haven: Yale University Press and Paris: Presses universitaires de France.

Brooks, Peter. 1984. *Reading for the Plot: Design and Intention in Narrative.* New York: A. A. Knopf.

Bunyan, John. *Pilgrim's Progress.*

Campbell, Joseph. 1956. *The Hero with a Thousand Faces.* Cleveland: Meridian.

Camus, Albert. *The Fall (La Chute).*

———. *The Plague (La Peste).*

Carroll, Noël. 2001. "On the Narrative Connection." In *New Perspectives on Narrative Perspective,* ed. Willie van Peer and Seymour Chatman, 21–41. Albany: State University of New York Press.

Castelvetro, Lodovico. *Poetica d'Aristotele vulgarizzata e sposta.*

Céline, Louis-Ferdinand. *Voyage au bout de la nuit (Journey to the End of the Night).*

Cent nouvelles nouvelles, Les.

Cervantes, Miguel de. *Don Quixote.*

———. "Rinconete and Cortadillo" (in *Novelas ejemplares*).

Charnes, Jean Antoine de. 1679. *Conversations sur la critique de la Princesse de Clèves.* Paris: Chez Claude Barbin.

Chateaubriand, François René de. *Atala.*

———. *René.*

Chatman, Seymour. 1980. *Story and Discourse: Narrative Structure in Fiction and Film.* Ithaca: Cornell University Press.

———. 1990. *The Rhetoric of Narrative in Fiction and Film.* Ithaca: Cornell University Press.

Chaucer, Geoffrey. *The Canterbury Tales*

———. *Troilus and Cressida.*

Chrétien de Troyes. 1959. *Le Roman de Perceval ou le conte du Graal.* Geneva: Droz, and Paris: Minard.

———. 1963. *Yvain* (*Le Chevalier au lion*). Paris: Champion.

———. *Cligés.*

———. *Érec et Énide.*

———. *Lancelot, ou le chevalier à la charrette.*

Climacus, John. *Climax* (*The Ladder of Perfection*). See John Rupert Martin.

Congreve, William. 1930. *Incognita: or, Love and Duty Reconcil'd. A Novel.* In *Shorter Novels: Seventeenth Century*, ed. Philip Henderson, 237–303. London: Dent.

Conrad, Joseph. *Nostromo.*

Corneille, Pierre. *Le Cid.*

Crane, Stephen. 1960. *The Red Badge of Courage and Other Writings.* Boston: Houghton Mifflin.

———. "A Mystery of Heroism."

Crébillon, Claude Prosper Jolyot de. *Le Sopha.*

Christie, Agatha. *Death on the Nile.*

Croce, Benedetto. 1951. "La storia ridotta sotto il concetto generale dell'arte." In *Primi saggi*, 3–41. Bari: Laterza.

Dante Alighieri. *Divina Commedia* (*The Divine Comedy*).

Danto, A. C. 1965. *Analytical Philosophy of History.* Cambridge: Cambridge University Press.

Defoe, Daniel. 1945. *Robinson Crusoe.* London: Dent, and New York: Dutton

———. 1964. *Moll Flanders.* New York: New American Library.

Descartes, René. *Discours de la méthode.*

Dickens, Charles. *Bleak House.*

———. *David Copperfield.*

———. *Little Dorrit.*

———. *Nicholas Nickleby.*

———. *Oliver Twist.*

Diderot, Denis. *Encyclopédie ou dictionnaire raisonné des sciences, des arts et des métiers.*

———. *Jacques le fataliste et son maître.*

Dostoevsky, Feodor Mikhailovitch. *Notes from the Underground.*

Doyle, Arthur Conan. *The Adventures of Sherlock Holmes* (includes "A Case of Identity").

Dreiser, Theodore. *Sister Carrie.*

Dryden, John. 1965. *An Essay of Dramatic Poesy.* Indianapolis: Bobbs-Merrill.

Dumas, Alexandre (fils). *La Dame aux camélias (Camille).*

Du Plaisir. 1975. *Sentiments sur les lettres et sur l'histoire avec des scrupules sur le style.* Geneva: Droz.

———. *La Duchesse d'Estramène.*

Eagleton, Terry. 1976. *Criticism and Ideology.* London: NLB.

Eisenstein, Sergei. 1949. "Dickens, Griffith and Film Today." In *Film Form*, ed. and trans. Jay Leyda, 195–255. New York: Harcourt, Brace.

Eliade, Mircea. 1959. *Cosmos and History: The Myth of the Eternal Return.* New York: Harper and Row.

Eliot, George. *Daniel Deronda.*

———. *Middlemarch: A Study of Provincial Life.*

Empson, William. 1950. *Some Versions of Pastoral.* Norfolk, Conn.: New Directions.

Enuma Elish (War of the Gods/Babylonian Genesis).

Eschenbach, Wolfram von. *Parzival.*

Felix. *Life of Saint Guthlac.*

Fénélon, François de Salignac de la Mothe-. *Télémaque.*

Fielding, Henry. *Joseph Andrews.*

———. *Tom Jones.*

The Filmic Character/Le Personnage au cinéma. 1997. Ed. Margrit Tröhler, Anne Goliot-Lété, Dominique Blüher, Claire Dupré la Tour, Marie-Françoise Grange. *Iris* 24.

Fitzgerald, F. Scott. *The Great Gatsby.*

Flaubert, Gustave. *L'Éducation sentimentale.*

———. *Madame Bovary.*

———. *Salammbô.*

Fletcher, Angus. 1964. *Allegory: The Theory of a Symbolic Mode.* Ithaca: Cornell University Press.

Foster, George M. 1961. "The Dyadic Contract: A Model for the Social Structure of a Mexican Peasant Village." *American Anthropologist* 63: 1173–92.

———. 1965. "Peasant Society and the Image of Limited Good." *American Anthropologist* 67: 293–315.

Fox, Edward. 1971. *History in Geographic Perspective.* New York: Norton.

Francis of Assisi, Saint. *Little Flowers of Saint Francis.*

Frank, Joseph. 1963. "Spatial Form in Modern Literature." In *The Widening Gyre: Crisis and Mastery in Modern Literature*, 3–62. New Brunswick: Rutgers University Press.

Franklin, Benjamin. *Autobiography.*

Frye, Northrop. 1957. *Anatomy of Criticism.* Princeton: Princeton University Press.

Galsworthy, John. *The Forsyte Saga.*

Garrett, Peter K. 1980. *The Victorian Multiplot Novel: Studies in Dialogical Form.* New Haven: Yale University Press.

Genette, Gérard. 1966. *Figures.* Paris: Seuil.

———. 1972. *Figures III.* Paris: Seuil.

———. 1980. *Narrative Discourse.* Trans. Jane E. Lewin. Ithaca: Cornell University Press.

———. 1983. *Nouveau discours du récit.* Paris: Seuil.

———. 1988. *Narrative Discourse Revisited.* Trans. Jane E. Lewin. Ithaca: Cornell University Press.

Gide, André. 1932. *Oeuvres completes d'André Gide.* Paris: Nouvelle Revue Française.

———. 1958a. *Les Caves du Vatican (Lafcadio's Adventures).* In *Romans: Récits et soties—Oeuvres lyriques*, 677–873. Paris: Pléïade.

———. 1958b. *Les Faux-monnayeurs (The Counterfeiters).* In *Romans: Récits et soties—Oeuvres lyriques*, 931–1248. Paris: Pléïade.

———. *L'Immoraliste.*

———. *La Porte étroite (Strait Is the Gate).*

———. *La Symphonie pastorale.*

Gillette, William. *Sherlock Holmes: A Drama in Four Acts.*

Girard, René. 1961. *Mensonge romantique et vérité romanesque.* Paris: Grasset.

Goethe, Johann Wolfgang von. *Faust.*

———. *Werther.*

———. *Wilhelm Meisters Lehrjahre.*

Goldmann, Lucien. 1964. *Pour une sociologie du roman.* Paris: Gallimard.

Goscinny, René, and Albert Uderzo. 1961. *Astérix le Gaulois.* Paris: Dargaud.

Gregory (the Great), Saint. 1878. "Homilies on Ezechiel, Book 2, Homily 5, Sections 8–9." In *Patrologia Cursus Completus*, Series Latina, ed. Jacques-Paul Migne, vol. 76, cols. 989–90 (Paris: Garnier).

———. *Life of Saint Benedict.*

Greimas, A. J. 1966. *Sémantique structurale.* Paris: Larousse.

Grossmann, F. 1973. *Pieter Bruegel: Complete Edition of the Paintings.* New York: Phaidon/Praeger.

Guilleragues, Gabriel de Lavergne, sieur de. *Les Lettres portugaises.*

Halliday, E. M. 1966. "Narrative Perspective in *Pride and Prejudice*." In Jane Austen, *Pride and Prejudice*, ed. Donald J. Gray, 431–37. New York: Norton.

Hammett, Dashiell. *The Maltese Falcon.*

Hardy, Thomas. *Tess of the D'Urbervilles.*

Harris, Joel Chandler. 1965. *Uncle Remus.* New York: Schocken.

Harvey, W. J. 1965. *Character and the Novel.* Ithaca: Cornell University Press.

Hawthorne, Nathaniel. 1962. *The Scarlet Letter. An Annotated Text, Backgrounds and Sources, Essays in Criticism.* Ed. Sculley Bradley, Richard Croom Beatty, and E. Hudson Long. New York: Norton.

———. 1851. *The House of Seven Gables.* Boston: Houghton Mifflin..

Heliodorus of Emesa. *Aethiopica (Theagenes and Chariclea).*

Hendricks, William O. 1973. "Methodology of Narrative Structural Analysis." *Semiotica* 7: 163–84.

Herman, David, Manfred Jahn, and Marie-Laure Ryan, eds. 2005. *Routledge Encyclopedia of Narrative Theory.* London: Routledge.

Herman, Luc, and Bart Vervaeck. 2005. *Handbook of Narrative Analysis.* Lincoln: University of Nebraska Press.

Herrad of Lansberg. *Hortus deliciarum.*

Hersey, John. 1946. *Hiroshima.* New York: Knopf.

Hesiod. *Theogony.*

Hesse, Hermann. *Steppenwolf.*

Homer. 1946. *The Odyssey.* Trans. E. V. Rieu. Baltimore: Penguin.

———. *The Iliad.*

Hugo, Victor. 1963. *Notre-Dame de Paris.* In *Romans* I. Paris: Le Seuil.

———. *Les Misérables.*

Jakobson, Roman. 1956. "Two Aspects of Language and Two Types of Aphasic Disturbances." In Jakobson and Morris Halle, *Fundamentals of Language,* 67–96. The Hague: Mouton.

James, Henry. 1934. "Preface to *The Tragic Muse.*" In *The Art of the Novel,* ed. R. P. Blackmur, 79–97. New York: Scribners.

———. *The Portrait of a Lady.*

———. *The Turn of the Screw.*

———. *What Maisie Knew.*

Jerome, Saint (Sophronius Eusebius Hieronymus). *Life of Saint Hilarion.*

———. *Life of Saint Paul of Thebes.*

Katzenellenbogen, Adolf. 1964. *Allegories of the Virtues and Vices in Mediaeval Art from Early Christian Times to the Thirteenth Century.* New York: Norton.

Kenner, Hugh. 1968. *The Counterfeiters.* Bloomington: Indiana University Press.

Kierkegaard, Søren. 1980. *The Concept of Anxiety: A Simple Psychologically Orienting Deliberation on the Dogmatic Issue of Hereditary Sin.* Princeton: Princeton University Press.

Klee, Paul. 1945. "Notes from His Diary." In *Artists on Art from the XIV to the XX Century*, ed. Robert Goldwater and Marco Treves, 441–43. New York: Pantheon.

Klein, H. Arthur. 1963. *Graphic Worlds of Peter Bruegel the Elder*. New York: Dover.

Koestler, Arthur. *Darkness at Noon*.

Laclos, Choderlos de. *Les Liaisons dangereuses*.

Lafayette, Madame (Marie Madeleine Pioche de La Vergne) de. 1961a. *La Princesse de Clèves*. In *Romans et nouvelles*, 237–395. Paris: Garnier.

——. 1961b. *Zaïde*. In *Romans et nouvelles*, 35–235. Paris: Garnier.

Langland, William (?). *Piers Plowman*.

La Rochefoucauld, François de. *Maximes*.

Lautréamont, Comte de (Isidore Lucien Ducasse). *Les Chants de Maldoror*.

Lawrence, D. H. 1960. *Women in Love*. New York: Viking.

——. 2003. "Nathaniel Hawthorne and *The Scarlet Letter*." In *Studies in Classic American Literature*, ed. Ezra Greenspan, Lindeth Vasey, and John Worthen, 81–95. Cambridge: Cambridge University Press. *Lazarillo de Tormes*.

Lesage, Alain René. *Le Diable boîteux*.

——. *Gil Blas de Santillane*.

Levin, Richard. 1971. *The Multiple Plot in English Renaissance Drama*. Chicago: University of Chicago Press.

Lévi-Strauss, Claude. 1976. "Structure and Form: Reflections on a Work by Vladimir Propp." In *Structural Anthropology* II, 115–45. New York: Basic Books.

Lewis, R. W. B. 1978. "The Return into Time: Hawthorne." In Nathaniel Hawthorne, *The Scarlet Letter: An Authoritative Text, Backgrounds and Sources, Criticism*, ed. Sculley Bradley, Richmond Croom Beatty, E. Hudson Long, and Seymour Gross, 342–47. 2nd ed. New York: Norton.

Longus. 1953. *Daphnis and Chloe*. In *Three Greek Romances*, ed. and trans. Moses Hadas, 3–68. Indianapolis: Bobbs-Merrill.

Lubbock, Percy. 1957. *The Craft of Fiction*. New York: Viking.

Lukács, Georg. 1963. *La Théorie du roman*. Paris: Gonthier.

Luther, Martin. 1960. *Three Treatises*. Philadelphia: Fortress.

Maatje, Frank. 1964. *Der Doppelroman: Eine literatursystematische Studie über duplicative Erzählstrukturen*. Groningen, Netherlands: J. B. Wolters.

MacCaffrey, Isabel. 1959. *Paradise Lost as "Myth."* Cambridge: Harvard University Press.

Machiavelli, Niccolò. 1964. *The Prince: A Bilingual Edition*. Ed. Mark Musa. New York: St. Martin's.

Malraux, André. 1946. *La Condition humaine (Man's Fate)*. Paris: Gallimard (Poche).

Mann, Thomas. *Buddenbrooks*.

Marguerite de Navarre. *L'Heptaméron*.

Marivaux, Pierre Carlet de Chamblain de. *Le Paysan parvenu*.

———. *La Vie de Marianne*.

Marsh, Charles. 2006. "Wayward Christian Soldiers." *International Herald Tribune*, 21 Jan., 6.

Marshburn, Joseph H., and Alan R. Velie. 1973. *Blood and Knavery: A Collection of English Renaissance Pamphlets and Ballads of Crime and Sin*. Rutherford, N.J.: Fairleigh Dickinson University Press.

Martin, John Rupert. 1954. *The Illustration of the Heavenly Ladder of John Climacus*. Princeton: Princeton University Press.

Martin, Wallace. 1986. *Recent Theories of Narrative*. Ithaca: Cornell University Press.

Martin du Gard, Roger. *Les Thibault*.

The Martyrdom of Saint Perpetua and Saint Felicitas.

Mérimée, Prosper. *Chronique du règne de Charles IX*.

Miller, J. Hillis. 1998. *Reading Narrative*. Norman: University of Oklahoma Press.

Milton, John. *Paradise Lost*.

Montaigne, Michel Eyquem de. *Essais*.

Montesquieu, Charles Louis de Secondat, baron de La Brède et de. *Les Lettres persanes*.

Nibelungenlied.

Nicholas, Brian. 1962. "The Novel as Social Document: *L'Assommoir*." In *The Moral and the Story*, ed. Ian Gregor and Brian Nicholas, 63–97. London: Faber and Faber.

Olrik, Axel. 1965. "The Epic Laws of Folk Narrative." In *The Study of Folklore*, ed. Alan Dundes, 129–41. Englewood Cliffs, N.J.: Prentice Hall.

Onega, Susana, and José Angel García Landa. 1996. *Narratology: An Introduction*. London: Longman.

O'Neill, Patrick. 1994. *Fictions of Discourse: Reading Narrative Theory*. Toronto: University of Toronto Press.

Ordoñez, Garci (or Rodríguez Montalvo). *Amadís of Gaul*.

Otloh. *Life of Saint Nicholas*.

Ovid (Publius Ovidius Naso). 1958. *Metamorphoses*. Trans. Horace Gregory. New York: Viking.

Pächt, Otto. 1962. *The Rise of Pictorial Narrative in Twelfth-Century England*. Oxford: Clarendon Press.

Pascal, Blaise. *Pensées*.

Phelan, James. 2006. "Narrative Theory, 1966–2006: A Narrative." In Robert Scholes, Robert Kellogg, and James Phelan, *The Nature of Narrative*, 283–336. 2nd ed. Oxford: Oxford University Press.

Poe, Edgar Allan. 1981a. "The Gold Bug." In *Tales of Mystery and Imagination*, 69–101. London: Dent.

——. 1981b. "Murders in the Rue Morgue." In *Tales of Mystery and Imagination*, 378–410. London: Dent.

——. 1981c. "The Purloined Letter." In *Tales of Mystery and Imagination*, 454–71. London: Dent.

——. 1981d. "Thou Art the Man." In *Tales of Mystery and Imagination*, 471–84. London: Dent.

The Poem of the Cid (*Cantar de mio Cid*). 1963. Trans. W. S. Merwin. In *Medieval Epics*, 441–590. New York: Modern Library.

Pöschl, Viktor. 1962. *The Art of Vergil: Image and Symbol in the Aeneid*. Trans. Gerda Seligson. Ann Arbor: University of Michigan Press.

Possidius. *Life of Augustine*.

Price, Martin. 1983. *Forms of Life: Character and Moral Imagination in the Novel*. New Haven: Yale University Press.

Prince, Gerald. 1973. *A Grammar of Stories: An Introduction*. The Hague: Mouton.

——. 1982. *Narratology: The Form and Functioning of Narrative*. Berlin: Mouton.

——. 2003 [1987]. *A Dictionary of Narratology*. 2nd ed. Lincoln: University of Nebraska Press.

Propp, Vladimir. 1970. *Morphologie du conte* (*Morphology of the Folktale*). Paris: Le Seuil.

Prudentius. *Pyschomachia*.

La Quête du Graal (*La Queste del Saint Graal*). 1965. Ed. Albert Béguin and Yves Bonnefoy. Paris: Le Seuil.

Rapin, René. 1674a. *Reflections on Aristotle's Treatise of Poesie, containing the necessary rational, and universal rules for epick, dramatick, and the other sorts of poetry*. Trans. Thomas Rymer. London: Printed by T. N. for H. Herringman.

——. 1674b. *Réflexions sur la Poétique d'Aristote, et sur les ouvrages des poètes anciens & modernes*. Paris: Chez F. Muguet.

Raynal, Maurice. 1966. "Conception et Vision." Trans. Jonathan Griffin. In Edward F. Fry, *Cubism*, 94–96. London: Thames and Hudson..

Remarque, Erich Maria. *All Quiet on the Western Front*.

Reverdy, Pierre. 1927. *Le Gant de crin*. Paris: Plon.

Richardson, Samuel. *Clarissa*.

——. *Pamela*.

Richardson, Brian. 1997. *Unlikely Stories: Causality and the Nature of Modern Narrative*. Newark: University of Delaware Press.

Rimmon-Kenan, Shlomith. 2002. *Narrative Fiction: Contemporary Poetics*. 2nd ed. London: Routledge.

Roberts, Andrew Michael, ed. 1993. *The Novel: A Guide to the Novel from Its Origins to the Present Day*. London: Bloomsbury.

Romains, Jules. *Les Hommes de bonnes volonté*.

Roman de Flamenca.

Roman de Renart.

Rougemont, Denis de. 1974. *Love in the Western World*. New York: Harper and Row.

Rousset, Jean. 1964. *Forme et signification: Essais sur les structures littéraires de Corneille à Claudel*. Paris: Corti.

Rutebeuf [no first name]. 1951. *Le Miracle de Théophile*. In *Jeux et sapience du moyen âge*, ed. Albert Pauphilet, 135–58. Paris: Pléïade.

Saint-Point, Valentine de. 1973. "Futurist Manifesto of Lust 1913." In *Futurist Manifestos*, ed. Umbro Apollonio, trans. J. C. Higgitt, 70–74. New York: Viking.

Saint-Réal, César Richard de. *Dom Carlos*.

Sartre, Jean-Paul. *La Nausée*.

Scaliger, Julius Caesar. *Poetices*.

Scarron, Paul. *Le Roman comique*.

Schapiro, Meyer. 1977. *Romanesque Art*. New York: George Braziller.

Scholes, Robert, and Robert Kellogg. 1966. *The Nature of Narrative*. Oxford: Oxford University Press.

Scholes, Robert, Robert Kellogg, and James Phelan. 2006. *The Nature of Narrative*. 2nd ed. Oxford: Oxford University Press.

Schwartz, Daniel R. 1994. "Joseph Conrad." In *Columbia History of the British Novel*, ed. John Richetti, 685–714. New York: Columbia University Press.

Scott, Walter. *Waverly*.

Scudéry, Madeleine de. *Le Grand Cyrus*.

Severini, Gino. 1973. "The Plastic Analogies of Dynamism: Futurist Manifesto 1913." In *Futurist Manifestos*, ed. Umbro Apollonio, trans. J. C. Higgitt, 118–25. New York: Viking.

Shakespeare, William. *King Lear*.

Shelley, Mary. *Frankenstein*.

Sheppard, J. T. 1969. *The Pattern of the Iliad*. New York: Barnes and Noble.

Shklovsky (Chklovski), Victor. 1973. "Comment est fait *Don Quichotte*." Trans. Guy Verret. In *Sur la théorie de la prose*, 107–45. Paris: Éditions l'Âge d'homme.

Simenon, Georges. *Le Commissaire Maigret.*

Sir Gawain and the Green Knight. 1974. Ed. W. R. J. Barron. Manchester: Manchester University Press.

Smith, Barbara Herrnstein. 1981. "Narrative Versions, Narrative Theories." In *On Narrative*, ed. W. J. T. Mitchell, 209–32. Chicago: University of Chicago Press.

The Song of Roland. 1978. Ed. Gerard J. Brault. 2 vols. University Park: Pennsylvania State University Press.

Spenser, Edmund. *The Faerie Queene.*

Spillane, Mickey. *I, the Jury.*

Stendhal (Henri Beyle). *Armance.*

——. *La Chartreuse de Parme* (*The Charterhouse of Parma*).

——. *Le Rouge et le noir* (*The Red and the Black*).

Stevenson, Robert Louis. *The Strange Case of Dr. Jekyll and Mr. Hyde.*

Stierle, Karlheinz. 1972. "L'Histoire comme exemple, l'exemple comme histoire." *Poétique* 10: 176–98.

Sue, Eugène. 1963. *Les Mystères de Paris.* Paris: Jean-Jacques Pauvert.

Sulpicius Severus. *Life of Saint Martin.*

Svevo, Italo. *La Coscienza di Zeno.*

Swift, Jonathan. *Battle of the Books.*

——. *Gulliver's Travels.*

Tacitus. *History.*

Tasso, Torquato. *Discorsi del poema eroico.*

——. *Gerusalemme liberata.*

Thackeray, William Makepeace. *History of Pendennis.*

Thomas à Kempis. *Imitation of Christ.*

Thoreau, Henry David. *Civil Disobedience.*

Thucydides. 1954. *History of the Peloponnesian War.* Trans. Rex Warner. London: Penguin.

Todorov, Tzvetan. 1971. "The Two Principles of Narrative." *Diacritics* 1, no. 1: 37–44.

Tolstoy, Leo. 1966. *War and Peace.* Ed. George Gibian. Trans. Louise and Aylmer Maude. New York: Norton.

Tomachevski, Boris. 1965. "Thématique." In *Théorie de la littérature*, ed. Tzvetan Todorov, 263–307. Paris: Seuil.

Toolen, Michael J. 1988. *Narrative: A Critical Linguistic Introduction.* London: Routledge.

Tristan and Iseult.

Trollope, Anthony. *The Last Chronicle of Barset.*

Turner, Paul. 1968. "Novels, Ancient and Modern." *Novel: A Forum on Fiction* 2, no. 1: 15–24.

Uitti, Karl. 1973. *Story, Myth, and Celebration in Old French Narrative Poetry, 1050–1200*. Princeton: Princeton University Press.

Urfé, Honoré d'. *L'Astrée*.

Valincour, Jean-Baptiste-Henry du Trousset de. 1678. *Lettres à Madame la Marquise sur le sujet de la Princesse de Clèves*. Paris: Chez Sébastien Mabre-Cramoisy.

Vance, Eugene. 1970. *Reading* The Song of Roland. Englewood Cliffs, N.J.: Prentice Hall.

Van Peer, Willie, and Seymour Chatman, eds. 2001. *New Perspectives on Narrative Perspective*. Albany: State University of New York Press.

Vergil (Publius Vergilius Maro). *The Aeneid*.

Vidocq, François Eugène. *Les Mémoires de Vidocq*.

Vie de Saint Alexis. 2000. Geneva: Droz.

Vigny, Alfred de. *Cinq-Mars*.

Voltaire (François-Marie Arouet). "Micromégas."

The Voyage of Brendan.

Wace. *Roman de Brut*.

Whitman, Cedric. 1958. *Homer and the Heroic Tradition*. Cambridge: Harvard University Press.

Wilder, Thornton. 1927. *The Bridge of San Luis Rey*. New York: Albert and Charles Boni.

Xenophon. 1953. *An Ephesian Tale*. In *Three Greek Romances*, ed. and trans. Moses Hadas, 71–126. Indianapolis: Bobbs-Merrill..

Young, Karl. 1933. *The Drama of the Medieval Church*. 2 vols. Oxford: Clarendon Press.

Zola, Émile. 1928. *Oeuvres complètes*. Ed. Maurice Le Blond. Paris: Bernouard.

——. 1967a. *L'Assommoir*. In *Les Rougon-Macquart* II, 371–796. Paris: Gallimard-Pléïade.

——. 1967b. *La Terre*. Paris: Fasquelle (Poche).

——. 1967c. "Notes générales sur la nature de l'oeuvre." In *Les Rougon-Macquart* V, 1742–45. Paris: Gallimard-Pléïade.

——. *La Faute de l'abbé Mouret*.

——. *Germinal*.

——. *Nana*.

——. *Le Roman expérimental*.

——. *Son Excellence Eugène Rougon*.

——. *Thérèse Raquin*.

——. *Le Ventre de Paris* (*The Fat and the Thin*).

Films

Antonioni, Michelangelo. *Zabriskie Point* (MGM, 1970).

Buñuel, Luis. *Viridiana* (José Esteban Alenda Distribución, 1961).

Cameron, James. *Titanic* (Twentieth Century Fox / Paramount, 1997).

Chaplin, Charles. *The Great Dictator* (United Artists, 1940).

Cooper, Merian C., and Ernest B. Schoedsack. *King Kong* (RKO, 1933).

Coppola, Francis Ford. *The Rain People* (Warner Bros, 1969).

Davies, Andrew. *Pride and Prejudice* (BBC, 1995).

De Mille, Cecil B. *Unconquered* (Paramount, 1947).

De Sica, Vittorio. *The Garden of the Finzi-Contini* (Central Cinema Company, 1970).

Douglas, Gordon. *Them!* (Warner Bros., 1954).

Eisenstein, Sergei. *Battleship Potemkin* (Goskino, 1925).

Fellini, Federico. *La Dolce Vita* (Cineriz, 1960).

———. *I Vitelloni* (ENIC, 1953).

Ford, John. *She Wore a Yellow Ribbon* (RKO, 1949).

———. *Wagonmaster* (Argosy, 1950).

Freeland, Thornton. *Flying Down to Rio* (RKO, 1933).

Fuller, Sam. *The Big Red One* (United Artists, 1980)

Garnett, Tay. *Bataan* (MGM, 1943).

Griffith, D. W. *The Birth of a Nation* (Epoch, 1915)

———. *The Cricket on the Hearth* (Biograph, 1909).

———. *Enoch Arden* (Biograph, 1911).

———. *Intolerance* (Triangle Corporation, 1916).

———. *Judith of Bethulia* (American Mutoscope & Biograph, 1913).

———. *The Lonedale Operator* (Biograph, 1911).

———. *The Lonely Villa* (Biograph, 1909).

———. *Ramona* (Biograph, 1910).

Guillermin, John. *Death on the Nile* (EMI, 1978).

———. *The Towering Inferno* (Twentieth Century Fox /Warner Bros., 1974).

Hitchcock, Alfred. *Notorious* (RKO, 1946).

Hopper, Dennis. *Easy Rider* (Columbia, 1969).

Julian, Rupert. *The Phantom of the Opera* (Universal, 1925).

Leonard, Robert Z. *New Moon* (MGM, 1940).

Ludwig, Edward. *The Fighting Seabees* (Republic, 1944)

Mamoulian, Rouben. *Silk Stockings* (MGM, 1957).

Meyer, Nicholas. *The Day After* (ABC, 1983).

Milestone, Lewis. *All Quiet on the Western Front* (Universal, 1930).

Minnelli, Vincente. *An American in Paris* (MGM, 1951).

———. *The Band Wagon* (MGM, 1953).

———. *Gigi* (MGM, 1958).

Penn, Arthur. *Bonnie and Clyde* (Warner Bros., 1967).

Renoir, Jean. *La Grande Illusion* (Cinédis, 1937).

———. *La Règle du jeu* (*Rules of the Game*) (Pathé, 1939).

Robson, Mark. *Earthquake* (Universal, 1974).

Seaton, George. *Airport* (Universal, 1970).

Spielberg, Steven. *Saving Private Ryan* (Paramount, 1999).

Truffaut, François. *The Bride Wore Black* (Les Artistes Associés (UA), 1968).

Van Dyke, W. S. *Sweethearts* (MGM, 1938).

Werker, Alfred L. *The Adventures of Sherlock Holmes* (Twentieth Century Fox, 1939).

Wise, Robert. *West Side Story* (United Artists, 1961).

Wyler, William. *The Best Years of Our Lives* (RKO, 1946).

Zinnemann, Fred. *Oklahoma!* (Todd, 1955).

Index

(Italic numbers indicate illustrations)

Campbell, Joseph, 4, 5, 171
Camus, Albert, 185, 248; *Fall, The*, 185; *La Peste*, 248
Canterbury Tales, The (Chaucer, Geoffrey), 248
carnivalesque, 221, 248–50
Caron, Leslie, 87
Carroll, Noël, 9, 85
"Case of Identity, A" (Doyle, Arthur Conan), 166
Castelvetro, Lodovico, 3, 322
category, 10, 248–50, 251, 253, 256, 257–60, 264–65, 267, 271–73, 276, 285–87
causality, 276–84
Caves du Vatican, Les. See Lafcadio's Adventures
Céline, Louis-Ferdinand, 177; *Journey to the End of the Night*, 177
Census at Bethlehem, The (Bruegel, Pieter), 204, 216
Cent nouvelles nouvelles, Les (Anonymous), 248
centrifugal, 191, 194–97, 211
centripetal, 194–97, 207, 208, 210–11, 214
Cervantes, Miguel de, 129, 132, 248; *Don Quixote*, 131, 149, 173, 178, 248, 253, 339
change, 9, 77
Chaplin, Charlie, 63; *Great Dictator, The*, 63
character, 8, 291, 305–307, 308–11, 312, 317, 321–22, 325, 340; as author of narrative, 155, 173–75, 181; as author stand-in, 257–62, 273–74, 277, 289, 318; as category, 248–50, 251, 253, 256, 257–60, 264–65, 267, 271–73, 276, 285–87; as celebrity, 212–16, 217–18, 221, 263–64; as interpreter of world, 162–70, 171, 182, 183–84, 189; as narrative material, 12–15; as subordinated to plot, 2, 5–8; causality and, 276–84; following and,

16, 17, 18, 21–22; in dual-focus epic, 28, 30–31, 42–48, 45–47, 48, 52–53, 55–57, 68, 70, 78, 82, 89–90, 183, 298; in dual-focus pastoral, 63, 66, 67; in multiple-focus narrative, 241, 242–43, 252, 256, 277, 282, 289, 303–305; in pictorial texts, 198–99, 200–204, 226, 236; in single-focus narrative, 99–100, 102–105, 106, 111, 113, 116, 118, 119, 126–27, 145–48, 152, 156–60, 178–80, 300–303; mapping and, 291–97, 308; metaphoric modulations and, 25; metonymic modulations and, 24–25; narrative drive and, 19–20; psychology of, 71, 76, 82, 102, 105, 114, 117, 119, 120–23, 132–34, 135, 142, 153, 168, 184; quest-driven, 125–31, 132–34, 135, 148–54; secondary, 136–40, 145–48, 152, 155, 159, 166, 170, 189, 244
Charisse, Cyd, 66, 88
Charnes, Jean Antoine de, 322
Chateaubriand, François René, 125, 148, 177; *Atala*, 177; *René*, 148, 177
Charterhouse of Parma, The (Stendhal [Henri Beyle]), 16
Chatman, Seymour, 14, 22
Chaucer, Geoffrey, 57, 248; *Canterbury Tales, The*, 248; *Troilus and Cressida*, 67
Chevalier, Maurice, 66, 72
Children's Games (Bruegel, Pieter), 204, 207, 210, 211, 234; as multiple-focus, 215, 222, 229, 267; perspective in, 206, 210, 214, 233, 235; spatial organization in, 205–206
Chouans, Les (Balzac, Honoré de), 57
Christ Carrying the Cross (Bruegel, Pieter), 216, 218–20, 219
Christianity 71, 334; apocalypse and, 84–86, 335–36; as artifactual, 164–65, 173–75, 186–88; dual-focus narrative and, 71–72,

79, 80, 85, 95, 97, 335–36; in graphic art, 191–94, 195–97, 216; single-focus narrative and, 117, 152, 153–54, 179, 323, 336

Christie, Agatha, 166; *Death on the Nile*, 166

Chronique du règne de Charles IX (Mérimée, Prosper), 178

Cid, Le (Corneille, Pierre), 3, 4, 246–47, 321

cinema. *See* film

Cinq-Mars (Vigny, Alfred de), 178

city, 125–26, 127, 129–30, 131, 151

City of God (Augustine), 56, 59, 71, 339

Civil Disobedience (Thoreau, Henry David), 111

Clair, René, 25

Cligés (Troyes, Chrétien de), 57, 243–44

Climacus, John, 153; *Climax*, 153–54

Cock, Jerome (Hieronymus), 197, 199, 213, 222, 224

Combat Between Carnival and Lent (Bruegel, Pieter), 209, 222

comics, 13–14; books, 78, 81, 97; strips, 25, 56, 165, 167, 188, 191, 327

Commissaire Maigret, Le (Simenon, Georges), 130

composition, 202–203; allegorical, 222, 224, 228, 229–30, 233, 234, 235; around empty center, 199, 200, 206–207, 218, 238; in works of Bruegel, 199–221, 228, 264

Condition humaine, La (Malraux, André), 26, 229, 247, 253; as multiple-focus, 248, 255, 267, 273–74, 287

Confessions (Augustine), 59, 339; as single-focus; 121, 147, 153, 163–65, 173

Congreve, William, 3, 322–23; *Incognita*, 322

Conques, Abbey Church of Sainte-Foy, 191, 192–93; as dual-focus, 193–94, 196–98;

description of, 192–94; *Tympanum* of West Entrance, 191

Conrad, Joseph, 273; *Nostromo*, 273

Conversion of Saint Paul, The (Bruegel, Pieter), 216, 220

Coscienza di Zeno, La (Svevo, Italo), 178, 185

Cooper, Merian, 56; *King Kong*, 56

Coppola, Francis Ford, 130; *Rain People, The*, 130

Corneille, Pierre, 3, 246, 321; *Le Cid*, 3, 4, 246–47, 321

corpus, 9–10

Cousin Pons, Le (Balzac, Honoré de), 125

Counterfeiters, The. See *Faux-monnayeurs, Les*

Crane, Stephen, 21; narrative technique of, 293–94

—*Red Badge of Courage*, 21; as single-focus, 67, 128, 135, 148, 150–51, 250, 251; as war story, 316–17; mapping of, 293–94, 314

Crébillon, Claude de, 177; *Le Sopha*, 177

Cricket on the Hearth, The (Griffith, D. W.), 324

Croce, Benedetto, 1

Cunning Bird Catcher, The (Bruegel, Pieter), 199, 200, 213

Curé de Tours, Le (Balzac, Honoré de), 125, 296–97

Dame aux camélias, La (Dumas, Alexandre [fils]), 13

Daniel Deronda (Eliot, George), 255

Dante, 126, 147, 153, 157; *Divine Comedy, The*, 126, 147, 153–54

Danto, A. C., 5

Daphnis and Chloe (Longus), 22; as dual-focus pastoral, 57, 63, 72, 120, 124; gender difference in, 73–77, 94, 331

Darkness at Noon (Koestler, Arthur), 148

Davies, Andrew, 319–20; *Pride and Prejudice* (BBC), 319–20

Da Vinci, Leonardo, 238; *Annunciation, The*, 238

Day After, The (Meyer, Nicholas), 248, 252

Death on the Nile (Christie, Agatha), 166

Decameron, The (Boccaccio), 248, 253, 254

definition, 6, 8, 9, 11

Defoe, Daniel, 4, 127–29, 157, 244, 333; *Moll Flanders*, 127–28, 129, 136, 148, 244, 332; *Robinson Crusoe*, 151, 163–63

Del Rio, Dolores, 66

De Mille, Cecil B., 56; *Unconquered*, 56

Deposition, The (Van der Weyden, Rogier), 220

Descartes, René, 188

De Sica, Vittorio, 57, 63; *Garden of the Finzi-Contini, The*, 57, 63

desire, 330–33; biblical, 131–34, 139–41; character psychology as, 120–34, 136, 148, 294; in saints' lives, 124–25, 129–30, 136; opposed to slot-logic, 123; ritual and, 120, 123

detective fiction, 11, 49, 88, 130, 167, 177; as single-focus narrative, 130–31, 133, 155–56, 162–63, 164–70, 171, 173, 185, 188; confession compared to, 163–65;

Diable boîteux, Le (Lesage, Alain-René), 177

Diary of a Seducer, The (Kierkegaard, Søren), 178

Dickens, Charles, 129, 253, 297, 325–26; *Little Dorrit*, 255; *Nicholas Nickleby*, 242, 255; *Oliver Twist*, 242

Diderot, Denis, 247, 253; *Encyclopédie*, 274; *Jacques le fataliste et son maître*, 253

diegesis, 14, 16–17, 23, 37

difference, 9, 58, 64

Divine Comedy, The (Dante), 126, 147, 153–54

Dolce Vita, La (Fellini, Federico), 121

Don Quixote (Cervantes, Miguel de), 131, 149, 173, 178, 248, 253, 339

Dostoevsky, Feodor, 178, 185; *Notes from the Underground*, 178, 185

Douglas, Gordon, 56; *Them!*, 56, 78

Doyle, Arthur Conan, 130, 175, 185, 326; "A Case of Identity," 166; *Adventures of Sherlock Holmes*, 130, 156, 175, 185

Dr. Jekyll and Mr. Hyde (Stevenson, Robert Louis), 326

Dreiser, Theodore, 129

Dryden, John, 241

dual-focus narrative, 55–98, 99, 101, 106, 122, 134–35, 140, 147–48, 152, 156, 167, 171, 230, 314, 324, 334, 338; and community, 49–50, 53–54; and historical fiction, 56; as amoebic, 76–78; character in, 28, 30–31, 42–48, 45–47, 48, 52–53, 55–57, 68, 70, 78, 82, 89–90, 183, 298; Christianity and, 71–72, 79, 80, 85, 95, 97, 335–36; compared to multiple-focus narrative, 241–43, 245–47, 248, 251, 254, 255–57, 263, 266–69, 271, 281, 285, 287–90; compared to single-focus narrative, 105–107, 115, 117–19, 131, 143, 183–86, 188, 189–90; definition of, 55–59; dependence on oppositions, 59, 66, 69, 70–72, 77–78, 82, 126–27, 139–41, 244, 318; economics and, 125–28, 328–29; epic mode of, 55–56, 57, 61, 66, 69, 72, 78, 87, 91, 96, 129, 158, 335–38; film and, 56, 63, 316–17, 325–27; group in, 55–56, 57, 66, 68, 70, 83, 119, 126; images and, 191–94, 197; Judaism and, 56, 60–61, 64, 70, 71, 79–80, 86, 96, 152–54, 188, 334–36; land in, 38–39, 50–51, 65, 72–73, 91, 94, 119, 125; marriage in, 55, 57, 72, 73, 84, 90, 93–94, 96, 101; narration and, 120–23; pastoral mode of, 56–57, 64, 66, 72, 73–78, 87, 91, 93–94, 96, 123, 125, 129, 157, 180, 319–20, 328–29, 331–32; plot of, 32–33,

history, 27; narrative and, 1; of film, 320–27, 338; of literature, 320–27, 338

History (Tacitus), 56

History of Pendennis (Thackeray, William Makepeace), 255

History of the Peloponnesian War (Thucydides), 56, 80

Hitchcock, Alfred, 63; *Notorious* 63

Hollywood, 56, 248, 263, 326; musicals and, 57, 66, 87–88, 97, 120, 129; Westerns and, 56, 78, 81, 97, 316–17

Homer, 2, 4; *Iliad, The,* 56, 68, 79–81, 98, 101, 122, 139, 152

—*Odyssey, The,* 2, 154, 159; as single-focus, 133–36, 144, 146–47, 176, 255; in *Poetics,* 4, 10, 80

Hommes de bonne volonté, Les (Romains, Jules), 254

Hopper, Dennis, 130; *Easy Rider,* 130

Hortus Deliciarum (Herrad of Lansberg), 86

House of Seven Gables, The (Hawthorne, Nathaniel), 22, 108; as dual-focus pastoral, 57, 64–65, 93–94

Hugo, Victor, 253, 258, 284, 325; technique of, 278–81

—*Les Misérables,* 16, 271

—*Notre-Dame de Paris,* 22, 249, 282; as multiple-focus, 248, 252, 255; modulation and, 24, 26, 276, 278–81; use of parallels in, 271–73

Hume, David, 323

Hussein, Saddam, 337

Hutchinson, Ann, 110

hyperbolic modulation 24, 25–26, 243–47, 263–65, 271, 276, 284, 289, 320, 324

Iliad, The (Homer), 56, 68, 79–81, 98, 101, 122, 139, 152

image, 13–14, 16, 268; deep-focus, 265–66; engravings, 197–202, 225–26, 228; illuminated manuscript, 305–307;

painting, 212, 213, 218, 221, 224, 230, 268, 327; pictorial text, 198, 212; style and, 217–21, 232

Imitation of Christ (Kempis, Thomas à), 153

Immoraliste, L' (Gide, André), 175

Intolerance (Griffith, D. W.), 242, 254, 267

Incognita (Congreve, William), 322

individual, 99–100; artifactual reading and, 163–70; central to single-focus narrative, 116, 142, 153, 317, 330–33; desire and, 123–25, 128, 131–34, 135; eccentricity of in single-focus narrative, 100–105, 107, 118, 119, 176, 189, 323; interiority and, 120–23, 148, 170, 281; multiple-focus narrative and, 263–65, 281; naming and, 132–33, 139; reformers as, 110–13, 118, 126, 174–75

integration, 42–48, 54, 59

I Vitelloni (Fellini, Federico), 267

Jacques le fataliste et son maître (Diderot, Denis), 253

Jakobson, Roman, 24

James, Henry, 4, 325; free indirect style, use of, 161, 173, 178; literary criticism of, 273, 284; *Portrait of a Lady,* 4, 244; *Turn of the Screw,* 178; use of by Lubbock, 4, 10; *What Maisie Knew,* 178

Jerome, 124, 126, 149; *Life of Saint Hilarion,* 124, 149

Joseph Andrews (Fielding, Henry), 248

Journey to the End of the Night (Céline, Louis-Ferdinand), 177

Judaism, 187–89; dual-focus epic and, 56, 60–61, 64, 70, 71, 79–80, 86, 96, 152–54, 188, 334–36; dual-focus pastoral and, 94–95, 96; law and, 174

Julian, Rupert, 24; *Phantom of the Opera, The,* 24

Kael, Pauline, 163

Kelly, Gene, 72, 87

Maatje, Frank, 241
MacCaffrey, Isabel, 67
Machiavelli, Niccolò, 146, 148, 182; *Prince, The*, 144, 148
MacDonald, Jeanette, 66
Madame Bovary (Flaubert, Gustave), 22, 312, 317–18; as single-focus, 120, 136–37, 149, 156–57, 242, 253, 294–95
Mad Meg (Bruegel, Pieter), 218, 222
Malraux, André, 273–74, 318
—*La condition humaine*, 26, 229, 247, 253; as multiple-focus, 248, 255, 267, 273–74, 287
Maltese Falcon, The (Hammett, Dashiell), 130
Mamoulian, Rouben, 25, 88; *Silk Stockings*, 88
Mann, Thomas, 254; *Buddenbrooks*, 254
Man's Fate. See *Condition humaine, La*
Mantegna, Andrea, 220, 238; *San Zeno Altarpiece*, 238
mapping, 291–97, 300, 301–302, 304–305, 307, 309–11, 312–13
Marivaux, Pierre, 127–29, 143–44, 146, 151, 175, 177, 182, 244, 325; *Paysan parvenu, Le*, 128, 129, 143–44, 147, 151; *Vie de Marianne, La*, 128, 244
marriage: as resolution for dual-focus pastoral, 55, 57, 72, 73, 84, 90, 93–94, 96, 101
Marsh, Charles, 337
Marshburn, Joseph H., 179
Martin, J. R., 22, 153
Martin du Gard, Roger, 254; *Les Thibault*, 254
Martyrdom of Saint Perpetua and Saint Felicitas, The (Anonymous), 85
Massacre of the Innocents, The (Bruegel, Pieter), 204
McClellan, Scott, 337
medieval narrative, 57, 71, 78, 88, 100, 128, 140, 151, 177, 185, 221, 245, 253, 286, 305–307, 323, 333–36, 339

Mémoires de Vidocq, Les (Vidocq, François), 131
memory, 13–14, 292
Mérimée, Prosper, 178, 325; *Chronique du règne de Charles IX*, 178
Metamorphoses (Ovid), 58
Metamorphoses, or the Golden Ass (Apuleius, Lucius), 176–77
metaphoric modulation, 24, 26, 33, 36, 37, 83, 84, 90, 92, 104, 153, 186, 245–47, 324; as alternating following-pattern, 30–33, 34–35, 37, 38, 40, 42, 44, 48, 53, 56, 66, 74, 82, 83, 84, 90, 92, 97, 244
metonymic modulation, 24–25, 26, 92, 104, 153–54, 186, 189, 244, 245–47, 320, 324
Meyer, Nicholas, 248; *Day After, The*, 248, 252
Middle Ages, 50, 80, 289
Middlemarch (Eliot, George), 242, 264, 272–73
Millard, Albert, 258–59
Miller, J. Hillis, 5, 11, 85
Milton, John, 67, 97; *Paradise Lost*, 67, 97
Minnelli, Vincente, 25, 66, 87; *An American in Paris*, 87; *Band Wagon, The*, 66; *Gigi*, 25, 66
Miracle de Théophile, Le (Rutebeuf), 141
Misérables, Les (Hugo, Victor), 16, 271
modulations (*see also* hyperbolic, meta-phoric, metonymic), 23, 26, 44, 83, 292, 304–305, 316, 323–24
Moll Flanders (Defoe, Daniel), 127–28, 129, 136, 148, 244, 332
Montaigne, Michel Eyquem de, 188
Montesquieu, Charles Louis de, 177; *Lettres persanes*, 177
More, Sir Thomas, 217
multiple-focus narrative, 191–240, 241–290, 317, 324, 228, 340; as anti-narrative, 252–53, 257, 259–60, 265, 270, 289; as

following-pattern of, 101–103, 104, 106, 111, 113–15, 117–18; gaze in, 103–105, 110, 114; importance of Puritanism to, 100, 103, 106–107, 108, 110, 114, 117; mapping of, 300–303, 308, 314; metonymic modulation in, 104

Scarron, Paul, 320

Schapiro, Meyer, 179, 191, 193

Schiller, Friedrich, 69

Schoedsack, Ernest, 56

Scholes, Robert, 10

Schwartz, Daniel, 273

Scott, Randolph, 23

Scott, Sir Walter, 178, 256, 325; *Waverly*, 178, 256

Scribe, Augustin, 324

Scudéry, Madeleine de, 180

Seaton, George, 248; *Airport*, 248

Sentiments sur les lettres (Du Plaisir), 322

Sermon of Saint John the Baptist, The (Bruegel, Pieter), 220

Seven Cardinal Vices, The (Bruegel, Pieter), 222

Seven Cardinal Virtues, The (Bruegel, Pieter), 222

Severini, Gino, 269

sexuality, 73–77, 123–27, 274–77

Shakespeare, William, 145; *King Lear*, 145

Shelley, Mary, 125, 131

Sheppard, J. T., 80

She Wore a Yellow Ribbon (Ford, John), 316–17

Shklovsky, Victor, 177

Silk Stockings (Mamoulian, Rouben), 88

Simenon, Georges, 130; *Le Commissaire Maigret*, 130

sin, 106, 107–108, 110, 117–18

single-focus narrative, 99–118, 119–90, 314, 317, 322, 324, 334, 338, 339; artifactual reading in, 162–70, 171, 175, 336;

bracketed tale in, 136–40, 154–56, 172; Bildungsroman as, 137–39, 143–48, 152–54, 158; character in, 99–100, 102–105, 106, 111, 113, 116, 118, 119, 126–27, 145–48, 152, 156–60, 178–80, 300–303; Christianity and, 117, 152, 153–54, 179, 323, 336; compared to dual-focus narrative, 99–100, 119, 143, 191; compared to multiple-focus narrative, 241–43, 245–47, 248, 251, 254–61, 262, 263–65, 266–69, 277–78, 281–84, 287–90; control of by protagonist, 102–105, 106, 110, 114–16, 120–23, 156–60, 176, 244, 285, 319–20, 323, 331–33; detective fiction as, 130–31, 133, 155–56, 162–63, 164–70, 171, 173, 185, 188; economics and, 127–28, 136, 141–42, 143–48, 151–54, 181, 189–90; gradational values in, 127–29, 142–44, 189, 330–34; image and, 191, 194–97, 229, 238; mirrored moments and, 157–60; morality in, 141–42, 143–48, 154; narration and, 133, 139, 147, 156, 172, 178; novel as, 100, 101, 106, 117, 128, 129–30, 135, 143, 145, 149, 155, 160, 168, 170, 172, 178, 188, 191, 319–20, 325, 333; plot of, 135; polysemy in, 112–13, 115, 178, 327; quest narrative as, 128–30, 137–40, 153, 171–72, 177, 178, 311, 318, 325–26; romance as, 128–30, 131, 149, 185, 188, 262, 339; saints' lives as, 124–26, 127–30, 136, 143, 149, 171, 175–76, 185, 339; text as, 102, 118, 138, 154, 172, 179; transformational approach and, 300–303, 306–307, 309; typological approach and, 291, 312–13, 316; vectoring and, 194–97, 208

Sir Gawain and the Green Knight (Anonymous), 128, 148

Smith, Barbara Herrnstein, 9–10, 11

social organization, 315, 327–34, 338

Son Excellence Eugène Rougon (Zola, Émile), 247, 257

Song of Roland, The (Anonymous), 55, 101; as dual-focus epic, 56, 59, 66, 68, 77, 78, 80, 81, 83, 87, 88, 98, 128, 147, 152, 154, 185, 251, 297; as war story, 316–17, 338; characterization through repetition in, 40–42, 46–48, 50–54; enjambment in, 43–45; following-pattern of, 29–38, 48–50, 53; integration and, 42–48, 50–51, 54; mapping of, 298–300, 308; metaphoric modulation of, 33–35; plot summary of, 29–30; polarity adjustment and, 48–54; symmetry of, 38, 40–42, 48, 54; traditional interpretation of, 28, 30–31

Sopha, Le (Crébillon, Claude de), 177

Sophocles, 4; *Oedipus Rex*, 4, 10, 167–68

space, 218; empty center and, 199, 200, 202, 204, 206, 212, 214, 216, 217, 236; fragmentation of, 219–21, 224, 232, 235–36; margins of pictorial, 200, 201, 213, 221, 236; multiple-focus use of, 197–240; narrative as, 202, 204, 217, 221, 229, 240

"Spanish Inn" stories, 248, 252, 254

spatialization, 32–33, 37–38, 41, 43, 78, 86, 90–91, 92–94, 96, 269, 312; conflict and, 78–96; dual-focus pastoral and, 63–66, 77, 92, 123, 244, 327–28; film and, 63; parallelism and, 33, 36, 38–39, 41, 42, 51, 55, 56, 123, 244; single-focus narrative and, 107, 109; synchronic, 77–78

speculation, 106–110, 112–13, 115–18

Spenser, Edmund, 320

Spielberg, Steven, 317; *Saving Private Ryan*, 317

Spillane, Mickey, 185

Sponde, Jean de, 25

stasis, 43, 45, 55–57, 78, 80, 93, 115, 142, 194

Stendhal [Henri Beyle], 16; *Armance*, 125; *Charterhouse of Parma, The*, 16

—*Red and the Black, The*, 21; as single-focus, 129, 136, 148, 149, 182; following-pattern of, 257, 314

Steppenwolf (Hesse, Hermann), 178, 185

Stevenson, Robert Louis, 326; *Dr. Jekyll and Mr. Hyde*, 326

Stierle, Karlheinz, 5

structuralism, 5–7, 8, 12, 296, 315

Sue, Eugène, 81, 130

—*Les Mystères de Paris*, 82, 130, 156; as multiple-focus, 271, 287, 318

Suicide of Saul, The (Bruegel, Pieter), 216

Sulpicius Severus, 125, 126; *Life of Saint Martin*, 125, 126

Summer (Bruegel, Pieter), 230, 238, 239, 240

Svevo, Italo, 178, 185; *La Coscienza di Zeno*, 178, 185

Sweethearts (Van Dyke, W. S), 66

Swift, Jonathan, 56, 177; *Battle of the Books*, 56; *Gulliver's Travels*, 177

symmetry, 38–42, 45, 58, 59, 191; slot-logic and, 40–41, 42, 43, 48, 49, 54, 97, 123

Symphonie pastorale, La (Gide, André), 136, 173, 175

syntagma, 91–92, 98

Tacitus, 56; *History*, 56

Tasso, Torquato, 3, 322

Télémaque (Fénelon, François), 137

television, 17, 191, 297

temporal development, 37, 63, 78, 90, 92–94, 327; cause-and-effect as, 32–33, 37–38, 43, 56, 86, 115, 142; diachronic, 77, 78, 80; images and, 212; single-focus narrative and, 90, 92–94, 115, 142, 156–60, 170, 269; traditional societies and, 96–97